THE SF BOOK OF LISTS

THE SF BOOK OF LISTS

MAXIM JAKUBOWSKI & MALCOLM EDWARDS

BERKLEY BOOKS, NEW YORK

THE SF BOOK OF LISTS

A Berkley Book/published by arrangement with
the authors

PRINTING HISTORY
Berkley trade paperback edition/November 1983

ISBN 0-425-06187-6

A BERKLEY BOOK ® TM 757,375
Berkley Books are published by The Berkley Publishing Group,
200 Madison Avenue, New York, New York 10016.
The name "BERKLEY" and the stylized "B" with design are
trademarks belonging to Berkley Publishing Corporation.
PRINTED IN THE UNITED STATES OF AMERICA

Introduction

Compiling lists is a simple and harmless pleasure to which few of us are wholly immune. Ask anyone for a list of their favourite books, movies, records, TV programmes, footballers – or whatever their interest happens to be – and they'll generally be all too happy to oblige. Compiling books of lists, however, enjoyable as it is, is also a sign of obsessiveness bordering on the maniacal. And compiling books of *science fiction and fantasy* lists is surely carrying things too far . . .

The SF and fantasy genres have always attracted list-makers. Long before respectable critics and scholars began to take a belated interest, most of the preliminary groundwork of indexing and bibliography and ordering of information had been carried out by dedicated fans making lists on file cards and publishing the results in small-circulation mimeograph pamphlets. The proliferation of theme anthologies testifies to the strength of the list-making instinct; look around and you can find anthologies on almost any theme you think of, as well as several you hoped nobody would ever be silly enough to come up with. So far we haven't quite reached such extremes as *Albanian Giant Ant Stories*, *Great Science Fiction About Breakfast Cereals* or *Bondage in the Fifth Dimension* – but we may not have long to wait.

Despite this record of devoted activity, SF and fantasy have remained relatively virgin territory for the list-maker. Until now, that is. When we started out to compile this *Complete Book of SF and Fantasy Lists* we rapidly drew up a list (naturally!) of a couple of hundred topics we thought would be informative and fun. As the research for the book progressed further ideas (some serious, some, to say the least, idiosyncratic) began cropping up with alarming regularity, threatening us with a project that could never be ended. Each list generated an idea for a further list, and that in turn threw up a third notion . . . and so on, *ad infinitum*. Eventually, when we had a book double the size originally envisaged, we had to call a halt, relegating another hundred or so notions into limbo (or possibly for a second volume) for fear of needlessly decimating another forest or of giving our publishers costing problems of the third kind. To call this the *Complete Book* is therefore not *strictly* accurate . . . but it looks good on the cover. The book may yet find its way on to a future list of not-strictly-accurate titles.

As the previous paragraph indicates, what we are aiming for in this book is a mixture of information and entertainment; of useful data and interesting trivia. We should further point out that the lists do not generally aim to be all-embracing. If we mention ten SF stories about giant carnivorous maggots, we do not mean that there are *only* ten stories on this vital theme, but we *do* mean that in our view these are ten of the most significant and memorable. Don't write and tell us we missed something; we didn't, we left it out deliberately!

Inevitably a book of this kind accumulates many debts of gratitude. We could make several lists of them. There are the people who sent us lists: Brian Aldiss, Isaac Asimov, David Langford, Nick Lowe, Richard Lupoff, Robert Silverberg, John Sladek, Brian Stableford, Ian Watson, and the editorial/sales departments of Berkley-Putnam, NAL, Sphere and Timescape. Thanks are due to the Science Fiction Foundation, for use of research facilities, and to Lloyd Currey for useful advice and information; to our agents Sheri Safran, Diana Price and Joyce Frommer; to our editors Andy McKillop and Victoria Schochet; to our wives Chris Atkinson and Dolores Jakubowski, for all the usual reasons; and to the late, great Philip Dick, without whom SF would have been a lot less interesting.

Malcolm Edwards and Maxim Jakubowski

June 1982

Great Aliens of Science Fiction

Alien creatures and intelligences are of course highly common in SF and the creation of new, weird species is an occupation all major authors come back to time and again. Editor Ian Summers and illustrator Wayne Douglas Barlowe got together to publish *Barlowe's Guide to Extraterrestrials* in 1979, a fascinating series of portraits of SF creatures from the pages of literature. Any selection of aliens is, because of the sheer availability of choice, a subjective one. We think Summers and Barlowe's compendium is first-class (and the pictures are great as well as incredibly faithful to the originating text).

The Abyormenite – from Hal Clement's *Cycle of Fire*
The Athsheans – from Ursula K. Le Guin's *The Word for World is Forest*
The Black Cloud – from Fred Hoyle's *The Black Cloud*
The Chulpex – from Avram Davidson's *Masters of the Maze*
The Cinruss – from James White's *Sector General* novels
The Cryer – from Joseph Green's *Conscience Interplanetary*
The Cygnan – from Donald Moffitt's *The Jupiter Theft*
The Cygnostik – from Michael Bishop's *A Little Knowledge*
The Czill – from Jack L. Chalker's *Midnight at the Well of Souls*
Demons – from Keith Laumer's *A Plague of Demons*
The Demu – from F. M. Busby's *Cage a Man*
The Dextrans – from David J. Lake's *The Right Hand of Dextra*
The Dilbians – from Gordon R. Dickson's *Spacial Delivery* and *Spacepaw*
The Dirdir – from Jack Vance's *The Dirdir*
The Garnishee – from Harry Harrison's *Star Smashers of the Galaxy Rangers*
The Gowachin – from Frank Herbert's *The Dosadi Experiment*
The Guild Steersmen – from Frank Herbert's *Dune Messiah*
The Ishtarians – from Poul Anderson's *Fire Time*
The Ixchel – from Madeleine L'Engle's *A Wrinkle in Time*
The Ixtl – from A. E. Van Vogt's *The Voyage of the Space Beagle*
The Lithians – from James Blish's *A Case of Conscience*
The Masters – from John Christopher's *Tripod* trilogy

The Medusans – from Jack Williamson's *The Legion of Space*
The Merseians – from Poul Anderson's *Ensign Flandry*
The Mesklinites – from Hal Clement's *Mission of Gravity*
Mother – from Philip José Farmer's *Strange Relations*
The Old Galactics – from James H. Schmitz's *Legacy*
The Old Ones – from H. P. Lovecraft's *At The Mountains of Madness*
The Overlords – from Arthur C. Clarke's *Childhood's End*
The Pnume – from Jack Vance's *The Pnume*
The Polarians – from Piers Anthony's *Cluster*
The Puppeteers – from Larry Niven's *Neutron Star* and *Ringworld*
The Radiates – from Naomi Mitchison's *Memoirs of a Spacewoman*
The Regul – from C. J. Cherryh's *The Faded Sun: Kesrith*
The Riim – from A. E. Van Vogt's *The Voyage of the Space Beagle*
The Ruml – from Gordon R. Dickson's *The Alien Way*
The Salamen – from Brian M. Stableford's *Wildeblood's Empire*
The Sirians – from Frederik Pohl's *The Age of the Pussyfoot*
The Slash – from Piers Anthony's *Kirlian Quest*
The Soft Ones – from Isaac Asimov's *The Gods Themselves*
Solaris – from Stanislaw Lem's *Solaris*
The Sulidor – from Robert Silverberg's *Downward to the Earth*
The Thing – from Don A. Stuart (John W. Campbells') *Who Goes There?*
The Thrint – from Larry Niven's *World of Ptavus*
The Tran – from Alan Dean Foster's *Icerigger*
The Tripeds – from Damon Knight's *Rule Golden*
The Tyreeans – from James Tiptree Jr's *Up the Walls of the World*
The Uchjinians – from Jack L. Chalker's *Exiles at the Well of Souls*
The Vegans – from Robert A. Heinlein's *Have Spacesuit Will Travel*
The Velantians – from E. E. Smith's *Children of the Lens*

Fifteen Important SF Stories about First Contact with Aliens

1. Brian Aldiss, *The Dark Light Years*
2. Arthur C. Clarke, *Childhood's End*
3. Arthur C. Clarke, *2001: A Space Odyssey*
4. Gordon R. Dickson, *The Alien Way*
5. Raymond Z. Gallun, 'Old Faithful'

6. Fred Hoyle, *The Black Cloud*
7. Fritz Leiber, *The Wanderer*
8. Murray Leinster, 'First Contact'
9. C. S. Lewis, *Out of the Silent Planet*
10. Katherine MacLean, 'Pictures Don't Lie'
11. Phillip Mann, *The Eye of the Queen*
12. David I. Masson, 'Not So Certain'
13. Larry Niven and Jerry Pournelle, *The Mote in God's Eye*
14. Ian Watson, *The Embedding*
15. Ivan Yefremov, 'The Heart of the Serpent'

Stories about first contact with aliens may stress either the mystical, wondrous aspects of it – or the difficulties, and even dangers. The former attitude is strongly expressed in two of the most popular recent SF films, *2001* and *Close Encounters of the Third Kind*; the latter approach is seen at its most primitive in a horde of monsters-from-outer-space movies. Most of the above concentrate on the implications for humanity of such contact, and on the practical difficulties of establishing contact with a truly alien being. They also include one of the rare polemical exchanges in science fiction. Murray Leinster's story lays stress on the necessity not to make known the location of your home planet to aliens (assuming your encounter is in deep space), lest they prove hostile; Yefremov's argues – perhaps optimistically – that any race advanced enough to undertake such journeys would have outgrown the paranoid and militaristic attitudes implied in Leinster's work.

Six SF Stories about Alien Languages

1. Brian Aldiss, 'Confluence' – not so much a story as an alien vocabulary, but the humorous definitions, for words we lack but would benefit from having (see following list) build up a picture of a different society
2. Samuel R. Delany, *Babel-17* – a complex study of alien language strongly based in linguistic theory
3. David I. Masson, 'Not So Certain' – a story of first contact with aliens told with sophisticated awareness of the linguistic problems

4. H. Beam Piper, 'Omnilingual' – the story of the discovery of a 'Rosetta Stone', which permits translation of an alien language; intelligently worked out
5. Jack Vance, *The Languages of Pao* – an interesting exploration of the idea that the limits of a culture's thought are set by its language: it is hard to think ideas which cannot be put into words
6. Ian Watson, *The Embedding* – a complex novel of human and alien linguistics

Fifteen Useful Pieces of Alien Vocabulary

Brian Aldiss's 'Confluence' presents a preliminary dictionary of the language spoken by the inhabitants of the planet Myrin. Some of these have little relevance to humans, but some more could usefully be added to our language.

1. *Ab we tel min*: The sensation that one neither agrees nor disagrees with what is being said to one, but that one simply wishes to depart from the presence of the speaker
2. *Bag rack*: Needless and offensive apologies
3. *Cham on th zam*: Being witty when nobody else appreciates it
4. *Har dar ka*: The complete understanding that all the soil of Myrin passes through the bodies of its earthworms every ten years
5. *Kundulum*: To be well and in bed with two pretty sisters
6. *Mal*: A feeling of being watched from within
7. *Mur on tig won*: The disagreeable experience of listening to oneself in the middle of a long speech and neither understanding what one is saying nor enjoying the manner in which it is being said
8. *Pat o bane ban*: The ten heartbeats preceding the first heartbeat of orgasm
9. *Shak ale man*: The struggle that takes place in the night between the urge to urinate and the urge to continue sleeping
10. *Shem*: A slight cold afflicting only one nostril; the thoughts that pass when one shakes hands with a politician
11. *Tok an*: Suddenly divining the nature and imminence of old age in one's thirty-first year
12. *U ri rhi*: Two lovers drunk together
13. *Uz*: Two very large people marrying after the prime of life

14. *Uz to kardin*: The realization in childhood that one is the issue of two very large people who married after the prime of life
15. *Yup pa*: A book in which everything is understandable except the author's purpose in writing it

Twenty-five Interesting Alien Worlds

1. *Anarres* - in Ursula Le Guin's *The Dispossessed*
2. *Arrakis* - in Frank Herbert's *Dune* series
3. *Belzagor* - in Robert Silverberg's *Downward to the Earth*
4. *BoskVeld* - in Michael Bishop's *Transfigurations*
5. *Chthon* - in Piers Anthony's *Chthon*
6. *Darkover* - in Marion Zimmer Bradley's *Darkover* series
7. *Dosadi* - in Frank Herbert's *The Dosadi Experiment*
8. *Durdane* - in Jack Vance's *Durdane* trilogy
9. *Gethen* - in Ursula Le Guin's *The Left Hand of Darkness*
10. *Helliconia* - in Brian Aldiss's *Helliconia Spring*
11. *Jem* - in Frederik Pohl's *Jem*
12. *Lithia* - in James Blish's *A Case of Conscience*
13. *Majipoor* - in Robert Silverberg's *Lord Valentine's Castle*
14. *Mesklin* - in Hal Clement's *Mission of Gravity*
15. *Norstrilia* - in Cordwainer Smith's *The Planet Buyer* and others
16. *Pe-Ellia* - in Phillip Mann's *The Eye of the Queen*
17. *Pern* - in Anne McCaffrey's *Dragon* series
18. *Pyrrus* - in Harry Harrison's *Deathworld*
19. *Riverworld* - in Philip José Farmer's *Riverworld* series
20. *Solaris* - in Stanislaw Lem's *Solaris*
21. *Tralfamadore* - in Kurt Vonnegut's *Slaughterhouse-Five*
22. *Trantor* - in Isaac Asimov's *Foundation* series
23. *Tschai* - in Jack Vance's *Planet of Adventure* series
24. *Wellworld* - in Jack Chalker's *Well of Souls* series
25. *Worlorn* - in George R. R. Martin's *Dying of the Light*

Twenty Lands of the Imagination

Every major fantasy author eventually creates an imaginary land, which he peoples with the most fantastic figments of his imagination.

This is a small selection of those which have become almost household names.

1. *The Beklan Empire* (Richard Adams' *Shardik*)
2. *Prydain* (Lloyd Alexander)
3. *Oz* (Frank Baum)
4. *The Four Lands* (Terry Brooks' *The Sword of Shannara*)
5. *Poictesme* (James Branch Cabell)
6. *The Land* (Stephen Donaldson)
7. *Yoknapatawpha County* (William Faulkner)
8. *Cimmeria* (Robert E. Howard)
9. *Earthsea* (Ursula K. Le Guin)
10. *Lankhmar* in the land of Newhon (Fritz Leiber)
11. *Narnia* (C. S. Lewis)
12. *The Duchy of Strackenz* (G. McDonald Fraser's *Flashman* books)
13. *Melniboné and the Young Kingdoms* (Michael Moorcock)
14. *The Commonwealth* (Roy Myers Myers' *Silverlock*)
15. *Dalarna* (Fletcher Pratt's *The Well of The Unicorn*)
16. *Hyperborea* (Clark Ashton Smith)
17. *Zoothique* (Clark Ashton Smith)
18. *Lilliput* (Jonathan Swift's *Gulliver's Travels*, also Laputa, Brobdingnag and the lands of the Houyhnhnms)
19. *Middle-Earth* (J. R. R. Tolkien)
20. *Islandia* (Austin Tappan Wright)

Thirteen Stories of Lost Worlds

1. Edgar Rice Burroughs, *At The Earth's Core* (plus half a dozen sequels). Novels set in the world of Pellucidar, existing inside the Earth (which is hollow)
2. Edgar Rice Burroughs, *The Land That Time Forgot* (a lost world near the South Pole)
3. Samuel Butler, *Erewhon* (a Utopian culture discovered in the heart of New Zealand)
4. Richard Cowper, 'The Web of the Magi' (a successful modern attempt to recreate the lost world story; this one is set in Asia Minor)

5. A. Conan Doyle, *The Lost World* (a plateau deep in the South American jungle houses many species long extinct elsewhere.)
6. H. Rider Haggard, *King Solomon's Mines* (a lost civilization in Africa)
7. H. Rider Haggard, *She* (and another)
8. James Hilton, *Lost Horizon* (the Tibetan lost world of Shangri-La)
9. Henry Kuttner, *Valley of the Flame* (a lost world in the Amazon jungle)
10. A. Merritt, *Dwellers in the Mirage* (an Asiatic lost race in a valley in Alaska)
11. A. Merritt, *The Face in the Abyss* (an Atlantean race survives in the Andes)
12. Joseph O'Neill, *Land Under England* (a totalitarian subterranean world)
13. John Wyndham, *The Secret People* (a lost race living under the Sahara; variously published as by John Beynon and John Beynon Harris)

The story of lost worlds, lost civilizations and lost races was enormously popular in the late nineteenth and early twentieth century; its king was undoubtedly Rider Haggard, who wrote many such works. As the twentieth century has progressed it has become increasingly difficult to find plausible lands beyond the map in which to set such stories. Only two of the entries to the list were published after 1940: Kuttner's, which is a pulp romance, and Cowper's, which is a pastiche of Haggard.

Roget's Imaginary Lands

Roget's Thesaurus is the long-established and recognized wordsmith's reference book. The 1982 edition includes a number of imaginary lands whose place in the English language is now considered permanent. These are gleaned from both legend and literature and comprise the following:

El Dorado
Happy Valley
The Isles of the Blest

Cockaigne
Ruritania
Shangri-La
Atlantis
Lyonesse
Middle-Earth
San Serriffe

San Serriffe is an apocryphal country invented as an April Fools' Day spoof by the British newspaper *The Guardian* in 1977. It has since been used by many other humorists. A short story by a writer from San Serriffe, Adam Barnett-Foster, was also included in the international SF anthology *Twenty Houses of the Zodiac* (ed M. Jakubowski, 1979).

Edgar Rice Burroughs Twelve Imaginary Lands

Edgar Rice Burroughs was a consummate world creator, not only dreaming up gaudy lost worlds or civilizations in his Tarzan books, but also conjuring up weird and exotic locales in SF novels. Although Rider Haggard can be considered the pioneer of the lost world yarn, Burroughs was the author who made it magical, adding the necessary colour and adventure to his creations that brought a whole new generation of readers to SF and fantasy, many of whom are now major writers in the field.

1. *Amtor* – another name for ERB's gripping, if unscientific, vision of the planet Venus
2. *The Land of the Ant Men* – hidden behind a thorn forest in Africa in a Tarzan adventure
3. *Barsoom* – John Carter's unforgettable planet Mars where monster races and beautiful princesses somehow coexist. A world of deserts and weird, dangerous species
4. *Caspak* – another lost world, on the island of Caprona, hidden from the rest of mankind in the South Pacific
5. *The Lost Empire* – where Tarzan comes face to face with the last remaining outpost of the glory that was ancient Rome
6. *The Moon* – not quite as we know it now, but hollow (in *The Moon Maid*)

14

7. *The Wild Island of Nadara* – where *The Cave Girl* is to be found
8. *Onthar and Thenar* – warring, mysterious lost lands of the dark African continent, discovered anew by Tarzan
9. *Opar* – the legendary city of gold. Another Tarzan rediscovery, since borrowed by Philip José Farmer
10. *Pal* – in Zaire, a lost world surrounded by impassable morasses which Tarzan soon overcomes
11. *Pellucidar* – the lost land at the centre of our hollow Earth
12. *Poloda* – in the Omos system, in *Beyond the Farthest Star*

The Tarzan Books

Created by Edgar Rice Burroughs in December 1911 and first published in the October 1912 edition of *All-Story*, *Tarzan of the Apes* is the all-time great hero of pulp adventure and, as such, characterizes much of what 'sense of wonder' science fiction at its best can achieve. The eponymous jungle hero has almost become a modern archetype and has spawned a legion of imitators (see list). His many appearances on film or TV have seen him portrayed by such varying specimens of virility as Elmo Lincoln, Buster Crabbe, Johnny Weissmuller, Lex Barker, Gordon Scott, Jock Mahoney, Mike Henry and, recently, Miles O'Keeffe in a curious silver screen version which did more for Bo Derek's nipples than it did for the perennial myth However, Burroughs' original novels are somewhat forgotten these days and we thought it would be nice to feature them, as they still contain many a treasure of imagination and fantasy. They are in order of publication.

Tarzan of the Apes (1914)
The Return of Tarzan (1915)
The Beasts of Tarzan (1916)
The Son of Tarzan (1917)
Tarzan and the Jewels of Opar (1918)
Jungle Tales of Tarzan (1919)
Tarzan the Untamed (1920)
Tarzan the Terrible (1921)
Tarzan and the Golden Lion (1923)
Tarzan and the Ant Men (1924)

The Tarzan Twins (1927)
Tarzan, Lord of the Jungle (1928)
Tarzan and the Lost Empire (1929)
Tarzan at the Earth's Core (1930)
Tarzan the Invincible (1931)
Tarzan Triumphant (1932)
Tarzan and the City of Gold (1933)
Tarzan and the Lion Man (1934)
Tarzan and the Leopard Men (1935)
Tarzan and the Tarzan Twins with Jad-Bal-Ja, the Golden Lion (1936)
Tarzan's Quest (1936)
Tarzan and the Forbidden City (1938)
Tarzan the Magnificent (1939)
Tarzan and 'The Foreign Legion' (1947)
Tarzan and the Madman (1964)
Tarzan and the Castaways (1964)
Tarzan and the Valley of Gold (this is the only authorized book featuring Tarzan not written by Edgar Rice Burroughs; it was authored by the famous SF and fantasy writer Fritz Leiber) (1966)

Eighteen Tarzan Clones

Although frowned upon by the Edgar Rice Burroughs estate, Tarzan has spawned a horde of jungle men (and women) imitators.

1. *Imaro* (Charles Saunders)
2. *Anjani the Mighty* (Earl Titan/John Russell Fearn)
3. *The Mighty Thunda, King of the Congo* (Buster Crabbe, 1952 serial)
4. *Shuna, White Queen of the Jungle* (John King)
5. *Azan the Ape Man* (Marco Garron)
6. *Ka-Zar* (Robert Byrd), also known as the King of Fang and Claw
7. *Ki-Gor, King of the Jungle* (John Murray Reynolds)
8. *Matalaa* (Red Star Adventures pulp character)
9. *Sheena, Queen of the Jungle* (1951)
10. *Hadon of Ancient Opar* (Philip José Farmer)
11. *Lord Grandrith* (Philip José Farmer)

12. *Kioga* (William L. Chester)
13. *Jan of the Jungle, Tam, Son of the Tiger* and *Kwa of the Jungle* (all Otis Adelbert Kline)
14. *Kaspa, the Lion Man* (C. T. Stonehall)
15. *Hathoo of the Elephants* (Post Wheeler)
16. *Bunduki* (J. T. Edson)

Six SF Novels about Supermen

1. Robert Heinlein, *Stranger in a Strange Land*
2. Frank Robinson, *The Power*
3. Olaf Stapledon, *Odd John*
4. John Taine, *Seeds of Life*
5. A. E. Van Vogt, *World of Null-A*
6. Stanley Weinbaum, *The New Adam*

Categories overlap: many telepaths (see p. 19) are also supermen, as are messiah figures (p. 65)

Ten Authors of Future Histories

A number of SF writers have written series of stories within a consistent framework. Sometimes these are linked by a chronology so that they become in essence histories of the future.

1. Poul Anderson – his *Technic History* series is long and complex, centring on the two characters Nicholas Van Rijn and Dominic Flandry
2. Isaac Asimov – his history of the decline and fall of a galactic empire is chronicled in the *Foundation* series, recently extended in *Foundation's Edge*
3. James Blish – his *Cities in Flight* series incorporates a detailed chronology
4. Gordon R. Dickson – his *Childe Cycle*, still far from complete after twenty-five years, will ultimately start well in the past and extend to the distant future

5. Robert Heinlein - his future history, *The Past Through Tomorrow*, was the first to be mapped in detail
6. Larry Niven - his *Known Space* series incorporates most of his major SF
7. H. Beam Piper - his *Federation* future history has only been clearly mapped out years after his death
8. Jerry Pournelle - his *CoDominium* history is carefully worked out, and also includes one of his collaborations with Larry Niven, *The Mote in God's Eye*
9. Cordwainer Smith - almost all his stories belong within his *Instrumentality of Mankind* series, a complex history of humanity's distant future
10. Olaf Stapledon, *Last and First Men* - an immensely detailed future history extending millions of years into the future

Fifteen SF Novels Featuring Mutants and Mutations

1. Poul Anderson, *Twilight World*
2. Isaac Asimov, *Foundation and Empire*
3. Philip K. Dick, *Dr Bloodmoney*
4. Daniel Galouye, *Dark Universe*
5. M. John Harrison, *The Committed Men*
6. Robert Heinlein, *Orphans of the Sky*
7. Russell Hoban, *Riddley Walker*
8. Henry Kuttner, *Mutant*
9. Walter Miller, *A Canticle for Leibowitz*
10. Edgar Pangborn, *Davy*
11. Robert Silverberg, *Nightwings*
12. Norman Spinrad, *The Iron Dream*
13. Olaf Stapledon, *Odd John*
14. A. E. Van Vogt, *Slan*
15. John Wyndham, *The Chrysalids*

Ten SF Novels Including Slavery

It is commonplace in SF for future societies to regress in their social and economic institutions while becoming ever more technologically sophisticated. Enslavement - either of intelligent aliens, or of humans, features in all these novels.

1. Piers Anthony, *Chthon*
2. Charles Harness, *The Paradox Men*
3. Robert Heinlein, *Citizen of the Galaxy*
4. Ursula Le Guin, *The Word for World is Forest*
5. John Norman, *Tarnsman of Gor* and sequels
6. Robert Silverberg, *Downward to the Earth*
7. Norman Spinrad, *The Iron Dream*
8. Norman Spinrad, *The Men in the Jungle*
9. A. E. Van Vogt, *Empire of the Atom*
10. Gene Wolfe, *The Fifth Head of Cerberus*

Seven SF Stories Taking Place in the Mind

These are SF stories which are literally 'all in the mind'. In the Brunner, Phillips, Silverberg and Zelazny, techniques - sometimes telepathic, sometimes mechanical - enable psychologists actually to enter the fantasies of disturbed patients, with varying results. In both Dick novels and in the Watson, the bulk of the novel takes place - as is gradually revealed - within the mental reality of one or more of the characters, which reaches out to encompass others.

1. John Brunner, *Telepathist* (*The Whole Man*)
2. Philip K. Dick, *Eye in the Sky*
3. Philip K. Dick, *Ubik*
4. Peter Phillips, 'Dreams are Sacred'
5. Robert Silverberg, 'A Sea of Faces'
6. Ian Watson, *Deathhunter*
7. Roger Zelazny, *The Dream Master*

Fifteen Important SF Novels about Telepathy

Telepathy - the ability to speak mind to mind - is an important SF theme. It is connected to other kinds of extra-sensory perception, and

19

also to stories about supermen, or mutation. The following are all important telepathy novels; many of them also include these other elements.

1. Alfred Bester, *The Demolished Man*
2. James Blish, *Jack of Eagles*
3. John Brunner, *Telepathist*
4. Algis Budrys, *Rogue Moon*
5. Robert Heinlein, *Time For the Stars*
6. Stephen King, *The Dead Zone*
7. Henry Kuttner, *Mutant*
8. Keith Roberts, *The Inner Wheel*
9. Joanna Russ, *And Chaos Died*
10. Eric Frank Russell, *Three to Conquer*
11. Robert Silverberg, *Dying Inside*
12. Theodore Sturgeon, *More Than Human*
13. Wilson Tucker, *Wild Talent*
14. A. E. Van Vogt, *Slan*
15. John Wyndham, *The Chrysalids*

The SF Bestiary:
Three Stories each about Intelligent Apes and Dogs,
Two Featuring Cats,
and One each about Mice, Newts, Rats and Skunks

The idea of animals being bred, mutated or simply evolving to the point where they achieve intelligence is a common one, often used to satiric ends. A few important stories featuring individual species are listed below. Others, in which a whole panoply of animals have intelligence, include most famously Wells' *Island of Dr Moreau*.

Apes are featured in
    Pierre Boulle, *Monkey Planet*
    Richard Cowper, *Clone*
    Peter van Greenaway, *Manrissa Man*
Cats are featured in
    Fritz Leiber, Space-Time for Springers
    Cordwainer Smith, *Ballad of Lost C'Mell* (Smith's great inter-

linked series of stories of the *Instrumentality of Mankind* feature a variety of animals biologically improved to human intelligence and near-human form, but cats predominate.)

Dogs appear in
Harlan Ellison, *A Boy and His Dog*
Clifford Simak, *City*
Olaf Stapledon, *Sirius*
Mice are revealed as Earth's dominant species in
Douglas Adams, *The Hitchhiker's Guide to the Galaxy*
Newts are used as slaves until they revolt in
Karel Capek, *War With the Newts*
Rats mutate into intelligence aboard a spaceship in
A. Bertram Chandler, *Giant Killer*
Skunks turn out to be skunky aliens in
Clifford Simak, Operation Stinky

Fifteen SF Novels about Immortals

Immortality as an idea and a literary theme long predates its use in science fiction. There is, for instance, the legend of the Wandering Jew, several times treated in novels: and one of the most famous early Gothic novels, Charles Maturin's *Melmoth the Wanderer* (1820), is about a man who receives near-immortality as a result of a pact with the devil. The central debate in stories about immortality is over whether it would be a benefit or a curse. The latter case tends to be argued more strongly – perhaps for predictable psychological reasons. Immortality, in such stories, is identified with stagnation, loss of creativity, sterility, and dreadful boredom – the reverse of creative, fecund, mortal life.

1. James Blish, *Cities in Flight*
2. Arthur C. Clarke, *The City and the Stars*
3. Raymond Z. Gallun, *The Eden Cycle*
4. James Gunn, *The Immortals*
5. H. Rider Haggard, *She*
6. Robert Heinlein, *Time Enough for Love* (and its predecessor, *Methuselah's Children*)

7. Michael Moorcock, *An Alien Heat* (and other novels in the *Dancers at the End of Time* sequence)
8. Frederik Pohl, *Drunkard's Walk*
9. Bob Shaw, *One Million Tomorrows*
10. Clifford Simak, *Way Station*
11. Norman Spinrad, *Bug Jack Barron*
12. Wilson Tucker, *The Time Masters*
13. A. E. Van Vogt, *The Weapon Shops of Isher* (and *The Weapon Makers*)
14. Jack Vance, *To Live Forever*
15. Roger Zelazny, *This Immortal*

Nine Generation Starship Stories

Travelling at anything less than the speed of light, a spaceship would take more than four years to reach the nearest star, and much longer to arrive anywhere with a prospect of habitable worlds. Such a journey might, in fact, take many hundreds of years, even with spaceships considerably faster than any we now possess, or could build. On such a journey what would become of the crew and their descendants? Would they remember the purpose of the trip? Would they even remember that they were making a trip? Several stories have explored the ramifications of this idea.

1. Brian Aldiss, *Nonstop* (alternative title *Starship*)
2. Edward Bryant and Harlan Ellison, *Phoenix Without Ashes* (based on Ellison's TV concept *The Starlost*)
3. Harry Harrison, *Captive Universe*
4. Robert Heinlein, *Orphans of the Sky*
5. Murray Leinster, *Proxima Centauri*
6. Harry Martinson, *Aniara*
7. Clifford Simak, *Target Generation*
8. E. C. Tubb, *The Space-Born*
9. Don Wilcox, *The Voyage That Lasted 600 Years*

In these stories humans – or aliens – have entirely abandoned their home world for a life in space, often travelling endlessly from star to star.

1. James Blish, *Cities in Flight* (an antigravity device enables entire cities to fly off the Earth, and they go out into the galaxy)
2. Arthur C. Clarke, *Rendezvous With Rama* (a mysterious alien spaceship visits the solar system without ever revealing its secrets, but it evidently is inhabited by an endlessly wandering, possibly all-machine civilization)
3. Donald Moffitt, *The Jupiter Theft* (eternally wandering aliens use entire gas giant planets as fuel for their ship, and come to the solar system to top up with Jupiter)
4. Larry Niven, *Ringworld* (the puppeteer civilization, featured here and in other Niven works, lives aboard a fleet of spaceships fleeing the destruction of the Galactic Core)
5. Alexei Panshin, *Rite of Passage* (a whole human society exists within a vast spaceship, like a generation starship)
6. Joan Vinge, *The Outcasts of Heaven's Belt* (the only habitable world in another planetary system has been rendered virtually uninhabitable through war; two conflicting civilizations now exist in environments created on less hospitable worlds, or in space)
7. George Zebrowski, *Macrolife* (a novel which develops the concepts of spacegoing civilizations being components of a new form of life – macrolife)

Ten Characters Who Have Promoted the Consumption of Coffee in Improbable Quarters of Space and Time
by Nick Lowe

1. *Kimball Kinnison.* Things are looking pretty desperate towards the climax of E. E. 'Doc' Smith's *Second Stage Lensmen.* In the most titanic space battle in all history, the great Boskonian armada is making interstellar dust of the forces of Civilization – and Gray

Lensman Kinnison, the one man who can save the day and keep the universe safe for democracy, lies shattered and nerveless, following his psychic combat with a warped Arisian brain! Fortunately for humanity, Kinnison is revived to full strength in a single paragraph merely by the ingestion of a large steak and a whole pot of Thralian coffee, brewed too strong for any but the Gray Lensman to swallow without getting the squitters all through the most important bit of the book.

2. *Tarl Cabot*, once of Earth, now interminably of Counter-Earth, is nevertheless slow to forsake the pleasures of his former home. With his good friend Elizabeth Cardwell, once a haughty terrestrial beauty but now a fulfilled Gorean slave-girl, he pauses from the rip-roaring excitement of John Norman's *Assassin of Gor* to enjoy a refreshing cup of the legendary black wine of Thentis, served them by the beautiful virgin slaves of the sinful city of Ar.

3. *The Lady Jessica Atreides* (mother, of course, of the hero of Frank Herbert's *Dune*) shows her keen interest in the economy of her adopted world by doing her bit for the Arrakeen coffee industry. Early in the novel she ingeniously sobers up a drunken minion by sousing him with spicy coffee; later, during her sojourn with the desert Fremen, she meditates for nearly a page on a cup of coffee that has momentarily become endowed with a mystical intensity of significance.

4. *Charli Bux*, Theodore Sturgeon's hero of 'If All Men were Brothers, Would you Let One Marry your Sister?', is driven by an overwhelming passion for Jamaican Blue Mountain to pursue his quest to the shunned utopia-world of Vexvelt, where the natives enjoy a life blessed with all manner of good things by the simple expedient of committing incest left, right and centre. I bet you didn't realize it was your clumsy neanderthal incest taboo that was preventing *you* from growing Blue Mountain coffee.

5. *Imperial Trader Horace Hussein Chamoun al-Shamlan Bury* is the man responsible for introducing the joys of caffeine to a whole alien civilization. After the 'Moties' in *The Mote in God's Eye* have given humanity its first contact with an extraterrestrial race, Larry Niven and Jerry Pournelle lost no time in giving the Moties their first contact with Blue Mountain and the other gourmet coffees of Earth. *The Mote* is one of several stories in which Jamaica is miraculously preserved from nuclear doom in order to keep future generations decently pepped.

6. *Paul Sanders,* in George R. R. Martin's 'With Morning Comes Mistfall', is anxious to boost tourism on Wraithworld, and this is no doubt why he has banned the use of all instant and synthetic coffees on the planet. So enticing do the attractions of real coffee prove that the story's characters take seven pages just to shift the action away from the café.

7. *Clee Garlock,* in E. E. 'Doc' Smith's *The Galaxy Primes,* is famous even before the story opens for needing a whole pot of coffee in the morning before he's any use to man or superman. The result is that five of the eight chapters in this astonishing novel begin with an explicit or obliquely mentioned pot of coffee for Garlock. Why Smith's characters seem unable to tolerate coffee in smaller doses than a litre is a riddle for future generations of critics.

8. *Empress Ettarre of the Twenty Universes* is just plain 'Star' to Oscar Gordon of Earth when they quest together for the Egg of the Phoenix in Heinlein's *Glory Road.* Oscar really ought to twig that there's more to his liberated Amazon sex-kitten than appears, when she prepares him for a heroic combat by making him a cup of extremely horrible coffee. This has the crafty effect of simultaneously perking him up and making him so cross and pugnacious he (literally) wipes up his monstrous opponent with his bare hands.

9. *Senior Medical Officer Onro of Regulus Base* is one of the most alarming victims of caffeine addiction in the interstellar age. No sooner has he been introduced to Helva XH-834, the spaceship with the larynx of gold, than he smashes up half her galley looking for some coffee, after having to make do with instant for two and a half weeks. Mercifully, he finds it before damaging Helva and himself beyond repair. (Anne McCaffrey, *The Ship Who Sang.*)

10. *Dan Brodersen,* Poul Anderson's irrepressible Danish entrepreneur in *The Avatar,* seems to be sustained on his epic journey across the unknown principally by regular doses of coffee and brandy, generally together. He spends a lot of time puffing on his dreadful smelly pipe, too, but that's another list.

Nick Lowe

Eight Stories about Intelligent Dolphins or Whales

1. Arthur C. Clarke, *Dolphin Island*
2. Robert Merle, *Day of the Dolphins*
3. Roy Meyers, *Dolphin Boy* (and sequels)
4. Joe Poyer, *Operation Malacca*
5. Robert Silverberg, 'Ishmael in Love'
6. Leo Szilard, 'The Voice of the Dolphins'
7. Ian Watson, *The Jonah Kit*
8. Roger Zelazny, 'Kjwalll'kje'k'koothaïlll'kej'k'

Thirteen SF Novels Set under the Sea

1. T. J. Bass, *The Godwhale*
2. Kenneth Bulmer, *City Under the Sea*
3. Arthur C. Clarke, *The Deep Range*
4. Hal Clement, *Ocean on Top*
5. Stanton A. Coblentz, *The Sunken World*
6. Richard Cowper, *Profundis*
7. Gordon R. Dickson, *The Space Swimmers*
8. Frank Herbert, *Under Pressure* (*The Dragon in the Sea*)
9. Henry Kuttner, *Fury*
10. Frederik Pohl and Jack Williamson, *Undersea Quest* (also *Undersea Fleet* and *Undersea City*)
11. Jules Verne, *20,000 Leagues Under the Sea*
12. Dennis Wheatley, *They Found Atlantis*
13. Jack Williamson, *The Green Girl*

Clarke's novel is a serious exploration of the possibilities of using the ocean's resources. In several of the others – Bass, Bulmer, Clement, Dickson, Williamson – humanity is adapted for undersea life. Herbert's and Verne's are submarine adventures, as is Cowper's (only his is a giant submarine in which live the survivors of the holocaust). Coblentz and Wheatley's novels have Atlantis preserved under the sea, and similiar undersea cities feature in the Pohl/ Williamson series and in *Fury* – although in the latter case the sea is on Venus.

Ten SF Stories Set on the Moon

1. Ben Bova, *Millennium*
2. Algis Budrys, *Rogue Moon*
3. Edgar Rice Burroughs, *The Moon Maid*
4. John W. Campbell, *The Moon is Hell*
5. Arthur C. Clarke, *Earthlight*
6. Arthur C. Clarke, *A Fall of Moondust*
7. Robert Heinlein, *The Moon is a Harsh Mistress*
8. E. C. Tubb, *Moon Base*
9. H. G. Wells, *The First Men in the Moon*
10. Jack Williamson, 'The Moon Era'

Fifteen SF Stories Set on Mars

1. Leigh Brackett, *Sword of Rhiannon*
2. Ray Bradbury, *The Martian Chronicles*
3. Edgar Rice Burroughs, *A Princess of Mars*
4 Arthur C. Clarke, *The Sands of Mars*
5. D. G. Compton, *Farewell, Earth's Bliss*
6. Philip K. Dick, *Martian Time-Slip*
7. Rex Gordon, *No Man Friday*
8. Robert Heinlein, *Red Planet*
9. C. S. Lewis, *Out of the Silent Planet*
10. Frederik Pohl, *Man Plus*
11. Christopher Priest, *The Space Machine*
12. John Varley, 'In The Hall of the Martian Kings'
13. Ian Watson, *The Martian Inca*
14. Stanley G. Weinbaum, 'A Martian Odyssey'
15. Roger Zelazny, 'A Rose for Ecclesiastes'

Ever since H. G. Wells's Martians set covetous eyes on Earth in *The War of the Worlds*, Mars and its inhabitants have been a favourite locale for SF writers. The above are a selection of the major stories largely set on the Red Planet, from Burroughs' and Brackett's romantic visions through to the arid realism of Compton and Dick.

Ten Stories Set on Venus

1. Poul Anderson, 'The Big Rain'
2. Poul Anderson, 'Sister Planet'
3. Ray Bradbury, 'The Long Rain'
4. Robert Heinlein, 'Logic of Empire'
5. Henry Kuttner, *Fury*
6. C. S. Lewis, *Perelandra*
7. Larry Niven, 'Becalmed in Hell'
8. Frederik Pohl, 'The Merchants of Venus'
9. Stanley G. Weinbaum, 'Paradise Planet'
10. Roger Zelazny, 'The Doors of His Face, the Lamps of His Mouth'

Venus has never established itself in the imaginations of SF writers and readers in the way Mars has. The most consistent image in these stories is that of a water world, or a planet lashed by perpetual storms. Niven's story presents a more modern picture.

Twelve Ways of Travelling in Time without a Time Machine

1. *Cryonics* By freezing the human body so that it can be thawed at some date in the future, as in Frederik Pohl's *The Age of the Pussyfoot*
2. *Dreaming* You may dream yourself into the future or the past, as in Michael Bishop's *No Enemy But Time*, Robert Graves' *Watch the North Wind Rise*
3. *Drugs* Taking drugs of various kinds does the trick in William Wallace Cook's *Marooned in 1492*, H. Rider Haggard's *The Ancient Allan*, and Michel Jeury's *Chronolysis*
4. *Falling into a radio telescope* The protagonist of James Blish's *Midsummer Century* is thrust into the distant future as a result of just such an accident
5. *Faster than light travel* The relativistic time-dilation effects in a spaceship travelling at close to the speed of light mean that many years normal time may pass in what is hours, or even minutes or seconds, to the travellers. This is explored in such books as Poul

Anderson's *Tau Zero*, L. Ron Hubbard's *Return to Tomorrow* and Larry Niven's *A World out of Time*

6. *Masturbation* A difficult one this, but Ray Nelson's protagonist pulls it off in 'Time Travel for Pedestrians'
7. *Mesmerism* A kind of suspended animation, induced through hypnosis, works in Edward Bellamy's *Looking Backward*
8. *Nuclear explosion* An H-bomb detonating in close proximity to a nuclear shelter thrusts it and its occupants into the future in Robert Heinlein's *Farnham's Freehold*
9. *Nuclear radiation* A nuclear accident transports the protagonist of Isaac Asimov's *Pebble in the Sky* far into the future
10. *Sleep* The simplest method is just to fall asleep and not wake up for a long time, as happened to Rip Van Winkle, and to the protagonist of *A Crystal Age* by W. H. Hudson
11. *Stasis field* A stasis field is a bit of pseudoscience. Inside it, nothing happens: time is halted. A man accidentally trapped in a stasis field journeys to the far future in Philip José Farmer's *The Stone God Awakens*; an alien from the distant past is loosed when a stasis field is broken in Larry Niven's *World of Ptavvs*
12. *Suspended animation* The most popular method of achieving travel into the future in nineteenth- and early twentieth-century SF, e.g. H. G. Wells's *When the Sleeper Wakes* and George Allan England's *Darkness and Dawn*. It has been used more recently in L. Sprage de Camp and P. Schuyler Miller's *Genus Homo*, and in Woody Allen's movie *Sleeper*

Ten Brain Twisting Time Paradox Stories

1. Isaac Asimov, *The End of Eternity*
2. Alfred Bester, 'The Men Who Murdered Mohammed'
3. David Gerrold, *The Man Who Folded Himself*
4. Robert Heinlein, 'All You Zombies—'
5. Robert Heinlein, 'By His Footsteps'
6. Robert Silverberg, 'Many Mansions'
7. Robert Silverberg, *Stepsons of Terra*
8. Robert Silverberg, *Up The Line*
9. William Tenn, 'The Brooklyn Project'
10. William Tenn, 'Me, Myself and I'

The Sleeper Awakes Ten Times

The theme of a character conserved in a state of suspended animation has often been an ideal shortcut for examining the perplexities of hypothetical societies and has long been a favourite of SF writers over the years. With the advent of cryogenics, it might soon no longer be a SF invention.

1. Edmund Cooper, *The Uncertain Midnight*
2. Erle Cox, *Out of the Silence*
3. Robert Heinlein, *The Door into Summer*
4. Washington Irving, *Rip Van Winkle*
5. Laurence Manning, *The Man Who Awoke*
6. Michael Moorcock, *The Warlord of the Air*
7. William Morris, *News from Nowhere*
8. Francis G. Rayer, *Tomorrow Never Comes*
9. Stanley G. Weinbaum, *The Black Flame*
10. H. G. Wells, *When the Sleeper Wakes*

Eight SF Stories Featuring Cryonics

Cryonics is the science of preserving people through freezing them, so that they can be thawed out later without cellular damage. It is already used on a limited scale by terminally-ill rich people, in the hope that when future medicine comes up with a cure for their ailment they will be thawed and restored. Thus cryonic freezing may be used as a convenient device for projecting a present-day individual into a future society, usually for satiric or salutary effect (as is the case with the Amosov, Bodelsen, Pohl and Reynolds novels). Alternatively it might be used as a way of preserving passengers during a long interstellar journey, as in the Tubb and White books. Simak's novel is concerned with the social problems large-scale cryonics might bring about. Carr's story is the most unusual: a post-holocaust setting in which the vaults of frozen individuals hoping for revival after the war become the target of tomb-robbers.

1. Nikolai Amosov, *Notes From the Future*
2. Anders Bodelsen, *Freezing Down*

3. Terry Carr, 'Ozymandias'
4. Frederik Pohl, *The Age of the Pussyfoot*
5. Mack Reynolds, *Looking Backward From the Year 2000*
6. Clifford Simak, *Why Call Them Back From Heaven?*
7. E. C. Tubb, *The Winds of Gath* (and sequels in the *Dumarest* series)
8. James White, *The Dream Millennium*

Nine Famous Imaginary Cities of Science Fiction

1. Bellona - in Samuel R. Delany's *Dhalgren*
2. Cinnabar - in Edward Bryan's *Cinnabar*
3. Diaspar - in Arthur C. Clarke's *The City and the Stars*
4. Metropolis - in Thea von Harbou's *Metropolis*
5. Todos Santos - in Larry Niven and Jerry Pournelle's *Oath of Fealty*
6. Trantor - in Isaac Asimov's *Foundation* series
7. Urbmon 116 - in Robert Silverberg's *The World Inside*
8. Vermilion Sands - in J. G. Ballard's *Vermilion Sands*
9. Viriconium - in M. John Harrison's *The Pastel City* and *A Storm of Wings*

Brian Aldiss's Ten Favourite Cities

1. *Norwich* Almost my home town, and England's finest provincial city. Stacked with history, churches, and pubs. A few miles away lie the sea and the Broads, and undiscovered Norfolk. The Norwich school of painters (Cotman *et al.*) knew a thing or two . . .
2. *Hong Kong* The city with the most beautiful harbour in the world. This harshly commercial city has a gentle light that must send painters mad. The way into and out of China, the world's biggest shopping spree. If you don't get a long loud buzz out of HK, you're dead.
3. *Rio de Janeiro* It's the doorstep to the South American continent. The mixture of Corbusier architecture, Copacabana beauties and chilled cashassa is irresistible. Generally warm and sunny. Rio requires stamina.

4. *Tours* An elegant French city on the Loire. Here, the south-bound visitor finds that the climate changes for the better. And within reach are all the fantastic fairy-tale castles of the Loire, not to be missed

5. *Copenhagen* This is the city I'd go to if I ever become a tax-exile. It's so civilized – a bit bland, it's true, but the gateway to the Scandinavian world

6. *Peking* The most awful city on my list, with a dreadful climate. You get bits of the Arctic down your neck by Christmas and bits of the Gobi down your throat in spring. But: it contains that thrilling sense of being capital of an empire almost inexhaustible in time and space

7. *Sydney* Not everyone's choice, but not many great cities have topless bathing beaches and spectacular scenery – that harbour with the opera house – within minutes of the heart of town. Also, those damned great oysters . . .

8. *Ohrid* A quiet city of the past, its Turkish houses sitting dreaming by Lake Ohrid, a lake divided by Albania and Yugoslavia. Great atmosphere, and the lake trout fantastic to eat. Also some golden ikons to see

9. *Los Angeles* You hate big brawling cities or you love them, depending on how lucky you got when you were there. I was lucky in LA and loved the place, together with its gentle, innocent, mystical people, perched on the edge of their infinite ocean

10 .*Singapore* My favourite city. The Garden City, its symbol an orchid. Beautiful, exciting, brash, etc. Full of charming attractive people and a high degree of racial harmony. Pleasantly hot all the year round. A great port, like many of the cities on my list

Brian W. Aldiss

Six Novels Portraying a Future New York

SF novels set in existing cities in the future are, of course, common enough. New York, for obvious reasons, is a particularly popular choice. Six of the most original and compelling visions are contained in these books:

1. Isaac Asimov, *The Caves of Steel*
2. James Blish, *Earthman, Come Home*
3. Algis Budrys, *Some Will Not Die*
4. Thomas M. Disch, *334*
5. Harry Harrison, *Make Room! Make Room!*
6. Frederik Pohl and C. M. Kornbluth, *The Space Merchants*

Five SF Stories about Doctors and Medicine

1. C. M. Kornbluth, 'The Little Black Bag' – in which a disbarred doctor finds a medical kit from the future
2. Murray Leinster, *Doctor to the Stars* – one novel in a series about spacefaring Doctor Calhoun, featuring different medical puzzles on a variety of planets
3. Ward Moore and Robert Bradford, *Caduceus Wild* – a medical dystopia that when published in book form had Bradford's name amputated
4. James White, *Star Surgeon* – one novel in his *Sector General* series, about problems in a hospital treating a wide variety of alien injuries and ailments (other titles include *Hospital Station*, *Major Operation* and *Ambulance Ship*)
5. Chelsea Quinn Yarbro, *Time of the Fourth Horseman* – a novel of a future plague which centres on the efforts of the medical profession to cope

Fourteen Novels in which the Earth is Invaded

1. Frederic Brown, *Martians Go Home!*
2. William R. Burkett, *Sleeping Planet*
3. Philip K. Dick, *The Game Players of Titan*
4. Thomas M. Disch, *The Genocides*
5. Jack Finney, *The Body Snatchers*
6. Robert Heinlein, *The Puppet Masters*
7. Frederik Pohl and C. M. Kornbluth, *Wolfbane*
8. Keith Roberts, *The Furies*
9. Eric Frank Russell, *Three to Conquer*
10. Robert Silverberg, *Nightwings*

11. Clifford Simak, *They Walked Like Men*
12. William Tenn, *Of Men and Monsters*
13. H. G. Wells, *The War of the Worlds*
14. John Wyndham, *The Kraken Wakes*

The first classic invasion novel was *The War of the Worlds*, where the Martian invaders are all-conquering until they fall victim to terrestrial germs to which they have no resistance. Alien invaders since have been very varied: rather stupid aliens in *Sleeping Planet*; agriculturalists who regard humans as inconvenient pests in *The Genocides*; spores which duplicate humans in *The Body Snatchers*; slug-like creatures which cling to people and control them in *The Puppet Masters*; enigmatic pyramidal aliens who drag Earth from its orbit in *Wolfbane*; giant wasps in *The Furies*; telepathic viruses in *Three to Conquer*; bowling-ball-shaped aliens in *Three to Conquer*; giant aliens in *Of Men and Monsters*; underwater dwellers in *The Kraken Wakes*; little green men in *Martians Go Home!*.

Eight Novels about Giant Objects Hitting the Earth (or Just Missing)

1. Edwin Balmer and Philip Wylie, *When Worlds Collide* (a stray planet enters the solar system and destroys the Earth)
2. John Baxter, *The Hermes Fall* (an asteroid hits the Earth)
3. Gregory Benford and William Rotsler, *Shiva Descending* (ditto)
4. Harry Harrison, *Skyfall* (a large spaceship threatens to fall out of orbit, causing massive destruction)
5. Fritz Leiber, *The Wanderer* (a planet, used by its inhabitants as a spaceship, arrives in the solar system; it does not actually hit the Earth, but the effects of its passage are catastrophic)
6. Larry Niven and Jerry Pournelle, *Lucifer's Hammer* (another meteor-hits-Earth story, presented in great detail)
7. R. C. Sherriff, *The Hopkins Manuscript* (the Moon collides with the Earth)
8. George H. Smith, *The Unending Night* (Mars collides with the Earth)

Five Novels of Future Floods

1. J. G. Ballard, *The Drowned World*
2. John Bowen, *After the Rain*
3. Garrett P. Serviss, *The Second Deluge*
4. S. Fowler Wright, *Deluge*
5. John Wyndham, *The Kraken Wakes*

Six Stories about Nuclear Reactors and Radiation

1. Lester del Rey, *Nerves*
2. Robert Heinlein, 'Blowups Happen'
3. Malcolm Jameson, *Atomic Bomb*
4. Daniel Keyes, *The Touch*
5. Henri Queffelec, *Frontier of the Unknown*
6. Thomas Scortia and Frank Robinson, *The Prometheus Crisis*

Four Novels of Diseases and Plagues

1. Michael Crichton, *The Andromeda Strain*
2. Richard Matheson, *I Am Legend*
3. George R. Stewart, *Earth Abides*
4. Chelsea Quinn Yarbro, *Time of the Fourth Horseman*

Eight Overpopulated Futures

1. Isaac Asimov, *The Caves of Steel*
2. J. G. Ballard, 'Billennium'
3. James Blish and Norman L. Knight, *A Torrent of Faces*
4. John Brunner, *Stand on Zanzibar*
5. Thomas M. Disch, *334*
6. Harry Harrison, *Make Room! Make Room!*
7. C. M. Kornbluth, 'The Marching Morons'
8. Robert Silverberg, *The World Inside*

Six SF Novels Discussing Sterility

1. Brian Aldiss, *Greybeard*
2. Richard Cowper, *The Twilight of Briareus*
3. M. John Harrison, *The Committed Men*
4. Michael Moorcock, *An Alien Heat*
5. Charles Platt, *The City Dwellers*
6. Bob Shaw, *One Million Tomorrows*

Can it be entirely coincidence that all these novels are by British authors? Probably not: the problems caused by sterility – like many other aspects of the disaster novel – can be seen as a metaphor for Britain's industrial decline, the loss of Empire, etc, etc. In Moorcock's and Shaw's novels sterility is the price paid for immortality: in the others it represents a problem to the race in the near future.

Five Novels of Ecological Catastrophe

1. John Brunner, *The Sheep Look Up* (pollution leads to the total destruction of the USA)
2. John Christopher, *The Death of Grass* (*No Blade of Grass*) (a blight on grasses and cereals leads to famine and the breakdown of civilization)
3. J. J. Connington, *Nordenholt's Million* (a bacteria destroy all the world's vegetation)
4. Ward Moore, *Greener Than You Think* (a new strain of grass multiplies wildly, and takes over everything)
5. Philip Wylie, *The End of a Dream* (well-depicted ecological collapse)

Fifteen Novels Set after the Nuclear Holocaust

The prospect of nuclear war and its terrible aftermath has naturally preoccupied SF writers since 1945. These are some of the notable novels based – in widely differing ways – on the idea.

1. Piers Anthony, *Sos the Rope* and sequels (collected as *Battle Circle*)
2. Angela Carter, *Heroes and Villains*
3. Philip K. Dick, *Dr Bloodmoney, or, How We Got Along After the Bomb*
4. Pat Frank, *Alas Babylon*
5. Daniel Galouye, *Dark Universe*
6. Peter van Greenaway, *The Crucified City*
7. M. John Harrison, *The Committed Men*
8. Judith Merril, *Shadow on the Hearth*
9. Walter M. Miller, *Canticle for Leibowitz*
10. Edgar Pangborn, *Davy* (and other novels with a common background: *The Judgment of Eve* and *The Company of Glory*)
11. Mordecai Roshwald, *Level 7*
12. Nevil Shute, *On the Beach*
13. Wilson Tucker, *The Long Loud Silence*
14. John Wyndham, *The Chrysalids*
15. Roger Zelazny, *Damnation Alley*

Twelve SF Stories of New Ice Ages

1. G. J. Arnaud's French series *La Compagnie des Glaces* (The Ice Company), which has already reached eleven volumes
2. John Boland, *White August*
3. John Christopher, *The World in Winter*
4. Arthur C. Clarke, 'The Forgotten Enemy'
5. Michael Coney, *Winter's Children*
6. Anna Kavan, *Ice*
7. Crawford Kilian, *Icequake*
8. Fritz Leiber, 'A Pail of Air'
9. Michael Moorcock, *The Ice Schooner*
10. Douglas Orgill and John Gribbin, *The Sixth Winter*
11. Robert Silverberg, *Time of the Great Freeze*
12. Kurt Vonnegut, *Cat's Cradle*

Most of these are relatively straightforward: Boland's, Christopher's, Clarke's, Kilian's and Orgill/Gribbin's tell of the coming of a new ice age; Arnaud's series, Coney's, Moorcock's and Silverberg's are about life long after it has set in. 'A Pail of Air' presents a situation in which the Earth has been separated from the sun and everything, atmosphere included, has frozen. Kavan's *Ice* is a surrealist fantasy of a psychiatric ice age of the mind which seeps through to the landscape in which the protagonist moves. *Cat's Cradle* has all the world's water turned into the unusable variant *ice-nine*.

An Unlucky Thirteen World-Destroying Catastrophes

1. *Drought* destroys civilization in J. G. Ballard's *The Drought* and Charles Eric Maine's *The Tide Went Out*
2. *Electricity* stops working in René Barjavel's *Ashes, Ashes*
3. *Gas* emitted by a volcano poisons all the world's population save one man in M. P. Shiel's *The Purple Cloud*
4. *Insects* cause havoc in Arthur Herzog's *The Swarm*, Thomas Page's *The Hephaestus Plague* and Keith Roberts's *The Furies* (in the last, the best of the three, they are giant alien wasps)
5. *Madness* afflicts the world in Edmund Cooper's *All Fools' Day*
6. *Metal Fatigue* has disastrous consequences in S. S. Held's *The Death of Iron* and Donald Suddaby's *The Death of Metal*
7. *Plague* wipes out nearly everyone in Mary Shelley's *The Last Man* and George R. Stewart's *Earth Abides*
8. *Plastic* is attacked by a voracious virus in Kit Pedler and Gerry Davis's *Mutant 59: The Plastic Eater*
9. *Polywater*, or a form of it, turns all the world's water into the useless substance *ice-nine* in Kurt Vonnegut's *Cat's Cradle*
10. *Religion* leads to the end of everything in Arthur C. Clarke's 'The Nine Billion Names of God': when they have all been printed out by computer, the universe ends
11. *Slowing rotation* of the Earth is the cause of catastrophe in J. B. S. Haldane's 'The Last Judgment'
12. *Sterility* is the problem in Brian Aldiss's *Greybeard*
13. *World-hatching* is unfortunate for those on the surface in Jack Williamson's 'Born of the Sun', in which we learn that the Earth is an egg containing a great embryonic being, hatched by the heat of the sun.

Spider Robinson's List of Silly Weapons

The Swordbroad: Invented by a tribe of fanatical male chauvinists, the Prix, this armament consisted of a wife gripped by the ankles and whirled like a flail (Prix warriors made frequent jocular allusion to the sharp cutting edge of their wives' tongue). The weapon died out, along with the Prix, in a single generation – for tolerably obvious reasons

The Rotator: A handgun in which the bullets are designed to rotate as well as revolve, presenting an approximately even chance of suicide with each use

The Bullista: A weapon of admittedly limited range which attempted to sow confusion among the enemy by firing live cows into their midst, placing them upon a dilemma of the horns (Also called the Cattling Gun)

The Arbalust: A modification of the bullista, which sought to demoralize and distract the enemy by peppering their encampments with pornographic pictures and literature – yet another dilemma of the horns

The Dogapult: Another modification of the bullista; self-explanatory

The Cross 'Bo: Yet another modification of the bullista, this weapon delivered a payload of enraged hoboes. Thus gunnery officers had a choice between teats, tits, mastiffs or bindlestiffs

The Blunderbus: A hunter-seeker weapon which destroys the steering box in surface mass transit

The Guided Missal: Originally developed as a specific deterrent to the Arbalust; as, however, it is hellishly more destructive, its use is now restricted by international convention to Sundays

The Slingshit: self-explanatory; still used in politics and in fandom. And, of course, such obvious losers as the *foot ax*, *relish gas*, *studded mice*, and the effective but disgusting *snotgun*

Source: *Silly Weapons Throughout History* in Spider Robinson's collection *Antinomy* (1980)

Ten Alternate Worlds Novels

Alternate worlds novels are those which try to answer the question: what would today's world be like if history had followed a different course? The most popular alternative – a different outcome to World War Two – receives its own list.

1. Kingsley Amis, *The Alteration* (the Reformation never happens, and the Catholic Church still rules Britain)
2. John Brunner, *Times Without Number* (the Spanish are dominant)
3. Ronald Clark, *Queen Victoria's Bomb* (the H-bomb arrives a few years early)
4. L. Sprague de Camp, *The Wheels of If* (America is colonized by the Norsemen)
5. Douglas C. Jones, *The Court Martial of George Armstrong Custer* (Custer survives the Little Big Horn)
6. MacKinlay Kantor, *If the South Had Won the Civil War* (self-explanatory)
7. Michael Moorcock, *The Warlord of the Air* (the two World Wars never happen, nor does the Russian Revolution)
8. Ward Moore, *Bring the Jubilee* (as with the Kantor, the South wins the Civil War)
9. Keith Roberts, *Pavane* (Spain conquers Britain in the sixteenth century and the Catholic Church still dominates the modern world)
10. Robert Silverberg, *The Gate of Worlds* (the Black Death is far more devastating, the USA is never colonized, and an Aztec Empire dominates modern America)

Twenty-five Victories for Hitler

A classic SF 'what if' theme which many authors have tackled often by the use of parallel universes where the worst happened.

1. Anthony Armstrong and Bruce Graeme, *When the Bell Rang*
2. Hilary Bailey, 'The Fall of Frenchy Steiner'
3. Otto Basil, *The Twilight Mar*

4. Douglas Brown and Christopher Serpell, *Loss of Eden*
5. Kevin Brownlow and Andrew Mollo, *It Happened Here* (movie)
6. Giles Cooper, *The Other Man*
7. Richard Cox, *Operation Sea Lion*
8. Len Deighton, *SS/GB*
9. Philip K. Dick, *The Man in the High Castle*
10. Gordon Eklund, 'Red Skies'
11. Harlan Ellison, 'The City on the Edge of Forever'
12. C. S. Forrester, 'If Hitler Had Invaded England'
13. Martin Hawkins, *When Adolf Came*
14. Keith Laumer, *Worlds of the Imperium*
15. Fritz Leiber, *The Big Time*
16. Norman Longmate, 'If Britain Had Fallen'
17. Kenneth McKay, *Invasion*
18. H. V. Morton, *I, James Blunt*
19. Frederic Mullally, 'Hitler Has Won'
20. Eric Norden, *The Ultimate Solution*
21. André Norton, *The Crossroads of Time*
22. Keith Roberts, 'Weinachtabend'
23. Sarban, *The Sound of his Horn*
24. Robert Silverberg, 'Trips'
25. Norman Spinrad, *The Iron Dream*

Ten SF Stories about Parallel Worlds

Parallel worlds and alternate worlds are different aspects of a similar idea, and the two concepts sometimes overlap. In parallel-worlds stories we imagine that there are other universes coexistent with ours but hidden from our perceptions; in these universes there may also be parallel Earths, either quite similar to our own or totally different. These parallel Earths may display the results of different historical events, the province of the alternate world story. The following use the alternate world aspect only in passing, if at all.

1. Isaac Asimov, *The Gods Themselves*
2. Richard Cowper, *Breakthrough*
3. Fred Hoyle, *October the First is Too Late*
4. R. A. Lafferty, 'The Hole on the Corner'

5. Keith Laumer, *Worlds of the Imperium* (and its sequels *The Other Side of Time* and *Assignment in Nowhere*)
6. Murray Leinster, 'Sidewise in Time'
7. Richard Meredith, *At the Narrow Passage* (and its sequels *No Brother, No Friend* and *Vestiges of Time*)
8. Alan Nourse, 'Tiger By the Tail'
9. H. Beam Piper, *Lord Kalvan of Otherwhen*
10. Clifford Simak, *Ring Around the Sun*

Fritz Leiber's List of Monsters

Frankenstein: 'that much misunderstood humble patchwork of humanity'

Yog-Sothoth: 'H. P. Lovecraft's somewhat uncheery vision of the ultimate god of gods'

Mr Hyde: 'that healthily dynamic alter ego of the pusillanimous *square* Dr Jekyll'

Helen Vaughan: 'Arthur Machen's she-satyr sneaking through *The Great God Pan*'

Alraune: 'Hans Heinz Ewer's last seed of a hanged murderer'

Charles Dexter Ward: 'Lovecraft's own projection of himself'

The Great Boyg: 'that living midnight forest from Ibsen's *Peer Gynt*'

Coeurl: 'who stalks magnificently through Van Vogt's *Black Destroyer*'

Richard III: 'who humped himself to rule all England'

Duke Ferdinand: 'the great grand-daddy of all wolfmen, from *The Duchess of Malfi*'

Svengali: 'the prototype of all power-hungry hypnotists'

Quasimodo: 'Hugo's deathless hunchback'

King Kong: 'another vastly misunderstood devotee of beauty'

The Phantom of the Opera: 'who made the sewers of Paris more livable'

Count Dracula: 'who subsisted on the blood of beautiful young ladies'

Cthulhu: 'Lovecraft's gigantic non-Euclidean undersea sleeper'

Nyarlathotep: 'a dark modern pharaoh–magician come out of Egypt'

The Wolf Man: 'lusty, satyrish old werewolf'

The Red Brain: 'Donald Wandrei's end-of-the-world creation'

It: 'whom Ted Sturgeon sent stumbling forever across forest and countryside'

Archimago: 'prototype of all queen-kidnapping, princess-starved, infant-enticing black magicians, from *The Faerie Queene*'
The Man Who Laughs: 'Hugo's creation with a face carved in infancy into a clown-mask'
The Mummy: 'whose only misdeed was that he wanted immortality'

'I love monsters,' begins Fritz Leiber in his remarkable article *Monsters and Monster-Lovers*, first given as a speech at an Oakland 1964 convention and since reprinted several times. The above list is excerpted from it.

Ten SF Stories Featuring Invisibility

1. Brian Aldiss, *The Saliva Tree* (1965)
2. Algis Budrys, *For Love* (1962)
3. C. H. Hinton, *Stella* (1895)
4. Jack London, *The Shadow and the Flash* (1903)
5. Edward Page Mitchell, *The Crystal Man* (1903)
6. Fitz-James O'Brien, *What Was It?* (1859)
7. Eric Frank Russell, *Sinister Barrier* (1939)
8. Bob Shaw, *A Wreath of Stars* (1976)
9. H. G. Wells, *The Invisible Man* (1897)
10. Philip Wylie, *The Murderer Invisible* (1931)

The early invisibility stories – such as Hinton, London, Mitchell and Wells – deal with scientific experiments which produce invisibility, usually to no good end. O'Brien's story is different – it is about an invisible predator (probably a vampire), and prefigures such stories of invisible aliens as Russell's and Aldiss's. Wylie's is a mad scientist story. Budrys's is the only modern SF story to try to come up with some convincing scientific jargon to 'explain' invisibility. Shaw's novel concerns the discovery of an 'anti-neutrino' world coexistent with our own, which is invisible until you put on special glasses.

Another sort of invisibility – where you are not invisible at all, but people nevertheless fail to see you – features in such stories as Gardner Dozois's *The Visible Man* (1975), Damon Knight's *The Country of the Kind* (1956) and Robert Silverberg's *To See The Invisible Man* (1963).

Ten SF Stories about Atlantis

Atlantis was a popular subject for science fiction in the early part of the century, but has lately been disregarded by most writers. The exceptions are Jane Gaskell's fantasy adventures, and Ursula Le Guin's story, which uses the rising of Atlantis in subtle metaphorical terms. Frena Bloomfield's lesser-known title is a juvenile fantasy of distinction.

1. Pierre Benoit, *L'Atlantide* (1919)
2. Frena Bloomfield, *Sky Fleet of Atlantis* (1979)
3. Stanton A. Coblentz, *The Sunken World* (1928)
4. Jules Verne, *Twenty Thousand Leagues Under the Sea* (1870)
5. Jane Gaskell, *The Serpent* (1963) and sequels
6. C. J. Cutcliffe Hyne, *The Lost Continent* (1900)
7. Ursula Le Guin, *The New Atlantis* (1975)
8. David M. Parry, *The Scarlet Empire* (1906)
9. E. E. Smith, *Triplanetary* (1934)
10. Dennis Wheatley, *They Found Atlantis* (1936)

Five SF Stories about Crucifixion

1. Brian Earnshaw, *Planet in the Eye of Time* (a time-travel story centred around the crucifixion)
2. Philip José Farmer, *To Your Scattered Bodies Go* (the crucifixion is re-enacted on Riverworld, a place where all Earth's dead are resurrected)
3. Harry Harrison, 'The Streets of Ashkelon' (a missionary on an alien planet is crucified by its natives)
4. Garry Kilworth, 'Let's Go to Golgotha' (another time-travel story, in which all the crowds watching the event prove to be time-travellers)
5. Michael Moorcock, *Behold The Man* (a time-traveller discovers Jesus to be a mental defective, and ultimately takes his place on the Cross)

Fourteen SF Stories about Clones

Clones and cloning have lately become one of the most popular SF subjects, as the dates given with the stories below will indicate – another instance of SF following somewhat behind science fact. But Van Vogt, at least, got there twenty-five years earlier.

1. Ben Bova, *The Multiple Man* (1976)
2. Arthur C. Clarke, *Imperial Earth* (1975)
3. Richard Cowper, *Clone* (1972)
4. Nancy Freedman, *Joshua, Son of None* (1973)
5. Joe Haldeman, *The Forever War* (1974)
6. Ursula Le Guin, 'Nine Lives' (1969)
7. Ira Levin, *The Boys From Brazil* (1976)
8. Evelyn Lief, *The Clone Rebellion* (1980)
9. Naomi Mitchison, *Solution Three* (1975)
10. Pamela Sargent, *Cloned Lives* (1976)
11. A. E. Van Vogt, *The World of Null-A* (1945)
12. John Varley, *The Ophiuchi Hotline* (1977)
13. Kate Wilhelm, *Where Late the Sweet Birds Sang* (1976)
14. Gene Wolfe, *The Fifth Head of Cerberus* (1972)

The Clone, a 1965 novel-length collaboration by Theodore L. Thomas and Kate Wilhelm is *not* about the theme of cloning, but describes a creature (that nothing could stop) born of a mix in the sewer system of various ingredients.

John Sladek's List of Seven Great Unexplained Mysteries of our Time (with Explanations)

The trouble with science today is that it has answers to all the wrong questions. No one is asking whether the laser is or is not a beam of coherent energy in the visible spectrum. No one is desperate to know what it is that ontogeny recapitulates, or whether E *really* equals mc^2. It is high time that scientists came out of their ivory laboratories, stopped messing around with silicon chips and transactional analysis, and tackled some of the real mysteries of our time:

1. *What's so great about the Great Pyramid?* Nearly everything. It contains millions or billions of pounds of stone or is it tons, I haven't got the exact figures here but it's very big. Modern scientists have discovered that if you put a razor blade under the Great Pyramid, *it will remain sharp throughout the night!* Because of the great weight of the Pyramid, however, this experiment has not yet been carried out. Still, rumours have it that a consortium of razor-blade companies are trying to buy up the patent and suppress it.

2. *How did Nostradamus manage to predict the rise of Clement Attlee?* Oddly enough, he didn't. This is one of the rare instances where the great sage of Provence made a wrong prediction. On the other hand, writing in 1556, he was right about millions of other future events, such as:

(a) Napoleon's invention of brandy, 1769
(b) Nepal invades Peru, 1999 (or World War Three, 1966)
(c) Martian invasion of California (undetected), last year
(d) Stock market steady for a time

3. *Could Stonehenge be a primitive computer, used by the Druids for figuring payrolls?* That must remain a mystery, an imponderable conundrum, a riddle wrapped in a dark enigma, an impenetrable veil of cloud-shrouded o'ercast secret of Sphinx-mute Nature

4. *Who killed Kennedy?* The assassination of President Kennedy in 1963 is one of the great baffling imponderable riddles of our time. Nearly everyone in the world remembers where he or she was at the time, especially if he or she happened to be in Dealey Plaza with a rifle. Yet the identity of the killer(s) remains a mystery. The Warren Commission found that:

(a) Kennedy was shot either by one person with one bullet or by several persons with several bullets, but probably not by several persons sharing the same bullet
(b) Lee Harvey Oswald may have entered the Texas Book Depository merely to deposit a Texas book
(c) It seems unlikely that the President was cleaning a gun in his car at the time
(d) Certain critical frames of film of the event were destroyed,

perhaps by the same hand that destroyed certain critical portions of the Watergate tapes

(e) I wasn't even in Dallas at the time, and I can prove it

5. *What is the truth about the Neapolitan Shroud?* This curious relic looks exactly like the more famous Turin Shroud, but it comes in three colours. Believers say it was a sacred burial shroud, sceptics maintain it was used to wrap fish. This has led to a sub-controversy over Christian fish-symbolism, Friday observance and whether it's okay to serve red wine with Cod Florentine.

The shroud bears the clear outline of a man with long blond hair and beard, blue eyes and Charlton Heston's nose. There is a distinct halo, 43cm in diameter and covered with gold leaf. All this is convincing enough, but what of the scientific evidence?

Scientific bodies subjected the shroud to every known test, with conflicting results: Carbon 14 test establishes its date as 1943, plus or minus 18,000 years. X-ray analysis shows the shroud to have an abscess in the upper left incisor that needs immediate attention. For chemical analysis, a small portion of one corner of the shroud was removed and the rest burnt, revealing it to be 'probably woven' out of some kind of 'fibre or thread'.

One recent test seems to clinch the shroud's authenticity, however. Scientists examining a small mark on the surviving corner have declared it to be the authentic laundry mark of Joseph of Arimathea.

6. *Has any human being been cloned, lately?* First, a few definitions. A clone is an exact genetic replica of someone, raised in a test tube and therefore inclined to be somewhat sensitive to the sound of breaking glass. A clone gets all of his or her chromosomes from one parent, and all of his or her allowance. Clones who develop Oedipal problems have only themselves to blame.

Why should anyone want to clone himself? For very rich men, there might be distinct tax advantages in claiming themselves as dependants. Clones can also sign your cheques, answer your phone and break in new shoes.

'The rich,' said Scott Fitzgerald to Ernest Hemingway, 'are not like you and me.' Soon this may no longer be the case. For soon the clones of the very rich will be everywhere. They will *be* you and me – *only more so.* Howard Hughes clones will be hiding away in thousands of Las Vegas hotel rooms, avoiding publicity. An army of J. Paul

Gettys is growing up in Brazil – already they know how to sign letters illegibly.

The prospect is frightening. China contemplates military cloning, or even the creation of a phalanx of waiters who look exactly alike. The resulting confusion, they hope, will bring about the final collapse of decadent Western civilization

7. *Is there intelligent life anywhere in the universe?* The UFO question remains a Number One mystery. In 1947 a retired Army major, flying his private plane over the Cascade mountains, saw a group of strange objects flying in formation below him. He circled for a closer look and saw that they were geese. The major did not report this unusual experience for fear of being branded a hoaxer or a lunatic.

Later, another retired major did report seeing Faust in Hell, and a journalistic distortion of the 'frying sorcerer' made world headlines. Suddenly everybody was seeing strange, unexplainable things in the sky. A retired Navy commander saw baskets of peaches flitting through the stratosphere. A Florida boy scout saw a flying tickertape machine that turned into a chicken salad sandwich without mayonnaise.

A Vermont police chief chased a flying saucer for two hours, unable to get its licence number. In New Mexico a giant saucer caused a family car to run out of gas. In Missouri there was funny interference on the radio. In Oregon some underwear was stolen off a clothesline.

Finally the Air Force was forced to investigate all such sightings of 'uninteresting flying objects', or UFOs, as they came to be called. The official Air Force report, now declassified, explains many of the sightings as natural phenomena (like peach baskets) or hoaxes or hallucinations or mirages or manifestations of the Cosmic Will. But there remains at bottom a tiny residue of saucer cases that cannot be explained or eliminated (this residue should not be confused with the residue in the bottom of saucers, which you can eliminate with a solution of baking soda and warm water, soak for one hour and then scrub). Here are a few of these remarkable cases:

(a) Avrel Gleans, 73, saw a bright light descend from the Western sky and land on his lawn sprinkler. As soon as the strange craft touched down, ten tiny George Washingtons leapt out, bound Mr Gleans hand and foot, and forced him to eat a magnetized hamburger.

(b) Roman Zipp, twelve but going on thirteen, took the only clear, detailed movie of a flying saucer. His film shows the craft to be a large, complex structure with portholes, flaming jets, coloured lights and an upper deck on which naked creatures can be seen playing shuffleboard. Unfortunately the drugstore refused to process such a film.

(c) Grantham Fassbinder, 48, an East Coast disc-jockey who runs an all-night phone-in programme, recorded the following conversation:

FASSBINDER: So you . . . you say you're from another planet?
CALLER: That's about it.
FASSBINDER: Well, uh, what planet?
CALLER: Does it matter? There are many planets known to us, planets rich in life-forms vastly superior to your puny so called human race.
FASSBINDER: Okay, why haven't you contacted us before?
CALLER: You are not yet ready, O puny man! Man knows so little, man is as a child, a selfish and ignorant child. Give up your nuclear weapons, stop eating meat, get to bed earlier. Then will ye grow in wisdom and understanding, then will ye be ready to venture in a silver ship beyond the vast dark interstellar reaches of stuff, to take your place among the intergalactic brotherhood of species. Ye have been warned!

Fassbinder ignored the warning, however, and remained sceptical. Yet later - exactly six years later, more or less - Grantham Fassbinder was arrested in Houston for not wearing a six-gun. Coincidences like that make you think.

(d) My uncle Clyde tells me he has met the aliens in person and gained their confidence by trading with them. He gave the creatures a Buddy Holly record and a novelty plastic dog turd, and in return they gave him half a ton of uncut diamonds.

'They reproduce,' he says, 'simply by shaking hands. So naturally they have to be very careful about overpopulation, especially at sales conferences. But they did give me a few tips about our own population problems.' He explained that in about twenty years, the earth will have over 731,000,000,000,000,000 inhabitants, and no one will have a place to sit down. From then on it gets worse: with half a million being born every second, people won't even have room to stand up, unless they form human pyramids. But in a short time, the pyramids will get too high, the earth will tip over, and we'll all fall off. How can we avoid this disaster?

'They say if we stop shaking hands right now, we just might have a chance. We could wear gloves, also – though a lot of people don't like it much, and anyway it's only 95 per cent safe.'

What does it all mean? Undoubtedly alien civilizations are trying to contact earth, probably to borrow money. As we know from movies, these aliens travel around the universe in a mother ship. From this, smaller craft descend to land on our planet, remaining to explore its surface until the mother ship tells them to come up and wash their hands for dinner.

John T. Sladek

Ten SF Private Eyes

Detectives of the future. Move over Sam Spade, Philip Marlowe, Hercule Poirot and the Continental Op. Your time is up!

1. *Lord d'Arcy*, a master detective in an alternate world where magic is operative; in Randall Garrett's *Too Many Magicians* and sequels
2. *Elijah Bailey*, a human detective with a robot sidekick working in underground cities; in Asimov's *Caves of Steel* and *The Naked Sun*
3. *Jan Darzek*, a private-eye on hire to the Council of The Supreme in Lloyd Biggle, Jr's *Watchers of the Dark* and sequels
4. *Rick Decard*, a bounty hunter searching for rogue androids; in Philip K. Dick's *Do Androids Dream of Electric Sheep?*
5. *Gil Hamilton*, psychic operative for ARM in Larry Niven's *Known Space* stories
6. *Miro Hetzel*, a canny galactic effectuator, in Jack Vance's stories collected under the same title
7. *Victor Slaughter*, a private detective in *Gomorrah* by Marvin Karlins and Lewis M. Andrews
8. *Matthew Swain*, a space-age hardboiled investigator closely modelled on Chandler's Marlowe in Mike McQuay's recent series

9. *Sybil Sue Blue*, a female galactic operator in Rosel George Brown's novels
10. *Anthony Villiers*, a suave operator in Alexei Panshin's *Star Well* and two sequels

Twelve SF Novels in Prehistoric Times

Paradoxically, science fiction has often taken place in prehistoric times. These novels generally follow two patterns with either modern men travelling back to the past by one means or another (Farmer, Aldiss, Silverberg, May, Bishop, Chilson, High) or they are presented as an anthropological study of the conditions and quirks of evolution in action (Auel, Rosny Ainé, London, Golding, Oliver).

1. Brian Aldiss, *An Age*
2. Jean Auel, *Clan of the Cave Bear*
3. Michael Bishop, *No Enemy But Mine*
4. Robert Chilson, *The Shores of Kansas*
5. Philip José Farmer, *Traitor to the Living*
6. William Golding, *The Inheritors*
7. Philip High, *Speaking of Dinosaurs*
8. Jack London, *Before Adam*
9. Julian May, *The Many-Colored Land*
10. Chad Oliver, *Mists of Dawn*
11. J. H. Rosny Ainé, *Quest for Fire* (and a score of other novels)
12. Robert Silverberg, *Hawksbill Station*

Nine SF Stories Featuring Dinosaurs

1. Brian Aldiss, 'Poor Little Warrior'
2. Piers Anthony, *Orn*
3. Ray Bradbury, 'A Sound of Thunder'
4. L. Sprague de Camp, 'A Gun for Dinosaur'
5. David Gerrold, *Deathbeast*
6. Anne McCaffrey, *Dinosaur Planet*
7. Robert Silverberg, 'Our Lady of the Sauropods'

51

8. Clifford Simak, 'Small Deer'
9. John Taine, *Seeds of Life*

Dinosaur stories were popular in early SF, and have lately taken on a new lease of life thanks to Adrian Desmond's theory that they were warm-blooded (see the Gerrold, McCaffrey and Silverberg stories). Aldiss, Bradbury and De Camp provide accounts of time-travellers hunting dinosaur; Simak offers an explanation of their sudden extinction; Anthony's novel includes an extended and convincing account of a human outwitting a rampaging tyrannosaurus; Taine's book has evolutionary mutation giving rise to reborn dinosaurs in the present day.

Twelve SF Voyages Beyond Death

What lies beyond death has always fascinated humanity. Since Dante explored the other side, many other writers have felt a need to venture into this most speculative of territories. Their excursions vary; some visit heaven or hell (Elkin, Niven/Pournelle, Moorcock, Hales) while others tread new ground in strange territories of the in-between (Farmer, Wyndham Lewis, Le Guin, Watson, Ellison, Swigart, Dann) but few of their visions offer any genuine reassurance.

1. Jack Dann, *Junction*
2. Stanley Elkin, *The Living End*
3. Harlan Ellison, 'The Region Between'
4. Philip José Farmer, *To Your Scattered Bodies Go*
5. E. E. Y. Hales, *Chariots of Fire*
6. Ursula K. Le Guin, *The Farthest Shore*
7. Wyndham Lewis, the *Human Age* trilogy
8. Michael Moorcock, *The Warhound and the World's Pain*
9. Larry Niven and Jerry Pournelle, *Inferno*
10. Rudy Rucker, *White Light*
11. Rob Swigart, *The Time Trip*
12. Ian Watson, *Death Hunter*

Fifteen Worlds of Women

Possibly because, until the last fifteen years or so, SF writing was very much a male enclave with just a few token women (like C. L. Moore and Leigh Brackett), the theme of 'when women rule' was an important one. As a result, stereotypes of women as castrator or amazon abounded in the pulps. This situation is now changing and, in retrospect, one can even detect a slight feminist bias in early utopias of this category. The theme of matriarchal societies has been, and continues to be, a major one in SF. This is a small selection of stories where women rule:

1. Poul Anderson, *Virgin Planet*
2. J. D. Beresford, *A World of Women*
3. Thomas Berger, *Regiment of Women*
4. Edward Bulwer-Lytton, *The Coming Race*
5. Angela Carter, *The Passion of New Eve*
6. L. Sprague de Camp, *Rogue Queen*
7. Philip José Farmer, *The Lovers*
8. David H. Keller, 'The Feminine Metamorphosis'
9. Charles Eric Maine, *World Without Men*
10. Mack Reynolds, *Amazon Planet*
11. Joanna Russ, *The Female Man*
12. Wilson Tucker, *Resurrection Days*
13. Monique Wittig, *Les Guérillères*
14. Philip Wylie, *The Disappearance*
15. John Wyndham, 'Consider Her Ways'

Fifteen Famous SF Computers

1. Abel in Lawrence Durrell's *Tunc* and *Nunquam*
2. Bossy in Mark Clifton and Frank Riley's *They'd Rather Be Right* (*The Forever Machine*)
3. Colossus in D. F. Jones' *Colossus*
4. Domino in Algis Budrys' *Michaelmas*
5. Epicac XIV in Kurt Vonnegut's *Player Piano*
6. Epiktistes in R. A. Lafferty's *Arrive at Easterwine*

7. Extro in Alfred Bester's *The Computer Connection* (*Extro*)
8. Hal 9000 in Arthur C. Clarke's *2001: A Space Odyssey*
9. Harlie in David Gerrold's *When Harlie Was One*
10. Mike in Robert Heinlein's *The Moon is a Harsh Mistress*
11. Multivac in various Isaac Asimov short stories
12. Proteus in Dean R. Koontz's *Demon Seed*
13. Shalmaneser in John Brunner's *Stand on Zanzibar*
14. Tench 889B in Philip K. Dick's *A Maze of Death*
15. UniComp in Ira Levin's *This Perfect Day*

Five More Stories of Mad, Megalomaniac or Godlike Computers

1. Isaac Asimov, 'The Last Question'. A computer ends up creating a universe
2. Fredric Brown, 'The Answer'. A computer decides it is God
3. Harlan Ellison, 'I Have No Mouth And I Must Scream'. Features a particularly vindictive mad computer
4. Frank Herbert, *Destination: Void* and *The Jesus Incident*. Another computer with ideas of Godhood
5. Robert Silverberg, 'Going Down Smooth'. A less destructive mad computer

Some of the computers in the previous list – notably Colossus and Proteus . . . and of course Hal 9000 – go more than a little mad.

Twelve Notable Robot Characters

Since Karel Capek coined the word robot in his play *RUR* (though in modern usage his robots are, in fact, androids), they have become a common part of the SF landscape. But they rarely become interesting in their own right; more often, as in Jack Williamson's *The Humanoids*, they are anonymous. Some robots, however, have achieved fame, and these are some of our favourites:

1. Adam Link, in Eando Binder's *Adam Link, Robot*
2. Brillo, in Ben Bova and Harlan Ellison's 'Brillo'

3. Helen O'Loy in Lester del Rey's 'Helen O'Loy'
4. Jaspcrodus, in Barrington J. Bayley's *The Soul of the Robot*
5. Jay Score, in Eric Frank Russell's *Men, Martians and Machines*
6. Jenkins, in Clifford Simak's *City*
7. Krag, in Edmond Hamilton's *Captain Future* series
8. Marvin, in Douglas Adams' *Hitchhiker's Guide to the Galaxy*
9. R. Daneel Olivaw in Isaac Asimov's *The Caves of Steel* and *The Naked Sun* (Asimov has, of course, written many robot stories; Olivaw is his most famous robot character, however)
10. Roderick, in John Sladek's *Roderick* and *Roderick at Random*
11. Spofforth, in Walter Tevis's *Mockingbird*
12. Tik-Tok, in L. Frank Baum's *Oz* series

Nine SF Stories of Living Worlds and Other Vast Living Entities

1. Michael Bishop, 'Rogue Tomato', in which the protagonist is transformed into a tomato the size of a planet
2. A. Conan Doyle, 'When the World Screamed', in which an attempt to drill towards the centre of the Earth reveals that it is a living entity
3. Frank Herbert, *Whipping Star*, in which sentient stars play a role
4. Fred Hoyle, *The Black Cloud*, in which a cloud of interstellar matter entering the solar system proves to be intelligent
5. R. A. Kennedy, *The Triuniverse*, an early (1912) novel of legendary eccentricity in which Mars reproduces by binary fission (and the Earth, reduced to the size of a pea, is carried off to Alpha Centauri)
6. Stanislaw Lem, *Solaris*, in which the planet-wide sea covering the world (or perhaps the whole world) proves to be a living organism
7. Laurence Manning, 'The Living Galaxy', whose title is self-explanatory
8. Olaf Stapledon, *Star Maker*, which again features intelligent stars
9. Jack Williamson, 'Born of the Sun', in which Earth proves to be one of the sun's eggs, and hatches in the course of the story

They Who Shrink: Fourteen Stories of Miniature Human Beings

1. Isaac Asimov, *Fantastic Voyage*
2. James Blish, 'Nor Iron Bars'
3. James Blish, 'Surface Tension'
4. Ray Cummings, *The Girl in the Golden Atom* and *Princess of the Atom*
5. Ray Cummings, *Beyond the Vanishing Point*
6. Alan Griff (Donald Suddaby), *Lost Men in the Grass*
7. Lindsay Gutteridge, *Cold War in a Country Garden* and sequels
8. Henry Hasse, 'He Who Shrank'
9. Tabitha King, *Small World*
10. Barry Malzberg, *The Men Inside*
11. Richard Matheson, *The Shrinking Man*
12. Captain S. P. Meek, 'Submicroscopic'
13. Fitz-James O'Brien, 'The Diamond Lens'
14. Gordon Williams, *The Micronauts*

Several of these stories – the Cummings novels, the Hasse and the Meek – rely on the outdated planetary theory of the atom, and surmise that each atom is a solar system just like ours. The reverse idea, that our solar system is but an atom in a much larger universe, is explored in Cummings's *Explorers Into Infinity*, Donald Wandrei's *Colossus*, and in a sense in Philip José Farmer's *The Unreasoning Mask*.

Seventeen Heroes and Heroines

In the good old days of pulp SF no story was complete without a square-jawed hero (also a black-hearted villain, absent-minded scientist, and beautiful daughter of same). These days authentic heroes are harder to find, but some still crop up – and some of the old names are still remembered.

1. *John Carter* (in Edgar Rice Burroughs's *Barsoom* series)
2. *Jason dinAlt* (in Harry Harrison's *Deathworld* series)
3. *Colonel John Falkenberg* (in Jerry Pournelle's *The Mercenary* and *West of Honor*)
4. *Dominic Flandry* (in Poul Anderson's *Ensign Flandry* and many others)

5. *F'lar* and *Lessa* (in Anne McCaffrey's *Dragon series*)
6. *Gilbert Gosseyn* (in A. E. Van Vogt's *World of Null-A* and *Pawns of Null A*)
7. *Donal Graeme* (in Gordon R. Dickson's *Dorsai!*)
8. *John Grimes* (in A. Bertram Chandler's *Rim World* series)
9. *Robert Hedrock* (in A. E. Van Vogt's *Weapon Shops of Isher* and *Weapon Makers*)
10. *Kimball Kinnison* (in E. E. Smith's *Lensman* series)
11. *Chet Kinsman* (in Ben Bova's *Kinsman* and *Millennium*)
12. *Professor Bernard Quatermass* (in Nigel Kneale's *Quatermass* series)
13. *Richard Seaton* (in E. E. Smith's *Skylark* series)
14. *Northwest Smith* (in C. L. Moore's *Northwest Smith* series)
15. *John Star* (in Jack Williamson's *Legion of Space* series)
16. *Eric John Stark* (in Leigh Brackett's *Skaith* series and others)
17. *Valentine* (in Robert Silverberg's *Lord Valentine's Castle*)

. . . And Eight Anti-Heroes

1. *Jerry Cornelius* (in Michael Moorcock's series)
2. *Thomas Covenant* (in Stephen Donaldson's series)
3. *Cudgel the Clever* (in Jack Vance's *Eyes of the Overworld*)
4. *Slippery Jim diGriz* (in Harry Harrison's *Stainless Steel Rat* series)
5. *Gully Foyle* (in Alfred Bester's *The Stars My Destination*)
6. *Kirth Gersen* (in Jack Vance's *Demon Princes* series)
7. *Magnus Ridolph* (in Jack Vance's *Many Worlds of Magnus Ridolph*)
8. *Nicholas Van Rijn* (in Poul Anderson's *Trader to the Stars* and others)

. . . And Eleven Villains

1. *Duncan Chalk* (in Robert Silverberg's *Thorns*)
2. *Blackie DuQuesne* (in E. E. Smith's *Skylark* series)
3. *Baron Vladimir Harkonnen* (in Frank Herbert's *Dune*)
4. *Damon Julian* (in George R. R. Martin's *Fevre Dream*)
5. *The Mule* (in Isaac Asimov's *Foundation* series)
6. *Ben Reich* (in Alfred Bester's *The Demolished Man*)
7-11. *Attel Malagate, Kokor Hekkus, Viole Falushe, Lens Larque* and *Howard Alan Treesong* (in Jack Vance's *Demon Princes* series)

Good villains are hard to come by. DuQuesne started out black as could be, but gained a following by being the strongest character in the series, and eventually turned out not too bad. The Mule and Ben Reich are both partly sympathetic. Julian is the epitome of evil, but is in some respects a pitiable character. Chalk and Harkonnen are both bloated sadists, with no endearing traits. And the five Demon Princes are *really* bad!

Eleven Novels about Mad Scientists

The mad scientist has long been one of the most enduring clichés of science fiction. It is therefore surprising to find that, possibly stung by criticism, modern SF authors have often deliberately avoided using such characters. Thus we have a variety of scientists as hero, visionary or misguided human being as opposed to the traditional creature of evil (and ultra-intelligence). The following are all, in one way or another, rather nasty. After all, isn't madness in the eye of the beholder?

1. Brian Aldiss, *Moreau's Other Island* (Mortimer Dart)
2. J. G. Ballard, *Crash* (Vaughan)
3. Angela Carter, *The Infernal Desire Machines of Dr Hoffman* (Dr Hoffman)
4. Frank Herbert, *Hellstrom's Hive* (Hellstrom)
5. William Kotzwinkle, *Dr Rat* (Dr Rat)
6. C. S. Lewis, *Out of the Silent Planet* (Weston)
7. Maurice Renard, *Le Docteur Lerne, Sous-Dieu – New Bodies for Old* (Dr Lerne)
8. Mary Shelley, *Frankenstein* (Baron Frankenstein)
9. Robert Louis Stevenson, *Dr Jekyll and Mr Hyde* (Dr Jekyll)
10. H. G. Wells, *The Island of Doctor Moreau* (Dr Moreau)
11. Chelsea Quinn Yarbro, *Time of the Fourth Horseman* (Mark Lebbreau)

Eleven SF Drugs

1. The Reality Pill in Chester Anderson's *The Butterfly Kid*
2. Can-D in Philip K. Dick's *The Three Stigmata of Palmer Eldritch*
3. Chew-Z in the same novel
4. JJ-180 in Philip K. Dick's *Now Wait For Last Year*
5. Substance D in Philip K. Dick's *A Scanner Darkly*
6. Trialine in Charles Harness's *The Catalyst*
7. Melange in Frank Herbert's *Dune* series
8. Soma in Aldous Huxley's *Brave New World*
9. M-A 19 in Michael Moorcock's 'The Deep Fix'
10. The Yellow Pill in Rog Phillips's 'The Yellow Pill'
11. Thionite in E. E. Smith's *Lensman* series

. . . And Ten More Stories on Drug Themes

1. Brian Aldiss, *Barefoot in the Head*
2. Philip K. Dick, 'Faith of our Fathers'
3. Philip K. Dick, *Flow My Tears, the Policeman Said*
4. Harlan Ellison, 'Shattered Like A Glass Goblin'
5. Michel Jeury, *Chronolysis* and sequels
6. Arthur Sellings, *The Uncensored Man*
7. Robert Silverberg, *Downward to the Earth*
8. Robert Silverberg, *A Time Of Changes*
9. Norman Spinrad, 'No Direction Home'
10. Norman Spinrad, 'The Weed of Time'

Fourteen Stories Featuring Futuristic Games and Sports

1. Richard Cowper, 'Out There Where The Big Ships Go'
2. Samuel F. Delany, *Triton*
3. Charles V. De Vet and Katherine MacLean, *Cosmic Checkmate*
4. Philip K. Dick, *Galactic Pot-Healer*
5. Philip K. Dick, *The Game-Players of Titan*
6. Philip K. Dick, *Solar Lottery*
7. William Harrison, 'Rollerball Murders'

8. Robert Sheckley, *The Tenth Victim*
9. Brian Stableford, *The Mind Riders*
10. A. E. Van Vogt, *World of Null-A*
11. Jack Vance, *Trullion: Alastor 2292*
12. Jack Vance, *The Face*
13. Gary K. Wolf, *Killerbowl*
14. Gary Wright, 'The Ultimate Racer'

Ten Chess-Influenced SF Stories

1. Poul Anderson, 'The Immortal Game'
2. Poul Anderson, 'The White King's War'
3. John Brunner, *The Squares of the City*
4. Edgar Rice Burroughs, *The Chessmen of Mars*
5. Victor Contoski, 'Von Gomm's Gambit'
6. Charles Harness, 'The Chessplayers'
7. Henry Kuttner, *The Fairy Chessmen*
8. Fritz Leiber, 'Midnight By The Morphy Watch'
9. Fritz Leiber, 'The 64-Square Madhouse'
10. Barry Malzberg, *The Tactics of Conquest*

Six SF Stories about Actors and the Theatre

1. John Brunner, *The Productions of Time*
2. Robert Heinlein, *Double Star*
3. Fritz Leiber, 'Four Ghosts in Hamlet'
4. Walter Miller, 'The Darfsteller'
5. C. L. Moore, *Doomsday Morning*
6. Jack Vance, *Showboat World*

Fifteen SF and Fantasy Stories Featuring Music and Musicians

1. Lloyd Biggle, *The Still, Small Voice of Trumpets*
2. James Blish, 'A Work of Art'

3. Michael Butterworth and Michael Moorcock, *Time of the Hawklords*
4. Samuel R. Delany, *The Einstein Intersection*
5. Philip K. Dick, *The Simulacra*
6. Thomas M. Disch, *On Wings of Song*
7. Anne McCaffrey, *The Crystal Singer*
8. Anne McCaffrey, *The Ship Who Sang*
9. Edgar Pangborn, 'The Music Master of Babylon'
10. Keith Roberts, 'Missa Privata'
11. Norman Spinrad, 'The Big Flash'
12. Jack Vance, *The Anome*
13. Jack Vance, *Space Opera*
14. Manly Wade Wellman, *Who Fears The Devil?* and sequels
15. Laurence Yep, *Sweetwater*

Nine Futuristic Arts

1. Cloud-sculpture, in J. G. Ballard's 'The Cloud Sculptors of Coral D'
2. Computer-assisted comic art, in Harry Harrison's 'Portrait of the Artist'
3. Dream construction, in Isaac Asimov's 'Dreaming is a Private Thing'
4. Free-fall dancing, in Spider and Jeanne Robinson's *Stardance*
5. Holographic sculpture, in William Rotsler's *Patron of the Arts*
6. Mask making, in Jack Vance's 'The Moon Moth'
7. Novel-writing by machine, in Fritz Leiber's *The Silver Eggheads*
8. Psycho-sculpture, in Robert Silverberg's *The Second Trip* (also sonic sculpture, in J. G. Ballard's 'The Singing Statues')
9. Re-creating civilizations, in Michael Moorcock's *Dancers at the End of Time* trilogy

Five Adam and Eve Stories

The story in which a group of space travellers land on an hospitable new world and we learn in the last paragraph that this planet is, in fact, Earth, and they include Adam and Eve among their number, is one of the basic SF clichés. Michael Moorcock, who saw many such stories as editor of *New Worlds*, dubbed them 'shaggy God' stories. Occasionally, however, they do make it into print . . .

1. Robert Arthur, 'Evolution's End' – featuring Aydem and Ayveh
2. Nelson S. Bond, 'Another World Begins' – in which Adam and Eve are escapees from the laboratory of an alien God
3. Eric Frank Russell, 'First Person Singular' – in which Edham and his chums from the planet Dise set up a Dise-like habitat on a new world; but Edham eventually abandons this Para-Dise with a native girl
4. Julius Jay Savarin, *Lemmus* (a trilogy) – in which Jael Adaamm comes from the Galactic Organizations and Dominions (G.O.D.) to colonize Earth
5. A. E. Van Vogt, 'Ship of Darkness' – in which the protagonist D'Ormand is christened Idorm by the girl he meets at the end

Ten Stories Featuring Matter Transmission

1. Poul Anderson, *The Enemy Stars*
2. John Brunner, *Web of Everywhere*
3. Algis Budrys, *Rogue Moon*
4. Thomas M. Disch, *Echo Round His Bones*
5. Joe Haldeman, *Mindbridge*
6. Harry Harrison, *One Step From Earth*
7. Larry Niven, 'Flash Crowd' and other stories
8. Bob Shaw, *Who Goes Here?*
9. Clifford Simak, *Way Station*
10. Roger Zelazny, *Today We Choose Faces*

Matter transmission is the technological equivalent of teleportation. You journey from *here* to *there* without apparently crossing the intervening space. The usual explanation is that your body is somehow broken down, its structure and constituents analysed, the information beamed to a receiver, where you are reconstituted. It sounds a chancy way to travel, but it is one which has become familiar to millions through its use in *Star Trek* ('Beam me up, Scottie').

Ten SF Stories about Terraforming

1. Poul Anderson, 'The Big Rain' (Venus)
2. Poul Anderson, *The Snows of Ganymede* (Ganymede)
3. Gregory Benford, *Jupiter Project* (Ganymede)
4. Arthur C. Clarke, *The Sands of Mars* (Mars)
5. Jack Chalker, *The Web of the Chozen* (other worlds)
6. David Gerrold, *Moonstar Odyssey* (an alien world)
7. Frank Herbert, *Dune* series (Arrakis)
8. Olaf Stapledon, *Last and First Men* (Venus)
9. Frederick Turner, *A Double Shadow* (Mars)
10. Ian Watson, *The Martian Inca* (Mars)

Terraforming is the term used for the process whereby planets are rendered suitable for human habitation. In SF, the process is usually carried out in the Solar System – as the locales listed above indicate – the assumption being that in the wider galaxy, if we get there, we will be able to search for and find Earthlike planets. The word was coined by Jack Williamson, in a series of stories not centrally concerned with terraforming.

Ten Cyborg Stories

A cyborg is a person with mechanical elements: in its simplest form, anyone with an artificial limb, or a cardiac pacemaker, could be described as a cyborg. In fiction this process is usually carried much further, as for instance in the popular TV series *The Six-Million Dollar Man* whose hero, Steve Austin, is a cyborg who as a result of the mechanisms fitted in his body is a virtual superman.

1. Barrington J. Bayley, *The Garments of Caean*
2. Algis Budrys, *Who?*
3. Martin Caidin, *Cyborg* (the novel on which *The Six-Million Dollar Man* was based)
4. D. G. Compton, *The Continuous Katherine Mortenhoe*
5. Samuel R. Delany, *Nova*
6. Damon Knight, 'Masks'

7. Anne McCaffrey, *The Ship Who Sang*
8. C. L. Moore, 'No Woman Born'
9. Cordwainer Smith, 'Scanners Live in Vain'
10. E. C. Tubb, *Dumarest* series

Eight Monsters (Not Necessarily Bug-Eyed)

1. The Clone, in Kate Wilhelm and Theodore L. Thomas's *The Clone*
2. Coeurl, in A. E. Van Vogt's *Voyage of the Space Beagle*
3. Frankenstein's creation, in Mary Shelley's *Frankenstein*
4. Golem, in Alfred Bester's *Golem-100*
5. Ixtl, in A. E. Van Vogt's *Voyage of the Space Beagle*
6. Puppet Masters, in Robert Heinlein's *The Puppet Masters*
7. Shambleau, in C. L. Moore's 'Shambleau'
8. Triffids, in John Wyndham's *Day of the Triffids*

Really good monsters (by which we mean really *bad* monsters!) are hard to come by in SF; perhaps conscious of the genre's pulp origins and bad reputation most writers studiously avoid such things. Even many of the nasties listed here have feelings and reasons for what they do, although you still wouldn't want to meet them on a dark night.

Eight SF Megastructures

1. Cageworld, in Colin Kapp's *Cageworld* series: a kind of lattice of artificial worlds around their sun
2. Gaea, in John Varley's *Titan* and sequels, a sentient enclosed world
3. Orbitsville, in Bob Shaw's *Orbitsville*: a Dyson sphere (that is, an artifical structure enclosing a sun, whose inhabitants live on the vast inner surface)
4. Ringworld, in Larry Niven's *Ringworld*: somewhat less than a Dyson sphere – a single hoop around the sun
5. Sector General, a gigantic space hospital in the series by James White

6. Space Colony, in Ben Bova's *Colony* and others: an artifical habitat built in space usually in a stable position in the Earth-Moon system
7. Space Elevator, in Arthur C. Clarke's *The Fountains of Paradise* and Charles Sheffield's *The Web of the Worlds*: literally an elevator built from the ground into orbit, providing (once built!) a cheap way of getting into space
8. Styth cities, in Cecelia Holland's *Floating Worlds*: artificial environments built in the outer atmosphere of the gas giant planets

Ten Novels of the Distant Future and the End of Time

1. Douglas Adams, *The Restaurant at the End of the Universe*
2. Brian Aldiss, *Hothouse*
3. Arthur C. Clarke, *The City and the Stars*
4. William Hope Hodgson, *The Night Land*
5. Michael Moorcock, the *Dancers at the End of Time* series
6. Doris Piserchia, *A Billion Days of Earth*
7. Robert Silverberg, *Son of Man*
8. Clark Ashton Smith, *Zoothique*
9. Jack Vance, *The Dying Earth*
10. H. G. Wells, *The Time Machine*

Stories of the extremely distant future, when our own time is less than a memory, provide an opportunity for exotic and apocalyptic imagery, but are by no means easy to write well. Adams's novel is a comedy partly set in the eponymous eatery; Moorcock's series are ironic comedies of decadent immortals; the remainder are extreme exercises of bizarre imagination.

Seven SF Messiahs

1. Paul Atreides (Muad'Dib), in Frank Herbert's *Dune*
2. John Cave, in Gore Vidal's *Messiah*
3. Colin Charteris, in Brian Aldiss's *Barefoot in the Head*

4. Jerry Cornelius, in Michael Moorcock's *The Final Programme*
5. Palmer Eldritch, in Philip K. Dick's *The Three Stigmata of Palmer Eldritch*
6. Valentine Michael Smith, in Robert Heinlein's *Stranger in a Strange Land*
7. Vornan-19, in Robert Silverberg's *The Masks of Time*

Most of these are ambiguous messiahs, at best; Heinlein's is nearest to the real thing, though the novel's purpose is iconoclastic and satiric rather than millenarian. Paul Atreides, too, is the real thing, but the novel is about his efforts to avoid the role, and its undesirable implications for the future.

Gay Science Fiction

One of the lists you will not find in this book is a list of gay SF authors. Such a list was compiled, as many such writers have openly come out and others have made no secret of their homosexuality. We felt, however, that such a list would be misconstrued (as would our other suppressed list of transsexual authors) in certain quarters. However, we thought it would be interesting to compile a short list of works where homosexuality features heavily and is integral to the plot rather than a sensationalistic future-life background perversion.

The Female Man, Joanna Russ
Triton, Samuel R. Delany
Various books in Marion Zimmer Bradley's *Darkover* series
'The World Well Lost', Theodore Sturgeon
The Ophiuchi Canal, John Varley
'Fair Eleanor is Dead', Raylin Moore
The Masks of Time, Robert Silverberg
Venus Plus X, Theodore Sturgeon

Ten Examples of Sex between Humans and Aliens

Perhaps the ultimate taboo and on SF writers have long shied away from. The liberalization of attitudes towards sex and Philip José

Farmer's daring experiments have opened the way for others shyly to go where few had gone before. Nevertheless, this is still a theme which writers haven't often tackled satisfactorily for lack of, possibly, sufficient biological speculation.

1. Jack Chalker in his *Well of Souls* series has invented a dizzy number of highly complex alien beings and thoroughly enjoys the sexual permutations thus offered for humans reincarnated as aliens. One should note a total lack of prurience here
2. Philip José Farmer in *The Lovers* shows a delicate relationship between a man and an alien female of human appearance, but with a different biological configuration
3. Naomi Mitchison in *Memoirs of a Spacewoman* also breaks taboos in hinting at sexual relations between humans and aliens
4. Catherine L. Moore in 'Shambleau' created one of the most beautiful but unforgettably sinister alien beings
5. François Mottier in his bawdy *Philip José Farmer Conquers the Universe* has the title character raped by despicable monsters. All in a spirit of fun
6. Larry Niven in his *Known Space* books invents the word 'Rishathra' to describe sex practices outside one's species (but within the hominids). However, apart from a brief fling with a bald, and not so alien woman in *Ringworld*, Niven gives few specific examples
7. Terry Pratchett in *Thoughtworld* presents sex between humans and others, but in very fuzzy terms
8. Andrew J. Offutt writing as John Cleve in the *Spaceways* series makes sex a frequent occurrence on the galactic lanes, but most of the relationships, despite heavy hints of perversion, appear to be between humanoids
9. Bruce Sterling in *Involution Ocean* depicts a touching love affair between a man and a female alien; any contact between them generates pain and, possibly death, complicating matters somewhat
10. James Tiptree's *And I Awoke and found me here on the Cold Hill's Side* is anything but explicit about the freak sexual encounters that occur in galactic spaceports, but the reticence is most chilling

Thirteen More SF Stories About Sex

Sex and SF were, until recently, held to be mutually incompatible subjects by many fans and critics (and writers too). In recent years SF incorporating sex has become reasonably commonplace; SF which uses sex, sexual relations and sexual roles as subject matter is less common, but includes the following:

1. Samuel Delany, 'Aye, and Gomorrah' (invents a new sexual perversion)
2. Gardner Dozois, *Strangers*
3. Philip José Farmer, *Flesh*
4. Philip José Farmer, *Strange Relations* (short stories)
5. Philip José Farmer, *Image of the Beast*
6. Robert A. Heinlein, *Stranger in a Strange Land*
7. Ursula Le Guin, *The Left Hand of Darkness* (in which the creation of a form of human which can be male, female or neuter allows a serious exploration of gender roles)
8. John Norman, the *Gor* series (SF and sado-masochistic fantasy, with women in bondage being the dominant motif)
9. Joanna Russ, *The Female Man* (a fiery feminist polemic)
10. Robert Silverberg, *The World Inside* (a world without privacy brings about a complete revision of sexual manners)
11. Theodore Sturgeon, 'If All Men Were Brothers, Would You Let One Marry Your Sister?' (a story about incest)
12. Theodore Sturgeon, *Venus Plus X*
13. John Wyndham, 'Consider Her Ways'

Fifteen Stories of Sex between Humans and Robots

1. Robert Bloch, 'The Tin You Love To Touch'
2. Lester del Rey, 'Helen O'Loy'
3. Lester del Rey, 'A Pound of Cure'
4. Jean-Claude Forest, *Barbarella*
5. J. W. Groves, 'Robots Don't Bleed'
6. Fritz Leiber, 'The Mechanical Bride'
7. Ira Levin, *The Stepford Wives*

8. J. T. McIntosh, 'Made in USA'
9. Sheila McLeod, *Xanthe and the Robots*
10. William Rotsler, 'Ship Me Tomorrow'
11. Josephine Saxton, 'Gordon's Women'
12. Robert Sheckley, 'Can You Feel Anything When I Do This?'
13. Robert Silverberg, *Tower of Glass*
14. Kate Wilhelm, 'Andover and the Android'
15. Robert F. Young, 'September Had Thirty Days'

Seven Controversial SF Stories

1. J. G. Ballard, *The Atrocity Exhibition*. Ballard's intense exploration of the media landscape and aberrant psychology in the form of a series of 'condensed novels' caused considerable debate on its magazine publication, and was withdrawn by its American publisher Doubleday after the edition had been printed. (It was eventually published in the US by Grove Press as *Love and Napalm: Export USA*)

2. Philip José Farmer, *The Lovers*. Credited with introducing sex into science fiction, Farmer's novel, though hardly startling to modern readers, certainly outraged many people when it appeared in the pulp magazine *Startling Stories* in 1952

3. Joe W. Haldeman, 'Hero'. Later incorporated into his award-winning novel *The Forever War*, this realistic and unsentimental account of future soldiery was strong enough to upset strait-laced readers of *Analog* magazine as late as 1972

4. Robert Heinlein, *Starship Troopers*. Allegedly written as a novel for young adults, rejected by Scribner's – for whom Heinlein had written a long succession of such books – and subsequently published as an adult book which won a Hugo, Heinlein's espousal of military virtues has been a cause of bitter controversy since

5. Robert Heinlein, *Stranger in a Strange Land*. Published in 1961 (although mostly written many years earlier), Heinlein's novel shocked on account of its treatment of such matters as free love and ritual cannibalism. Later became a bible for elements of the late 1960s counter-culture, and later still by Charles Manson, as a partial inspiration for his murderous deeds

6. Michael Moorcock, *Behold the Man*. Previous stories had dealt with time-travel to the period of the crucifixion; Moorcock caused offence by showing the historical Christ as a drooling idiot, and having his time-traveller take his place on the Cross
7. Norman Spinrad, *Bug Jack Barron*. Somewhat experimental in style, and sexually outspoken for the SF of its time, Spinrad's novel was reviled by old-time SF fans and critics (Donald A. Wollheim, founder of DAW Books, called it 'degenerate'), and its serialization in the British magazine *New Worlds* led it into trouble with its distributors, and caused a question to be asked in the British House of Commons about public money being used to subsidize filth (the magazine being in receipt of an Arts Council grant at the time)

Eight Real SF Authors Who Make Appearances in SF Stories

1. *Forrest J. Ackerman* appears in *Blown* by Philip José Farmer
2. *Poul Anderson* is the protagonist of Philip K. Dick's story 'Waterspider', which is partly set at an SF convention and has parts for A. E. Van Vogt, Anthony Boucher and several others
3. *J. G. Ballard* is the name of the narrator of J. G. Ballard's novel *Crash*
4. *Cecil Corwin*, a successful pseudonym of C. M. Kornbluth, is killed off by his creator in Kornbluth's 'MS Found in a Chinese Fortune Cookie'
5. *Philip K. Dick* appears as a character in *Valis*, by Philip K. Dick
6. *Philip José Farmer* is the protagonist of the novel *Philip José Farmer Conquers the Universe*, by French author François Mottier
7. *Mary Shelley* is a major character in Brian Aldiss's *Frankenstein Unbound*
8. *H. G. Wells* makes a number of appearances, for instance in Brian Aldiss's 'The Saliva Tree', Karl Alexander's *Time After Time*, and Christopher Priest's *The Space Machine*

Five Crime Novels Featuring SF Writers and/or Fans

1. Anthony Boucher: *Rocket to the Morgue* (1942), a murder mystery centred on SF writers and fans, with thinly-disguised portraits of many real people
2. Wilson Tucker: *The Chinese Doll* (1946), a crime novel incorporating many references to contemporary SF fanzines and fans
3. Mack Reynolds: *Case of the Little Green Men* (1951), partly set at a world SF convention
4. Isaac Asimov: *Murder at the ABA* (1976), a murder mystery featuring Asimov as a character
5. William Marshall: *Sci-Fi* (1981), set at a science fiction convention (actually a media convention) in the Far East

Four Books Full of SF In-Jokes

SF writers probably mix with one another more than writers in most other areas of literature, and the urge to make jokey acknowledgment of this in print is probably correspondingly stronger. Usually this simply takes the form of giving characters the names of real-life friends or associates – a practice which has become known in SF circles as 'Tuckerizing', as Wilson Tucker is its most consistent exponent – but sometimes it goes further

1. James Blish, *Black Easter*: The white magicians are mostly given names of various SF writers, and their characterizations are a series of in-jokes. (Blish himself appears as Fr Atheling – 'William Atheling' being a pseudonym of his)
2. Steven Eisler, *Space Wars, Worlds and Weapons*: This large-format illustrated book, evidently pseudonymously written (though the author's identity remains a secret) has extended picture captions almost all of which are in-jokes about British SF writers and fans
3. David Gerrold and Larry Niven, *The Flying Sorcerers*: The gods invoked by the characters in this humorous novel are almost all thinly-disguised jokes on various SF writers
4. Michael Moorcock, *Barbarians of Mars* (*Masters of the Pit*): In this, the third of the 'Michael Kane' series, the first chapter features an aerial journey over an archipelago of islands with such names as Golana, Drallab and K'cocroom. (Read them backwards)

Four Instances of Migrating Characters

Another species of in-joke is that in which a character from one story makes a 'guest appearance' in another. Here are four SF examples: there are doubtless many more.

1. Gregory Benford's *Timescape* provides a walk-on part for David Selig, protagonist of Robert Silverberg's *Dying Inside*
2. Robert Heinlein's *The Number of the Beast* contains a great many guest appearances as the characters voyage from one fictional universe to another – including L. Frank Baum's Oz, Edgar Rice Burroughs's Barsoom and E. E. Smith's Lensman universe
3. L. Ron Hubbard's 'The Case of the Friendly Corpse', published in *Unknown* in 1941, introduces one of the magazine's most popular characters, Harold Shea, hero of De Camp and Pratt's *Incomplete Enchanter* series. Hubbard even goes so far as to kill him off, though he turned up unscathed in authentic later adventures
4. Richard Lupoff's *Sacred Locomotive Flies* has a part for Jack Barron, of *Bug Jack Barron* (by Norman Spinrad) fame

Six Authors of SF Parodies

1. James Blish (with Judith Ann Lawrence) parodied a number of writers in the story 'Getting Along', among them Mary Shelley, Wells, Merritt and Lovecraft
2. James Cawthorn parodied J. G. Ballard briefly but accurately in 'Ballard of a Whaler'
3. Arthur C. Clarke parodied H. P. Lovecraft in 'At the Mountains of Murkiness'
4. Randall Garrett has published a book, *Take-Off*, parodying various writers
5. Richard Lupoff, writing as 'Ova Hamlet' has parodied Ellison, Moorcock and others
6. John Sladek has written a series of short parodies, included in *The Best of John Sladek*; the targets include Asimov, Ballard, Clarke, Dick, Heinlein and others

David Langford's Twelve Favourite SF Clichés

1. *There are secrets of the Universe with which Man should not meddle!* This line from the closing scenes of all too many SF/horror films is also the moral of the first SF novel, *Frankenstein.* Earlier still, the biblical legend of Babel can only be a warning against meddling with the secrets of high-rise apartment blocks

2. *The tentacled aliens preyed on Earth's fairest daughters!* And the covers of endless pulp SF magazines showed them doing it. What was never explained was why the alien selection criteria were so similar to that of breast-fixated Earthlings, or what the aliens (with their undoubtedly different genetic makeup, protein needs and sexual apparatus) proposed to *do* with the unfortunate victims

3. *The Brass Brassière* was of course the customary garb of Earth's fairest daughters, on magazine covers if not in the stories within; it was endemic through a particular trademark of pulp artist Garle Bergey. Did wearers warm them up before putting them on each morning? Were countless young males later disappointed when the real things failed to have that perfect conicality? Did countless young females consider themselves unfairly short-changed, on this evidence? There are secrets of the Universe . . .

4. *The eccentric scientific genius lived alone with his beautiful daughter* This ménage is traceable back to *The Tempest*, where Miranda does at least tend to doze off during Prospero's monologues ('Thou attend'st not!'). Her spiritual descendants are all too prone to encourage him: 'Gee, Professor, I know you told me already, but how *does* the dimension-buster valve work?'

5. *With terrible irony, the monster had destroyed its own creator!* This and its variants seemed a jolly good idea in *Frankenstein* or Capek's *RUR.* Later it induced terrible yawns. Even Asimov's ingeniously foolproof robots spend altogether too much time exploiting loopholes in his Three Laws in order to destroy or at least inconvenience their creators. Taking this theme about as far as it can go, someone in a short Barrington Bayley story assassinates God

6. *Man – the toughest, meanest, deadliest, most unrelenting critter in the Universe!* Adolescent readers of Heinlein's novels were surprised

73

and gratified to be described approximately thus. 'This is the race that shall rule the sevagram,' some van Vogt aliens conclude after brief inspection of our toughness; they fail to mention what a sevagram may be. And in del Rey's 'For I Am A Jealous People', God switches sides to aid the vile aliens against us: sure enough, the hero (a priest) decides God has picked an opponent his own size (See 5)

7. *With a fibre-wrenching jerk, the mighty ship burst into hyperspace* or went FTL, or activated the Interstellar Jump, or engaged fifth gear. Any old doubletalk will do to evade Einstein's speed-of light limitation; the common factor of most faster-than-light propulsion systems was noted in M. John Harrison's review title 'To the Stars and Beyond on the Fabulous Anti-Syntax Drive'

8. *The awesomely omniscient Brain dwarfed any mere human intellect* Two varieties here. One is the overgrown organic brain (*Donovan's Brain*), often housed in the smooth-domed shell which gave one critic nightmares of boiled eggs and gigantic teaspoons. Although more formidable are super-computers as in Fredric Brown's 'Answer' ('Yes – *now* there is a God!'), which fortunately can be disabled by feeding them insoluble, paradoxical problems. Hero: 'Why is a mouse when it spins?' Omniscient computer: 'Because . . . *crackle crackle fzzzt*'

9. *Whipping out his blaster, the Lensman loosed a rain of lethal fire!* The heavy-duty blaster – in later incarnations a mere laser – was always useful for melting airlock doors, disabling control panels in a shower of sparks, or incinerating hordes of ravening spear-carriers. Major characters tend to be mysteriously immune, as in *Star Wars*, where the fewness of hits actually scored by Imperial Storm Troopers makes you wonder how they even acquired an Empire in the first place

10. *Those danged radiation-spawned Mutants can read your mind!* It's amazing what writers of after-the-Bomb stories can achieve with a little chromosome damage: a huge range of psionic powers, extra arms, legs, wings, scales or feathers, and only once in a while a little cosmetic cancer. Comparison of these fantasies with the actual lives of certain Japanese unfortunates is felt to be in rather bad taste

11. *And I shall call you Eve!* Thus the last man to the last woman after the holocaust, in a favourite version of the 'shaggy-God story', long thought dead but now revived at the hands of Doris Lessing. In other variants God is an alien, the serpent is a visiting physicist, or the spirit which moves on the face of the waters proves to be Arthur C. Clarke

12. *Invaders from Space!* The clichés above are traditional; this one is manifestly an Idea Whose Time Has Come. Rather than the expected crop of shaggy-God stories, a recent SF competition drew dozens of tales in which an invading fleet battles its way through the planetary defences and despite enormous losses touches down at last on the target area – whereupon great fiery letters appear in the sky, saying GAME OVER – PLEASE INSERT COIN

David Langford

The Years of Futures Past

In this section we present a detailed chronicle of the best science fiction through the years, in chronological order. Chronology is vital to an understanding of SF's development: only thus can you see the crucial years in which, for some reason, several seminal works appear; only thus can you appreciate the sudden flowering of great careers, like Verne's in the 1860s, or Wells' in the 1890s or Heinlein's in the 1940s. Where others' choices of the best exist – in award and award nominations, or in best-of-the-year anthologies, we have presented these; elsewhere the choices are ours.

Important Nineteenth-century SF Novels

The Last Man	Jean-Baptiste de Grainville (1805)
Frankenstein	Mary Shelley (1818)
Symzonia	Captain Adam Seaborn (1820)
A Voyage to the Moon	Joseph Atterley (1827)
The Narrative of A. Gordon Pym	Edgar Allan Poe (1837)
Five Weeks in a Balloon	Jules Verne (1863)
Journey to the Centre of the Earth	Jules Verne (1864)
From the Earth to the Moon	Jules Verne (1865)
Round the Moon	Jules Verne (1870)
20,000 Leagues Under the Sea	Jules Verne (1870)
The Coming Race	Edward Bulwer-Lytton (1871)

The Battle of Dorking	Sir George Chesney (1871)
Erewhon	Samuel Butler (1872)
The Mysterious Island	Jules Verne (1875)
Across the Zodiac	Percy Greg (1880)
Flatland	E. A. Abbott (1884)
After London	Richard Jeffries (1885)
The Strange Case of Dr Jekyll and Mr Hyde	Robert Louis Stevenson (1886)
Robur the Conqueror	Jules Verne (1886)
A Crystal Age	W. H. Hudson (1887)
She	H. Rider Haggard (1887)
War in the Twentieth Century	Albert Robida (1887)
Looking Backward 2000-1887	Edward Bellamy (1888)
A Strange MS Found in a Copper Cylinder	James de Mille (1888)
A Connecticut Yankee in King Arthur's Court	Mark Twain (1889)
Urania	Camille Flammarion (1889)
News from Nowhere	William Morris (1890)
La Fin du Monde	Camille Flammarion (1893)
Angel of the Revolution	George Griffith (1894)
The Time Machine	H. G. Wells (1895)
Propellor Island	Jules Verne (1895)
The Island of Dr Moreau	H. G. Wells (1896)
The Invisible Man	H. G. Wells (1897)
Two Planets	Kurd Lasswitz (1897)
The War of the Worlds	H. G. Wells (1898)
When the Sleeper Wakes	H. G. Wells (1899)

Notable SF Achievements 1900-10

The Moon Metal	Garrett P. Serviss (1900)
The Lost Continent	C. J. Cutcliffe Hyne (1900)
Honeymoon in Space	George Griffith (1901)
First Men in the Moon	H. G. Wells (1901)
The Purple Cloud	M. P. Shiel (1901)
Lord of the Sea	M. P. Shiel (1901)
The Napoleon of Notting Hill	G. K. Chesterton (1904)

78

The Food of the Gods	H. G. Wells (1904)
Master of the World	Jules Verne (1904)
Lt Gulliver Jones: His Vacation	Edwin Lester Arnold (1905)
With the Night Mail	Rudyard Kipling (1905)
A Modern Utopia	H. G. Wells (1905)
In the Days of the Comet	H. G. Wells (1906)
Before Adam	Jack London (1906)
The Iron Heel	Jack London (1907)
The War in the Air	H. G. Wells (1908)
The House on the Borderland	William Hope Hodgson (1908)
The Machine Stops	E. M. Forster (1909)
Quest for Fire	J. H. Rosny (1909)

Notable SF Achievements 1911-20

Ralph 124C41+	Hugo Gernsback (1911)
The Hampdenshire Wonder	J. D. Beresford (1911)
The Lost World	Arthur Conan Doyle (1912)
Under the Moons of Mars	Edgar Rice Burroughs (1912)
Darkness and Dawn	George Allan England (1912)
The Night Land	William Hope Hodgson (1912)
The Second Deluge	Garrett P. Serviss (1912)
The Gods of Mars	Edgar Rice Burroughs (1913)
At the Earth's Core	Edgar Rice Burroughs (1914)
The World Set Free	H. G. Wells (1914)
The Star Rover	Jack London (1915)
Pellucidar	Edgar Rice Burroughs (1915)
The Messiah of the Cylinder	Victor Rousseau (1917)
The Moon Pool	A. Merritt (1918)
The Runaway Skyscraper	Murray Leinster (1919)
The Girl in the Golden Atom	Ray Cummings (1919)
When the World Shook	H. Rider Haggard (1919)
We	Yevgeny Zamyatin (1920)
The Metal Monster	A. Merritt (1920)
A Voyage to Arcturus	David Lindsay (1920)
Beyond the Planet Earth	Konstantin Tsiolkovsky (1920)

Notable SF Achievements 1921-5

RUR	Karel Capek (1921)
The Blind Spot	Austin Hall and Homer Eon Flint (1921)
Capillaria	Frigyes Karinthy (1922)
The Absolute at Large	Karel Capek (1922)
Nordenholt's Millions	J. J. Connington (1923)
Men Like Gods	H. G. Wells (1923)
The Clockwork Man	E. V. Odle (1923)
The Radio Man	Ralph Milne Farley (1924)
Krakatit	Karel Capek (1925)
The Makropoulos Secret	Karel Capek (1925)

1926: Best SF of the Year

SHORT STORIES

The Coming of the Ice	G. Peyton Wertenbaker
A Runaway World	Clare Winger Harris
Across Space	Edmond Hamilton
The Night Wire	H. F. Arnold

NOVELS

Beyond the Pole	A. Hyatt Verrill
Emperor of the If	Guy Dent
Metropolis	Thea von Harbou

1927: Best SF of the Year

SHORT STORIES

The Red Brain	Donald Wandrei
The Machine Man of Ardathia	Francis Flagg
Around the Universe	Ray Cummings
The Colour out of Space	H. P. Lovecraft
The Moon Menace	Edmond Hamilton
The Tissue-Culture Kings	Julian Huxley

NOVELS

The Master Mind of Mars	E. R. Burroughs
Deluge	S. Fowler Wright

1928: Best SF of the Year

SHORT STORIES

Armageddon 2419 AD	Philip Francis Nowlan
A Biological Experiment	David H. Keller
The Revolt of the Pedestrians	David H. Keller
The Moon of Doom	Earl Bell
Out of the Sub-Universe	R. F. Starzl
The Miracle of the Lily	Clare Winger Harris
The Eight Green Men	G. G. Pendarves
In Amundsen's Tent	John Martin Leahy

NOVELS

Crashing Suns	Edmond Hamilton
The Skylark of Space	E. E. Smith and Lee Hawkins Garby
The Island of Captain Sparrow	S. Fowler Wright
The Spacious Adventures of the Man in the Street	Eimar O'Duffy

1929: Best SF of the Year

SHORT STORIES

Barton's Island	Harl Vincent
The Eternal Man	D. D. Sharp
The Airlords of Mars	Philip Francis Nowlan
The Darkness on Fifth Avenue	Murray Leinster
The Last Man	Wallace West
The Killing Flash	Hugo Gernsback

NOVELS

Cities in the Air	Edmond Hamilton
Outside the Universe	Edmond Hamilton
The Human Termites	David H. Keller
The World Below	S. Fowler Wright

1930: Best SF of the Year

SHORT STORIES

The Black Star Passes	John W. Campbell Jr
When the Atoms Failed	John W. Campbell Jr
The Power and the Glory	Charles Willard Diffin
The Day of the Beast	D. D. Sharp
The Man Who Saw the Future	Edmond Hamilton
Piracy Preferred	John W. Campbell Jr
The Ivy War	David H. Keller

NOVELS

The Universe Wreckers	Edmond Hamilton
Brigands of the Moon	Ray Cummings
Murder Madness	Murray Leinster
Gladiator	Philip Wylie
Last and First Men	Olaf Stapledon
The Green Girl	Jack Williamson
White Lily	John Taine
The Iron Star	John Taine
Paradise and Iron	Miles J. Breuer

1931: Best SF of the Year

SHORT STORIES

The Man Who Evolved	Edmond Hamilton
The Jameson Satellite	Neil R. Jones
Submicroscopic	Captain S. P. Meek

Tetrahedra of Space	P. Schuyler Miller
The World of the Red Sun	Clifford D. Simak
Beyond the Singing Flame	Clark Ashton Smith
The Voice from the Ether	Lloyd Arthur Eshbach
Hawk Carse	Anthony Gilmore
Out Round Rigel	Robert H. Wilson
The Fifth Dimension Catapult	Murray Leinster
The City of the Singing Flame	Clark Ashton Smith
The Conquest of Gola	Leslie F. Stone
If Lee Had Not Won the Battle of Gettysburg	Winston Churchill

NOVELS

The Exiles of Time	Ray Cummings
Seeds of Life	John Taine
Spacehounds of IPC	E. E. Smith
The Weigher of Souls	André Maurois

1932: Best SF of the Year

SHORT STORIES

Tumithak of the Corridors	Charles R. Tanner
The Moon Era	Jack Williamson
The Asteroids of Gold	Clifford D. Simak
The Light from Infinity	Lloyd Arthur Eshbach
Wave of Compulsion	Raymond Z. Gallun
The Lost Machine	John Beynon Harris
The Thing in the Cellar	David H. Keller
The Cities of Ardathia	Francis Flagg
The Planet of the Double Sun	Neil R. Jones

NOVELS

Wandl the Invader	Ray Cummings
When Worlds Collide	Philip Wylie and Edwin Balmer
Brave New World	Aldous Huxley
The Time Stream	John Taine
To-Morrow's Yesterday	John Gloag

1933: Best SF of the Year

SHORT STORIES

Into the Meteorite Orbit	Frank Kelly
The Man Who Awoke	Laurence Manning
Tumithak in Shawm	Charles R. Tanner
Ancestral Voices	Nat Schachner
The Island of Unreason	Edmond Hamilton
Shambleau	C. L. Moore
A Race Through Time	Donald Wandrei
A Child is Born	David H. Keller
The Battery of Hate	John W. Campbell Jr
The Superior Judge	J. Paul Suter

NOVELS

The Intelligence Gigantic	John Russell Fearn
The Shape of Things to Come	H. G. Wells
When Worlds Collide	Philip Wylie and Edwin Balmer

1934: Best SF of the Year

SHORT STORIES

The Distortion Out of Space	Francis Flagg
The Man Who Stopped the Dust	John Russell Fearn
Bright Illusion	C. L. Moore
Colossus	Donald Wandrei
Born of the Sun	Jack Williamson
Sideways in Time	Murray Leinster
Old Faithful	Raymond Z. Gallun
Valley of Dreams	Stanley G. Weinbaum
A Martian Odyssey	Stanley G. Weinbaum
Twilight	Don A. Stuart
A Matter of Size	Harry Bates
One Prehistoric Night	Philip Barshofsky
The Wall	Howard Graham
The Lost Language	David H. Keller
The Last Man	Frank Belknap Long

The Other	Howard Graham
The Mole Pirate	Murray Leinster

NOVELS

Rebirth	Thomas Calvert
The Skylark of Valeron	E. E. Smith
The Legion of Space	Jack Williamson
Adrift in the Stratosphere	A. M. Lowe
Triplanetary	E. E. Smith
The Strange Invaders	Alun Llewellyn
After Worlds Collide	Edwin Balmer and Philip Wylie

1935: Best SF of the Year

SHORT STORIES

The Son of Old Faithful	Raymond Z. Gallun
Flight on Titan	Stanley G. Weinbaum
Proxima Centauri	Murray Leinster
The Accursed Galaxy	Edmond Hamilton
The Ultimate Metal	Nat Schachner
Davy Jones's Ambassador	Raymond Z. Gallun
The Cosmic Pantograph	Edmond Hamilton
The Red Peri	Stanley G. Weinbaum
The Mad Moon	Stanley G. Weinbaum
Alas, All Thinking	Harry Bates
The Lotus Eaters	Stanley G. Weinbaum
Prowlers of the Wasteland	Harl Vincent
The Phantom Dictator	Wallace West
Night	Don A. Stuart
The Galactic Circle	Jack Williamson
The Adaptive Ultimate	John Jessel (Stanley G. Weinbaum)
Parasite Planet	Stanley G. Weinbaum
Worlds of If	Stanley G. Weinbaum

NOVELS

The Mightiest Machine	John W. Campbell Jr
The Liners of Time	John Russell Fearn

The Green Man of Graypec	Festus Pragnell
Odd John	Olaf Stapledon
Land Under England	Joseph O'Neill
The Green Child	Herbert Read
The Secret People	John Beynon (John Wyndham)

1936: Best SF of the Year

SHORT STORIES

Mathematica	John Russell Fearn
The Circle of Zero	Stanley G. Weinbaum
He Who Shrank	Henry Hasse
The Human Pets of Mars	Leslie F. Stone
The Brain-Stealers of Space	John W. Campbell Jr
Devolution	Edmond Hamilton
Uncertainty	John W. Campbell Jr
The Isotope Man	Nat Schachner
The Shadow Out of Time	H. P. Lovecraft
The Time Decelerator	A. Macfadyen Jr
The Council of Drones	W. K. Sonneman
Tryst in Time	C. L. Moore

NOVELS

The Incredible Invasion	Murray Leinster
The Cometeers	Jack Williamson
At the Mountains of Madness	H. P. Lovecraft
War With the Newts	Karel Capek
Planet Plane	John Beynon (John Wyndham)

1937: Best SF of the Year

SHORT STORIES

Other Eyes Watching	John W. Campbell Jr
Minus Planet	John D. Clark
Space Blister	John D. Clark

Past, Present and Future	Nat Schachner
The Sands of Time	P. Schuyler Miller
Within the Pyramid	R. De Witt Miller
Seeker of Tomorrow	Eric Frank Russell and Leslie Johnson
The Blue Spot	Jack Williamson
Beyond Infinity	Chan Corbett
Forgetfulness	Don A. Stuart

NOVELS

Galactic Patrol	E. E. Smith
Star Maker	Olaf Stapledon
Star-begotten	H. G. Wells
Sugar in the Air	E. C. Large
The Thought-Reading Machine	André Maurois
The Young Men Are Coming	M. P. Shiel
To Walk the Night	William F. Sloane

1938: Best SF of the Year

SHORT STORIES

The Merman	L. Sprague de Camp
Rule 18	Clifford D. Simak
The Men and the Mirror	Ross Rocklynne
Who Goes There?	Don A. Stuart
Seeds of the Dusk	Raymond Z. Gallun
Robot's Return	Robert Moore Williams
Beyond Space and Time	Joel Townsley Rogers
The Dead Spot	Jack Williamson
Dead Knowledge	Don A. Stuart
The Smile of the Sphinx	William F. Temple
Helen O'Loy	Lester Del Rey
Hyperpilosity	L. Sprague de Camp
Pithecanthropus Erectus	Manly Wade Wellman
The Robot and the Lady	Manly Wade Wellman
The Shadow on the Screen	Henry Kuttner
Slave of the Flames	Robert Bloch
The House of Ecstasy	Ralph Milne Farley

The Garden of Adompha	Clark Ashton Smith
Roads	Seabury Quinn
A Matter of Form	H. L. Gold

NOVELS

The Legion of Time	Jack Williamson
Out of the Silent Planet	C. S. Lewis
Saurus	Eden Philpotts
The Adventure of Wyndham Smith	S. Fowler Wright
Three Thousand Years	Thomas Calvert McClary

1939: Best SF Short Stories of the Year*

I, Robot	Eando Binder
The Strange Flight of Richard Clayton	Robert Bloch
Trouble with Water	H. L. Gold
Cloak of Aesir	Don A. Stuart
The Day is Done	Lester Del Rey
The Ultimate Catalyst	John Taine
The Gnarly Man	L. Sprague de Camp
Black Destroyer	A. E. Van Vogt
Greater Than Gods	C. L. Moore
Trends	Isaac Asimov
The Blue Giraffe	L. Sprague de Camp
The Misguided Halo	Henry Kuttner
Heavy Planet	Milton A. Rothman
Life-Line	Robert A. Heinlein
Ether Breather	Theodore Sturgeon
Pilgrimage	Nelson Bond
Rust	Joseph E. Kelleam
The Four-Sided Triangle	William F. Temple
Star Bright	Jack Williamson
Misfit	Robert A. Heinlein

*Isaac Asimov and Martin H. Greenberg *The Great SF Stories 1*

88

1939: Best SF Novels of the Year

Sinister Barrier	Eric Frank Russell
Lest Darkness Fall	L. Sprague de Camp
One Against the Legion	Jack Williamson
Grey Lensman	E. E. Smith
The New Adam	Stanley G. Weinbaum
Divide and Rule	L. Sprague de Camp
After Many A Summer	Aldous Huxley
The Hopkins Manuscript	R. C. Sherriff

1940: Best SF Stories of the Year*

Requiem	Robert A. Heinlein
The Dwindling Sphere	Willard Hawkins
The Automatic Pistol	Fritz Leiber
Hindsight	Jack Williamson
Postpaid to Paradise	Robert Arthur
Coventry	Robert A. Heinlein
Into the Darkness	Ross Rocklynne
Dark Mission	Lester Del Rey
It	Theodore Sturgeon
Vault of the Beast	A. E. Van Vogt
The Impossible Way	Oscar J. Friend
Quietus	Ross Rocklynne
Blowups Happen	Robert A. Heinlein
Strange Playfellow	Isaac Asimov
The Warrior Race	L. Sprague de Camp
Farewell to the Master	Harry Bates
Butyl and the Breather	Theodore Sturgeon
The Exalted	L. Sprague de Camp
Old Man Mulligan	P. Schuyler Miller

*Asimov and Greenberg *The Great SF Stories 2*

1940: Best SF Novels of the Year

Typewriter in the Sky	L. Ron Hubbard
Darker Than You Think	Jack Williamson
If This Goes On	Robert A. Heinlein
Final Blackout	L. Ron Hubbard
Slan	A. E. Van Vogt

1941: Best SF Short Stories of the Year*

Mechanical Mice	Eric Frank Russell (as Maurice Hugi)
And He Built a Crooked House	Robert A. Heinlein
Shottle Bop	Theodore Sturgeon
The Rocket of 1955	C. M. Kornbluth
They	Robert A. Heinlein
Evolution's End	Robert Arthur
Microcosmic God	Theodore Sturgeon
Jay Score	Eric Frank Russell
Universe	Robert A. Heinlein
Liar!	Isaac Asimov
Solution Unsatisfactory	Robert A. Heinlein
Time Wants a Skeleton	Ross Rocklynne
The Words of Guru	C. M. Kornbluth
The Seesaw	A. E. Van Vogt
Armageddon	Fredric Brown
Adam and no Eve	Alfred Bester
Solar Plexus	James Blish
Nightfall	Isaac Asimov
A Gnome There Was	Henry Kuttner and C. L. Moore
By His Bootstraps	Robert A. Heinlein (as Anson MacDonald)
Snulbug	Anthony Boucher
Hereafter, Inc.	Lester Del Rey

*Asimov and Greenberg *The Great SF Stories 3*

1941: Best SF Novels of the Year

Methuselah's Children	Robert A. Heinlein
Sixth Column	Robert A. Heinlein (as Anson MacDonald)

1942: Best SF Short Stories of the Year*

The Star Mouse	Fredric Brown
The Wings of Night	Lester Del Rey
Cooperate - Or Else!	A. E. Van Vogt
Foundation	Isaac Asimov
The Push of a Finger	Alfred Bester
Asylum	A. E. Van Vogt
Proof	Hal Clement
Nerves	Lester Del Rey
Barrier	Anthony Boucher
The Twonky	Lewis Padgett
QRM-Interplanetary	George O. Smith
The Weapons Shop	A. E. Van Vogt
Mimic	Donald Wollheim

1942: Best SF Novels of the Year

Beyond this Horizon	Robert A. Heinlein (as Anson MacDonald)
The Comet Kings	Edmond Hamilton
Second Stage Lensman	E. E. Smith
Islandia	Austin Tappan Wright
Darkness and the Light	Olaf Stapledon

*Asimov and Greenberg *The Great SF Stories 4*

1943: Best SF Short Stories of the Year*

The Cave	P. Schuyler Miller
The Halfling	Leigh Brackett
Mimsy Were the Borogoves	Lewis Padgett
Q.U.R.	Anthony Boucher
Clash by Night	Lawrence O'Donnell
Exile	Edmond Hamilton
Daymare	Fredric Brown
Doorway Into Time	C. L. Moore
The Storm	A. E. Van Vogt
The Proud Robot	Lewis Padgett
Symbiotica	Eric Frank Russell
The Iron Standard	Lewis Padgett

1943: Best SF Novels of the Year

Gather, Darkness	Fritz Leiber
Donovan's Brain	Curt Siodmak
Judgement Night	C. L. Moore
The Book of Ptath	A. E. Van Vogt
Perelandra	C. S. Lewis
The Weapon Makers	A. E. Van Vogt
Conjure Wife	Fritz Leiber
The Glass Bead Game	Hermann Hesse

1944: Best SF Short Stories of the Year

City	Clifford D. Simak
Far Centaurus	A. E. Van Vogt
Killdozer!	Theodore Sturgeon
No Woman Born	C. L. Moore
When the Bough Breaks	Lewis Padgett
The Veil of Astellar	Leigh Brackett

*Asimov and Greenberg *The Great SF Stories 5*

The Children's Hour	Lawrence O'Donnell
Deadline	Cleve Cartmill
Arena	Fredric Brown
Catch That Rabbit	Isaac Asimov
The Changeling	A. E. Van Vogt
A Can of Paint	A. E. Van Vogt
Wanderers of Time	John Russell Fearn
Lazarus Come Forth	Ray Bradbury
As Never Was	P. Schuyler Miller
Huddling Place	Clifford D. Simak
Desertion	Clifford D. Simak

1944: Best SF Novels of the Year

Renaissance	Raymond F. Jones
Sirius	Olaf Stapledon
Ape and Essence	Aldous Huxley

1945: Best SF Short Stories of the Year

First Contact	Murray Leinster
Giant Killer	A. Bertram Chandler
The Mixed Men	A. E. Van Vogt
The Waveries	Fredric Brown
Blind Alley	Isaac Asimov
Heir Apparent	A. E. Van Vogt
The Ethical Equations	Murray Leinster
Three Blind Mice	Lewis Padgett
The Lion and the Unicorn	Lewis Padgett
Line to Tomorrow	Lewis Padgett
The Critters	Frank Belknap Long
The Power	Murray Leinster
Dead Hand	Isaac Asimov
Paradoxical Escape	Isaac Asimov
The Piper's Son	Lewis Padgett
Beggars in Velvet	Lewis Padgett

1945: Best SF Novels of the Year

The World of $\overline{A}$	A. E. Van Vogt
That Hideous Strength	C. S. Lewis
Destiny Times Three	Fritz Leiber
The Mule	Isaac Asimov

1946: Best SF Short Stories of the Year

Loophole	Arthur C. Clarke
Placet is a Crazy Place	Fredric Brown
Alexander the Bait	William Tenn
The Million-Year Picnic	Ray Bradbury
Metamorphosite	Eric Frank Russell
Rocket to Limbo	Margaret St Clair
A Logic Named Joe	Will F. Jenkins
Memorial	Theodore Sturgeon
Rescue Party	Arthur C. Clarke
The Bottled Man	Ross Rocklynne
Vintage Season	Lawrence O'Donnell
Mewhu's Jet	Theodore Sturgeon
Tepondicon	Carl Jacobi
What Hath Me?	Henry Kuttner
Evidence	Isaac Asimov
Call Him Demon	Henry Kuttner
Absalom	Henry Kuttner

1946: Best SF Novels of the Year

Slan	A. E. Van Vogt
The Fairy Chessmen	Lewis Padgett
Pattern for Conquest	George O. Smith

1947: Best SF Short Stories of the Year

Tomorrow's Children	Poul Anderson and F. N. Waldrop
Time and Time Again	H. Beam Piper
E for Effort	T. L. Sherred
With Folded Hands	Jack Williamson
The Star King	Edmond Hamilton
Thunder and Roses	Theodore Sturgeon
Little Lost Robot	Isaac Asimov
Hobbyist	Eric Frank Russell
The Fires Within	Arthur C. Clarke
Rocket Summer	Ray Bradbury
Zero Hour	Ray Bradbury
Maturity	Theodore Sturgeon
Child's Play	William Tenn
The Equalizer	Jack Williamson

1947: Best SF Novels of the Year

Greener Than You Think	Ward Moore
Fury	Lawrence O'Donnell (Henry Kuttner)
Children of the Lens	E. E. Smith
The End is Not Yet	L. Ron Hubbard
Doppelgangers	H. F. Heard

1948: Best SF Short Stories of the Year*

Mars is Heaven!	Ray Bradbury
Ex Machina	Lewis Padgett
The Strange Case of John Kingman	Murray Leinster
Doughnut Jockey	Eric Fennell
Thang	Martin Gardner
Period Piece	J. J. Coupling

*E. F. Bleiler and T. E. Dikty *The Best Science Fiction Stories 1949*

Knock	Fredric Brown
Genius	Poul Anderson
And the Moon Be Still as Bright	Ray Bradbury
No Connection	Isaac Asimov
In Hiding	Wilmar H. Shiras
Happy Ending	Henry Kuttner

1948: Best Novels of the Year

. . . And Searching Mind	Jack Williamson
Dreadful Sanctuary	Eric Frank Russell
What Mad Universe	Fredric Brown
The Players of $\bar{A}$	A. E. Van Vogt
Against the Fall of Night	Arthur C. Clarke

1949: Best SF Short Stories of the Year*

Private Eye	Henry Kuttner
Doomsday Deferred	Will F. Jenkins
The Hurkle is a Happy Beast	Theodore Sturgeon
Eternity Lost	Clifford D. Simak
Easter Eggs	Robert S. Carr
Opening Doors	Wilmar H. Shiras
Five Years in the Marmalade	Robert W. Krepps
Dwellers in Silence	Ray Bradbury
Mouse	Fredric Brown
Refuge for Tonight	Robert Moore Williams
The Life-Work of Professor Muntz	Murray Leinster
Flaw	John D. MacDonald
The Man	Ray Bradbury

---

*Bleiler and Dikty, *The Best Science Fiction Stories 1950*

1949: Best SF Novels of the Year

Earth Abides	George R. Stewart (Winner of the 1951 International Fantasy Award)
Nineteen Eighty-Four	George Orwell
Seetee Shock	Jack Williamson (as Will Stewart)
Needle	Hal Clement
Flight Into Yesterday	Charles L. Harness
And Now You Don't	Isaac Asimov
Seven Days In New Crete	Robert Graves

1950: Best SF Short Stories of the Year*

The Santa Claus Planet	Frank Morton Robinson
The Gnurrs Come from the Voodvork Out	Reginald Bretnor
The Mindworm	C. M. Kornbluth
The Star Ducks	Bill Brown
Not to be Opened	Roger F. Young
Process	A. E. Van Vogt
Forget-Me-Not	William F. Temple
Contagion	Katherine MacLean
Trespass	Poul Anderson and Gordon Dickson
Oddy and Id	Alfred Bester
To Serve Man	Damon Knight
Summer Wear	L. Sprague de Camp
Born of Man and Woman	Richard Matheson
Fox in the Forest	Ray Bradbury
The Last Martian	Fredric Brown
The New Reality	Charles L. Harness
Two Face	Frank Belknap Long
Coming Attraction	Fritz Leiber

*Bleiler and Dikty, The Best Science Fiction Stories 1951

1950: Best SF Novels of the Year

Pebble in the Sky	Isaac Asimov
The Martian Chronicles	Ray Bradbury
The Voyage of the Space Beagle	A. E. Van Vogt
The Dreaming Jewels	Theodore Sturgeon
The Wizard of Linn	A. E. Van Vogt
The Hand of Zei	L. Sprague de Camp

1951: Best SF Short Stories of the Year*

The Other Side	Walter Kubilius
Of Time and Third Avenue	Alfred Bester
The Marching Morons	C. M. Kornbluth
A Peculiar People	Betsy Curtis
Extending the Holdings	David Grinnell
The Tourist Trade	Wilson Tucker
The Two Shadows	William F. Temple
Balance	John Christopher
Brightness Falls From the Air	Idris Seabright
Witch War	Richard Matheson
At No Extra Cost	Peter Phillips
Nine-Finger Jack	Anthony Boucher
Appointment in Tomorrow	Fritz Leiber
The Rats	Arthur Porges
Men of the Ten Books	Jack Vance
Dark Interlude	Mack Reynolds and Fredric Brown
The Pedestrian	Ray Bradbury
Generation of Noah	William Tenn

1951: Best SF Novellas of the Year†

Izzard and the Membrane	Walter M. Miller
And Then There Were None	Eric Frank Russell

*Bleiler and Dikty *The Best Science Fiction Stories 1952*
†Bleiler and Dikty, *Year's Best Science Fiction Novels 1952*

Flight to Forever	Poul Anderson
The Hunting Season	Frank M. Robinson
Seeker of the Sphinx	Arthur C. Clarke

1951: Best SF Novels of the Year

The Day of the Triffids	John Wyndham
The Sands of Mars	Arthur C. Clarke
The Weapon Shops of Isher	A. E. Van Vogt
The Puppet Masters	Robert A. Heinlein
Iceworld	Hal Clement
Prelude to Space	Arthur C. Clarke
The Disappearance	Philip Wylie

1952: Best SF Short Stories of the Year*

The Fly	Arthur Porges
Ararat	Zenna Henderson
Counter-Transference	William F. Temple
The Conqueror	Mark Clifton
Machine	John Jakes
The Middle of the Week After Next	Murray Leinster
The Dreamer	Alfred Coppel
The Moon is Green	Fritz Leiber
I Am Nothing	Eric Frank Russell
Command Performance	Walter M. Miller
Survival	John Wyndham
Game for Blondes	John D. MacDonald
The Girls from Earth	Frank M. Robinson
Lover, When You're Near Me	Richard Matheson
Fast Falls the Eventide	Eric Frank Russell

*Bleiler and Dikty, *The Best Science Fiction Stories 1953*

1952: Best SF Novellas of the Year*

Firewater	William Tenn
Category Phoenix	Boyd Ellanby
Surface Tension	James Blish
The Gadget had a Ghost	Murray Leinster
Conditionally Human	Walter M. Miller

1952: Hugo Award for Best SF Novel of the Year

The Demolished Man	Alfred Bester

1952: Best SF Novels of the Year

City	Clifford D. Simak (Winner of the 1953 International Fantasy Award)
Takeoff	C. M. Kornbluth
Player Piano	Kurt Vonnegut Jr
Jack of Eagles	James Blish
The Space Merchants	Frederik Pohl and C. M. Kornbluth
The Currents of Space	Isaac Asimov
Gunner Cade	Cyril Judd
Limbo	Bernard Wolfe
The Sound of His Horn	Sarban
Big Planet	Jack Vance
The Long Loud Silence	Wilson Tucker
You Shall Know Them	Vercors

1953: Best SF Short Stories of the Year†

Icon of the Imagination	Fritz Leiber
DP!	Jack Vance

*Bleiler and Dikty, *Year's Best Science Fiction Novels 1953*
†Bleiler and Dikty, *The Best Science Fiction Stories 1954*

The Big Holiday	Fritz Leiber
The Collectors	G. R. Dewey and G. Dancy
One in Three Hundred	J. T. McIntosh
Wonder Child	J. Shallit
Crucifixus Etiam	Walter M. Miller
The Model of a Judge	William Morrison
The Last Day	Richard Matheson
Time is the Traitor	Alfred Bester
Lot	Ward Moore
Yankee Exodus	Ruth Goldsmith
What Thin Partitions	Mark Clifton and Alex Apostolides
A Bad Day for Sales	Fritz Leiber

1953: Best SF Novellas of the Year*

The Enormous Room	H. L. Gold and Robert W. Krepps
Assignment to Aldebaran	Kendall Foster Crossen
The Oceans Are Wide	Frank M. Robinson
The Sentimentalists	Murray Leinster
Second Variety	Philip K. Dick

1953: Best SF Novels of the Year

More than Human	Theodore Sturgeon (Winner of the 1954 International Fantasy Award)
Fahrenheit 451	Ray Bradbury
Childhood's End	Arthur C. Clarke
Bring the Jubilee	Ward Moore
Police Your Planet	Lester Del Rey
Mission of Gravity	Hal Clement
The Caves of Steel	Isaac Asimov
The Syndic	C. M. Kornbluth
The Kraken Wakes	John Wyndham
The Lights in the Sky are Stars	Fredric Brown
One	David Karp

*Bleiler and Dikty *Year's Best Science Fiction Novels 1954*

1954: Best SF Short Stories of the Year*

The Cold Equations	Tom Godwin
Of Course	Chad Oliver
Dominions Beyond	Ward Moore
Guilty As Charged	Arthur Porges
Careless Love	A. C. Friborg
Memento Homo	Walter M. Miller
Mousetrap	André Norton
Christmas Trombone	Raymond E. Banks
One Thousand Miles Up	Frank M. Robinson
How-2	Clifford D. Simak
Heirs Apparent	Robert Abernathy
John's Other Practice	Winston Marks
The Inner Worlds	William Morrison
The Will	Walter M. Miller
Felony	J. Causey
The Littlest People	Raymond E. Banks
One Way Street	Jerome Bixby
Axolotl	Robert Abernathy
Exile	Everett B. Cole
Nightmare Blues	Frank Herbert

1954: Hugo Award for Best SF Novel of the Year

They'd Rather Be Right	Mark Clifton and Frank Riley

1954: International Fantasy Award

A Mirror For Observers	Edgar Pangborn

*Dikty, *The Best Science Fiction Stories and Novels 1955*

Other Major SF Novels of 1954

I Am Legend	Richard Matheson
Gladiator-At-Law	Frederik Pohl and C. M. Kornbluth
Brain Wave	Poul Anderson
Messiah	Gore Vidal
Wild Talent	Wilson Tucker

1955: Best SF Short Stories of the Year*

Jungle Doctor	Robert F. Young
Judgment Day	L. Sprague de Camp
The Game of Rat and Dragon	Cordwainer Smith
The Man Who Always Knew	Algis Budrys
Dream Street	Frank M. Robinson
You Created Us	Tom Godwin
Swenson, Dispatcher	R. De Witt Miller
Thing	Paul Janvier
I Do Not Love Thee, Dr Fell	Robert Bloch
Clerical Error	Mark Clifton
A Canticle for Leibowitz	Walter M. Miller
The Cyber and Justice Holmes	Frank Riley
The Shores of Night	Thomas N. Scortia

1955: Best SF Short Stories of the Year†

The Stutterer	R. R. Merliss
The Golem	Avram Davidson
Junior	Robert Abernathy
The Cave of Night	James E. Gunn
The Hoofer	Walter M. Miller
Bulkhead	Theodore Sturgeon
Sense from Thought Divide	Mark Clifton

*Dikty *The Best Science Fiction Stories and Novels 1956*
†Judith Merril, *SF: The Year's Greatest Science Fiction and Fantasy*

Pottage	Zenna Henderson
Nobody Bothers Gus	Algis Budrys
The Last Day of Summer	E. C. Tubb
One Ordinary Day, With Peanuts	Shirley Jackson
The Ethicators	Willard Marsh
Birds Can't Count	Mildred Clingerman
Of Missing Persons	Jack Finney
Dreaming is a Private Thing	Isaac Asimov
The Country of the Kind	Damon Knight
The Public Hating	Steve Allen
Home There's No Returning	Henry Kuttner and C. L. Moore

Hugo Awards, 1955

BEST SF NOVELETTE

The Darfsteller	Walter M. Miller

BEST SF SHORT STORY

Allamagoosa	Eric Frank Russell (awarded in 1955)
The Star	Arthur C. Clarke (awarded in 1956)

1955: Best Novels of the Year

The End of Eternity	Isaac Asimov
Earthman Come Home	James Blish
The Long Tomorrow	Leigh Brackett
This Fortress World	James E. Gunn
Hell's Pavement	Damon Knight
Star Bridge	Jack Williamson and James E. Gunn
The Chrysalids	John Wyndham
Under Pressure	Frank Herbert
The Long Way Home	Poul Anderson
Call Him Dead	Eric Frank Russell

104

Solar Lottery	Philip K. Dick
The Body Snatchers	Jack Finney

1956: Best SF Short Stories of the Year*

The Man Who Liked Lions	John B. Daley
The Cosmic Expense Account	C. M. Kornbluth
The Far Look	Theodore L. Thomas
When Grandfather Flew to the Moon	E. L. Malpass
The Doorstep	Reginald Bretnor
Silent Brother	Algis Budrys
Stranger Station	Damon Knight
Each an Explorer	Isaac Asimov
Put Them All Together, They	
Spell Monster	Ray Russell
Digging the Weans	Robert Nathan
Take a Deep Breath	Roger Thorne
Grandma's Lie Soap	Robert Abernathy
Compounded Interest	Mack Reynolds
Prima Belladonna	J. G. Ballard
The Other Man	Theodore Sturgeon
The Damndest Thing	Garson Kanin
The Anything Box	Zenna Henderson

Hugo Awards, 1956

BEST SF NOVEL

Double Star   Robert A. Heinlein

BEST SF NOVELETTE

Exploration Team   Murray Leinster

*Judith Merril *SF: The Year's Greatest Science Fiction and Fantasy: Second Annual Volume*

Other Major SF Novels of 1956

The Death of Grass	John Christopher
The Power	Frank M. Robinson
Slave Ship	Frederik Pohl
The Naked Sun	Isaac Asimov
The Stars My Destination	Alfred Bester
The Door Into Summer	Robert A. Heinlein
The City and the Stars	Arthur C. Clarke
The World Jones Made	Philip K. Dick
The Shrinking Man	Richard Matheson

1957: Best SF Short Stories of the Year*

2066: Election Day	Michael Shaara
The Mile-Long Spaceship	Kate Wilhelm
The Last Victory	Tom Godwin
Call Me Joe	Poul Anderson
Didn't He Ramble	Chad Oliver
The Queen's Messenger	John J. McGuire
The Other People	Leigh Brackett
Into Your Tent I'll Creep	Eric Frank Russell
Nor Dust Corrupt	J. McConnell
Nightsound	Algis Budrys
The Tunesmith	Lloyd Biggle Jr
Hunting Machine	Carol Emshwiller

1957: Best SF Short Stories of the Year†

Let's Be Frank	Brian Aldiss
The Fly	George Langelaan
Let's Get Together	Isaac Asimov

*Dikty, *Best Science Fiction Stories and Novels, 9th Series*
†Judith Merril, *SF: The Year's Greatest Science Fiction and Fantasy: Third Annual Volume*

The Wonder Horse	George Byram
You Know Willie	Theodore R. Cogswell
Near Miss	Henry Kuttner
Game Preserve	Rog Phillips
Now Let Us Sleep	Avram Davidson
Wilderness	Zenna Henderson
Flying High	Eugène Ionesco
The Edge of the Sea	Algis Budrys

1957: Best SF Novels of the Year

Earthman's Burden	Poul Anderson and Gordon R. Dickson
They Shall Have Stars	James Blish
The Deep Range	Arthur C. Clarke
The Black Cloud	Fred Hoyle
Wolfbane	Frederik Pohl and C. M. Kornbluth
The Dawning Light	Robert Randall
Citizen of the Galaxy	Robert A. Heinlein
Cycle of Fire	Hal Clement
Eye in the Sky	Philip K. Dick
The Green Odyssey	Philip José Farmer
The Midwich Cuckoos	John Wyndham
On the Beach	Nevil Shute

1958: Best SF Short Stories of the Year*

Pelt	Carol Emshwiller
Triggerman	J. F. Bone
The Prize of Peril	Robert Sheckley
Hickory, Dickory, Kerouac	Richard Gehman
The Yellow Pill	Rog Phillips
River of Riches	Gerald Kersh
Satellite Passage	Theodore Thomas
Casey Agonistes	Richard M. McKenna

*Judith Merril, SF: The Year's Greatest Science Fiction and Fantasy: Fourth Annual Volume

Space-Time for Springers	Fritz Leiber
Or All the Seas with Oysters	Avram Davidson
Ten-Story Jigsaw	Brian Aldiss
Fresh Guy	E. C. Tubb
The Beautiful Things	Arthur Zirul
The Comedian's Children	Theodore Sturgeon
The Short-Short Story of Mankind	John Steinbeck

1958: Hugo Awards

BEST SF NOVEL

The Big Time   Fritz Leiber

BEST SF SHORT STORY

Or All the Seas with Oysters   Avram Davidson

(*Note*: The above awards were presented at the 1958 Los Angeles Solacon convention and covered works published during the preceding twelve months. From 1959, works eligible for the Hugo Awards had to be published during the course of the preceding year. This explains why there are two sets of awards for 1958, although technically the second set of awards was given out in 1959.)

1958: Hugo Awards and Nominations

BEST SF NOVEL

A Case of Conscience	**James Blish** (Winner)
Have Spacesuit-Will Travel	Robert A. Heinlein
Time Killer	Robert Sheckley
We Have Fed Our Sea	Poul Anderson
Who?	Algis Budrys

BEST SF NOVELETTE

The Big Front Yard	**Clifford D. Simak** (Winner)
Captivity	Zenna Henderson

A Deskful of Girls	Fritz Leiber
The Miracle-Workers	Jack Vance
Rat in the Skull	Rog Phillips
Reap the Dark Tide	C. M. Kornbluth
Second Game	Katherine MacLean and Charles V. DeVet
Unwilling to School	Pauline Ashwell

BEST SHORT STORY

That Hell-Bound Train	**Robert Bloch** (Winner)
The Advent on Channel Twelve	C. M. Kornbluth
The Edge of the Sea	Algis Budrys
The Man Who Murdered Mohammed	Alfred Bester
Nine Yards of Other Cloth	Manly Wade Wellman
Rum-Titty-Titty-Tum-Ta-Tee	Fritz Leiber
Space to Swing a Cat	Stanley Mullen
Theory of Rocketry	C. M. Kornbluth
They've Been Working On . . .	Anton Lee Baker
Triggerman	J. F. Bone

Best SF Short Stories of 1959*

The Handler	Damon Knight
The Other Wife	Jack Finney
No Fire Burns	Avram Davidson
No, No, Not Rogov!	Cordwainer Smith
The Shoreline at Sunset	Ray Bradbury
The Dreamsman	Gordon R. Dickson
Multum in Parvo	Jack Sharkey
Flowers for Algernon	Daniel Keyes
A Death in the House	Clifford D. Simak
Mariana	Fritz Leiber
An Inquiry Concerning the Curvature of the Earth's Surface and Diverse Investigations of a Metaphysical Nature	Roger Price

*Judith Merril *Year's Best SF: Fifth Annual Edition*

A Day at the Beach	Carol Emshwiller
What the Left Hand was Doing	Darrel T. Langart
The Sound Sweep	J. G. Ballard
Plenitude	Will Worthington
The Man Who Lost the Sea	Theodore Sturgeon
Make a Prison	Lawrence Block
What Now, Little Man?	Mark Clifton

1959: Hugo Awards and Nominations

BEST SF NOVEL

Starship Troopers	**Robert A. Heinlein** (Winner)
Dorsai!	Gordon R. Dickson
The Pirates of Ersatz	Murray Leinster
The Sirens of Titan	Kurt Vonnegut Jr
That Sweet Little Old Lady	Mark Phillips

BEST SF NOVELETTE OR SHORT STORY

Flowers for Algernon	**Daniel Keyes** (Winner)
The Alley Man	Philip José Farmer
Cat and Mouse	Ralph Williams
The Man Who Lost the Sea	Theodore Sturgeon
The Pi Man	Alfred Bester

Best SF Short Stories of 1960*

Double, Double, Toil and Trouble	Holley Cantine
The Never Ending Penny	Bernard Wolfe
The Fellow Who Married the Maxill Girl	Ward Moore
Something Invented Me	R. C. Phelan
I Remember Babylon	Arthur C. Clarke
Report on the Nature of the Lunar Surface	John Brunner

*Judith Merril, *Year's Best SF: Sixth Annual Edition*

Chief	Henry Slesar
The Large Ant	Howard Fast
A Rose by Other Name	Christopher Anvil
Enchantment	Elizabeth Emmett
Beach Scene	Marshall King
Creature of the Snows	William Sambrot
Abominable	Fredric Brown
The Man on Top	Reginald Bretnor
David's Daddy	Rosel George Brown
Something Bright	Zenna Henderson
In the House, Another	Joseph Whitehill
The Brotherhood of Keepers	Dean McLaughlin
Hemingway in Space	Kingsley Amis
Mine Own Ways	Richard McKenna
Old Hundredth	Brian Aldiss

1960: Hugo Awards and Nominations

BEST SF NOVEL

A Canticle for Leibowitz	**Walter M. Miller** (Winner)
Deathworld	Harry Harrison
The High Crusade	Poul Anderson
Rogue Moon	Algis Budrys
Venus Plus X	Theodore Sturgeon

BEST SHORT FICTION

The Longest Voyage	**Poul Anderson** (Winner)
The Lost Kafoozalum	Pauline Ashwell
Need	Theodore Sturgeon
Open to me, My Sister	Philip José Farmer

1961: Best SF Short Stories of the Year*

A Passage From the Stars	Kaatje Hurlbut
Among the Dangs	George P. Elliott
Immediately Yours	Robert B. Hale

*Judith Merril, *The Year's Best SF: 7th Annual Edition*

1961: Hugo Awards and Nominations

BEST SF NOVEL

Stranger in a Strange Land	**Robert A. Heinlein** (Winner)
Dark Universe	Daniel F. Galouye
The Fisherman	Clifford D. Simak
Second Ending	James White
Sense of Obligation	Harry Harrison

BEST SF SHORT FICTION

the **Hothouse** series	**Brian Aldiss** (Winner)
Lion Loose	James H. Schmitz
Monument	Lloyd Biggle Jr
Scylla's Daughter	Fritz Leiber
Status Quo	Mack Reynolds

1962: Best SF Short Stories of the Year*

The Unsafe Deposit Box	Gerald Kersh
Seven-Day Terror	R. A. Lafferty
The Toy Shop	Harry Harrison
The Face in the Photo	Jack Finney
The Circuit Riders	R. C. Fitzpatrick
Such Stuff	John Brunner
The Man Who Made Friends with Electricity	Fritz Leiber
Kings Who Die	Poul Anderson
The Unfortunate Mr Morky	Vance Aandhal
Christmas Treason	James White
A Miracle of Rare Device	Ray Bradbury
All the Sounds of Fear	Harlan Ellison
One of Those Days	William F. Nolan
The Day Rembrandt Went Public	Arnold M. Auerbach
Ms Found in a Bus	Russell Baker
The Insane Ones	J. G. Ballard
Leprechaun	William Sambrot
Change of Heart	George Whitley

Angela's Satyr	Brian Cleeve
Puppet Show	Fredric Brown
Hang Head, Vandal	Mark Clifton
The Martian Star-Gazers	Frederik Pohl
Planetary Effulgence	Bertrand Russell
Deadly Game	Edward Wellen
Subcommittee	Zenna Henderson
The Piebald Hippogriff	Karen Henderson
Home from the Shore	Gordon R. Dickson

1962: Hugo Awards and Nominations

BEST SF NOVEL

The Man in the High Castle	**Philip K. Dick** (Winner)
A Fall of Moondust	Arthur C. Clarke
Little Fuzzy	H. Beam Piper
Sword of Aldones	Marion Zimmer Bradley
Sylva	Vercors

BEST SF SHORT FICTION

The Dragon Masters	**Jack Vance** (Winner)
Myrrha	Gary Jennings
The Unholy Grail	Fritz Leiber
When You Care, When You Love	Theodore Sturgeon
Where is the Bird of Fire?	Thomas Burnett Swann

*Judith Merril, *The Year's Best SF: 8th Annual Edition*

1963: Best SF Short Stories of the Year*

Bernie the Faust	William Tenn
Fortress Ship	Fred Saberhagen
Mr Waterman	Peter Redgrove
Mrs Pigafetta Swims Well	Reginald Bretnor
They Don't Make Life Like They Used To	Alfred Bester
The Great Nebraska Sea	Allen Danzig
The Faces Outside	Bruce McAllister
A Slight Case of Limbo	Lloyd Biggle Jr
237 Talking Statues	Fritz Leiber
Mourning Song	Charles Beaumont
The JewBird	Bernard Malamud
One the Fourth Planet	J. F. Bone
Poppa Needs Shorts	Walt and Leigh Richmond
Double Standard	Fredric Brown
Interview	Frank A. Javor
Eight O'Clock in the Morning	Ray Nelson
The Earth Dwellers	André Maurois
The Nobel Prize Winners	W. J. J. Gordon
Hot Planet	Hal Clement
Confessions of the First Number	Cliff Owsley
The Ming Vase	E. C. Tubb
A Bargain with Cashel	Gerald Kersh
Drunkboat	Cordwainer Smith

1963: Hugo Awards and Nominations

BEST SF NOVEL

Here Gather the Stars	**Clifford D. Simak** (Winner)
Cat's Cradle	Kurt Vonnegut Jr
Dune World	Frank Herbert
Glory Road	Robert A. Heinlein
Witch World	André Norton

*Judith Merril, *The Year's Best SF: 9th Annual Edition*

No Truce with Kings   **Poul Anderson** (Winner)
Code Three   Rick Raphael
A Rose for Ecclesiastes   Roger Zelazny
Savage Pellucidar   Edgar R. Burroughs

1964: Best SF Short Stories of the Year*

Automatic Tiger   Kit Read
The Carson Effect   Richard Wilson
The Shining Ones   Arthur C. Clarke
Pacifist   Mack Reynolds
The New Encyclopaedist   Stephen Becker
The Legend of Joe Lee   John D. MacDonald
Gas Mask   James D. Houston
A Sinister Metamorphosis   Russell Baker
Sonny   Rick Raphael
*The Last Secret Weapon
  of the Third Reich*   Josef Nesvadba
Descending   Thomas M. Disch
Decadence   Romain Gary
Be Of Good Cheer   Fritz Leiber
It Could Be You   Frank Roberts
A Benefactor of Humanity   James T. Farrell
Synchromocracy   Hap Carwood
The Pirokin Effect   Larry Eisenberg
The Twerlik   Jack Sharkey
A Rose for Ecclesiastes   Roger Zelazny
The Terminal Beach   J. G. Ballard
Problem Child   Arthur Porges
The Wonderful Dog Suit   Donald Hall
The Mathenauts   Norman Kagan
Family Portrait   Morgan Kent

The Red Egg	José Maria Gironella
The Power of Positive Thinking	M. E. White
A Living Doll	Robert Wallace
Training Talk	David R. Bunch
A Miracle Too Many	Philip H. Smith
	and Alan E. Nourse
The Last Lonely Man	John Brunner
The Man Who Found Proteus	Robert Rohrer
Yachid and Yechida	Isaac Bashevis Singer

1964. Best SF Short Stories of the Year†

Greenplace	Tom Purdom
Men of Good Will	Ben Bova and
	Myron L. Lewis
Bill for Delivery	Christopher Anvil
Four Brands of Impossible	Norman Kagan
A Niche in Time	William F. Temple
Sea Wrack	Edward Jesby
For Every Action	C. C. MacApp
Vampires Ltd.	Josef Nesvadba
The Last Lonely Man	John Brunner
The Star Party	Robert Lory
The Weather in the Underworld	Colin Free
Oh, to Be a Blobel!	Philip K. Dick
The Unremembered	Edward Mackin
What Happened to Sergeant Masuro?	Harry Mulisch
Now is Forever	Thomas M. Disch
The Competitors	Jack B. Lawson
When the Change-Winds Blow	Fritz Leiber

*Judith Merril, *The Year's Best SF: 10th Annual Edition*
†Wollheim and Carr, *World's Best Science Fiction: 1965*

1964: Hugo Awards and Nominations

BEST SF NOVEL

The Wanderer   **Fritz Leiber** (Winner)
Davy   Edgar Pangborn
The Planet Buyer   Cordwainer Smith
The Whole Man   John Brunner

BEST SF SHORT STORY

Soldier, Ask Not   **Gordon R. Dickson** (Winner)
Little Dog Gone   Albert F. Young
Once A Cop   Rick Raphael

1965: Best SF Short Stories of the Year*

Something Else	Robert Tilley
The Volcano Dances	J. G. Ballard
Slow Tuesday Night	R. A. Lafferty
Better than Ever	Alex Kirs
Coming-of-Age Day	A. K. Jorgsensson
The Wall	Josephine Saxton
The Survivor	Walter Moudy
Moon Duel	Fritz Leiber
Project Inhumane	Alexander B. Malec
Those Who Can, Do	Bob Kurosaka
Susan	Alistair Bevan
Yesterdays' Gardens	Johnny Byrne
The Roaches	Thomas M. Disch
Game	Donald Barthelme
J Is For Jeanne	E. C. Tubb
Terminal	Ron Goulart
The Plot	Tom Herzog
Investigating the Bidwell Endeavors	David R. Bunch
There's a Starman in Ward 7	David Rome
Eyes Do More Than See	Isaac Asimov
Maelstrom II	Arthur C. Clarke

1965: Best SF Short Stories of the Year†

*Judith Merril, The Year's Best SF: 11th Annual Edition
†Wollheim and Carr, World's Best Science Fiction: 1966

Vanishing Point	Jonathan Brand
In Our Block	R. A. Lafferty
Masque of the Red Shift	Fred Saberhagen
The Captive Djinn	Christopher Anvil
The Good News Days	Fritz Leiber

1965: Hugo Awards and Nominations

BEST SF NOVEL

. . . And Call Me Conrad	**Roger Zelazny** (Joint Winner)
Dune	**Frank Herbert** (Joint Winner)
The Moon is a Harsh Mistress	Robert A. Heinlein
Skylark DuQuesne	E. E. Smith
Squares of the City	John Brunner

BEST SF SHORT FICTION

'Repent, Harlequin!' Said the Ticktockman	**Harlan Ellison** (Winner)
Day of the Great Shout	Philip José Farmer
The Doors of His Face The Lamps of His Mouth	Roger Zelazny
Marque and Reprisal	Poul Anderson
Stardock	Fritz Leiber

1965: Nebula Awards and Nominations

BEST SF NOVEL

Dune	**Frank Herbert** (Winner)
All Flesh is Grass	Clifford D. Simak
The Clone	Theodore Thomas and Kate Wilhelm
Dr Bloodmoney	Philip K. Dick
The Escape Orbit	James White
The Genocides	Thomas M. Disch
Nova Express	William Burroughs
A Plague of Demons	Keith Laumer

120

Rogue Dragon	Avram Davidson
The Ship That Sailed the	
Time Stream	C. C. Edmondson
The Star Fox	Poul Anderson
The Three Stigmata of	
Palmer Eldritch	Philip K. Dick

BEST SF NOVELLA

He Who Shapes	**Roger Zelazny** (Joint Winner)
The Saliva Tree	**Brian Aldiss** (Joint Winner)
The Ballad of Beta-2	Samuel R. Delany
The Mercurymen	C. C. McApp
On the Storm Planet	Cordwainer Smith
Research Alpha	A. E. Van Vogt and James H. Schmitz
Rogue Dragon	Avram Davidson
Under Two Moons	Frederik Pohl

BEST SF NOVELETTE

The Doors of His Face, The	
Lamps of His Mouth	**Roger Zelazny**
Adventure of the Extraterrestrial	Mack Reynolds
At the Institute	Norman Kagan
The Decision Makers	Joseph Green
The Earth Merchants	Norman Kagan
Four Ghosts in Hamlet	Fritz Leiber
Goblin Night	James Schmitz
Half a Loaf	R. C. Fitzpatrick
Laugh Along with Franz	Norman Kagan
The Life of your Time	Michael Karageorge
Maiden Voyage	J. W. Schutz
The Masculinist Revolt	William Tenn
The Masque of the Red Shift	Fred Saberhagen
102 H-Bombs	Thomas M. Disch
Planet of Forgetting	James H. Schmitz
Shall We Have A Little Talk?	Robert Sheckley
The Shipwrecked Hotel	James Blish and Norman Knight
Small One	E. Clayton McCarty
Vanishing Point	Jonathan Brand

BEST SF SHORT STORY

'Repent Harlequin!' Said the Ticktockman

Harlan Ellison (Winner)

There were thirty other stories also nominated, from the pens of James Schmitz, Larry Niven, Edgar Pangborn, Alex Kirs, Ron Goulart, Thomas M. Disch, Gordon Dickson, Fritz Leiber, Roger Zelasny, Richard Wilson, Isaac Asimov, John Christopher, Donald Barthelme, Avram Davidson, R. A. Lafferty, H. L. Gold, Robert Rohrer, Mack Reynolds, Jane Beauclerk, Richard Olin, James Durham, Clifford D. Simak, Ted White and L. McCombs, J. G. Ballard, Scott Nichols, and Lin Carter.

1966: Best SF Short Stories of the Year*

In Seclusion	Harvey Jacobs
The Food Farm	Kit Reed
Gogol's Wife	Tommaso Landolfi
The Balloon	Donald Barthelme
The Cloud Sculptors of Coral D	J. G. Ballard
Luana	Gilbert Thomas
During the Jurassic	John Updike
The Fall of Frenchy Steiner	Hilary Bailey
Light of Other Days	Bob Shaw
Beyond the Weeds	Peter Tate
Crab-Apple Crisis	George MacBeth
The Primary Education of the Camiroi	R. A. Lafferty
When I Was Miss Dow	Sonya Dorman
Confluence	Brian Aldiss
Journey from Ellipsia	Hortense Calisher
An Ornament to His Profession	Charles L. Harness
Narrow Valley	R. A. Lafferty
They Do Not Always Remember	William Burroughs
The Winter Flies	Fritz Leiber
When I First Read . . .	Dick Allen
You: Coma: Marilyn Monroe	J. G. Ballard
And More Changes Still	Henri Michaux
The Other	Katherine MacLean

| Chicken Icarus | Carol Emshwiller |
| The Star-Pit | Samuel R. Delany |

1966: Best SF Short Stories of the Year†

We Can Remember It For You Wholesale	Philip K. Dick
Light of Other Days	Bob Shaw
The Keys to December	Roger Zelazny
Nine Hundred Grandmothers	R. A. Lafferty
Bircher	A. A. Walde
Behold the Man	Michael Moorcock
Bumberboom	Avram Davidson
Day Million	Frederik Pohl
The Wing of a Bat	Paul Ash
The Man From When	Dannie Plachta
Amen and Out	Brian Aldiss
For a Breath I Tarry	Roger Zelazny

1966: Hugo Awards and Nominations

BEST SF NOVEL

The Moon is a Harsh Mistress	**Robert A. Heinlein** (Winner)
Babel-17	Samuel R. Delany
Day of the Minotaur	Thomas Burnett Swann
Flowers for Algernon	Daniel Keyes
Too Many Magicians	Randall Garrett
The Witches of Karres	James H. Schmitz

*Judith Merril, *SF 12*
†Wollheim and Carr, *World's Best Science Fiction: 1967*

BEST SF NOVELETTE

The Last Castle   **Jack Vance** (Winner)
The Alchemist   Charles L. Harness
Apology to Inky   Robert M. Green Jr
Call Him Lord   Gordon R. Dickson
The Eskimo Invasion   Hayden Howard
For A Breath I Tarry   Roger Zelazny
The Manor of Rose   Thomas Burnett Swann
An Ornament to His Profession Charles L. Harness
The Moment of the Storm   Roger Zelazny

BEST SF SHORT STORY

Neutron Star   **Larry Niven** (Winner)
Comes Now the Power   Roger Zelazny
Delusions for a Dragon Slayer Harlan Ellison
Man in his Time   Brian Aldiss
Mr Jester   Fred Saberhagen
Rat Race   Raymond F. Jones
The Secret Place   Richard McKenna

1966: Nebula Awards and Nominations

BEST SF NOVEL

Babel-17   **Samuel R. Delany** (Joint Winner)
Flowers for Algernon   **Daniel Keyes** (Joint Winner)
The Moon is a Harsh Mistress Robert A. Heinlein

BEST SF NOVELLA

The Last Castle   **Jack Vance** (Winner)
The Alchemist   Charles L. Harness
Clash of Star Kings   Avram Davidson

BEST SF NOVELETTE

Call Him Lord   **Gordon R. Dickson** (Winner)
Apology to Inky   Robert M. Green Jr
An Ornament to his Profession Charles L. Harness

The Eskimo Invasion	Hayden Howard
The Moment of the Storm	Roger Zelazny

BEST SF SHORT STORY

The Secret Place	**Richard McKenna** (Winner)
Light of Other Days	Bob Shaw
Man in his Time	Brian Aldiss

1967: Best SF Short Stories of the Year*

Hawksbill Station	Robert Silverberg
Ultimate Construction	C. C. Shackleton
1937 A.D.!	John T. Sladek
Fifteen Miles	Ben Bova
Blackmail	Fred Hoyle
The Vine	Kit Reed
Interview with a Lemming	James Thurber
The Wreck of the Ship 'John B'	Frank M. Robinson
The Left-Hand Way	A. Bertram Chandler
The Forest of Zil	Kris Neville
The Assassination of John Fitzgerald Kennedy Considered as a Downhill Motor Race	J. G. Ballard
Answering Service	Fritz Leiber
The Last Command	Keith Laumer
Mirror of Ice	Gray Wright
Pretty Maggie Moneyeyes	Harlan Ellison

1967: Best SF Short Stories of the Year†

See Me Not	Richard Wilson
Driftglass	Samuel R. Delany
Ambassador at Verdammt	Colin Kapp

*Harry Harrison and Brian Aldiss, *Best SF: 1967*
†Wollheim and Carr, *World's Best Science Fiction: 1968*

The Man Who Never Was	R. A. Lafferty
The Billiard Ball	Isaac Asimov
Hawksbill Station	Robert Silverberg
The Number You Have Reached	Thomas M. Disch
The Man Who Loved the Faioli	Roger Zelazny
Population Implosion	Andrew J. Offutt
I Have No Mouth and I Must Scream	Harlan Ellison
The Sword Swallower	Ron Goulart
Coranda	Keith Roberts
Thus We Frustrate Charlemagne	R. A. Lafferty
Handicap	Larry Niven
Full Sun	Brian Aldiss
It's Smart to Have an English Address	D. G. Compton

1967: Hugo Awards and Nominations

BEST SF NOVEL

Lord of Light	**Roger Zelazny** (Winner)
The Butterfly Kid	Chester Anderson
Chthon	Piers Anthony
The Einstein Intersection	Samuel R. Delany
Thorns	Robert Silverberg

BEST SF NOVELLA

Riders of the Purple Wage	**Philip José Farmer** (Joint Winner)
Weyr Search	**Anne McCaffrey** (Joint Winner)
Damnation Alley	Roger Zelazny
Hawksbill Station	Robert Silverberg
The Star-Pit	Samuel R. Delany

BEST SF NOVELETTE

Gonna Roll the Bones	**Fritz Leiber** (Winner)
Faith of our Fathers	Philip K. Dick
Pretty Maggie Moneyeyes	Harlan Ellison
Wizard's World	Andre Norton

BEST SF SHORT STORY

**I Have No Mouth,
And I Must Scream**   **Harlan Ellison** (Winner)
Aye, and Gomorrah   Samuel R. Delany
The Jigsaw Man   Larry Niven

1967: Nebula Awards and Nominations

BEST SF NOVEL

The Einstein Intersection   **Samuel R. Delany** (Winner)
Thorns   Robert Silverberg
Chthon   Piers Anthony
The Eskimo Invasion   Hayden Howard
Lord of Light   Roger Zelazny

BEST SF NOVELLA

Behold the Man   **Michael Moorcock** (Winner)
Weyr Search   Anne McCaffrey
Hawksbill Station   Robert Silverberg
Riders of the Purple Wage   Philip José Farmer
*If All Men Were Brothers Would You
   Let One Marry Your Sister?*   Theodore Sturgeon

BEST SF NOVELETTE

Gonna Roll the Bones   **Fritz Leiber** (Winner)
The Keys to December   Roger Zelazny
Pretty Maggie Moneyeyes   Harlan Ellison
Flatlander   Larry Niven
This Mortal Mountain   Roger Zelazny

BEST SF SHORT STORY

Aye, and Gomorrah   **Samuel R. Delany** (Winner)
Baby, You Were Great   Kate Wilhelm
Answering Service   Fritz Leiber
The Doctor   Theodore Thomas
Driftglass   Samuel R. Delany
Earthwoman   Reginald Bretnor

1968: Best SF Stories of the Year*

Budget Planet	Robert Sheckley
Appointment on Prila	Bob Shaw
Lost Ground	David I. Masson
The Annex	John D. MacDonald
Segregationist	Isaac Asimov
Final War	K. M. O'Donnell
Golden Acres	Kit Reed
Criminal in Utopia	Mack Reynolds
One Station of the Way	Fritz Leiber
Sweet Dreams, Melissa	Stephen Goldin
To The Dark Star	Robert Silverberg
Like Young	Theodore Sturgeon

1968: Best SF Short Stories of the Year†

Street of Dreams, Feet of Clay	Robert Sheckley
Backtracked	Burt Filer
Kyrie	Poul Anderson
Going Down Smooth	Robert Silverberg
The Worm That Flies	Brian Aldiss
Masks	Damon Knight
Time Considered as a Helix of Semi-Precious Stones	Samuel R. Delany
Hemeac	E. G. Von Wald
The Cloudbuilders	Colin Kapp
This Grand Carcass	R. A. Lafferty
A Visit to Cleveland General	Sydney J. Van Scyoc
The Selchey Kids	Laurence Yep
Welcome to the Monkey House	Kurt Vonnegut Jr
The Dance of the Changer and the Three	Terry Carr
Sword Game	H. H. Hollis
Total Environment	Brian Aldiss

*Harrison and Aldiss, *Best SF: 1968*
†Wollheim and Carr, *World's Best Science Fiction 1969*

The Square Root of Brain	Fritz Leiber
Starsong	Fred Saberhagen
Fear Hound	Katherine MacLean

1968: Hugo Awards and Nominations

BEST SF NOVEL

Stand on Zanzibar	**John Brunner** (Winner)
Goblin Reservation	Clifford D. Simak
Nova	Samuel R. Delany
Past Master	R. A. Lafferty
Rite of Passage	Alexei Panshin

BEST SF NOVELLA

Nightwings	**Robert Silverberg** (Winner)
Dragonrider	Anne McCaffrey
Hawk Among the Sparrows	Dean McLaughlin
Lines of Power	Samuel R. Delany

BEST SF SHORT STORY

The Beast that Shouted Love at the Heart of the World	**Harlan Ellison** (Winner)
All the Myriad Ways	Larry Niven
The Dance of the Changer and the Three	Terry Carr
Mask	Damon Knight
The Steiger Effect	Besty Curtis

BEST SF NOVELETTE

The Sharing of the Flesh	**Poul Anderson** (Winner)
Getting Through University	Piers Anthony
Mother to the World	Richard Wilson
Total Environment	Brian Aldiss

BEST SF NOVEL

Rite of Passage   **Alexei Panshin** (Winner)
Black Easter   James Blish
Do Androids Dream of Electric Sheep? Philip K. Dick
The Masks of Time   Robert Silverberg
Past Master   R. A. Lafferty
Stand on Zanzibar   John Brunner

BEST SF NOVELLA

Dragon Rider   **Anne McCaffrey** (Winner)
The Day Beyond Forever   Keith Laumer
Hawk Among the Sparrows   Dean McLaughlin
Lines of Power   Samuel R. Delany
Nightwings   Robert Silverberg

BEST SF NOVELETTE

Mother to the World   **Richard Wilson** (Winner)
Final War   K. M. O'Donnell
Once There Was a Giant   Keith Laumer
Total Environment   Brian Aldiss
The Guerilla Trees   H. H. Hollis
The Listeners   James E. Gunn
The Sharing of the Flesh   Poul Anderson

BEST SF SHORT STORY

The Planners   **Kate Wilhelm** (Winner)
*The Dance of the Changer and
  the Three*   Terry Carr
Idiot's Mate   Robert Taylor
Kyrie   Poul Anderson
Masks   Damon Knight
Sword Game   H. H. Hollis

1969: Best SF Short Stories of the Year*

The Muse	Anthony Burgess
Working in the Spaceship Yards	Brian Aldiss
The Schematic Man	Frederik Pohl
The Snows are Melted, the Snows are Gone	James Tiptree Jr
Eco-Catastrophe!	Paul Ehrlich
The Castle on the Crag	P. G. Wyal
Nine Lives	Ursula K. Le Guin
The Killing Ground	J. G. Ballard
The Dannold Cheque	Ken W. Purdy
Womb to Womb	Joseph Wesley
Like Father	Jon Hartridge
The Electric Ant	Philip K. Dick
The Man Inside	Bruce McAllister
Now Hear the Word of the Lord	Algis Budrys

1969: Best SF Short Stories of the Year†

A Man Spekith	Richard Wilson
After the Myths Went Home	Robert Silverberg
Death by Ecstasy	Larry Niven
One Sunday in Neptune	Alexei Panshin
For the Sake of Grace	Suzette Haden Elgin
Your Haploid Heart	James Tiptree Jr
Therapy 2000	Keith Roberts
Sixth Sense	Michael Coney
A Boy and his Dog	Harlan Ellison
And So Say All of Us	Bruce McAllister
Ship of Shadows	Fritz Leiber
Nine Lives	Ursula K. Le Guin
The Big Flash	Norman Spinrad

*Harrison and Aldiss, Best SF: 1969
†Wollheim and Carr, World's Best Science Fiction 1970

1969: Hugo Awards and Nominations

BEST SF NOVEL

The Left Hand of Darkness
Bug Jack Barron
Macroscope
Slaughterhouse-Five
Up the Line

Ursula K. Le Guin (Winner)
Norman Spinrad
Piers Anthony
Kurt Vonnegut Jr
Robert Silverberg

BEST SF NOVELLA

Ship of Shadows
A Boy and his Dog
Dramatic Mission
To Jorslem
We All Die Naked

Fritz Leiber (Winner)
Harlan Ellison
Anne McCaffrey
Robert Silverberg
James Blish

BEST SF SHORT STORY

Time Considered as a Helix of Semi-Precious Stones
Deeper Than Darkness
Not Long Before the End
Passengers
Winter's King

Samuel R. Delany (Winner)
Gregory Benford
Larry Niven
Robert Silverberg
Ursula K. Le Guin

1969: Nebula Awards and Nominations

BEST SF NOVEL

The Left Hand of Darkness
Bug Jack Barron
Isle of the Dead
The Jagged Orbit
Up the Line
Slaughterhouse-Five

Ursula K. Le Guin (Winner)
Norman Spinrad
Roger Zelazny
John Brunner
Robert Silverberg
Kurt Vonnegut Jr

BEST SF NOVELLA

A Boy and His Dog

Harlan Ellison (Winner)

To Jorslem	Robert Silverberg
Dramatic Mission	Anne McCaffrey
Ship of Shadows	Fritz Leiber
Probable Cause	Charles L. Harness

BEST SF NOVELETTE

Time Considered as a Helix of Semi-Precious Stones	**Samuel R. Delany** (Winner)
Deeper Than The Darkness	Gregory Benford
Nine Lives	Ursula K. Le Guin
The Big Flash	Norman Spinrad

BEST SF SHORT STORY

Passengers	**Robert Silverberg** (Winner)
Not Before the End	Larry Niven
The Man Who Learned Loving	Theodore Sturgeon
The Last Flight of Dr Ain	James Tiptree Jr
Shattered Like a Glass Goblin	Harlan Ellison

*1970: Best SF Short Stories of the Year**

Gone Fishin'	Robin Scott Wilson
The Ugupu Bird	Slawomir Mrozek
Black is Beautiful	Robert Silverberg
The Lost Face	Josef Nesvadba
Gorman	Jerry Farber
Mary and Joe	Naomi Mitchison
Oil-Mad Bug-Eyed Monsters	Hayden Howard
A Pedestrian Accident	Robert Coover
The Asian Shore	Thomas M. Disch
Traffic Problems	William Earls
Erem	Gleb Anfilov
Car Sinister	Gene Wolfe
'Franz Kafka' by Jorge Luis Borges	Alvin Greenberg
Pacem Est	Kris Neville and K. M. O'Donnell

*Harrison and Aldiss, *Best SF: 1970*

133

1970: Best SF Short Stories of the Year*

Slow Sculpture	Theodore Sturgeon
Bird in the Hand	Larry Niven
Ishmael in Love	Robert Silverberg
Invasion of Privacy	Bob Shaw
Waterclap	Isaac Asimov
Continued on Next Rock	R. A. Lafferty
The Thing in the Stone	Clifford D. Simak
Nobody Lives on Burton Street	Gregory Benford
Whatever Became of the McGowans?	Michael Coney
The Last Time Around	Arthur Sellings
Greyspun's Gift	Neal Barrett Jr
The Shaker Revival	Gerald Jonas
Dear Aunt Annie	Gordon Eklund
Confessions	Ron Goulart
Gone Are the Lupo	H. B. Hickey

1970: Hugo Awards and Nominations

BEST SF NOVEL

Ringworld	**Larry Niven** (Winner)
Tau Zero	Poul Anderson
Tower of Glass	Robert Silverberg
Star Light	Hal Clement
The Year of the Quiet Sun	Wilson Tucker

BEST SF NOVELLA

Ill Met in Lankhmar	**Fritz Leiber** (Winner)
Beast Child	Dean R. Koontz
The Region Between	Harlan Ellison
The Thing in the Stone	Clifford D. Simak
The World Outside	Robert Silverberg

*Wollheim and Carr, *World's Best Science Fiction 1971*

Best SF Short Story

Slow Sculpture	**Theodore Sturgeon** (Winner)
Continued on Next Rock	R. A. Lafferty
Jean Dupres	Gordon R. Dickson
Brillo	Ben Bova and Harlan Ellison
In the Queue	Keith Laumer

1970: Nebula Awards and Nominations

Best SF Novel

Ringworld	**Larry Niven** (Winner)
And Chaos Dies	Joanna Russ
Tower of Glass	Robert Silverberg
The Year of the Quiet Sun	Wilson Tucker
Fourth Mansions	R. A. Lafferty
The Steel Crocodile	D. G. Compton

Best SF Novella

Ill Met in Lankhmar	**Fritz Leiber** (Winner)
The Thing in the Stone	Clifford D. Simak
The Region Between	Harlan Ellison
April Fools' Day Forever	Kate Wilhelm
Fatal Fulfillment	Poul Anderson

Best SF Novelette

Slow Sculpture	**Theodore Sturgeon** (Winner)
Continued on Next Rock	R. A. Lafferty
The Asian Shore	Thomas M. Disch
The Shaker Revival	Gerald Jonas
The Second Inquisition	Joanna Russ
Dear Aunt Annie	Gordon Eklund

Best SF Short Story

No Award	
The Island of Doctor Death	Gene Wolfe
Entire and Perfect Chrysolite	R. A. Lafferty

A Dream at Noonday	Gardner Dozois
In the Queue	Keith Laumer
The Creation of Bennie Good	James Sallis
By the Falls	Harry Harrison
A Cold Dark Night with Snow	Kate Wilhelm

1971: Best SF Short Stories of the Year*

Occam's Scalpel	Theodore Sturgeon
The Queen of Air and Darkness	Poul Anderson
In Entropy's Jaws	Robert Silverberg
The Sliced-Crosswise Only-on- Tuesday World	Philip José Farmer
A Meeting with Medusa	Arthur C. Clarke
The Frayed String on the Stretched Forefinger of Time	Lloyd Biggle Jr
How Can We Sink When We Can Fly?	Alexei Panshin
No Direction Home	Norman Spinrad
Vaster Than Empires and More Slow	Ursula K. Le Guin
All The Last Wars at Once	George Alec Effinger
The Fourth Profession	Larry Niven

1971: Best SF Short Stories of the Year†

Doctor Zombie and His Little Furry Friends	Robert Sheckley
Conquest	Barry N. Malzberg
Gehenna	Barry N. Malzberg
A Meeting with Medusa	Arthur C. Clarke
The Genius	Donald Barthelme
Angoulême	Thomas M. Disch
Statistician's Day	James Blish
The Hunter at his Ease	Brian Aldiss

*Terry Carr, The Best Science Fiction of the Year
†Harrison and Aldiss, Best SF: 1971

The Cohen Dog Exclusion Act	Steven Schrader
Gauntlet	Richard E. Peck
The Pagan Rabbi	Cynthia Ozick
An Uneven Evening	Steve Herbst
Ornithan thropus	B. Alan Burhoe
No Direction Home	Norman Spinrad

1971: Best SF Short Stories of the Year*

The Fourth Profession	Larry Niven
Gleepsite	Joanna Russ
The Bear With the Knot On His Tail	Stephen Tall
The Sharks of Pentreath	Michael Coney
A Little Knowledge	Poul Anderson
Real Time World	Christopher Priest
All Pieces of a River Shore	R. A. Lafferty
With Friends Like These	Alan Dean Foster
Aunt Jennie's Tonic	Leonard Tushnet
Timestorm	Eddy C. Bertin
Transit of Earth	Arthur C. Clarke
Gehenna	Barry N. Malzberg
One Life, Furnished in Early Poverty	Harlan Ellison
Occam's Scalpel	Theodore Sturgeon

1971: Hugo Awards and Nominations

BEST SF NOVEL

To Your Scattered Bodies Go	**Philip José Farmer** (Winner)
Dragonquest	Anne McCaffrey
Jack of Shadows	Roger Zelazny
The Lathe of Heaven	Ursula K. Le Guin
A Time of Changes	Robert Silverberg

*Donald Wollheim, *The 1972 Annual World's Best SF*

BEST SF NOVELLA

The Queen of Air and Darkness   **Poul Anderson** (Winner)
Dread Empire   John Brunner
The Fourth Profession   Larry Niven
A Meeting with Medusa   Arthur C. Clarke
A Special Kind of Morning   Gardner Dozois

BEST SF SHORT STORY

Inconstant Moon   **Larry Niven** (Winner)
All the Last Wars at Once   George Alec Effinger
The Autumn Land   Clifford D. Simak
The Bear with the Knot on his Tail   Stephen Tall
Sky   R. A. Lafferty
Vaster Than Empires and More Slow   Ursula K. Le Guin

1971: Nebula Awards and Nominations

BEST SF NOVEL

A Time of Changes   **Robert Silverberg** (Winner)
The Byworlder   Poul Anderson
Half Past Human   T. J. Bass
The Lathe of Heaven   Ursula K. Le Guin
Margaret and I   Kate Wilhelm

BEST SF NOVELLA

The Missing Man   **Katherine McLean** (Winner)
Being There   Jerzy Kozinski
The God House   Keith Roberts
The Infinity Box   Kate Wilhelm
The Plastic Abyss   Kate Wilhelm

BEST SF NOVELETTE

Queen of Air and Darkness   **Poul Anderson** (Winner)
A Special Kind of Morning   Gardner Dozois
Mount Charity   Edgar Pangborn

138

Poor Man, Beggar Man	Joanna Russ
The Encounter	Kate Wilhelm

Best SF Short Story

Good News from the Vatican	**Robert Silverberg** (Winner)
Horse of Air	Gardner Dozois
The Last Ghost	Stephen Goldin
Heathen God	George Zebrowski

1972: Best SF Short Stories of the Year*

The Meeting	Frederik Pohl and C.M. Kornbluth
Nobody's Home	Joanna Russ
Fortune Hunter	Poul Anderson
The Fifth Head of Cerberus	Gene Wolfe
Caliban	Robert Silverberg
Conversational Mode	Grahame Leman
Their Thousandth Season	Edward Bryant
Eurema's Dam	R. A. Lafferty
Zero Gee	Ben Bova
Sky Blue	Alexei and Cory Panshin
Miss Omega Raven	Naomi Mitchison
Patron of the Arts	William Rotsler
Grasshopper Time	Gordon Eklund
Hero	Joe Haldeman
When We Went to See the End of the World	Robert Silverberg
Painwise	James Tiptree Jr

1972: Best SF Short Stories of the Year†

In the Matter of the Assassin Merefirs	Ken W. Purdy
As For Our Fatal Continuity . . .	Brian Aldiss

*Terry Carr, *The Best Science Fiction of the Year 2*
†Harrison and Aldiss, *Best SF: 1972*

The Old Folks	James E. Gunn
From Sea to Shining Sea	Jonathan Ela
Weinachtabend	Keith Roberts
The Years	Robert F. Young
Darkness	André Carneiro
Words of Warning	Alex Hamilton
Out, Wit!	Howard L. Myers
An Imaginary Journey to the Moon	Victor Sabah
The Head and the Hand	Christopher Priest
Hero	Joe Haldeman

1972: Best SF Short Stories of the Year*

Goat Song	Poul Anderson
The Man Who Walked Home	James Tiptree Jr
Oh, Valinda!	Michael Coney
The Gold at the Starbow's End	Frederik Pohl
To Walk a City's Street	Clifford D. Simak
Rorqual Maru	T. J. Bass
Changing Woman	W. MacFarlane
Willie's Blues	Robert J. Tilley
Long Shot	Vernor Vinge
Thus Love Betrays Us	Phyllis MacLennon

1972: Hugo Awards and Nominations

BEST SF NOVEL

The Gods Themselves	**Isaac Asimov** (Winner)
The Book of Skulls	Robert Silverberg
A Choice of Gods	Clifford D. Simak
Dying Inside	Robert Silverberg
There Will Be Time	Poul Anderson
When Harlie Was One	David Gerrold

*Donald Wollheim, *The 1973 Annual World's Best SF*

BEST SF NOVELLA

The Word for World is Forest	**Ursula K. Le Guin** (Winner)
The Fifth Head of Cerberus	Gene Wolfe
The Gold at Starbow's End	Frederik Pohl
Hero	Joe Haldeman
The Mercenary	Jerry Pournelle

BEST SF NOVELETTE

Goat Song	**Poul Anderson** (Winner)
Basilisk	Harlan Ellison
A Kingdom by the Sea	Gardner Dozois
Painwise	James Tiptree Jr
Patron of the Arts	William Rotsler

BEST SF SHORT STORY

Eurema's Dam	**R. A. Lafferty** (Joint Winner)
The Meeting	**Frederik Pohl** and
And I Awoke And Found Me Here	**C. M. Kornbluth** (Joint Winner)
on the Cold Hill's Side	James Tiptree Jr
When it Changed	Joanna Russ
When We Went to See the End of	
the World	Robert Silverberg

1972: Nebula Awards and Nominations

BEST SF NOVEL

The Gods Themselves	**Isaac Asimov** (Winner)
The Sheep Look Up	John Brunner
What Entropy Means to Me	George Alec Effinger
When Harlie Was One	David Gerrold
The Book of Skulls	Robert Silverberg
Dying Inside	Robert Silverberg
The Iron Dream	Norman Spinrad

BEST SF NOVELLA

A Meeting with Medusa
Son of the Morning
The Word for World is Forest
With the Bentfin Boomer Boys on
  Little Old New Alabama
The Gold at Starbow's End
The Fifth Head of Cerberus

Arthur C. Clarke (Winner)
Phyllis Gottlieb
Ursula K. Le Guin

Richard A. Lupoff
Frederik Pohl
Gene Wolfe

BEST SF NOVELETTE

Goat Song
The Animal Fair
A Kingdom by the Sea
Basilisk
In the Deadlands
Patron of the Arts
The Funeral

Pohl Anderson (Winner)
Alfred Bester
Gardner Dozois
Harlan Ellison
David Gerrold
William Rotsler
Kate Wilhelm

BEST SF SHORT STORY

When It Changed
On the Downhill Side
Shaffery Among the Immortals
And I Awoke and Found Me Here on
  the Cold Hill's Side
Against the Lafayette Escadrille

Joanna Russ (Winner)
Harlan Ellison
Frederik Pohl

James Tiptree Jr
Gene Wolfe

1973: Best SF Short Stories of the Year*

Something Up There Likes Me
The World As Will and Wallpaper
Breckenridge and the Continuum
Rumfuddle
Tell Me All About Yourself
The Deathbird

Alfred Bester
R. A. Lafferty
Robert Silverberg
Jack Vance
F. M. Busby
Harlan Ellison

*Terry Carr, *The Best Science Fiction of the Year 3*

142

Of Mist, and Grass, and Sand	Vonda N. McIntyre
The Death of Dr Island	Gene Wolfe
The Ones Who Walk Away from Omelas	Ursula K. Le Guin
Sketches Among the Ruins of my Mind	Philip José Farmer
The Women Men Don't See	James Tiptree Jr

1973: Best SF Short Stories of the Year*

Roller Ball Murder	William Harrison
Mason's Life	Kingsley Amis
Welcome to the Standard Nightmare	Robert Sheckley
Serpent Burning on an Altar	Brian Aldiss
We Are Very Happy Here	Joe Haldeman
The Birds	Thomas M. Disch
The Wind and the Rain	Robert Silverberg
Ten Years Ago	Max Beerbohm
Parthen	R. A. Lafferty
The Man Who Collected the First of September 1973	Tor Age Bringsvaerd
Captain Nemo's Last Adventure	Josef Nesvadba
La Befana	Gene Wolfe
The Window in Dante's Hell	Michael Bishop
Sister Francetta and the Pig Baby	Kenneth Bernard
Escape	Ilya Varshafsky
Early Bird	Theodore Cogswell and Theodore Thomas

1973: Best SF Short Stories of the Year†

A Suppliant in Space	Robert Sheckley
Parthen	R. A. Lafferty
Doomship	Frederik Pohl and Jack Williamson
Weed of Time	Norman Spinrad

*Harrison and Aldiss, *Best SF: 1973*
†Donald Wollheim, *The 1974 Annual World's Best SF*

A Modest Genius	Vadim Shefner
The Deathbird	Harlan Ellison
Evane	E. C. Tubb
Moby, Too	Gordon Eklund
Death and Designation Among the Asadi	Michael Bishop
Construction Shack	Clifford D. Simak

1973: Hugo Awards and Nominations

BEST SF NOVEL

Rendezvous with Rama	**Arthur C. Clarke** (Winner)
The People of the Wind	Poul Anderson
The Man Who Folded Himself	David Gerrold
Time Enough for Love	Robert A. Heinlein
Protector	Larry Niven

BEST SF NOVELLA

The Girl Who Was Plugged In	**James Tiptree Jr** (Winner)
Death and Designation Among the Asadi	Michael Bishop
The White Otters of Childhood	Michael Bishop
Chains of the Sea	Gardner Dozois
The Death of Doctor Island	Gene Wolfe

BEST SF NOVELETTE

The Deathbird	**Harland Ellison** (Winner)
City on the Sand	George Alec Effinger
Of Mist, And Grass, And Sand	Vonda N. McIntyre
He Fell Into a Dark Hole	Jerry Pournelle
Love Is The Plan, The Plan Is Death	James Tiptree Jr

BEST SF SHORT STORY

The Ones Who Walk Away from Omelas	**Ursula K. Le Guin** (Winner)
Wings	Vonda N. McIntyre
With Morning Comes Mistfall	George R. R. Martin
Construction Shack	Clifford D. Simak

1973: Nebula Awards and Nominations

BEST SF NOVEL

Rendezvous With Rama   **Arthur C. Clarke** (Winner)
Time Enough for Love   Robert A. Heinlein
Gravity's Rainbow   Thomas Pynchon
The People of the Wind   Poul Anderson
The Man Who Folded Himself   David Gerrold

BEST SF NOVELLA

The Death of Doctor Island   **Gene Wolfe** (Winner)
The White Otters of Childhood   Michael Bishop
Junction   Jack Dann
*Death and Designation Among
    the Asadi*   Michael Bishop
Chains of the Sea   Gardner Dozois

BEST SF NOVELETTE

**Of Mist, and Grass, and
    Sand**   **Vonda N. McIntyre** (Winner)
Case and the Dreamer   Theodore Sturgeon
The Deathbird   Harlan Ellison
The Girl Who Was Plugged In   James Tiptree Jr

BEST SF SHORT STORY

**Love Is The Plan, the Plan
    Is Death**   **James Tiptree Jr** (Winner)
A Thing of Beauty   Norman Spinrad
Wings   Vonda N. McIntyre
With Morning Comes Mistfall   George R. R. Martin
Shark   Edward Bryant
*How I Lost the Second World War
    and Helped Turn Back the
    German Invasion*   Gene Wolfe

1974: Best SF Short Stories of the Year*

We Purchased People	Frederik Pohl
Pale Roses	Michael Moorcock
The Hole Man	Larry Niven
Born with the Dead	Robert Silverberg
The Author of the Acacia Seeds and Other Extracts from the Journal of the Association of Therolinguistics	Ursula K. Le Guin
Dark Icarus	Bob Shaw
A Little Something for us Tempunauts	Philip K. Dick
On Venus, Have We Got a Rabbi	William Tenn
The Engine at Heartspring's Center	Roger Zelazny
If the Stars are Gods	Gordon Eklund and Gregory Benford

1974: Best SF Short Stories of the Year†

After King Kong Fell	Philip José Farmer
When Petals Fall	Sydney J. Van Scyoc
Paleontology: An Experimental Science	Robert R. Olsen
The Women Men Don't See	James Tiptree Jr
Listen with Big Brother	Brian Aldiss
The Rise of Airstrip One	Clive James
Owing to Circumstances Beyond Our Control 1984 Has Been Unavoidably Detained	Alan Coren
Lost and Found	Thomas Baum
The Four-Hour Fugue	Alfred Bester
The Scream	Kate Wilhelm
The Executioner's Beautiful Daughter	Angela Carter
Songs of War	Kit Reed
Time Deer	Craig Strete
A Typical Day	Doris Piserchia
Programmed Love Story	Ian Watson

*Terry Carr, The Best Science Fiction of the Year 4
†Harrison and Aldiss, Best SF: 1974

1974: Best SF Short Stories of the Year*

A Song for Lya	George R. R. Martin
Deathsong	Sydney J. Van Scyoc
A Full Member of the Club	Bob Shaw
The Sun's Tears	Brian Stableford
The Gift of Garigolli	Frederik Pohl and C. M. Kornbluth
The Four-Hour Fugue	Alfred Bester
Twig	Gordon R. Dickson
Cathadonian Odyssey	Michael Bishop
The Bleeding Man	Craig Strete
Stranger in Paradise	Isaac Asimov

1974: Hugo Awards and Nominations

BEST SF NOVEL

The Dispossessed	**Ursula K. Le Guin** (Winner)
Fire Time	Poul Anderson
Flow My Tears, The Policeman Said	Philip K. Dick
The Inverted World	Christopher Priest
The Mote in God's Eye	Larry Niven and Jerry Pournelle

BEST SF NOVELLA

A Song for Lya	**George R. R. Martin** (Winner)
Assault on a City	Jack Vance
Born with the Dead	Robert Silverberg
Riding the Torch	Norman Spinrad
Strangers	Gardner Dozois

BEST SF NOVELETTE

Adrift just off the Islets of Langerhans Latitude 38°54'N, Longitude 77°00'13"W	**Harlan Ellison** (Winner)

*Donald Wollheim, *The 1975 Annual World's Best SF*

After the Dreamtime	Richard A. Lupoff
A Brother to Dragons, A Companion of Owls	Kate Wilhelm
Extreme Prejudice	Jerry Pournelle
Midnight by the Morphy Watch	Fritz Leiber
Nix Olympica	William Walling
That Thou Art Mindful of Him	Isaac Asimov

BEST SF SHORT STORY

The Hole Man	**Larry Niven** (Winner)
A Cathadonian Odyssey	Michael Bishop
The Day Before the Revolution	Ursula K. Le Guin
The Four-Hour Fugue	Alfred Bester
Schwartz Between the Galaxies	Robert Silverberg

1974: Nebula Awards and Nominations

BEST SF NOVEL

The Dispossessed	**Ursula K. Le Guin** (Winner)
Flow My Tears, The Policeman Said	Philip K. Dick
334	Thomas M. Disch
The Godwhale	T. J. Bass

BEST SF NOVELLA

Born with the Dead	**Robert Silverberg** (Winner)
A Song for Lya	George R. R. Martin
On the Street of the Serpents	Michael Bishop

BEST SF NOVELETTE

If the Stars are Gods	**Gordon Eklund** and **Gregory Benford** (Winners)
The Rest is Silence	Charles L. Grant
Twilla	Tom Reamy

BEST SF SHORT STORY

The Day Before the Revolution   **Ursula K. Le Guin** (Winner)
The Engine at Heartspring's Center   Roger Zelazny
After King Kong Fell   Philip José Farmer

1975: Best SF Short Stories of the Year*

Down to a Sunless Sea   Cordwainer Smith
Retrograde Summer   John Varley
The Hero as Werewolf   Gene Wolfe
The Silent Eyes of Time   Algis Budrys
Croatoan   Harlan Ellison
Doing Lennon   Gregory Benford
The New Atlantis   Ursula K. Le Guin
Clay Suburb   Robert F. Young
The Storms of Windhaven   Lisa Tuttle and George R. R. Martin
Child of all Ages   P. J. Plauger
In the Bowl   John Varley
Sail the Tide of Mourning   Richard A. Lupoff

1975: Best SF Short Stories of the Year†

A Scraping at the Bones   Algis Budrys
Changelings   Lisa Tuttle
The Santa Claus Compromise   Thomas M. Disch
A Galaxy Called Rome   Barry N. Malzberg
The Custodians   Richard Cowper
The Linguist   Stephen Robinett
Settling the World   M. John Harrison
The Chaste Planet   John Updike
End Game   Joe Haldeman
A Dead Singer   Michael Moorcock

*Terry Carr, *The Best Science Fiction of the Year 5*
†Harrison and Aldiss, *Best SF: 1975*

1975: Best SF Short Stories of the Year*

Catch That Zeppelin!   Fritz Leiber
The Peddler's Apprentice   Vernor Vinge
The Bees of Knowledge   Barrington J. Bayley
The Storms of Windhaven   Lisa Tuttle and
                                          George R. R. Martin
The Engineer and the Executioner   Brian Stableford
Allegiances   Michael Bishop
Child of all Ages   P. J. Plauger
Helbent 4   Stephen Robinett
The Protocols of the Elders of
  Britain   John Brunner
The Custodians   Richard Cowper

1975: Hugo Awards and Nominations

BEST SF NOVEL

The Forever War   **Joe Haldeman** (Winner)
The Computer Connection   Alfred Bester
Inferno   Larry Niven and Jerry Pournelle
The Stochastic Man   Robert Silverberg
Doorways in the Sand   Roger Zelazny

BEST SF NOVELLA

Home Is the Hangman   **Roger Zelazny** (Winner)
The Silent Eyes of Time   Algis Budrys
The Custodians   Richard Cowper
The Storms of Windhaven   Lisa Tuttle and George R. R. Martin
ARM   Larry Niven

BEST SF NOVELETTE

The Borderland of Sol   **Larry Niven** (Winner)
The New Atlantis   Ursula K. Le Guin

---

*Donald Wollheim, *The 1976 Annual World's Best SF*

. . . And 7 Times Never Kill a Man	George R. R. Martin
Tinker	Jerry Pournelle
San Diego, Lightfoot Sue	Tom Reamy

BEST SF SHORT STORY

Catch That Zeppelin!	**Fritz Leiber** (Winner)
Doing Lennon	Gregory Benford
Rogue Tomato	Michael Bishop
Croatoan	Harlan Ellison
Sail the Tide of Mourning	Richard A. Lupoff
Child of all Ages	P. J. Plauger

1975: Nebula Awards and Nominations

BEST SF NOVEL

The Forever War	**Joe Haldeman** (Winner)
The Mote in God's Eye	Larry Niven and Jerry Pournelle
Dhalgren	Samuel R. Delany

BEST SF NOVELLA

Home Is the Hangman	**Roger Zelazny** (Winner)
The Storms of Windhaven	Lisa Tuttle and George R. R. Martin
A Momentary Taste of Being	James Tiptree Jr

BEST SF NOVELETTE

San Diego, Lightfoot Sue	**Tom Reamy** (Winner)
A Galaxy Called Rome	Barry N. Malzberg
The Final Fighting of	
Fion MacCumhail	Randall Garrett

BEST SF SHORT STORY

Catch That Zeppelin!	**Fritz Leiber** (Winner)
Child of all Ages	P. J. Plauger
Shatterday	Harlan Ellison

1976: Best SF Short Stories of the Year*

I See You	Damon Knight
The Phantom of Kansas	John Varley
Seeing	Harlan Ellison
The Death of Princes	Fritz Leiber
The Psychologist Who Wouldn't Do Awful Things to Rats	James Tiptree Jr
The Eyeflash Miracles	Gene Wolfe
An Infinite Summer	Christopher Priest
The Highest Dive	Jack Williamson
Meathouse Man	George R. R. Martin
Custer's Last Jump	Steven Utley and Howard Waldrop
The Bicentennial Man	Isaac Asimov

1976: Best SF Short Stories of the Year†

Appearance of Life	Brian Aldiss
Overdrawn at the Memory Bank	John Varley
Those Good Old Days of Liquid Fuel	Michael Coney
The Hertford Manuscript	Richard Cowper
Natural Advantage	Lester Del Rey
The Bicentennial Man	Isaac Asimov
The Cabinet of Oliver Naylor	Barrington J. Bayley
My Boat	Joanna Russ
Houston, Houston, Do You Read?	James Tiptree Jr
I See You	Damon Knight

1976: Hugo Awards and Nominations

BEST SF NOVEL

Where Late the Sweet Birds Sang   **Kate Wilhelm** (Winner)

*Terry Carr, *The Best Science Fiction of the Year* 6
†Donald Wollheim, *The 1977 Annual World's Best SF*

Children of Dune	Frank Herbert
Man Plus	Frederik Pohl
Mindbridge	Joe Haldeman
Shadrach in the Furnace	Robert Silverberg

BEST SF NOVELLA

By Any Other Name	**Spider Robinson** (Joint Winner)
Houston, Houston, Do You Read?	**James Tiptree Jr** (Joint Winner)
Piper at the Gates of Dawn	Richard Cowper
The Samurai and the Willow	Michael Bishop

BEST SF NOVELETTE

The Bicentennial Man	Isaac Asimov (Winner)
The Diary of the Rose	Ursula K. Le Guin
Gotta Sing, Gotta Dance	John Varley
The Phantom of Kansas	John Varley

BEST SF SHORT STORY

Tricentennial	**Joe Haldeman** (Winner)
A Crowd of Shadows	Charles L. Grant
Custom Fitting	James White
I See You	Damon King

1976: Nebula Awards and Nominations

BEST SF NOVEL

Man Plus	Frederik Pohl (Winner)
Where Late the Sweet Birds Sang	Kate Wilhelm
Inferno	Larry Niven and Jerry Pournelle
Shadrach in the Furnace	Robert Silverberg
Triton	Samuel R. Delany
Islands	Marta Randall

BEST SF NOVELLA

Houston, Houston, Do You Read?   **James Tiptree** (Winner)
The Samurai and the Willow   Michael Bishop
The Eyeflash Miracles   Gene Wolfe
Piper at the Gates of Dawn   Richard Cowper

BEST SF NOVELETTE

The Bicentennial Man   **Isaac Asimov** (Winner)
Custer's Last Jump   Steven Utley and
      Howard Waldrop
In the Bowl   John Varley
His Hour Upon the Stage   Grant Carrington
The Diary of the Rose   Ursula K. Le Guin

BEST SF SHORT STORY

A Crowd of Shadows   **Charles L. Grant** (Winner)
Breath's A Ware That Will Not Keep   Thomas Monteleone
Back to the Stone Age   Jake Saunders
Stone Circle   Lisa Tuttle
Mary-Margaret Road-Grader   Howard Waldrop
Tricentennial   Isaac Asimov

1977: Best SF Short Stories of the Year*

Lollipop and the Tar Baby   John Varley
Stardance   Spider and Jeanne Robinson
The House of Compassionate Sharers   Michael Bishop
The Screwfly Solution   Raccoona Sheldon
Aztecs   Vonda N. McIntyre
Tropic of Eden   Lee Killough
Victor   Bruce McAllister
The Family Monkey   Lisa Tuttle
A Rite of Spring   Fritz Leiber

*Terry Carr, *The Best Science Fiction of the Year* 7

1977: Best SF Short Stories of the Year*

In The Hall of the Martian Kings	John Varley
A Time to Live	Joe Haldeman
The House of Compassionate Sharers	Michael Bishop
Particle Theory	Edward Bryant
The Taste of the Dish and the Savor of the Day	John Brunner
Jeffty is Five	Harlan Ellison
The Screwfly Solution	Raccoona Sheldon
Eyes of Amber	Joan D. Vinge
Child of the Sun	James E. Gunn
Brother	Clifford D. Simak

1977. Hugo Awards and Nominations

BEST SF NOVEL

Gateway	**Frederik Pohl** (Winner)
The Forbidden Tower	Marion Zimmer Bradley
Lucifer's Hammer	Larry Niven and Jerry Pournelle
Time Storm	Gordon R. Dickson
Dying of the Light	George R. R. Martin

BEST SF NOVELLA

Stardance	**Spider and Jeanne Robinson** (Winner)
In the Hall of the Martian Kings	John Varley
Aztecs	Vonda N. McIntyre
A Snark in the Night	Gregory Benford
The Wonderful Secret	Keith Laumer

BEST SF NOVELETTE

Eyes of Amber	**Joan D. Vinge** (Winner)
Ender's Game	Orson Scott Card

*Donald Wollheim, *The 1978 Annual World's Best SF*

The Screwfly Solution	Raccoona Sheldon
Prismatica	Samuel R. Delany
The Ninth Symphony of Ludwig	
Van Beethoven and Other Lost Songs	Carter Scholz

BEST SF SHORT STORY

Jeffty is Five	**Harlan Ellison** (Winner)
Air Raid	John Varley
Dog Day Evening	Spider Robinson
Lauralyn	Randall Garrett
Time-Sharing Angel	James Tiptree Jr

1977: Nebula Awards and Nominations

BEST SF NOVEL

Gateway	**Frederik Pohl** (Winner)
In the Ocean of Night	Gregory Benford
Cirque	Terry Carr
Moonstar Odyssey	David Gerrold
Sword of the Demon	Richard A. Lupoff

BEST SF NOVELLA

Stardance	**Spider and Jeanne Robinson** (Winner)
Aztecs	Vonda N. McIntyre

BEST SF NOVELETTE

The Screwfly Solution	**Raccoona Sheldon** (Winner)
A Rite of Spring	Fritz Leiber
Particle Theory	Edward Bryant
The Stone City	George R. R. Martin
The Ninth Symphony of Ludwig	
Van Beethoven and Other Lost Songs	Carter Scholz

Best SF Short Story

Jeffty Is Five   **Harlan Ellison** (Winner)
Air Raid   John Varley
The Hibakusha Gallery   Edward Bryant
Tin Woodman   Dennis Bailey, David Bailey and
                                         Dave Bischoff
Camera Obscura   Thomas Monteleone

1978: Best SF Short Stories of the Year*

The Barbie Murders   John Varley
A Hiss of Dragon   Gregory Benford and
                                         Marc Laidlaw

Black Glass   Fritz Leiber
To Bring in the Steel   Donald Kingsbury
The Very Slow Time Machine   Ian Watson
Devil You Don't Know   Dean Ing
Count the Clock That Tells the Time Harlan Ellison
View From a Height   Joan D. Vinge
The Morphology of the Kirkham Wreck Hilbert Schenck
Vermeer's Window   Gordon Eklund
The Man Who Had No Idea   Thomas M. Disch
Death Therapy   James Patrick Kelly
The Persistence of Vision   John Varley
Old Folks at Home   Michael Bishop
Shipwright   Donald Kingsbury
Seven American Nights   Gene Wolfe
Fireship   Joan D. Vinge
The Watched   Christopher Priest

*Terry Carr, *The Best Science Fiction of the Year* 8 and *The Best Science Fiction Novellas of the Year* 1

1978: Best Short Stories of the Year*

Come to the Party	Frank Herbert and F. M. Busby
Creator	David Lake
Dance Band on the Titanic	Jack L. Chalker
Cassandra	C. J. Cherryh
In Alien Flesh	Gregory Benford
SQ	Ursula K. Le Guin
The Persistence of Vision	John Varley
We Who Stole the Dream	James Tiptree Jr
Scattershot	Greg Bear
Carruthers' Last Stand	Dan Henderson

1978: Hugo Awards and Nominations

BEST SF NOVEL

Dreamsnake	**Vonda N. McIntyre** (Winner)
The Faded Sun: Kesrith	C. J. Cherryh
The White Dragon	Anne McCaffrey
Blind Voices	Tom Reamy
Up the Walls of the World	James Tiptree Jr

BEST SF NOVELLA

The Persistence of Vision	**John Varley** (Winner)
Enemies of the System	Brian Aldiss
The Watched	Christopher Priest
Fireship	Joan D. Vinge
Seven American Nights	Gene Wolfe

BEST SF NOVELETTE

Hunter's Moon	**Poul Anderson** (Winner)
Mikal's Songbird	Orson Scott Card
The Man Who Had No Idea	Thomas M. Disch
Devil You Don't Know	Dean Ing
The Barbie Murders	John Varley

*Donald Wollheim, *The 1979 Annual World's Best SF*

BEST SF SHORT STORY

Cassandra	**C. J. Cherryh** (Winner)
Stone	Edward Bryant
Count the Clock That Tells the Time	Harlan Ellison
View From a Height	Joan D. Vinge
The Very Slow Time Machine	Ian Watson

1978: Nebula Awards and Nominations

BEST SF NOVEL

Dreamsnake	**Vonda N. McIntyre** (Winner)
The Faded Sun: Kesrith	C. J. Cherryh
Blind Voices	Tom Reamy
Strangers	Gardner Dozois
Kalki	Gore Vidal

BEST SF NOVELLA

The Persistence of Vision	**John Varley** (Winner)
Seven American Nights	Gene Wolfe

BEST SF NOVELETTE

A Glow of Candles, a Unicorn's Eye	**Charles L. Grant** (Winner)
Mikal's Songbird	Orson Scott Card
Devil You Don't Know	Dean Ing

BEST SF SHORT STORY

Stone	**Edward Bryant** (Winner)
Cassandra	C. J. Cherryh
A Quiet Revolution from Death	Jack Dann

1979: Best SF Short Stories of the Year*

Galatea Galante, the Perfect Popsy	Alfred Bester
Sandkings	George R. R. Martin
Time Shards	Gregory Benford
In the Country of the Blind, No One Can See	Melissa Michaels
Re-deem the Time	David Lake
Down and Out in Ellfive Prime	Dean Ing
The Exit Door Leads In	Philip K. Dick
Options	John Varley
In Trephonius's Cave	James P. Girard
Fireflood	Vonda N. McIntyre
No More Pencils, No More Books	John Morressy
The Vacuum-packed Picnic	Rick Gauger
The Thaw	Tanith Lee
In a Petri Dish Upstairs	George Turner
Enemy Mine	Barry B. Longyear
The Moon Goddess and the Son	Donald Kingsbury
Palely Loitering	Christopher Priest
Songhouse	Orson Scott Card
Ker-Plop	Ted Reynolds

1979: Best SF Short Stories of the Year†

The Way of Cross and Dragon	George R. R. Martin
The Thirteenth Utopia	Somtow Sucharitkul
Options	John Varley
Unaccompanied Sonata	Orson Scott Card
The Story Writer	Richard Wilson
Daisy, in the Sun	Connie Willis
The Locusts	Larry Niven and Steve Barnes
The Thaw	Tanith Lee
Out There Where the Big Ships Go	Richard Cowper

*Terry Carr, *The Best Science Fiction of the Year* 9 and *The Best Science Fiction Novellas of the Year* 2
†Donald Wollheim, *The 1980 Annual World's Best SF*

| Can These Bones Live? | Ted Reynolds |
| The Extraordinary Voyages of Amélie Bertrand | Joanna Russ |

1979: Hugo Awards and Nominations

BEST SF NOVEL

The Fountains of Paradise	**Arthur C. Clarke** (Winner)
Harpist in the Wind	Patricia McKillip
Jem	Frederik Pohl
On Wings of Song	Thomas M. Disch
Titan	John Varley

BEST SF NOVELLA

Enemy Mine	**Barry B. Longyear** (Winner)
The Battle of the Abaco Reefs	Hilbert Schenck
Ker-Plop	Ted Reynolds
The Moon Goddess and the Son	Donald Kingsbury
Songhouse	Orson Scott Card

BEST SF NOVELETTE

Sandkings	**George R. R. Martin** (Winner)
Fireflood	Vonda N. McIntyre
Homecoming	Barry B. Longyear
The Locusts	Larry Niven and Steven Barnes
Options	John Varley
Palely Loitering	Christopher Priest

BEST SF SHORT STORY

The Way of Cross and Dragon	**George R. R. Martin** (Winner)
Can These Bones Live?	Ted Reynolds
Daisy, in the Sun	Connie Willis
giANTS	Edward Bryant
Unaccompanied Sonata	Orson Scott Card

BEST SF NOVEL

The Fountains of Paradise	**Arthur C. Clarke** (Winner)
On Wings of Song	Thomas M. Disch
Titan	John Varley
Jem	Frederik Pohl
The Road to Corlay	Richard Cowper
Juniper Time	Kate Wilhelm

BEST SF NOVELLA

Enemy Mine	**Barry B. Longyear** (Winner)
Fireship	Joan D. Vinge
The Tale of Gorgik	Samuel R. Delany
The Battle of the Abaco Reefs	Hilbert Schenck
Mars Masked	Frederik Pohl
The Story Writer	Richard Wilson

BEST SF NOVELETTE

Sandkings	**George R. R. Martin** (Winner)
Options	John Varley
The Ways of Love	Poul Anderson
Camps	Jack Dann
The Pathways of Desire	Ursula K. Le Guin
The Angel of Death	Michael Shea

BEST SF SHORT STORY

giANTS	**Edward Bryant** (Winner)
Unaccompanied Sonata	Orson Scott Card
The Way of Cross and Dragon	George R. R. Martin
The Extraordinary Voyages of	
Amélie Bertrand	Joanna Russ
Red as Blood	Tanith Lee
Vernalfest Morning	Michael Bishop

1980: Best Short Stories of the Year*

Grotto of the Dancing Deer	Clifford D. Simak
Scorched Supper on New Niger	Suzy McKee Charnas
Ginungagap	Michael Swanwick
Frozen Journey	Philip K. Dick
The Ugly Chickens	Howard Waldrop
Nightflyers	George R. R. Martin
Beatnik Bayou	John Varley
Window	Bob Leman
Tell Us A Story	Zenna Henderson
Le Croix	Barry N. Malzberg
Martian Walkabout	F. Gwynplaine MacIntyre
Slow Music	James Tiptree Jr

1980: Best SF Short Stories of the Year†

Variation on a Theme From Beethoven	Sharon Webb
Beatnik Bayou	John Varley
Elbow Room	Marion Zimmer Bradley
The Ugly Chickens	Howard Waldrop
Prime Time	Norman Spinrad
Nightflyers	George R. R. Martin
A Spaceship Made From Stone	Lisa Tuttle
Window	Bob Leman
The Summer Sweet, The Winter Wild	Michael Coney
Achronos	Lee Killough

1980: Hugo Awards and Nominations

BEST SF NOVEL

The Snow Queen	**Joan D. Vinge** (Winner)
Beyond the Blue Event Horizon	Frederik Pohl

*Terry Carr, The Best Science Fiction of the Year 10
†Donald Wollheim, The 1981 Annual World's Best SF

Lord Valentine's Castle	Robert Silverberg
The Ringworld Engineers	Larry Niven
Wizard	John Varley

BEST SF NOVELLA

Lost Dorsai	**Gordon R. Dickson** (Winner)
All the Lies That Are My Life	Harlan Ellison
The Brave Little Toaster	Thomas M. Disch
Nightflyers	George R. R. Martin
One Wing	George R. R. Martin and Lisa Tuttle

BEST SF NOVELETTE

The Cloak and the Staff	**Gordon R. Dickson** (Winner)
The Autopsy	Michael Shea
Beatnik Bayou	John Varley
The Lordly Ones	Keith Roberts
Savage Planet	Barry B. Longyear
The Ugly Chickens	Howard Waldrop

BEST SF SHORT STORY

Grotto of the Dancing Deer	**Clifford D. Simak** (Winner)
Cold Hands	Jeff Duntemann
Guardian	Jeff Duntemann
Our Lady of the Sauropods	Robert Silverberg
Spidersong	Susan C. Petrey

1980: Nebula Awards and Nominations

BEST SF NOVEL

Timescape	**Gregory Benford** (Winner)
The Snow Queen	Joan D. Vinge
The Shadow of the Torturer	Gene Wolfe
Mockingbird	Walter Tevis
The Orphan	Robert Stallman
Beyond the Blue Event Horizon	Frederik Pohl

BEST SF NOVELLA

Unicorn Tapestry	**Suzy McKee Charnas** (Winner)
The Brave Little Toaster	Thomas M. Disch
The Autopsy	Michael Shea
There Beneath the Silky-Trees and	
Whelmed in Deeper Gulphs Than Me	Avram Davidson
Lost Dorsai	Gordon R. Dickson
Dangerous Games	Marta Randall

BEST SF NOVELETTE

The Ugly Chickens	**Howard Waldrop** (Winner)
Strata	Edward Bryant
The Way Station	Stephen King
The Feast of St Janis	Michael Swanwick
Ginungagap	Michael Swanwick
Beatnik Bayou	John Varley

BEST SF SHORT STORY

Grotto of the Dancing Deer	**Clifford D. Simak** (Winner)
Secret of the Heart	Charles L. Grant
A Sunday Visit to Great-Grandfather	Craig Strete
Window	Bob Leman
The War Beneath the Tree	Gene Wolfe

1981: Nebula Awards and Nominations

BEST SF NOVEL

The Claw of the Conciliator	**Gene Wolfe** (Winner)
Radix	A. A. Attanasio
The Vampire Tapestry	Suzy McKee Charnas
Little, Big	John Crowley
Riddley Walker	Russell Hoban
The Many-Colored Land	Julian May

BEST SF NOVELLA

The Saturn Game	**Poul Anderson** (Winner)

Swarmer, Skimmer	Gregory Benford
Amnesia	Jack Dann
In the Western Tradition	Phyllis Eisenstein
True Names	Vernor Vinge
The Winter Beach	Kate Wilhelm

BEST SF NOVELETTE

The Quickening	**Michael Bishop** (Winner)
Sea Changeling	Mildred Downey Broxon
The Thermals of August	Edward Bryant
The Fire When It Comes	Parke Godwin
Mummer Kiss	Michael Swanwick
Lirios: A Tale of the Quintana Roo	James Tiptree Jr

BEST SF SHORT STORY

The Bone Flute	**Lisa Tuttle** (Winner)
Going Under	Jack Dann
The Quiet	George Florance-Guthridge
Johnny Mnemonic	William Gibson
Venice Drowned	Kim Stanley Robinson
Zeke	Timothy R. Sullivan
Disciples	Gardner Dozois
The Pusher	John Varley

*1981: Best SF Short Stories of the Year**

The Saturn Game	Poul Anderson
Walk the Ice	Mildred Downey Broxon
Trial Sample	Ted Reynolds
The Pusher	John Varley
Venice Drowned	Kim Stanley Robinson
Walden Three	Michael Swanwick
Second Comings – Reasonable Rates	Pat Cadigan
Forever	Damon Knight
Emergence	David R. Palmer

*Terry Carr, *The Best SF of the Year* 11

You Can't Go Back	R. A. Lafferty
Walpoogisnacht	Roger Zelazny
The Woman the Unicorn Loved	Gene Wolfe
Serpent's Teeth	Spider Robinson
The Thermals of August	Edward Bryant
Going Under	Jack Dann
The Quiet	George Florance-Guthridge
Swarmer, Skimmer	Gregory Benford

*1981: Best US Short Stories of the Year**

Blind Spot	Jayge Carr
Highliner	C. J. Cherryh
The Pusher	John Varley
Polyphemus	Michael Shea
Absent Thee From Felicity A While . . .	Somtow Sucharitkul
Out Of The Everywhere	James Tiptree Jr
Slac	Michael P. Kube-McDowell
The Cyphertone	S. C. Sykes
Through All Your Houses Wandering	Ted Reynolds
The Last Day of Christmas	David J. Lake

*Donald Wollheim, *The 1982 Annual World's Best SF*

The All-Time Top Eighteen Authors (1966)

1. Isaac Asimov (80.4%)
2. Robert A. Heinlein (80%)
3. Arthur C. Clarke (66.9%)
4. A. E. Van Vogt (44.9%)
5. Poul Anderson (42.8%)
6. H. G. Wells (39.1%)
7. Clifford Simak (33.3%)
8. Theodore Sturgeon (32.3%)
9. Ray Bradbury (30%)
10.= Murray Leinster (24.4%)
10.= E. E. Smith (24.4%)
12. Andre Norton (21%)
13. Eric Frank Russell (20.5%)
14. Henry Kuttner/C. L. Moore (18.8%)
15. L. Sprague de Camp (18.1%)
16. Alfred Bester (15.4%)
17. Edgar Rice Burroughs (14.9%)
18. James Blish (14.5%)

(Reader survey reported in *Analog*. Readers were invited to nominate ten authors)

The All-Time Top Twenty-two Authors (1973)

1. Robert A. Heinlein (179 votes)
2. Isaac Asimov (136)
3. Arthur C. Clarke (85)
4. Robert Silverberg (81)
5. Poul Anderson (74)
6. Theodore Sturgeon (72)
7. Harlan Ellison (54)
8.= Clifford Simak (41)
8.= Roger Zelazny (41)
10. Samuel R. Delany (39)
11. Ray Bradbury (38)
12. Philip K. Dick (36)
13. Larry Niven (29)

14.= Philip José Farmer (26)
14.= Cordwainer Smith (26)
16.= Ursula Le Guin (25)
16.= Andre Norton (25)
18. John Brunner (20)
19.= Keith Laumer (16)
19.= A. E. Van Vogt (16)
19.= H. G. Wells (16)
22. Fritz Leiber (15)

(Reader survey reported in *Locus*)

The Twenty-two Most Popular SF Writers in Britain (1975)

1. Isaac Asimov (57%)
2. Arthur C. Clarke (43%)
3. Robert A. Heinlein (32%)
4. A. E. Van Vogt (25%)
5. Frank Herbert (22%)
6. John Wyndham (16%)
7. Brian Aldiss (15%)
8.= Ray Bradbury (13%)
8.= Harry Harrison (13%)
8.= Michael Moorcock (13%)
11.= E. E. Smith (12%)
11.= Larry Niven (12%)
13.= Poul Anderson (11%)
13.= James Blish (11%)
13.= Clifford Simak (11%)
13.= Roger Zelazny (11%)
17.= Edmund Cooper (10%)
17.= Philip K. Dick (10%)
19.= Eric Frank Russell (9%)
19.= H. G. Wells (9%)
21.= Ursula Le Guin (8%)
21.= Philip José Farmer (8%)

(In 1975 the magazine *Science Fiction Monthly* conducted a reader survey, which included a question about favourite authors. The figures are the percentages of replies which mentioned a given writer)

The All-Time Top Twenty-six Authors (1977)

1. Robert A. Heinlein (297 votes)
2. Isaac Asimov (238)
3. Arthur C. Clarke (198)
4. Ursula Le Guin (170)
5. Robert Silverberg (140)
6. Larry Niven (131)
7. Harlan Ellison (124)
8. Roger Zelazny (109)
9. Fritz Leiber (94)
10. Philip K. Dick (86)
11. Theodore Sturgeon (81)
12. Poul Anderson (79)
13. Jack Vance (73)
14. Ray Bradbury (57)
15. Alfred Bester (56)
16. Samuel R. Delany (45)
17.= Philip José Farmer (41)
17.= Cordwainer Smith (41)
19. Frank Herbert (40)
20. J. R. R. Tolkien (38)
21. Gordon Dickson (36)
22.= Clifford Simak (35)
22.= H. G. Wells (35)
24. John Brunner (32)
25. Frederik Pohl (31)
26. Kate Wilhelm (30)

(Reader survey reported in *Locus*)

The Forty Most Popular SF Short Stories (1971)

1. Isaac Asimov, 'Nightfall' (*49 votes*)
2.= Arthur C. Clarke, 'The Star' (*42 votes*)
2.= Robert Heinlein, 'The Green Hills of Earth' (*42 votes*)
2.= Daniel Keyes, 'Flowers for Algernon' (*42 votes*)
5. Roger Zelazny, 'A Rose for Ecclesiastes' (*36 votes*)
6. Bob Shaw, 'Light of Other Days' (*29 votes*)

7.= Arthur C. Clarke, 'The Nine Billion Names of God' (*27 votes*)
7.= Harlan Ellison, 'Repent Harlequin!' Said the Ticktockman' (*27 votes*)
9.= Arthur C. Clarke, 'Rescue Party' (*26 votes*)
9.= Tom Godwin, 'The Cold Equations' (*26 votes*)
9.= Murray Leinster, 'First Contact' (*26 votes*)
9.= Robert Heinlein, 'By His Bootstraps' (*26 votes*)
13.= Theodore Sturgeon, 'Microcosmic God' (*23 votes*)
13.= C. M. Kornbluth, 'The Little Black Bag' (*23 votes*)
15.= Isaac Asimov, 'The Last Question' (*22 votes*)
15.= Harlan Ellison, 'I Have No Mouth and I Must Scream' (*22 votes*)
17.= Clifford Simak, 'The Big Front Yard' (*21 votes*)
17.= Arthur C. Clarke, 'The Sentinel' (*21 votes*)
17.= James Blish, 'Surface Tension' (*21 votes*)
20. Jerome Bixby, 'It's A *Good* Life' (*20 votes*)
21.= John W. Campbell, 'Twilight' (*19 votes*)
21.= Stanley G. Weinbaum, 'A Martian Odyssey' (*19 votes*)
21.= Robert Heinlein, 'And He Built A Crooked House' (*19 votes*)
21.= Henry Kuttner, 'Mimsy Were The Borogoves' (*19 votes*)
21.= Roger Zelazny, 'For A Breath I Tarry' (*19 votes*)
26.= John W. Campbell, 'Who Goes There?' (*18 votes*)
26.= Cordwainer Smith, 'The Game of Rat and Dragon' (*18 votes*)
28.= Robert Heinlein, 'The Roads Must Roll' (*17 votes*)
28.= Eric Frank Russell, 'Dear Devil' (*17 votes*)
30.= Robert Heinlein, 'All You Zombies' (*16 votes*)
30.= Robert Heinlein, 'The Long Watch' (*16 votes*)
30.= H. Beam Piper, 'Omnilingual' (*16 votes*)
30.= Eric Frank Russell, 'Allamagoosa' (*(16 votes*)
30.= Cordwainer Smith, 'A Planet Named Shayol' (*16 votes*)
35.= Robert Heinlein, 'The Year of the Jackpot' (*15 votes*)
35.= Robert Heinlein, 'The Man Who Sold The Moon' (*15 votes*)
35.= Wilmar Shiras, 'In Hiding' (*15 votes*)
35.= Theodore Sturgeon, 'Killdozer' (*15 votes*)
35.= Fredric Brown, 'Arena' (*15 votes*)
35.= Harlan Ellison, 'A Boy and His Dog' (*15 votes*)

(Results of poll announced in *Analog*, October 1971. 108 readers voted)

The Thirty-four Best SF Short Stories Published Before 1940 (1971)

1.= John W. Campbell, 'Twilight' (*25 votes*)
1.= John W. Campbell, 'Who Goes There?' (*25 votes*)
3. Stanley G. Weinbaum, 'A Martian Odyssey' (*20 votes*)
4. Lester del Rey, 'Helen O'Loy' (*19 votes*)
5. John W. Campbell, 'Night' (*17 votes*)
6. John W. Campbell, 'Forgetfulness' (*14 votes*)
7.= A. E. Van Vogt, 'Black Destroyer' (*13 votes*)
7.= John Wyndham, 'The Lost Machine' (*13 votes*)
9. Isaac Asimov, 'Marooned off Vesta' (*12 votes*)
10.= P. Schuyler Miller, 'The Sands of Time', (*11 votes*)
10.= E. M. Forster, 'The Machine Stops' (*11 votes*)
12.= Murray Leinster, 'Proxima Centauri' (*10 votes*)
12.= H. P. Lovecraft, 'The Colour Out of Space' (*10 votes*)
14.= Philip Francis Nowlan, 'Armageddon: 2419 AD' (*9 votes*)
14.= Robert Heinlein, 'Life Line' (*9 votes*)
16.= Robert Moore Williams, 'Robot's Return' (*8 votes*)
16.= Stanley G. Weinbaum, 'The Adaptive Ultimate' (*8 votes*)
16.= Eando Binder, 'I, Robot' (*8 votes*)
19.= H. G. Wells, 'The New Accelerator' (*7 votes*)
19.= H. G. Wells, 'The Country of the Blind' (*7 votes*)
19.= Henry Hasse, 'He Who Shrank' (*7 votes*)
19.= Murray Leinster, 'Politics' (*7 votes*)
19.= L. Sprague de Camp, 'The Blue Giraffe' (*7 votes*)
19.= Lester del Rey, 'The Faithful' (*7 votes*)
25.= H. G. Wells, 'The Crystal Egg' (*6 votes*)
25.= C. L. Moore, 'Shambleau' (*6 votes*)
25.= R. DeWitt Miller, 'Within the Pyramid' (*6 votes*)
25.= H. P. Lovecraft, 'The Shadow Out Of Time' (*6 votes*)
25.= Murray Leinster, 'Sidewise in Time' (*6 votes*)
25.= Murray Leinster, 'The Runaway Skyscraper' (*6 votes*)
25.= Ray Cummings, 'The Girl in the Golden Atom' (*6 votes*)
25.= Raymond Z. Gallun, 'Seed of the Dusk' (*6 votes*)
25.= Raymond Z. Gallun, 'Old Faithful' (*6 votes*)
25.= Edmond Hamilton, 'He That Hath Wings' (*6 votes*)

(Results of poll announced in *Analog*, November 1971. While being asked to choose the best SF short stories ever, readers were also invited to send lists confined to SF published before 1940. Thirty-three readers obliged, with the above results)

The Eight Most Popular SF Series (1971)

1. Isaac Asimov's *Robot* series (*46 votes*)
2. Zenna Henderson's *People* series (*43 votes*)
3. Clifford Simak's *City* series (*25 votes*)
4. Henry Kuttner's *Gallegher* series (*23 votes*)
5. Larry Niven's *Known Space* series (*22 votes*)
6. A. E. Van Vogt's *Space Beagle* series (*20 votes*)
7. James Schmitz' *Telzey Amberdon* series (*17 votes*)
8. Christopher Anvil's *Pandora's Planet* series (*15 votes*)

(Results of poll announced in *Analog*, October 1971. As well as voting for favourite short stories, readers were invited to vote for their favourite short story series, with these results)

The Seventeen Basic SF Titles (1949)

1. H. G. Wells: *Seven Famous Novels* (9 votes)
2.= Aldous Huxley: *Brave New World* (7)
2.= Olaf Stapledon: *Last and First Men* (7)
4.= Healy and McComas (eds): *Adventures in Time and Space* (6)
4.= A. E. Van Vogt: *Slan* (6)
4.= H. G. Wells: *Short Stories of H. G. Wells* (6)
7.= August Derleth (ed.): *Strange Ports of Call* (5)
7.= S. Fowler Wright: *The World Below* (5)
9.= A. Conan Doyle: *The Lost World* (4)
9.= William F. Sloane: *To Walk the Night* (4)
9.= Olaf Stapledon: *Sirius* (4)
9.= Philip Wylie: *Gladiator* (4)
13.= John W. Campbell: *Who Goes There?* (3)
13.= Groff Conklin (ed): *The Best of Science Fiction* (3)
13.= Erle Cox: *Out of the Silence* (3)
13.= Olaf Stapledon: *Star Maker* (3)
13.= John Taine: *Before the Dawn* (3)

(Survey conducted by August Derleth and reported in the *Arkham Sampler*. Derleth polled twelve writers, editors and critics for their choices)

The Twenty-Eight All-Time Best SF Books (1952)

1. Healy and McComas (eds): *Adventures in Time and Space*
2. A. E. Van Vogt: *Slan*
3. H. G. Wells: *Seven Famous Novels*
4. Robert Heinlein: *The Man Who Sold The Moon*
5. John W. Campbell: *Who Goes There?*
6. Groff Conklin (ed): *The Best of Science Fiction*
7. Ray Bradbury: *The Martian Chronicles*
8. Robert Heinlein: *The Green Hills of Earth*
9. Bleiler and Dikty (eds): *The Science Fiction Omnibus*
10. Ray Bradbury: *The Illustrated Man*
11. L. Sprague de Camp: *Lest Darkness Fall*
12. Donald A. Wollheim (ed): *Portable Novels of Science*
13. E. E. Smith: *Grey Lensman*
14. A. E. Van Vogt: *World of Null-A*
15. Isaac Asimov: *Foundation*
16. John W. Campbell (ed): *Astounding Science Fiction Anthology*
17. George Orwell: *1984*
18. Eric Frank Russell: *Sinister Barrier*
19. H. G. Wells: *Short Stories of H. G. Wells*
20. Groff Conklin (ed): *A Treasury of Science Fiction*
21. Lester del Rey: *And Some Were Human*
22. Aldous Huxley: *Brave New World*
23. Isaac Asimov: *I, Robot*
24. John W. Campbell: *The Moon is Hell*
25. Robert Heinlein: *Beyond This Horizon*
26. A. E. Van Vogt: *The Weapon Makers*
27. Jack Williamson: *The Humanoids*
28. S. Fowler Wright: *The World Below*

(Reader survey reported in *Astounding Science Fiction*)

The Twenty-six All-Time Best SF Books (1956)

1. Healy and McComas (eds): *Adventures in Time and Space* (51 votes)
2. Clifford Simak: *City* (50)

3.= Ray Bradbury: *The Martian Chronicles* (48)
3.= Theodore Sturgeon: *More Than Human* (48)
5. A. E. Van Vogt: *Slan* (44)
6. Robert Heinlein: *The Man Who Sold The Moon* (40)
7. Alfred Bester: *The Demolished Man* (39)
8. John W. Campbell (ed): *Astounding Science Fiction Anthology* (37)
9.= Arthur C. Clarke: *Childhood's End* (35)
9.= George Orwell: *1984* (35)
9.= A. E. Van Vogt: *World of Null-A* (35)
12. Isaac Asimov: *Foundation* (32)
13.= John W. Campbell: *Who Goes There?* (31)
13.= Olaf Stapledon: *To the End of Time* (omnibus) (31)
15. Aldous Huxley: *Brave New World* (30)
16. H. G. Wells: *Seven Famous Novels* (29)
17. Robert Heinlein: *The Green Hills of Earth* (28)
18.= Hal Clement: *Mission of Gravity* (27)
18.= Jack Williamson: *The Humanoids* (27)
20. L. Sprague de Camp: *Lest Darkness Fall* (26)
21. Isaac Asimov: *I, Robot* (25)
22.= Ray Bradbury: *The Illustrated Man* (23)
22.= Arthur C. Clarke: *The City and the Stars* (23)
22.= Frederik Pohl and C. M. Kornbluth: *The Space Merchants* (23)
25.= Ray Bradbury: *Fahrenheit 451* (22)
25.= Arthur C. Clarke: *Prelude to Space* (22)

(Reader survey reported in *Astounding Science Fiction*)

The Twenty-seven All-Time Best SF Books (1966)

1. Isaac Asimov: *The Foundation Trilogy* (67.4%)
2. H. G. Wells: *Seven Famous Novels* (59.4%)
3. A. E. Van Vogt: *Slan* (50.5%)
4. Isaac Asimov: *The Rest of the Robots* (omnibus) (45.7%)
5. Alfred Bester: *The Demolished Man* (44.2%)
6. Arthur C. Clarke: *Childhood's End* (41.2%)
7. Arthur C. Clarke: *The City and the Stars* (40.6%)
8. Ray Bradbury: *The Martian Chronicles* (38.9%)
9. Clifford Simak: *City* (38.6%)

175

10. Walter M. Miller: *A Canticle for Leibowitz* (38.1%)
11. Robert Heinlein: *Starship Troopers* (37.7%)
12. Isaac Asimov: *I, Robot* (37.2%)
13. Olaf Stapledon: *To the End of Time* (omnibus) (36.7%)
14. Robert Heinlein: *The Man Who Sold the Moon* (35.2%)
15. Hal Clement: *Mission of Gravity* (34.5%)
16. Alfred Bester: *The Stars My Destination* (33.8%)
17. Robert Heinlein: *Stranger in a Strange Land* (32.9%)
18. A. E. Van Vogt: *The World of Null-A* (31.9%)
19. Theodore Sturgeon: *More Than Human* (31.4%)
20. Healy and McComas, (eds): *Adventures in Time and Space* (30.7%)
21. Frank Herbert: *Dune* (27.3%)
22. Frederik Pohl and C. M. Kornbluth: *The Space Merchants* (26.3%)
23. John Wyndham: *Re-birth (The Chrysalids)* (26.1%)
24. Robert Heinlein: *Waldo & Magic, Inc.* (25.6%)
25. A. E. Van Vogt: *The Weapon Shops of Isher* (24.1%)
26. Robert Heinlein: *Methuselah's Children* (23.7%)
27. Clifford Simak: *Way Station* (22.4%)

(Reader survey reported in *Analog*. Readers were allowed to nominate up to twenty-five titles)

The Twenty-six All-Time Best SF Novels (1975)

1. Frank Herbert: *Dune* (104 votes)
2. Arthur C. Clarke: *Childhood's End* (97)
3. Ursula Le Guin: *The Left Hand of Darkness* (90)
4. Robert Heinlein: *Stranger in a Strange Land* (63)
5. Walter M. Miller: *A Canticle for Leibowitz* (57)
6. Isaac Asimov: *The Foundation Trilogy* (53)
7. Alfred Bester: *The Stars My Destination* (50)
8. Robert Heinlein: *The Moon is a Harsh Mistress* (41)
9. Theodore Sturgeon: *More Than Human* (40)
10. Roger Zelazny: *Lord of Light* (35)
11. John Brunner: *Stand on Zanzibar* (34)
12. Larry Niven: *Ringworld* (32)
13. Ursula Le Guin: *The Dispossessed* (31)
14. Alfred Bester: *The Demolished Man* (30)

15. J. R. R. Tolkien: *Lord of the Rings* (29)
16. Hal Clement: *Mission of Gravity* (25)
17.= Arthur C. Clarke: *The City and the Stars* (23)
17.= Philip José Farmer: *To Your Scattered Bodies Go* (23)
19. Robert Silverberg: *Dying Inside* (23)
20 = Arthur C. Clarke: *Rendezvous with Rama* (20)
20.= H. G. Wells: *The Time Machine* (20)
22.= Philip K. Dick: *The Man in the High Castle* (17)
22.= Robert Heinlein: *Starship Troopers* (17)
22.= Ray Bradbury: *The Martian Chronicles* (16)
24.= Frederik Pohl and C. M. Kornbluth: *The Space Merchants* (16)
24.= H. G. Wells: *War of the Worlds* (16)

(Reader survey reported in *Locus*)

The Fifteen Best SF Short Stories Published Before 1965

In order to compile their Hall of Fame anthologies, the Science Fiction Writers of America polled their members to discover their opinion of the best SF published before the institution of the Nebula Awards. In the short-story category the results were as follows, in order of votes received:

1. 'Nightfall', by Isaac Asimov
2. 'A Martian Odyssey', by Stanley G. Weinbaum
3. 'Flowers for Algernon', by Daniel Keyes
4.= 'Microcosmic God', by Theodore Sturgeon
4.= 'First Contact', by Murray Leinster
6. 'A Rose for Ecclesiastes', by Roger Zelazny
7.= 'The Roads Must Roll', by Robert Heinlein
7.= 'Mimsy Were the Borogoves', by Lewis Padgett
7.= 'Coming Attraction', by Fritz Leiber
7.= 'The Cold Equations', by Tom Godwin
11. 'The Nine Billion Names of God', by Arthur C. Clarke
12. 'Surface Tension', by James Blish
13.= 'The Weapon Shop', by A. E. Van Vogt
13.= 'Twilight', by John W. Campbell
15.= 'The Star', by Arthur C. Clarke

The Twenty-four SF Novelettes and Novellas Published Before 1965

The SFWA Hall of Fame exercise was subsequently extended to longer stories, with the following results (in alphabetical order, as the order of popularity was not revealed).

1. *Call Me Joe*, by Poul Anderson
2. *The Martian Way*, by Isaac Asimov
3. *Earthman, Come Home*, by James Blish
4. *The Fireman*, by Ray Bradbury
5. *Rogue Moon*, by Algis Budrys
6. *Who Goes There?*, by John W. Campbell
7. *The Spectre General*, by Theodore Cogswell
8. *Nerves*, by Lester del Rey
9. *The Machine Stops*, by E. M. Forster
10. *Universe*, by Robert Heinlein
11. *The Marching Morons*, by C. M. Kornbluth
12. *Vintage Season*, by Henry Kuttner and C. L. Moore
13. *A Canticle for Leibowitz*, by Walter M. Miller
14. *The Midas Plague*, by Frederik Pohl
15. *And Then There Were None*, by Eric Frank Russell
16. *The Witches of Karres*, by James Schmitz
17. *E for Effort*, by T. L. Sherred
18. *In Hiding*, by Wilmar H. Shiras
19. *The Big Front Yards*, by Clifford Simak
20. *The Ballad of Lost C'Mell*, by Cordwainer Smith
21. *Baby is Three*, by Theodore Sturgeon
22. *The Moon Moth*, by Jack Vance
23. *The Time Machine*, by H. G. Wells
24. *With Folded Hands*, by Jack Williamson

Barry Malzberg's Best SF Short Stories of All Time

In his book of essays on science fiction, *The Engines of the Night*, Malzberg chooses his best stories, which he qualifies as follows:

They are not ranked in order of descending merit (it is foolish enough to find a top ten without going on to arrange them), the judgment is based upon literary excellence (seminal stories such as Weinbaum's 'A Martian Odyssey' as influences upon the genre have had far greater effect than most of the stories on this list but the work is being judged *sui generis*) and, of course, as a single if informed opinion it is liable to challenge and dispute, not least from the list-maker himself who a year or two from now might want to change three-quarters of it . . .

1. Henry Kuttner and C. L. Moore – *Vintage Season*
2. James Tiptree Jr – *Her Smoke Rose Up Forever*
3. Edward Bryant – *Particle Theory*
4. J. G. Ballard – *The Terminal Beach*
5. Henry Kuttner and C. L. Moore – *Private Eye*
6. Robert Silverberg – *Sundance*
7. Damon Knight – *Anachron*
8. Alfred Bester – *The Men Who Murdered Mohammed*
9. Alfred Bester – *Fondly Fahrenheit*
10. T. L. Sherred – *E For Effort*

For good measure, Malzberg goes on to give ten runners-up, 'listed once more in no particular order and with the understanding that any one or all of them could probably be traded in for any one or all of the top ten':

11. Theodore Sturgeon – *Baby is Three*
12. Alfred Bester – *They Don't Make Life Like They Used To*
13. Isaac Asimov – *The Dead Past*
14. Carter Scholz – *The Ninth Symphony of Ludwig van Beethoven and Other Lost Songs*
15. Carter Scholz – *The Eve of the Last Apollo*
16. James Tiptree Jr – *The Psychologist Who Wouldn't Do Awful Things to Rats*
17. William Tenn – *The Party of the Two Parts*
18. Henry Kuttner and C. L. Moore – *The Children's Hour*
19. Jack Dann – *Timetipping*

The Most Acclaimed Stories in Astounding/Analog

For many years the magazine *Astounding Science Fiction* (later *Analog*) ran a regular readers' poll to determine the most popular stories in each issue. Readers would rank the stories in order of preference, and these figures would be used to obtain an average figure. For a story to obtain a score of 1.00 exactly, every reader who voted would have to rank it first or equal first in the issue. This happened five times in the history of the magazine, four times with episodes of serials:

1. December 1940. A. E. Van Vogt – *Slan* (part 4)
2. August 1941. Robert A. Heinlein – *Methuselah's Children* (part 2)
3. April 1942. Robert A. Heinlein (as Anson MacDonald) – *Beyond This Horizon* (part 1)
4. September 1942. Lester del Rey – *Nerves*
5. September 1945. A. E. Van Vogt – *The World of Null-A* (part 2)

The most remarkable of these is probably *Nerves*, as two of the competing stories – *Barrier* by Anthony Boucher and *The Twonky* by Henry Kuttner – have frequently been reprinted. It should be noted that it has been suggested that long-time editor John W. Campbell often fiddled the figures to suit his own opinions.

The Ten Most Anthologized Modern SF Stories

William B. Contento's *Index to Science Fiction Anthologies and Collections* is an exhaustive compilation of such books published up to June 1977. From its pages we have culled this list of the most frequently anthologized stories, discounting appearances in an author's own collection.

1. Isaac Asimov – *Nightfall* (16 anthologies)
2.= Harlan Ellison – *'Repent Harlequin!' Said the Ticktockman* (14)
2.= Tom Godwin – *The Cold Equations* (14)
4. Arthur C. Clarke – *The Nine Billion Names of God* (13)
5.= J. G. Ballard – *Billennium* (11)
5.= Ursula Le Guin – *Nine Lives* (11)

7.= Jerome Bixby - *It's a Good Life* (10)
7.= Fredric Brown - *Arena* (10)
7.= Arthur C. Clarke - *The Star* (10)
7.= Frederik Pohl - *Day Million* (10)

The Ten Most Popular SF Books in Russia (1967)

Science fiction is exceptionally popular in the USSR, though only selected overseas works are translated. Accurate sales figures are hard to come by, but print runs of 200,000 copies - which sell out instantly - are not uncommon. In 1967 the magazine *Fantastyka* took a poll to find its readers' favourite SF books. Not surprisingly, the list is dominated by the Strugatsky brothers, who stand head and shoulders above any of their contemporaries in reputation.

1. Arkady and Boris Strugatsky, *Hard to Be A God*
2. Arkady and Boris Strugatsky, *Monday Beings On Saturday*
3. Ray Bradbury, *The Martian Chronicles*
4. Stanislaw Lem, *Solaris*
5. Stanislaw Lem, *The Invincible*
6. Arkady and Boris Strugatsky, *Far Rainbow*
7. Robert Sheckley, *Stories*
8. Isaac Asimov, *I, Robot*
9. Stanislaw Lem, *Return to the Stars*
10. Arkady and Boris Strugatsky, *The Final Circle of Paradise*

Authors' Pets: Their Favourite Stories

There have been several anthologies collecting authors' favourite SF stories. The following list has been compiled from:

Leo Margulies and Oscar J. Friend (eds) *My Best Science Fiction Story*, 1949 (MF); August Derleth (ed), *The Outer Reaches*, 1951 (AD); Harry Harrison (ed), *SF: Author's Choice*, 1968 (HH1); Harry Harrison (ed) *SF: Author's Choice 2*, 1970 (HH2); Harry Harrison (ed) *SF: Author's Choice 3*, 1971 (HH3); Harry Harrison (ed) *SF: Author's Choice 4*, 1974 (HH4).

Various writers have collected their best stories in volume form (Aldiss, Blish, Malzberg, etc.) or the choice of their stories was effected by other editors. These, more detailed, choices have not been included here.

Brian Aldiss	*Judas Danced* (HH1)
	Auto-Ancestral Fracture (HH2)
	Sober Noises of Morning in a Marginal Land (HH3)
	Old Hundredth (HH4)
Poul Anderson	*Interloper* (AD)
	The Last of the Deliverers (HH1)
Piers Anthony	*Phog* (HH3)
Isaac Asimov	*Robot AL76 Goes Astray* (MF)
	Death Sentence (AD)
	Founding Father (HH1)
J. G. Ballard	*End-Game* (HH1)
Arthur K. Barnes	*Grief of Baghdad* (MF)
Alfred Bester	*Fondly Fahrenheit* (HH2)
Eando Binder	*The Teacher from Mars* (MF)
James Blish and Damon Knight	*Tiger Ride* (HH1)
Robert Bloch	*Almost Human* (MF)
Nelson Bond	*This is the Land* (AD)
Ray Bradbury	*Zero Hour* (MF)
	Ylla (AD)
Fredric Brown	*Nothing Sirius* (MF)
John Brunner	*Fair* (HH4)
Algis Budrys	*Contact Between Equals* (HH2)
John W. Campbell	*Blindness* (MF)
Cleve Cartmill	*Visiting Yokel* (MF)
	The Green Cat (AD)
A. Bertram Chandler	*Late* (HH2)
Arthur C. Clarke	*The Forgotten Enemy* (HH4)
Theodore Cogswell	*Consumer's Report* (HH1)
Avram Davidson	*The Power of Every Root* (HH3)
L. Sprague de Camp	*The Hibited Man* (MF)
	Git Along (AD)
	Proposal (HH1)
Gordon Dickson	*Warrior* (HH4)
Thomas M. Disch	*Et In Arcadia Ego* (HH4)

Sonya Dorman	*The Deepest Blue in the World* (HH3)
Harlan Ellison	*O Ye of Little Faith* (HH3)
Carol Emshwiller	*But Soft, What Light* (HH4)
Paul Ernst	*The Thing in the Pond* (MF)
Philip José Farmer	*Sail On! Sail On!* (HH1)
John Russell Fearn	*Wanderer of Time* (MF)
Daniel F. Galouye	*Diplomatic Coop* (HH2)
H. L. Gold	*Love in the Dark* (HH2)
James Gunn	*The Misogynist* (HH4)
Edmond Hamilton	*The Inn Outside the World* (MF)
Robert A. Heinlein	*The Green Hills of Earth* (MF)
Frank Herbert	*Missing Link* (HH1)
L. Ron Hubbard	*The Professor was a Thief* (MF)
George Clayton Johnson	*All of Us Are Dying* (HH4)
Langdon Jones	*The Coming of the Sun* (HH3)
David H. Keller	*Service First* (AD)
Henry Kuttner	*Don't Look Now* (MF)
	Shock (AD)
Fritz Leiber	*The Ship Sails at Midnight* (AD)
	Myths my Great-Granddaughter Taught Me (HH1)
Murray Leinster	*The Lost Race* (MF)
	The Power (AD)
Frank Belknap Long	*The House of the Rising Winds* (MF)
	The Critters (AD)
Katherine MacLean	*Syndrome Johnny* (HH1)
Barry N. Malzberg	*The Falcon and the Falconer* (HH3)
David I Masson	*The Transfinite Choice* (HH3)
Sam Merwin	*The Carrier* (MF)
Michael Moorcock	*The Tank Trapeze* (HH3)
Larry Niven	*Bordered in Black* (HH3)
Alan Nourse	*The Expert Touch* (HH2)
Chad Oliver	*A Stick for Harry Eddington* (HH2)
Frederik Pohl	*Day Million* (HH1)
Fletcher Pratt	*Doctor Grimshaw's Sanitarium* (MF)
	Pardon My Mistake (AD)
Kit Reed	*At Central* (HH3)
Mack Reynolds	*Retaliation* (HH1)
Frank Morton Robinson	*The Fire and the Sword* (HH4)
James H. Schmitz	*Just Curious* (HH2)

Robert Sheckley	*The Autumn Land* (HH4)
Robert Silverberg	*Bad Medicine* (HH4)
Clifford D. Simak	*To See the Invisible Man* (HH2)
	Goodnight, Mr James (AD)
Clark Ashton Smith	*The Uncharted Isle* (MF)
	The Plutonian Drug (AD)
Norman Spinrad	*The Last Hurrah of the Golden Horde* (HH3)
Theodore Sturgeon	*Thunder and Roses* (MF)
	Farewell to Eden (AD)
John Taine	*The Ultimate Catalyst* (MF)
Robert Taylor	*A Sense of Beauty* (HH4)
James Tiptree Jr	*The Last Light of Dr Ain* (HH4)
Jack Vance	*Ullward's Retreat* (HH4)
A. E. Van Vogt	*Project Space-Ship* (MF)
	Co-Operate or Else (AD)
	Heir Unapparent (HH2)
Donald Wandrei	*Finality Unlimited* (AD)
Manly Wade Wellman	*Space Station No 1* (MF)
Jack Williamson	*Star Bright* (MF)
Roger Zelazny	*The Man Who Loved the Faioli* (HH4)

Isaac Asimov's 'Ten Books I Most Enjoyed Writing'

1. *In Memory Yet Green* and *In Joy Still Felt* (my autobiography, written as one volume, though published as two)
2. *Asimov's Guide to Shakespeare* (again written as one volume though published as two)
3. *Asimov's Biographical Guide to Science and Technology* (third edition just published)
4. *Murder at the ABA* (straight mystery) (UK title *Authorised Murder*)
5. *The Gods Themselves* (my favourite science fiction novel)
6. *Asimov's Annotated Don Juan* (dealing with Byron's comic epic; *not* a sex manual or an autobiography)
7. *The Naked Sun* (science fiction novel)
8. *The Caves of Steel* (science fiction novel)
9. *Nine Tomorrows* (science fiction short story collection)
10. *Exploring the Earth and the Cosmos* (published in 1982)

Isaac Asimov's 'Ten Science Fiction Stories I Like Best'

1. The Last Question
2. The Bicentennial Man
3. The Ugly Little Boy
4. The Mule
5. Dreaming is a Private Thing
6. Strikebreaker
7. Breeds There A Man?
8. Galley Slave
9. The Dead Past
10. Nightfall

Best New Writers of the Year
(The John W. Campbell Jr Award)

1973: Jerry Pournelle
1974: Spider Robinson and Lisa Tuttle (Tic)
1975: P. J. Plauger
1976: Tom Reamy
1977: C. J. Cherryh
1978: Orson Scott Card
1979: Stephen R. Donaldson
1980: Barry B. Longyear
1981: Somtow Sucharitkul
1982: Alexis Gililand

The Ten Most Unjustly Neglected SF Novels Ever Written
by Brian Stableford

1. *The Revolt of Man* by Walter Besant (1882) It is the twentieth century and *the suffragettes have taken over the world!* A masterpiece of unintentional comedy

2. *The Ghost of Guy Thyrle* by Edgar Fawcett (1895) The disembodied consciousness of Guy Thyrle crosses the universe in the hope of finding release from his condition. An impressive early cosmic voyage

185

3. *The Mortgage on the Brain* by Vincent Harper (1904) Hard-headed psychologists prove that the soul does not exist. A lurid speculative solution to the mind/body problem

4. *Theodore Savage* by Cicely Hamilton (1922) Mankind bombs itself back to the Stone Age and becomes re-brutalized in the space of a single generation. A bleak tale ahead of its time

5. *The Clockwork Man* by E. V. Odle (1923) A cyborg whose life is regulated by a 'clock' attached to the back of his head is cast into the twentieth century by a mechanical malfunction. The best scientific romance of the twenties

6. *The Man With Six Senses* by Muriel Jaeger (1927) An early conscientious attempt to envisage the psychological effects of living with a sixth sense

7. *The Spacious Adventures of the Man in the Street* by Eimar O'Duffy (1928) A magnificent counter-Earth satire, putting the boot into sexual morality, politics and religion

8. *The Imitation Man* by John Hargrave (1931) A scientist follows an ancient alchemical recipe and creates a homunculus. There is an awful lot of sex in the story considering when it was written

9. *Winter's Youth* by John Gloag (1934) A sharp political satire in which the ruling class nearly precipitates revolution by promoting a longevity-treatment while the world lurches towards the holocaust

10. *The Thought-Reading Machine* by André Maurois (1938) A machine which records people's thoughts becomes briefly fashionable, until it is realized that the thoughts in people's heads aren't really of any great significance. A useful antidote to ESP melodramas

Brian Stableford

Unreadable and Overrated SF Novels

There are probably hundreds of books which fit this category. Those listed below are among the few that I have got a long way into but failed to finish. At least one is by a writer I otherwise greatly admire.

1. Isaac Asimov, *The Gods Themselves*
2. Samuel R. Delany, *Dhalgren*
3. Philip K. Dick, *Valis*
4. Larry Niven and Jerry Pournelle, *The Mote in God's Eye*
5. Joan Vinge, *The Snow Queen*

(Malcolm Edwards)

A healthy disagreement here. I enjoyed *The Gods Themselves* and *Dhalgren* (although I agree the latter can be hard-going) and finished (but dislike) the Niven–Pournelle opus. *Valis* I couldn't finish, much to my consternation and *The Snow Queen* I couldn't even begin, despite several attempts.

I'd add Brian Aldiss's *The 80-Minute Hour* to any list of unreadable books, although like Dick he is an author I hold in high esteem. And I would also include a sterling Robert Heinlein trio: *I Will Fear No Evil*, *Time Enough for Love* and *The Number of the Beast*.

I'm a persistent reader who seldom gives up once I have begun, even if from an early stage I know the book is up to no good; however, I'd like to list a few books, considered as important in most circles, but which I find immensely overrated.

1. Samuel R. Delany, *Triton*
2. Ursula K. Le Guin, *The Dispossessed**
3. George R. R. Martin and Lisa Tuttle, *Windhaven*
4. Christopher Priest, *The Space Machine*
5. Spider and Jeanne Robinson, *Stardance*

(Maxim Jakubowski)

*And *I* disagree strongly about this! (ME)

The Apollo Award

The *Prix Apollo*, possibly Europe's most prestigious SF award, was founded by writer, publisher and critic Jacques Sadoul in 1972. Together with a panel of leading French writers and critics (who have over the years numbered many non-SF personalities like Alain

Robbe-Grillet, Michel Butor, François Le Lionnais, Jacques Bergier as well as Michel Demuth, René Barjavel, Francis Lacassin, Michel Lancelot, the jury select the best SF novel to have appeared in the French language during the course of the preceding year. Characteristically, the award has only once been given to a local writer although the 1982 award surprised many by being given to a much lesser-known American author who happens to be resident in Paris.

1972	Roger Zelazny	*Isle of the Dead*
1973	John Brunner	*Stand on Zanzibar*
1974	Norman Spinrad	*The Iron Dream*
1975	Ian Watson	*The Embedding*
1976	Robert Silverberg	*Nightwings*
1977	Philippe Curval	*Cette Chère Humanité* (translated in 1981 as *Brave Old World*)
1978	Frank Herbert	*Hellstrom's Hive*
1979	Frederik Pohl	*Gateway*
1980	John Varley	*The Persistence of Vision*
1981	Kate Wilhelm	*Juniper Time*
1982	Scott Baker	*Symbiote's Crown*

Forty-three Famous Astounding/Analog *Serials*

A list of famous stories which first appeared in the pages of *Astounding/Analog* would prove virtually endless; there is a whole series of anthologies devoted to this famous magazine. We thought it would be interesting to list, however, some famous novels which began their life as *Astounding/Analog* serials. If anything, it shows the sheer importance of the magazine in the history of SF.

1. A. E. Van Vogt's *The World of Null-A* (Aug.–Oct. 1945) now known as *The World of Ā*
2. A. E. Van Vogt's *The Weapon Makers* (Feb.–Apr. 1943)
3. C. L. Mocre's *Judgment Night* (Aug.–Sep. 1943)
4. Jack Williamson's . . . *And Searching Mind* (Mar.–May 1948) now known as *The Humanoids*
5. Robert Heinlein's *Methuselah's Children* (July–Sep. 1941)
6. Fritz Leiber's *Gather Darkness!* (May–July 1943)

7. Robert Heinlein's *Double Star* (Feb.-Apr. 1956)
8. Robert Heinlein's *Beyond this Horizon* (Apr.-May 1942) as Anson MacDonald
9. Gordon Dickson's *The Tactics of Mistake* (Oct. 70-Jan. 1971)
10. Robert Heinlein's *Sixth Column* (Jan.-Mar. 1941) as Anson MacDonald now known as *The Day After Tomorrow*
11. Isaac Asimov's *The Naked Sun* (Oct.-Dec. 1956)
12. Anne McCaffrey's *Dragonrider* (Dec. '67-Jan. 1968)
13. Robert Heinlein's *Citizen of the Galaxy* (Sep.-Dec. 1957)
14. Raymond F. Jones' *Renaissance* (July-Oct. 1944)
15. Henry Kuttner's *Fury* (May-July 1947) as Lawrence O'Donnell
16. Harry Harrison's *The Ethical Engineers* (July-Aug. 1963) now known as *Deathworld 2*
17. Frank Herbert's *Children of Dune* (Jan.-Apr. 1976)
18. Frank Herbert's *Dune World* (Dec. 63-Feb. 1964) now known as *Dune*
19. A. E. Van Vogt's *Slan* (Sep.-Dec. 1940)
20. Frank Herbert's *Under Pressure* (Nov. '55-Jan. 1056)
21. A. E. Vogt's *The Players of Null A* (Oct. '48-Jan. 1949)
22. E. E. Smith's *Second Stage Lensman* (Nov. '41-Feb. 1942)
23. Hal Clement's *Mission of Gravity* (Apr.-July 1953)
24. Harry Harrison's *Deathworld* (Jan.-Mar. 1960)
25. Poul Anderson's *Satan's World* (May-Aug. 1968)
26. Eric Frank Russell's *Dreadful Sanctuary* (June-Aug. 1948)
27. Randall Garrett's *Too Many Magicians* (Aug.-Nov. 1966)
28. Poul Anderson's *The High Crusade* (July-Sep. 1960)
29. James Blish's *A Life for the Stars* (Sep.-Oct. 1962)
30. Roger Zelazny's *Doorways in the Sand* (June-Aug. 1975)
31. Lewis Padgett's *The Fairy Chessmen* (Jan.-Feb. 1946)
32. Robert Silverberg's *Shadrach in the Furnace* (Aug.-Oct. 1976)
33. Hal Clement's *Needle* (May-June 1949)
34. Isaac Asimov's *The Currents of Space* (Oct.-Dec. 1952)
35. Mark Clifton and Frank Riley's *They'd Rather Be Right* (Aug.-Nov. 1954)
36. Jack Williamson's *The Legion of Space* (Apr.-Sept. 1934)
37. E. E. Smith's *The Skylark of Valeron* (Aug. '34-Feb. 1935)
38. John W. Campbell's *The Mightiest Machine* (Dec. '34-Apr. 1935)
39. H. P. Lovecraft's *At The Mountains of Madness* (Feb.-Apr. 1936)
40. Jack Williamson's *The Cometeers* (May-Aug. 1936
41. Jack Williamson's *The Legion of Time* (May-July 1938)

42. Clifford Simak's *Cosmic Engineers* (Feb.–Apr. 1939)
43. E. E. Smith's *Grey Lensman* (Oct. '39–Jan. 1940)

Twelve Notable SF and Fantasy Series

1. The *Darkover series*, by Marion Zimmer Bradley. Bradley has published well over a dozen books in the series, and a fan club, The Friends of Darkover, write their own additions to the series, three books of which have been published
2. The *Deathworld* series, by Harry Harrison. Limited so far to three volumes, the adventures of Jason dinAlt on various hostile worlds have nevertheless attracted a strong following
3. The *Dragon* series, by Anne McCaffrey. Consisting of three adult and three juvenile books, this is one of the most popular of all SF series
4. The *Dray Prescot* series, by Kenneth Bulmer (writing as Alan Burt Akers and subsequently as Dray Prescot). Influenced strongly by Edgar Rice Burroughs, this series has reached twenty-seven volumes at time of writing, and is still going strong
5. The *Dumarest* series, by E. C. Tubb. Running neck and neck with the Dray Prescot series (above), this saga of Earl Dumarest searching the galaxy for his legendary home world (Earth) has reached twenty-seven volumes without Earth yet in sight
6. The *Dune* series, by Frank Herbert. Perhaps the most commercially successful of all SF books, this series currently comprises four volumes, with a fifth on the way
7. The *Elric* series, by Michael Moorcock. In fact, the Elric series proper consists at present of six books, but owing to Moorcock's habit of making links between virtually all his published books, it could at a pinch be extended to some forty others
8. The *Fafhrd/Gray Mouser* series by Fritz Leiber. This is the longest running current series, the first story having appeared in 1939. At present it comprises six books plus a few short pieces. Sword and sorcery with a nicely ironic line in anti-heroism
9. The *Gor* series by John Norman. Up to sixteen volumes at time of writing, this series has provided less and less originality and more and more sadomasochism and bondage; its audience has grown

correspondingly. More interesting as psychopathology than as fiction

10. The *Perry Rhodan* series, by various authors. Over a hundred books have been translated into English, but that is only the tip of the iceberg. Over a thousand have appeared in its native Germany – and over 500 of a companion series, *Atlan!*

11. The *Riverworld* series, by Philip José Farmer. Originally conceived as a single novel in the early 1950s, this has now expanded to four novels, plus some short stories, with more promised

12. The *Stainless Steel Rat* series, by Harry Harrison. Four novels have so far been published, with more promised

Harlan Ellison's Top Eight SF Writers (1974)

In the course of a lengthy book review column, Ellison referred to James Tiptree Jr as 'one of our top eight writers at this moment'. He then went on: 'I'd like to dispense with the politic gibberish usually intended by the phrase "eight top writers" as a substitute for actually *naming* the best, and lay myself on the line with the eight I think rise head and shoulders above all the others working in our genre today. I exclude myself only out of a decorous sense of humility, as is my wont.'

1. Kate Wilhelm
2. R. A. Lafferty
3. James Tiptree Jr
4. Thomas M. Disch
5. Robert Silverberg
6. Barry Malzberg
7. Gene Wolfe
8. Joanna Russ

Source: *F&SF*, May 1974

The Five Most Useful SF Reference Books

1. Donald B. Day (compiler), *Index to the Science Fiction Magazines, 1926-50* (1952). Compiled as a labour of love, this index set high bibliographic standards for later companion volumes (notably the 1951-55 *Index* compiled under the auspices of the MIT SF Society), and is absolutely indispensable to anyone wishing to find their way around SF magazines, as are the following books
2. Donald H. Tuck, *The Encyclopedia of Science Fiction and Fantasy* (2 vols, 1974 and 1978). Though dogged by publication delays, and thus less useful than it might have been (cut-off date is 1968, since when a lot has happened), this remains an essential reference book largely because of the comprehensiveness of its bibliographic information. (A third volume was to appear, but there is no sign of it yet)
3. Peter Nicholls and John Clute (eds), *The Encyclopedia of Science Fiction* (1979). By far the best one-volume reference work available, and the one to have if you only have one. Encyclopedic in scope, if less detailed biographically than Tuck's book, and generally highly accurate. A second edition would be even more welcome
4. L. W. Currey, *Science Fiction and Fantasy Authors* (1979). A book primarily for collectors, but of general value because of the scrupulous accuracy of its bibliographic information, whose compilation and presentation is a model of scrupulous scholarship
5. Neil Barron (ed), *Anatomy of Wonder*, 2nd ed (1981). A great improvement on the first edition, valuable though that was. The best critical guide available, with annotations for close on 2,000 books, and particularly strong coverage of foreign language SF. Also a wealth of ancillary information

NB: This list does not include Pierre Versin's *Encyclopédie de l'Utopie et de la SF* (1972), a work comparable in scope to the Nicholls/Clute volume, but of less value to the English-speaking user, owing to its being in French

. . . and Five Fairly Useless Reference Books

1. Brian Ash, *Who's Who in Science Fiction* (1976). A derivative and inaccurate set of potted biographies
2. George S. Elrick, *Science Fiction Handbook for Readers and Writers* (1978). An eccentric and amateurish compilation of generally useless information
3. David Kyle, *The Illustrated Book of Science Fiction Ideas and Dreams* (1977). A follow-up to *The Pictorial History of Science Fiction*, this shows every sign of being thrown together in an enormous hurry. Much of it consists of as much quotation from various stories as could be got away with inside the copyright laws, strung together with perfunctory exposition
4. Colin Lester (ed), *The International SF Yearbook* (1978). A good idea, but compiled according to a lunatic system, and laid out in a manner which makes it impossible to use.
5. Franz Rottensteiner, *The Science Fiction Book* (1975). Rottensteiner is an iconoclastic Austrian critic, who has had a good time lambasting American SF over the years. An odd choice to produce a coffee-table book, he produced an odd book, scrappily arranged and lacking either useful information or critical bite

Stephen King's List of Important Fantasy and Horror Books

Richard Adams, *Watership Down*
J. G. Ballard, *Concrete Island*
Charles Beaumont, *Hunger*
Robert Bloch, *Pleasant Dreams*
Robert Bloch, *Psycho*
Ray Bradbury, *Something Wicked This Way Comes*
Joseph Payne Brennan, *The Shapes of Midnight*
Fredric Brown, *Nightmares and Geezenstacks*
Ramsey Campbell, *The Doll Who Ate His Mother*
Ramsey Campbell, *The Parasite*
Roald Dahl, *Kiss Kiss*
Roald Dahl, *Someone Like You*
Stephen R. Donaldson, The *Thomas Covenant* trilogy
Harlan Ellison, *Deathbird Stories*

Harlan Ellison, *Strange Wine*
Jack Finney, *The Body Snatchers*
Jack Finney, *The Third Level*
Jack Finney, *Time and Again*
William Golding, *Lord of the Flies*
Charles L. Grant, *The Sound of Midnight*
Davis Grubb, *Twelve Tales of Horror*
James Herbert, *The Spear*
William Hjortsberg, *Fallen Angel*
Shirley Jackson, *The Haunting of Hill House*
Shirley Jackson, *The Lottery and other stories*
Gerald Kersh, *Men Without Bones*
William Kotzwinkle, *Dr Rat*
Jerzy Kozinski, *The Painted Bird*
Fritz Leiber, *Our Lady of Darkness*
Ursula Le Guin, *The Lathe of Heaven*
Ira Levin, *Rosemary's Baby*
Michael McDowell, *The Amulet*
Michael McDowell, *Cold Moon Over Babylon*
Bernard Malamud, *The Magic Barrel*
Robert Marasco, *Burnt Offerings*
Richard Matheson, *I Am Legend*
Richard Matheson, *The Shrinking Man*
Joyce Carol Oates, *Nightside*
Flannery O'Connor, *A Good Man is Hard to Find*
Thomas Pynchon, *V.*
Ray Russell, *Sardonicus*
Joan Samson, *The Auctioneer*
Sarban, *The Sound of His Horn*
Anne Rivers Siddons, *The House Next Door*
Isaac Bashevis Singer, *The Seance and other stories*
Peter Straub, *Ghost Story*
Peter Straub, *Shadowland*
Theodore Sturgeon, *Some of your Blood*
Thomas Tryon, *The Other*
Les Whitten, *Progeny of the Adder*
Thomas Williams, *Tsuga's Children*
T. M. Wright, *Strange Seed*
John Wyndham, *The Day of the Triffids*
(From *Danse Macabre*, 1981)

NAL Bestsellers as at March 1982

1. *2001: A Space Odyssey*, Arthur C. Clarke (2,600,000)
2. *The Green Hills of Earth*, Robert Heinlein (1,303,000)
3. *The Puppet Masters*, Robert Heinlein (1,260,000)
4. *Revolt in 2100*, Robert Heinlein (1,123,000)
5. *The Man Who Sold the Moon*, Robert Heinlein (1,033,000)
6. *Door into Summer*, Robert Heinlein (950,000)
7. *Beyond this Horizon*, Robert Heinlein (949,000)
8. *Day After Tomorrow*, Robert Heinlein (935,000)
9. *Methuselah's Children*, Robert Heinlein (919,000)
10. *Double Star*, Robert Heinlein (805,000)

Berkley Bestsellers

1. *Stranger in a Strange Land*, Robert A. Heinlein (3,028,347)
2. *Dune Messiah*, Frank Herbert (2,257,576)
3. *Children of Dune*, Frank Herbert (2,051,788)
4. *Dune*, Frank Herbert (1,841,386)
5. *The Once and Future King*, T. H. White (1,728,953)
6. *Time Enough for Love*, Robert A. Heinlein (1,219,069)
7. *The Time Machine*, H. G. Wells (1,119,907)
8. *The Moon is a Harsh Mistress*, Robert Heinlein (817,013)
9. *Starship Troopers*, Robert Heinlein (690,013)
10. *The Dosadi Experiment*, Frank Herbert (678,088)

These figures are total numbers of copies in print. The return rate on these books is negligible but if you want you can subtract 10 per cent for a total sales figure. *Dune* was published by Ace for a number of years before Berkley took it over, so its figures represent only Berkley sales, and not the total sales of the title

Timescape's cumulative bestseller list as of January 1982

1. *The Mote in God's Eye*, Larry Niven and Jerry Pournelle
2. *The Book of the Dun Cow*, Walter Wangerin Jr

3. *Inferno,* Larry Niven and Jerry Pournelle
4. *Timescape,* Gregory Benford
5. *The Mercenary,* Jerry Pournelle
6. *Colony,* Ben Bova
7. *The Starchild Trilogy,* Frederik Pohl and Jack Williamson
8. *The Entropy Effect,* Vonda McIntyre
9. *The White Hart,* Nancy Springer
10. *Where Late the Sweet Birds Sang,* Kate Wilhelm
11. *West of Honor,* Jerry Pournelle
12. *The Last Defender of Camelot,* Roger Zelazny
13. *The Demu Trilogy,* F. M. Busby
14. *High Justice,* Jerry Pournelle
15. *Birth of Fire,* Jerry Pournelle
16. *The Silver Sun,* Nancy Springer
17. *The Sable Moon,* Nancy Springer
18. *The Shadow of the Torturer,* Gene Wolfe
19. *The Demolished Man,* Alfred Bester
20. *The Weapon Shops of Isher,* A. E. Van Vogt
21. *Golem 100,* Alfred Bester
22. *E Pluribus Unicorn,* Theodore Sturgeon
23. *The Ruins of Isis,* Marion Zimmer Bradley
24. *The Road to Corlay,* Richard Cowper
25. *Journey,* Marta Randall
26. *The Best of Poul Anderson*
27. *Retief and the Warlord,* Keith Laumer
28. *The Eyes of the Overworld,* Jack Vance
29. *Retief's War,* Keith Laumer
30. *The Best Science Fiction of the Year No 10,* ed Terry Carr
31. *The Devil's Game,* Poul Anderson
32. *Retief, Emissary to the Stars,* Keith Laumer
33. *The Best of Keith Laumer*
34. *Juniper Time,* Kate Wilhelm
35. *The Cosmic Rape,* Theodore Sturgeon
36. *The Voyage of the Space Beagle,* A. E. Van Vogt
37. *The Blessing Papers,* William Barnwell
38. *The Weapon Makers,* A. E. Van Vogt
39. *Dangerous Games,* Marta Randall
40. *Beauty,* Robin McKinley

Sphere Books Bestsellers

Star Wars, George Lucas (1,089,219)
Close Encounters of the Third Kind, S. Spielberg (602,019)
The Empire Strikes Back, Donald F. Glut (547,101)
Splinter of the Mind's Eye, A. D. Foster (196,431)
Pebble in the Sky, I. Asimov (131,999)
The Empire Strikes Back (junior ed), Donald F. Glut (122,687)
Fade Out, Patrick Tilley (113,094)
Ringworld, Larry Niven (111,081)
Star Fire, Ingo Swann (83,804)
Stainless Steel Rat's Revenge, H. Harrison (82,873)
The Best of Arthur C. Clarke, A. C. Clarke (82,177)
Blake's Seven, Trevor Hoyle (80,317)
The Best of Isaac Asimov, I. Asimov (78,884)
Timescape, Gregory Benford (76,645)
Invasion of the Body Snatchers, Jack Finney (74,706)
Stainless Steel Rat Saves the World, H. Harrison (74,012)

The Ten Longest-Serving SF and Fantasy Writers

1. Frank Belknap Long (first published fantasy *The Desert Lich*, 1924)
2. E. Hoffman Price (first published fantasy *Rajah's Gift*, 1925)
3. Manly Wade Wellman (first published fantasy *Back to the Beast*, 1927)
4. Jack Williamson (first published SF *The Metal Man*, 1928)
5. Raymond Z. Gallun (first published SF *The Space Dwellers* and *The Crystal Ray*, 1929)
6. Clifford Simak (first published SF *World of the Red Sun*, 1931)
7. Robert Bloch (first published *Lilies*, 1934)
8. André Norton (first SF story *People of the Crater* announced in 1935, though it failed to appear until 1947 because the publisher ran out of money)
9. L. Sprague de Camp (first published SF *The Isolinguals*, 1937)
10. Frederik Pohl (first published SF *Elegy to a Dead Planet: Luna* (poem), 1937)

(The list on p. 197 refers only to the *SF and fantasy* writing careers of authors who are still living and have published recently enough to be considered active. It does not include writers who are still active only as editors, such as H. L. Gold and Donald A. Wollheim (first story 1934 in each case); or writers who are still alive but no longer active, such as Stanton A. Coblentz (first SF of 1928), C. L. Moore (1933) and William F. Temple (1935); or writers who are now dead but had SF/fantasy writing careers of comparable lengths, such as Murray Leinster (publishing career 1919-69) and H. G. Wells (1894-1941); or writers who had careers in other fields before turning to SF, such as A. E. Van Vogt, who sold his first story in 1932, but his first SF in 1939)

Eight Long-Interrupted Careers

1. *Arthur Tofts: 32 years* (1940-72) Tofts published five stories between 1938 and 1940, then was not heard of again until he started contributing to Roger Elwood anthologies in 1972, after his retirement. He published a couple of novels before his death in 1980
2. *Julian May: 28 years* (1953–81) May published a couple of short stories, including the anthologized 'Dune Roller'. She then fell silent until *The Many-Colored Land* was published, to great acclaim
3. *Hilbert Schenck: 24 years* (1953–77) Schenck published a story in *F&SF* in 1953, after which there was nothing (excepting a few short poems, which we don't count) until 1977, when he emerged as a writer of great promise with such stories as 'The Morphology of the Kirkham Wreck'
4. *Donald Kingsbury: 23 years* (1953–71) Kingsbury is another writer who published a couple of stories, went away, and then returned to build a promising career
5. *E. Hoffman Price: 18 years* (1953–71) One of the longest-serving SF or fantasy writers, Price took a long break from the genres during this period
6. *Raymond Z̧. Gallun: 13 years* (1961–74) Gallun has had more than one break from SF publishing, but this was the longest
7. *Alfred Bester: 9 years* (1963–72) Bester published no fiction in this

period, though he was active as a freelance writer in other fields

8. *Bob Shaw: 9 years* (1956–65) Shaw published a number of stories in the mid-'50s, but was dissatisfied, and took a self-imposed break until he felt mature enough to resume his career

Five Famous Authors Who Started Their Careers in the SF Magazines

1. *Tennessee Williams* (first published story was *The Vengeance of Nitocris*, which appeared in *Weird Tales*, August 1928, under the byline Thomas Lanier Williams – the author's given name. Williams was just fourteen years old when the story was published)

2. *Howard Fast* (first published story was *Wrath of the Purple* in *Amazing Stories*, October 1932. Fast has published occasional SF throughout his career, and has stated that by choice he would write nothing else)

3. *John D. Macdonald* (first published story *Cosmetics* in *Astounding Science Fiction*, February 1948. Macdonald wrote prolifically for the SF pulp magazines before embarking on his career as a thriller writer)

4. *John Jakes* (first published story *Machine* in *F&SF*, April 1952. Jakes wrote about 20 SF and fantasy novels and many short stories before his 'Bicentennial' series made him one of America's all-time best-selling writers)

5. *Stephen King* (first published story *The Glass Door* in *Startling Mystery Stories*, Autumn 1967, a very-obscure, low-budget magazine)

The Ubiquitous Isaac Asimov

A true legend in his own time, Isaac Asimov has written well over 200 books. Although he began primarily as a science fiction author and remains one of the leading names in the field to this day, he soon became an expert popularizer of science and has covered virtually every scientific discipline in book form, dictionaries and text-books

199

(ranging from biochemistry to physics, astronomy, ecology, every facet of astronomy and the planets, photosynthesis, etc.). However, this list highlights the more unusual subjects, usually outside the realm of science, he has also covered in book form (we have excluded single articles or the list would have proved endless)

Races (*Races and People*, 1955)
Myths (*Words from the Myths*, 1961)
Genesis (*Words from Genesis*, 1962)
Exodus (*Words from Exodus*, 1963)
The Greeks (*The Greeks*, 1965)
The Slide Rule (*An Easy Introduction to the Slide Rule*, 1965)
Rome (*The Roman Republic*, 1966 and *The Roman Empire*, 1967)
Egypt (*The Egyptians*, 1967)
The Near East (*The Near East*, 1968)
The Dark Ages (*The Dark Ages*, 1968)
History (*Words from History*, 1968)
The Bible (*Asimov's Guide to the Bible*, Vol 1, 1968 and Vol 2, 1969)
England (*The Shaping of England*, 1969)
Shakespeare (*Asimov's Guide to Shakespeare*, 1970)
Constantinople (*Constantinople*, 1970)
Smut (*The Sensuous Dirty Old Man*, 1971)
Humor (*Isaac Asimov's Treasury of Humor*, 1971)
France (*The Shaping of France*, 1972)
Don Juan (*Asimov's Annotated 'Don Juan'*, 1972)
The USA (*The Shaping of North America*, 1973)
Dinosaurs (*How Did We Find Out About Dinosaurs?*, 1973)
Germs (*How Did We Find Out About Germs?*, 1974)
Paradise Lost (*Asimov's Annotated 'Paradise Lost'*, 1974)
Vitamins (*How Did We Find Out About Vitamins?*, 1974)
Limericks (*Lecherous Limericks*, 1975 and sequels)
Poetry (*Familiar Poems Annotated*, 1976)
Sherlock Holmes (*Asimov's Sherlockian Limericks*, 1977)
Earthquakes (*How Did We Find Out About Earthquakes?*, 1978)
Autobiography (*In Memory Yet Green*, 1979 and sequel)

Twelve SF and Fantasy Suicides

A high proportion of creative artists have taken their own lives.

Relatively few have done so, however, in the SF and fantasy fields; let us hope the low batting average continues.

1. Neil Bell, a prolific British author whose real name was Stephen Southwold, in 1964
2. Karin Boye, the Danish author of *Kallocain*, in 1941
3. Claude F. Cheinisse, the French writer in 1982, after murdering his two daughters and his mother in a fit of depression
4. David R. Daniels, an occasional *Astounding* contributor, in 1936
5. Egon Friedell, the Austrian author of *The Return of the Time Machine*, in 1938
6. Romain Gary, a well-known personality of French diplomatic and literary circles, many of whose novels are borderline fantasy; in 1980, a few years after the suicide of his wife, the actress Jean Seberg
7. Peter George, the British author of *Red Alert*, which became Kubrick's *Dr Strangelove* movie; in 1966
8. Robert E. Howard, the creator of Conan, in 1936
9. Johanne Marsais, a young but promising French writer, in her early twenties in 1980
10. H. Beam Piper, while at the height of his SF success, in 1964
11. Edward Lucas White, fantasy author of *Lukundoo*; in 1934
12. Robert H. Wilson, the author of just two stories *Out Around Rigel* and *A Flight Into Time*; in 1931 while still in his twenties

Eight of the Longest SF/Fantasy Novels

Of course, it all depends on what you call a novel. SF and fantasy are full of series, some of which may run into millions of words, and if they were put in a single volume any of them might be called a novel as they feature the same characters in a progression of adventures. However, we only class a multi-volume work as a novel if there is clear evidence that it was conceived – and generally written – as a single work, and broke into several books for practical purposes.

1. Samuel R. Delany, *Dhalgren*. Published in 1975, Delany's blockbuster runs to 879 pages, and probably close on 400,000 words
2. Stephen Donaldson, *Chronicles of Thomas Covenant the Unbeliever*. Published in 1977 in three volumes, but written and sold as a single massive work, this has a continuous narrative which

clearly establishes it as a three-volume novel rather than a trilogy. Its length is about 500,000 words

3. Stephen King, *The Stand*. Published in 1978, this 823-page monster was reportedly cut from a substantially longer type-script! Even so, it runs to over 350,000 words

4. Kurt Lasswitz, *Auf Zwei Planeten* (*Twin Planets*). This massive novel, first published in 1897, has never been published in its entirety in English. An abridged translation runs to about 200,000 words; the original is much longer

5. J. R. R. Tolkien, *Lord of the Rings*. Like Stephen Donaldson's later work, this was written as a single narrative and split into three books for publishing convenience. It is about 450,000 words long

6. Gene Wolfe, *The Book of the New Sun*. Published in four volumes during 1980-2, this was carefully written and rewritten over a period of several years beforehand, and its continuous narrative establishes it as a four-volume novel. At time of writing the fourth volume is still to appear, but the work can be predicted to span about 1,100 pages and 400,000 words in all

7. Austin Tappan Wright, *Islandia*. Wright spent much of his life working out this imaginary realm in enormous detail. Eleven years after his death a novel was published, culled from his work. Though it contains only a portion of his work it spans 1,018 pages and perhaps 450,000 words

8. Roger Zelazny, *The Chronicles of Amber*. Published in five volumes between 1970 and 1977, this is a work Zelazny began to plan in 1967, at which time he predicted its length at 250,000 words. In the event it is nearer 375,000, and certainly makes little sense unless read as a single work

Six SF Short Stories Whose Combined Word Length Equals That of This Heading

The short-short story (roughly 1,000 words or fewer) is very popular in science fiction, but few short-shorts can rival the following. Word lengths given do not include the words of the title.

1. Edward Wellen: *If Eve Had Failed To Conceive* (0 words)

2. Edward Wellen: *Why Booth Did Not Shoot Lincoln* (0 words)
3. Forrest J. Ackerman: *Atomigeddon 2419 AD* (2 words)
4. Duane Ackerson: *The Sign at the End of the Universe* (3 words)
5. Roger Deeley: *The Shortest SF Story Ever Told* (3 words)
6. E. Michael Blake: *Science Fiction for Telepaths* (6 words)

Thirty Famous Writers Who Have Published SF

There are many famous writers who are closely identified with science fiction, such as Verne and Wells. But a surprising number of others, including many giants of world literature, have dabbled in the genre.

1. Kingsley Amis (*The Alteration, Russian Hide and Seek*)
2. John Barth (*Giles Goat-Boy*)
3. Anthony Burgess (*A Clockwork Orange, The Wanting Seed*)
4. Samuel Butler (*Erewhon*)
5. G. J. Chesterton (*The Napoleon of Notting Hill*)
6./7. Joseph Conrad and Ford Madox Ford (*The Inheritors*)
8. Fyodor Dostoevsky (*The Dream of a Ridiculous Man*)
9. Lawrence Durrell (*Tunc, Nunquam*)
10. C. S. Forester (*The Peacemaker*)
11. E. M. Forster (*The Machine Stops*)
12. William Golding (*Envoy Extraordinary*)
13. Robert Graves (*Watch the North Wind Rise*)
14. L. P. Hartley (*Facial Justice*)
15. Nathaniel Hawthorne (*The Birthmark*)
16. John Hersey (*The Child Buyer, White Lotus, My Petition for More Space*)
17. Hermann Hesse (*The Glass Bead Game*)
18. Aldous Huxley, (*Brave New World, After Many A Summer*)
19. Rudyard Kipling (*Easy as ABC, With the Night Mail*)
20. Doris Lessing (*Memoirs of a Survivor, Canopus in Argos: Archives*)
21. Jack London (*The Iron Heel, The Star Rover*)
22. Herman Melville (*The Bell Tower*)
23. Vladimir Nabokov (*Ada*)
24. Thomas Pynchon (*Gravity's Rainbow*)
25. Alan Sillitoe (*Travels in Nihilon*)

26. George Bernard Shaw (*Back to Methuselah*)
27. Anthony Trollope (*The Fixed Period*)
28. Gore Vidal (*Messiah, Kalki*)
29. Evelyn Waugh (*Scott-King's Modern Europe, Love Among the Ruins*)
30. Angus Wilson (*The Old Men at the Zoo*)

Six Writers Who Published More Than a Million Words of SF/Fantasy by Their Thirtieth Birthday

A million words is a lot of fiction – equivalent to fifteen or sixteen ordinary-length novels. To get this amount into print you need to start young and be fairly prolific from the outset. Those who have managed it include:

1. John Brunner (born September 1934; published 25 novels by February 1964, in addition to countless short stories)
2. R. L. Fanthorpe (born February 1935; published over 100 novels by the end of 1964)
3. Dean R. Koontz (born July 1945; published 18 novels by the end of 1974)
4. Michael Moorcock (born December 1939; published 17 novels, plus a huge mass of other material, by mid-1969)
5. Robert Silverberg (born January 1935; had published 20 solo novels, plus 2 collaborations, plus hundreds of short stories, by the end of 1964)
6. Brian Stableford (born July 1948; published 20 novels by the end of 1977)

Other contenders for this dubious honour must include three prolific contributors to the pulp magazines: Otto ('Eando') Binder, Henry Kuttner and Jack Williamson

The Six Most Prolific SF Novelists

1. R. L. Fanthorpe – *120 novels*
2. John Russell Fearn – *90 novels*

3. E. C. Tubb - *89 novels*
4. Kenneth Bulmer - *80 novels*
5. André Norton - *80 novels*
6. Ron Goulart - *69 novels*

With the exception of Fanthorpe these authors have also published novels - sometimes in great numbers - outside the SF/fantasy genres; these are not included in the totals. (If they were, Bulmer would no doubt be the leader.) Britons can take pride (or otherwise) in the fact that the first four names on the list are all British; on the other hand certain American pulp writers of the 1930s and '40s, much of whose work was fringe SF - such as Walter Gibson (*The Shadow*) and Lester Dent (*Doc Savage* and *The Avenger*) - can rival anybody for prolificacy. These figures were compiled in March 1982; by the time this book appears the totals will doubtless have advanced in several cases.

Six SF Authors Whose Claim to Fame Rests on a Single Story

1. Jerome Bixby ('It's A *Good* Life')
2. Tom Godwin ('The Cold Equations')
3. Daniel Keyes ('Flowers for Algernon')
4. T. L. Sherred ('E for Effort')
5. George R. Stewart ('Earth Abides')
6. Bernard Wolfe ('Limbo')

Apart from Stewart, all have published other SF stories and novels, but were it not for the above their names would hardly be remembered. As it is their fame is secure.

Seventeen Major Writers Who Haven't Published in Astounding/Analog

Although not the oldest magazine in existence in the SF field, *Astounding Science Fiction*, now *Analog*, still holds the title of the most prestigious. This is very much due to the editorial influence of the great John W. Campbell Jr who single-handedly ushered in what is now known as 'The Golden Age of SF'. It is generally assumed that all the big names in the field have, at one time or another in their careers, contributed to the magazine. This is, however, not so. These are the famous writers who have never figured on its contents page.

1. Brian W. Aldiss
2. J. G. Ballard
3. Robert Bloch
4. Ray Bradbury
5. Samuel R. Delany
6. Thomas M. Disch
7. Philip José Farmer
8. Daniel F. Galouye
9. R. A. Lafferty
10. Ursula K. Le Guin
11. Richard A. Lupoff
12. Richard Matheson
13. Michael Moorcock
14. Ward Moore
15. Keith Roberts
16. John Sladek
17. Cordwainer Smith

Astounding/Analog's Most Prolific Authors

Astounding/Analog's roll-call of writers is most prestigious. Based on *The Complete Index to Astounding/Analog*, published by Robert Weinberg, here is a list detailing the record number of appearances in the magazine (fiction only) of its major contributors*:

1. Poul Anderson (82 appearances)
2. Randall Garrett (77)
3. Christopher Anvil (74)
4. Murray Leinster (60)
5. Nat Schachner (60)
6. A. E. Van Vogt (59)

*As of December 1979

7. Mack Reynolds (57)
8. Jack Williamson (56)
9. Eric Frank Russell (54)
10. Isaac Asimov (50)
11. Gordon Dickson (48)
12. Clifford Simak (45)
13. Raymond Gallun (43)
14. Henry Kuttner (43)
15. Harry Harrison (41)
16. George O. Smith (41)
17. James Schmitz (39)
18. L. Ron Hubbard (37)
19. Malcolm Jameson (37)
20. Robert Heinlein (36)

Eight Corporate SF Authors

Forming yourself into a company has, under certain circumstances, tax advantages for writers, and of late more and more have been doing it. Some of these companies have rather prosaic names – e.g. John Brunner's copyrights are held by Brunner Fact and Fiction Ltd – but some are less obvious:

1. Brian Aldiss – Southmoor Serendipity
2. Isaac Asimov – Nightfall, Inc.
3. Gregory Benford – Abbenford Associates
4. Harlan Ellison – The Kilimanjaro Corporation
5. Alan Dean Foster – Thranx, Inc.
6. Robert Silverberg – Agberg, Ltd
7. Brian Stableford – Cosmic Perspectives Ltd
8. Peter Straub – The Seafront Corporation

The Science Fiction Plutocracy

Inflation being what it is, it is misleading simply to list big advances. This year's record is sure to be beaten next year. (At present the record stands at $2 million, this being the advance reportedly paid for Carl Sagan's first novel, *Contact*. As Sagan has never published SF and the novel shows no sign of appearing at time of writing, we note this information, but leave him off the list.) The following is an informed guess at the twelve most prosperous SF writers.

1. *Isaac Asimov* In his autobiography, Asimov gives year by year details of his income, until he evidently becomes embarrassed at its size. In 1962 he was earning $72,000 a year. By 1970, the only subsequent figure cited, he was up to $200,000. At the time of writing his new novel, *Foundation's Edge*, has a minimum $500,000 paperback offer in the USA. It's a safe bet he's a millionaire

2. *Ray Bradbury* Bradbury does not publish details of massive sales, or boast about his income; nor does he publish much fiction these days. Nevertheless, his work is constantly reprinted, new material appears in the highest paying markets, and he commands very large lecture fees. Despite his low profile, Bradbury is a certainty for this list

3. *Arthur C. Clarke* In the early 1970s it was Clarke who made SF readers – and perhaps some writers – aware of the top writers' earning power when he signed an American three-book contract for $500,000. (The books were *Rendezvous with Rama*, *Imperial Earth*, and *The Fountains of Paradise*. The publishers probably got a bargain.) More recently Clarke was the first mainstream SF author to move into the seven-figure bracket when his sequel to *2001 – 2010: Odyssey Two* – sold for $1 million

4. *Stephen R. Donaldson* Donaldson is the dark horse in this race. A couple of years ago he would have been nowhere, but with the fifth Thomas Covenant book, *The One Tree*, high on the bestseller lists on both sides of the Atlantic, and sales of its predecessors booming nicely, he is obviously leaping into contention

5. *Harlan Ellison* Like Bradbury, Ellison makes no massive novel sales, owing to his incapacity for writing novels. However, he is free with details of his income from short stories, journalism and lectures, and it apparently amounts to around $100,000 per year, making him comfortably plutocratic, if possibly the least wealthy of the writers on this list

6. *Robert Heinlein* With a massive backlist, and thirteen titles

featured on just two publishers' all-time bestseller lists (see elsewhere in this book), Heinlein hardly needs recent success to assure his place. However, his $500,000 advance for *Number of the Beast* and the undisclosed but larger sum paid for *Friday*, provide further confirmation

7. *Frank Herbert* The largest advance paid to a mainstream SF author is the $1.5 million which Herbert received for US rights alone on the fifth *Dune* novel. Added to that was another $750,000 for a fringe-SF novel, *The White Plague*. With the first three *Dune* books all having sold well over 2 million copies in their US editions, the fourth having been a massive bestseller in hardcover and trade paperback, and the first book having sold to the movies for around a million dollars, it's small wonder that Herbert was able to buy his very own Hawaiian island

8. *Stephen King* King is the bestselling phenomenon of modern American fiction. When he switched publishers a few years ago he commanded $2 million for a three-book contract. Each of those three books – *The Dead Zone*, *Firestarter* and *Cujo* – was a No 1 bestseller, so it was money well spent for the publisher. His earlier novels have probably sold even more, particularly *The Shining*, and he recently signed a contract for a collaboration with Peter Straub, *The Talisman*, for between one and two million dollars. It's reasonable to assume that King enjoys moderate financial security

9. *Anne McCaffrey* No figures are available about McCaffrey's books, but with *The White Dragon* a national bestseller, and its predecessors going through multiple printings and hundreds of thousands of copies, she almost certainly belongs here

10. *Larry Niven and Jerry Pournelle* Two authors for the price of one here – but it's a hefty price. Niven started with an advantage, being the scion of a wealthy family with a trust fund to cushion him against adversity. It was not until he teamed up with Pournelle, however, that he hit the real financial bigtime in SF. Their novel *Lucifer's Hammer* sold to paperback for what was then an SF record of $236,500. More recently a forthcoming novel – called variously *The Foot*, *Footfall*, or *The Heel of Vishnu* – fetched $600,000, and another book, *The Moat Around Murcheson's Eye*, also commanded an unspecified six-figure sum

11. *Robert Silverberg* Silverberg has hit the SF jackpot only once, with *Lord Valentine's Castle*, which sold US rights for $127,500.

However, in his early years Silverberg was one of the most prolific writers of all time – in or out of SF – and invested his income shrewdly. He was rumoured to be a millionaire by the time he was thirty

12. *Kurt Vonnegut* Specific figures are not available, but since the publication of *Slaughterhouse Five* Vonnegut has been one of the major American bestsellers, and must be considered in the Stephen King league

Five Notable SF Lawsuits

1. Donald A. Wollheim and others vs. Hugo Gernsback. In 1934 Gernsback published Wollheim's first story in *Wonder Stories*, but did not pay him. Wollheim contacted other contributors to the magazine, found several of them in a similar position, and got together with some to take legal action. Gernsback settled out of court for a reported $75, of which $10 went in legal fees

2. Donald A. Wollheim vs James Blish, Chester Cohen, Virginia Kidd, Damon Knight, Robert A. W. Lowndes, Judith Merril, and Larry Shaw. All were members of the most famous of SF fan groups, the Futurians. Wollheim's close friend John Michel had been romantically involved with Merril, but broke it off – he claimed at Wollheim's insistence. The seven defendants published a fanzine denouncing Wollheim, who responded with a libel suit. It was eventually dropped, but cost the defendants $600 in legal fees, and left some lasting bitterness. This happened in 1945, but it is said that Blish and Wollheim did not speak for some thirty years afterwards

3. Judith Merril vs Harlan Ellison and Metropolitan-Goldwyn-Mayer. Merril sued over an episode of *The Man From UNCLE*, scripted by Ellison, and containing a character Merril claimed to be slanderously based on herself. The case was settled out of court for a reported $5,000

4. Harlan Ellison and Ben Bova vs ABC-TV and Paramount Pictures. Ellison and Bova claimed that the 1973 TV series *Future Cop* plagiarized their short story 'Brillo' and a TV adaptation thereof. They won the case in 1980 and were awarded $337,000 ($154,000 actual damages and $183,000 punitive damages), but settled for $285,000 to avoid appeals and further legal costs.

More wrangling followed when the defendants claimed that Ellison had slandered and libelled them in various remarks

5. A. E. Van Vogt vs 20th Century Fox. This case was settled amicably in 1980 without reaching court. It was based on similarities between the movie *Alien* and Van Vogt's story 'Discord in Scarlet' (which forms part of his novel *Voyage of the Space Beagle*). No direct plagiarism was alleged, and eventually a settlement of $50,000 was agreed

My Six Favourite Fan Letters (by Ian Watson)

1. From Joe X— (American soldier, New York State):
Hey Ian! I been reading your books, man. Far out! Like, where do you get your dope, man? Do you snort it man, raw? I bet you do that tantric fucking too . . . You sure know your needles, man, i.e. 'Thy Blood Like Milk.' But I liked it!! I like all your shit, man. Does that make me nuts too??

2. From P. Y. N—. (France):
I find this novel interesting, though your knowledge of Go seems elementary . . .

3. From X—. (Oregon):
If you fuck with your readers' heads, you can expect a bloody nose . . .

4. From F. X . (Connecticut):
I just finished reading your book and think the following people would interest your Khidr. Greta Woodrow in Westport Connecticut who has bent 21 metals under laboratory conditions during Tesla Convention. Dan Elkins in Kentucky wrote *Secret of the UFOs* in nexus with Andrija. He was in synchron when Trundell was burned to death by Venus.

5. From R. X—. (California):
In the October issue of your magazine appeared 'The Dog Flea Version'. The author's name was Ian Watson. Several years ago, I had a good friend by that name . . .

6. From M. X—. (Florida):
The question I want answered most badly is, did the whales themselves impart any of the ideas to you?

Ian Watson

Professions of SF writers

Authors have, by tradition, interesting lives if one were to believe the often bizarre succession of professions they have held according to dustjacket blurbs and biographical information. Reality is often more prosaic. In listing the following examples, we have automatically omitted writers who have been editors, scientists, agents, doctors, teachers, journalists, librarians or standard academics. In all cases we have selected professions which the author has been in for an appreciable amount of time to avoid the paraphernalia of holiday and temporary occupations. This list could be much longer but is geared either to the unusual or to areas which one least expects from the writers in question.

Mark Adlard, sales manager in the steel industry
Pierre Barbet, pharmacist
T. J. Bass, pathologist and consultant to the National Joggers Association
Gregory Benford, professor of physics
James Blish, public relations officer for a tobacco company
Jesse F. Bone, professor of veterinary medicine
Edward Bryant, disc jockey
David R. Bunch, cartographer
Francis Carsac, professor of prehistory
A. Bertram Chandler, ship's master
D. G. Compton, abridger for *Reader's Digest*
Michael Coney, hotel manager and forestry official
Glen Cook, various production line work for General Motors
L. P. Davies, optician
Charles V. de Vet, postal worker
Dominique Douay, cabinet secretary in French government
G. C. Edmondson, blacksmith
Ivan Efremov, paleontologist
Suzette Haden Elgin, professor of linguistics
R. L. Fanthorpe, school headmaster
Mark Geston, attorney-at-law
Charles Harness, patents attorney
Maxim Jakubowski, fruit-juice salesman
Michel Jeury, castle janitor

Neil R. Jones, insurance claims examiner
Lee Killough, radiographer
Russell Kirk, professor of politics
Katherine Kurtz, police technician
Keith Laumer, diplomat (embassy secretary)
R. W. Mackleworth, insurance sales manager
William F. Nolan, greetings cards designer
John Norman, professor of philosophy
Chad Oliver, professor of anthropology
Jerry Pournelle, political campaign manager
Christopher Priest, accountant
Seabury Quinn, editor of the *Morticians Trade Journal*
Rudy Rucker, lecturer in the philosophy of mathematics
Josephine Saxton, restaurant cook
Cordwainer Smith, diplomat and professor of Asiatic studies
E. E. Smith, organic chemist (specialized for years in seeking a way to
    enable sugar to stick to doughnuts)
Theodore Thomas, patents lawyer
James Tiptree Jr, psychologist
E. C. Tubb, shirt salesman
Wilson Tucker, cinema projectionist
Vernor Vinge, professor of mathematics
Karl Edward Wagner, psychiatrist
William Jon Watkins, professor of humanities
Stefan Wul, dentist
Robert F. Young, foundry inspector
Roger Zelazny, social security claims representative

SF and Fantasy Writers Who Gave It Up and Did Better Doing Something Else
by Richard A. Lupoff

1. Steve Allen (became television star)
2. Alan Arkin (became successful actor)
3. Benjamin Disraeli (became Prime Minister of England)
4. Joe Gores (became mystery writer, *Hammett*, etc.)
5. L. Ron Hubbard (became founder and world head of Dianetics
   and Scientology)
6. John Jakes (became best-selling historical novelist)

213

7. Frederick T. Jane (became world's leading authority on ships and aircraft)
8. Frank K. Kelly (became Presidential speech-writer for Harry S. Truman)
9. Salvatore A. Lombino (became leading 'straight' novelist Evan Hunter *and* mystery writer Ed McBain)
10. John D. MacDonald (became leading author of general bestsellers (*Condominium*) and mysteries ('Travis McGee' series, etc.))
11. Edison Tesla Marshall (dropped the Tesla and became writer of million-selling historical romances)
12. Frank M. Robinson and Thomas Scortia (became co-authors, of best-selling 'techno-thrillers' (*The Glass Inferno*, etc.))
13. Thomas Lanier Williams (as Tennessee Williams, became world-famous playwright)

Richard A. Lupoff

Twenty Scientists Who Are Also SF Writers, and Vice Versa

Tradition has it that science fiction is predominantly read by people with technical training. Many scientists have dabbled with indifferent success in SF. This list includes only people who have reached a position of some eminence in either science or science fiction or (more rarely) both.

1. Isaac Asimov (Until 1958, when he became a full-time writer, Asimov was Associate Professor of Biochemistry at Boston University. He still retains the title)
2. Gregory Benford (a full Professor of Physics at the University of California and acknowledged authority on certain aspects of advanced particle theory – as well as being an award-winning SF writer – Benford qualifies as the most successful modern combiner of the two roles)
3. Arthur C. Clarke (Though Clarke's formal scientific training was completed after he published his pioneering paper on communications satellites, and though he has never truly been a working scientist, his accomplishments certainly qualify him for inclusion)
4. Robert L. Forward (An expert on theories of spaceflight, and

author of many influential scientific papers on the subject – some of which have inspired such writers as Larry Niven and Jerry Pournelle – Dr Forward is also the author of the Hugo Award nominated novel *Dragon's Egg*)

5. J. B. S. Haldane (An eminent twentieth-century biologist, Professor Haldane also wrote the SF novel *The Man With Two Memories*)

6. Fred Hoyle (Britain's most noted astronomer, recipient of a knighthood, Hoyle has also written or collaborated on many SF novels, the most notable of which remains his first, *The Black Cloud*)

7. Julian Huxley (Brother of Aldous Huxley, famous biologist, first Director-General of UNESCO, Huxley is also the author of an often reprinted SF story, 'The Tissue-Culture Kings', first published in *Amazing Stories* in 1927)

8. Philip Latham (This was the pseudonym used in his SF – which included two juvenile novels – by noted American astronomer Robert S. Richardson)

9. Stanislaw Lem (The most famous East European SF writer, author of *Solaris*, Lem trained as a medical doctor, but has published a variety of scientific papers and books. His magnum opus, not so far translated into English, is *Summa Technologiae*, described as 'a breathtakingly brilliant survey of possible social, informational, cybernetic, cosmogonic and biological engineering')

10. Willy Ley (A German-born scientist who emigrated to the USA in 1935, Ley was one of the pioneers of the theory and practice of rocket propulsion. He was also a noted scientific popularizer and published SF under the pseudonym 'Robbert Willey')

11. Patrick Moore (An astronomer who has become a TV personality in the UK, Moore is also the author of more than a dozen SF adventures for children, as well as a book about SF)

12. Carl Sagan (The pre-eminent scientific popularizer of our day, Sagan has not so far published any SF – but he has contracted to write an SF novel for a huge advance)

13. E. E. Smith (Author of the much-loved *Skylark* and *Lensman* series, Smith spent his working life as a research chemist; one project which occupied much of his time was to find a method to make the sugar stick on to doughnuts!)

14. Boris Strugatsky (One half of the writing brothers Strugatsky –

who are to Russian SF what Asimov, Clarke and Le Guin rolled into one are to the West – Boris Strugatsky worked as a computer mathematician at a Russian observatory before becoming a full-time writer)

15. Leo Szilard (An important physicist, who worked on the Manhattan Project, and after World War II threw his energies into working for atomic weapons control, Szilard also published a book of SF stories, *The Voice of the Dolphin*)

16. John Taine (One of the most popular and imaginative SF writers of the 1920s and '30s, 'Taine' was a pseudonym for Eric Temple Bell, a Scottish-born mathematician who became a US citizen and published many books on his subject)

17. Konstantin Tsiolkovsky (Along with Robert Goddard in the USA and Hermann Oberth in Germany, Tsiolkovsky was one of the three pioneers of rocketry. He also dramatized his ideas in fiction, most notably the novel *Beyond the Planet Earth*)

18. W. Grey Walter (Pioneer in the field of electroencephalography, and author of a basic study of the brain, Dr Grey Walter also wrote an SF novel variously titled *Further Outlook* and *The Curve of the Snowflake*)

19. H. G. Wells (Wells trained as a biologist under Darwin's most famous disciple, Thomas Huxley, and published two textbooks before turning to fiction)

20. Norbert Wiener (The virtual creator of the modern science of cybernetics, Wiener published two SF stories under the pseudonym 'W. Norbert'

Ten Favourite Scientific Errors
(by David Langford)

1. *The Cannon Into Space* In Jules Verne's *From the Earth to the Moon*, astronauts are fired at escape velocity from an immense cannon. Considering how much damage the human body can suffer on rapid acceleration to a few tens of kilometres per hour – as when hit by a car – it's not hard to appreciate that the sudden jerk forward to Earth's escape velocity of 40,000kph would convert the bold astronauts to a thin, displeasing layer of slime on their capsule's floor. (Later the projectile falls back to Earth. If it fell from infinity it would hit at no more than 40,000kph. It falls from

the Moon and hits at about 185,000kph. The passengers are unhurt).

2. *The Magical Gravity Screen* 'Cavorite' is the wonderful stuff in H. G. Wells's *The First Men In The Moon*, which blocks off the pull of gravity and lets his spacecraft float up like a balloon. Even in 1901 there was obviously something wrong with the idea, since it defied fundamental laws of physics by making energy available for nothing – in the story, the mere existence of Cavorite causes a tornado as the air above it rises weightlessly. Einstein's General Theory of Relativity later explained that gravity isn't a simple 'force' but a basic curving of space/time: to cancel gravity while keeping the mass which causes it is like trying to have a mountain without a slope. In 1948, long after this was understood, the real-life Gravity Research Foundation was set up to find a Cavorite equivalent; having become respectable in recent years, the Foundation is no longer believed to be trying very hard.

3. *Where No Helicopter Has Gone Before* There are sinister goings-on up on the Moon. A lady scientist escapes various difficulties. She flees in a helicopter . . . This would be worth a guffaw even if perpetrated in the primordial days of 1930s pulp SF: in fact the book is Judith Merril's *The Tomorrow People* (1960). Readers will hardly need to be reminded that helicopter blades don't push very effectively against near-perfect vacuum. Since sound can't travel in vacuum either (a sound wave being a compression of the air or other material) all those filmic meteoroids which go *whoooosh* past spacecraft also need to be taken with a pinch of sodium chloride.

4. *The Giant Spider In Splints* You've seen the film. Enormously enlarged by radiation, vitamins or fertilizer, the giant spider crashes jerkily through the forest, uttering strange cries . . . Assume this is quite a small giant spider, scaled up from (say) five millimetres to five metres in height: a modest factor of one thousand. So the spider's legs will be a thousand times thicker; their cross-sectional area (a measure of their strength) will be a thousand squared or a million times greater. But the volume and therefore the weight of the whole spider is scaled up by a thousand *cubed* – a thousand *million*. Those legs are carrying a weight one thousand times greater than they're equipped for; the unfortunate spider feels as though it had 999 similar monsters on its back. Its legs break under its own weight, its body collapses

squishily, the world is saved from the domination of giant spiders, and the film company goes bust.

5. *Next: The Giant Spiderweb* Even Brian Aldiss nods, and his *Hothouse* features some unlikely celestial mechanics. In the early versions of the story the Moon no longer circles the Earth but drifts along in a parallel orbit, stationary relative to Earth: and great 'spiders' spin webs between them. In fact, if the Moon stopped moving relative to Earth, it would fall down. The revised novel *Hothouse* adjusts this slightly by moving the Moon (how?) to the stable 'Trojan' position 150 million kilometres from both Sun and Earth – too far away even to be seen, let alone show as the 'silver half globe' of the book. We'll pass over the fact that the 150 million kilometre spiderweb would need to be many times stronger than the strongest fibres feasible today, if it were not to come apart thanks to the pull of its own weight . . .

6. *That Fearful Violet Ray* In book after book, lethal rays have blazed through space as mighty interstellar dreadnoughts open fire on one another – they come particularly thick and fast in the works of E. E. Smith. Just as the phenomenon was dying out in more respectable SF, it gained a further foothold in films and TV. What's the matter with rays, now we all know that lasers exist? It's the 'blazing through space' which fails to convince. There is no air in space. Therefore there are no air molecules. Therefore a beam of radiation will not be scattered, and without some scattered light it can't be seen. The target may glow, or flash, or puff into vapour, but between it and the beam weapon there's nothing photogenic. An example from an author who should know better: Fritz Leiber's *The Wanderer*, where the laser beams are not only visible in vacuum, but continue to be visible after the firing has stopped.

7. *Piggy's Glasses* William Golding's *Lord of the Flies* is only borderline SF/fantasy; but let's put it on record that not only straightforward SF authors make elementary mistakes of detail. Piggy is the myopic – short-sighted – boy in the story, whose glasses are commandeered for use as burning-lenses to start a fire. Unfortunately the corrective lenses for short sight would be concave. Such lenses don't concentrate the sun's rays, but spread them out. Unless the party included long-sighted or elderly wearers of glasses, it would be back to rubbing sticks together, or

(the pulp SF solution) constructing a small atomic generator from available materials.

8. *Ring Around the Sun* Pausing only to mention that early editions of Larry Niven's *Ringworld* had the Earth rotating in the wrong direction . . . let's look at the Ringworld itself. An artificial world, it's a 150 million kilometre (radius) ring with its sun in the middle. The set-up is gravitationally unstable in the plane of the ring, the Ringworld being balanced in the sun's gravity field in such a way that the tiniest nudge will send it off-centre with increasing acceleration until it hits the sun. (Niven's attempt to patch this up in a sequel, with endless 'attitude jets' bolted round the Ringworld's edge, was not really very convincing.) A world which is a hollow *sphere* with the sun in the middle – Bob Shaw's *Orbitsville* – is neither stable nor unstable in this way: with no more mathematical tools than were used by Isaac Newton, it can be calculated that the hollow sphere and its contents will drift independently of one another. Several authors including Wells failed to understand this: Ross Rocklynne's 'At the Centre of Gravity' features the plight of men trapped at the 'centre of gravity' of a hollow planet. In fact there would be no internal gravity field to keep them there, and by industrious spitting they could propel themselves to freedom.

9. *In the Country of the Blind, Everyone's Invisible* 'An invisible man would of course be blind' is a favourite ploy of clever sods who (like the present writer) enjoy picking holes in stories. If someone were perfectly invisible, his retinas would stop no light, and therefore he would be unable to see. As it happens – and despite what it says in the *Encyclopedia of SF* – H. G. Wells was aware of this; in *The Invisible Man* he was careful to arrange that his antihero's retinas should mysteriously remain *just* visible. The trouble with Wells's invisibility process is that it involves altering the refractive index of the body so you disappear in air, just as a cheap glass tumbler *almost* disappears in water thanks to the nearly identical refractive indexes of water and low-grade glass. Unfortunately refractive index is linked to physical density – or in plain language, to be invisible in air you need to be as light as air. SF also offers devices to make you invisible by 'bending light around you'. These cannot be recommended as Best Buys, since attempts to sketch what actually happens to light-rays suggest

219

that people will see things behind the 'invisible' wearer as distorted, mirror-imaged and upside down.

10. *The Fateful Glow of Radiation* Arthur C. Clarke speaks of the faint glow of dying atoms; Sturgeon's *Venus Plus X* ends with people watching the sky 'shimmer' and 'sparkle' with fallout. It may or may not be reassuring to know that the radiation which kills you is not the sort you can see, and that fallout looks like plain dust or like nothing at all - a far cry from Sturgeon's loony vision of cascading Christmas glitter. (There *are* substances which can be triggered by high-energy 'hard' radiation into emitting visible light via fluorescence or phosphorescence; what you see is not so much the actual debris of 'dying atoms' as a sort of ricochet.) Another implausibility, alas, is Jack Williamson's serum against radiation sickness (*Seetee Shock*). Considering what radiation actually does to living cells, this is rather like the idea of vaccination against assault and battery.

David Langford

Fifteen SF Writers Who Were Also Important Editors

1. Anthony Boucher (edited the magazine *F&SF* for ten years)
2. Ben Bova (editor of *Analog*, and subsequently *Omni*)
3. John W. Campbell (editor of *Astounding/Analog* for over thirty years)
4. Terry Carr (editor at Ace Books, and of the *Universe* series)
5. Lester Del Rey (editor of several 1950s magazines, and now fantasy editor of Del Rey Books)
6. Samuel Delany (editor of the *Quark* series of anthologies)
7. Harry Harrison (editor of various magazines in the 1950s and '60s)
8. Damon Knight (editor of the magazine *Worlds Beyond* and the *Orbit* series)
9. Michael Moorcock (editor of *New Worlds*)
10. Frederik Pohl (editor of *Galaxy, If* and various other magazines)
11. Keith Roberts (editor of *Impulse*)
12. Robert Sheckley (fiction editor of *Omni*)
13. Robert Silverberg (editor of the *New Dimensions* series)
14. E. C. Tubb (editor of *Authentic SF* in the 1950s)
15. Ted White (editor of *Amazing* and *Fantastic* 1969–78)

1. Anthony Boucher, who edited *Fantasy & Science Fiction* from 1949 to 1960 or so, was notorious for his keen interest in cats, Catholicism, detective fiction, and opera. Randall Garrett and I, thinking to cash in on Tony's various obsessive interests, did a story about a nun's cat who solves a mystery puzzle, and I think we worked opera into it somewhere, too. Tony didn't buy the story. I don't think he even noticed he was being spoofed.

2. Howard Browne, editor of *Amazing Stories* in the mid 1950s, hated science fiction. He made no secret of his preference for mystery stories, but his employers wouldn't let him edit a mystery-story magazine. Generally he wrote his own (excellent) detective novels in the magazine's office on company time, but somehow he managed to put an issue out every month. I doubt that he ever read what he published.

3. John W. Campbell Jr, editor of *Astounding* and *Analog* for three decades, was of Scottish ancestry and believed that Scots were the chosen master race of the galaxy. Garrett and I, in that same cynical era long ago, concocted a proposal for a novel in which the protagonist was named something like Rupert Murdoch – a super-Earthman. Campbell liked the idea but suggested that we throw out the protagonist and tell the story from the viewpoint of the aliens. We did, and it became *The Shrouded Planet*, a serial in ASF in 1957.

   A little earlier, because someone suggested that unconscious anti-Semitism might be the reason I was having trouble getting Campbell to buy my stories, I devised the pseudonym 'Calvin M. Knox' as the most Protestant name I could think of, the 'M', however, standing for Moses. Campbell bought the first 'Knox' story he saw. However, he also bought a Silverberg-byline story a week or two later, and when I told him, eventually, the rumours of his anti-Semitism that had led me to invent the pseudonym, he said, 'Have you ever noticed in my magazine the stories of a certain Isaac Asimov?'

4. Horace L. Gold, the founding editor of *Galaxy*, suffered from wartime psychological debilities that left him confined to his apartment. At the time I began writing for *Galaxy* he was also

unwilling to meet new people, and so we conducted all our business by telephone, even though we lived in the same city. When Horace began to feel a little more tranquil, I was allowed to go downtown and visit him. A few years later, when he was even further along the road to recovery, he actually went out of his house, and almost at once was involved in a severe automobile accident, which probably left him wondering if it had been worthwhile to recover. But eventually he completely overcame his agoraphobia and these days he lives in Los Angeles and travels about freely, to the amazement of those who knew him thirty years ago.

5. Frederik Pohl, when he succeeded Gold as editor of *Galaxy*, changed the title of nearly every story I sold to him despite my protests. (I gather he changed a lot of other people's titles, too.) I vowed that if I ever became an editor and bought stories from Pohl, I'd change *their* titles, too. Years later I did indeed become an editor and bought a story from Pohl. I couldn't think of a better title for it.

©Agberg, Ltd

Five Del Rey Novels Written by Paul W. Fairman

1. *Prisoners of Space*
2. *The Runaway Robot*
3. *The Scheme of Things*
4. *Siege Perilous*
5. *Tunnel Through Time*

Why are these novels published under del Rey's name if Fairman wrote them? The explanation is actually quite simple. Del Rey apparently suffered a massive writer's block for many years, but not through any shortage of ideas. These five novels were written by Fairman in the mid-1960s from detailed outlines provided by del Rey; Fairman thus functioned as a ghost writer.

Three SF Plagiarisms

Plagiarism is a charge more commonly made than sustained. Accidental similarities between stories frequently occur, and authors may reproduce something from a story they have read years ago without being conscious that they are doing so. Occasionally, however, there is no doubt whatever, as an author copies someone else's work verbatim.

1. Allen Glasser, 'Across the Ages', published in the August 1933 *Amazing Stories*, was later shown to be plagiarized from his own earlier story, 'The Haze of Heat'
2. Irwin Ross, 'To Kill a Venusian', published in the October 1971 *Worlds of If* is an almost word-for-word copy of a quite famous story by Anthony Boucher, 'Nine-Fingered Jack', which appeared in the August 1951 *Fantasy and Science Fiction*
3. Gardner F. Fox's undistinguished novel *Escape Across the Cosmos*, published in 1964, has the unusual distinction of being plagiarized *twice* (presumably by the same person), as *Titans of the Universe* by James Harvey and *Star Chase* by Brian James Royal

Thirty-one Well Known Names of SF Who Are in Fact Pseudonyms

1. Piers Anthony (Piers A. D. Jacob)
2. Christopher Anvil (Harry C. Crosby)
3. Pierre Barbet (Claude Avice)
4. T. J. Bass (Thomas J. Basser)
5. Charles Beaumont (Charles Nutt)
6. Hannes Bok (Wayne Woodard)
7. Anthony Boucher (William A. P. White)
8. John Boyd (Boyd Upchurch)
9. C. J. Cherryh (Carolyn Cherry)
10. John Christopher (C. S. Youd)
11. Hal Clement (Harry Stubbs)
12. Richard Cowper (John Murry)
13. Ralph Milne Farley (Roger S. Hoar)
14. Jack Finney (Walter B. Finney)

15. Rex Gordon (S. B. Hough)
16. Stuart Gordon (Richard Gordon)
17. Murray Leinster (Will F. Jenkins)
18. C. C. MacApp (Caroll M. Capps)
19. J. T. McIntosh (James M. MacGregor)
20. Charles Eric Maine (David McIlwain)
21. John Norman (John F. Lange)
22. George Orwell (Eric Blair)
23. Arthur Sellings (Robert Arthur Ley)
24. Cordwainer Smith (Paul Linebarger)
25. John Taine (Eric Temple Bell)
26. William Tenn (Philip Klass)
27. James Tiptree Jr (Alice Sheldon)
28. Ian Wallace (John Wallace Pritchard)
29. Hugh Walters (Walter L. Hughes)
30. Stefan Wul (Pierre Pairault)
31. John Wyndham (John Wyndham Parkes Lucas Beynon Harris)

What is a pseudonym? Sometimes contractions of their names ordinarily used by writers are mistakenly referred to as pseudonyms, such as Algis Budrys (Algirdas Budrys), Lester del Rey (Ramon Alvarez del Rey), Mack Reynolds (Dallas McCord Reynolds) or Jack Vance (John Holbrook Vance). This is mistaken, however, as these are the names the individuals use in day-to-day life; one might equally well say that Ray Bradbury and Larry Niven are pseudonyms, because they use contractions of their given names! Equally, names which have legally been changed are not pseudonyms, so that David Gerrold, Judith Merril and André Norton are not on the above list, though they were born Jerrold Friedmann, Juliet Grossman and Alice Norton respectively. Of those names on the list, Hannes Bok, Anthony Boucher and C. J. Cherryh are borderline for the same reason.

Seventeen SF Authors Who Have Also Published SF Books under Pseudonyms

It's quite common for writers to publish books in other areas under pseudonyms (particularly if they are hack writing), and also for writers to appear in magazines under pseudonyms – particularly when an individual magazine publishes a lot of a writer's work, but does not want his or her name dominating the contents page. The following have all published SF or fantasy books under other names.

1. Isaac Asimov (Paul French)
2. John Brunner (Gill Hunt, Keith Woodcott)
3. Kenneth Bulmer (Alan Burt Akers, Manning Norvil, Tully Zetford, etc.)
4. Edmund Cooper (Richard Avery)
5. John Russell Fearn (Vargo Statten, Volsted Gridban, etc.)
6. Randall Garrett (Darrel T. Langart)
7. Henry Kuttner and C. L. Moore (Lewis Padgett)
8. Barry Malzberg (K. M. O'Donnell)
9. Douglas R. Mason (John Rankine)
10. André Norton (Andrew North)
11. John Phillifent (John Rackham)
12. Fletcher Pratt (George U. Fletcher)
13. Robert Silverberg (Ivar Jorgenson, Clavin M. Knox, David Osborne)
14. E. C. Tubb (Charles Grey, Volsted Gridban, Gregory Kern, etc.)
15. Jack Williamson (Will Stewart)
16. Donald A. Wollheim (David Grinnell)
17. John Wyndham (John Beynon)

The Six Silliest SF Pseudonyms

SF writers do sometimes give themselves some strange aliases, but none are dafter than these . . .

1. *Ray Cosmic* (used by John S. Glasby)
2. *Volsted Gridban* (used by John Russell Fearn and E. C. Tubb)
3. *Vector Magroon* (unknown: possibly Fearn)
4. *Deutero Spartacus* (used by R. L. Fanthorpe)
5. *Vargo Statten* (used by John Russell Fearn)
6. *Pel Torro* (used by R. L. Fanthorpe)

This list is another whitewash for British authors, who are evidently unrivalled in their silliness!

Fourteen Anagrams

Crossword-solvers start here. It's possible to get differing anagrams from writers' names, particularly if one incorporates the middle initial or full middle name. For instance, while Brian Aldiss yields 'rabid snails', Brian *W.* Aldiss presents the alternative, 'I was bland, sir!', and Brian *Wilson* Aldiss gives us 'ribald swain's loins'. The following is a selection of anagrams, with the number of letters of each part of the name indicated afterwards. Some of the anagrams include clues to the answer, but we aren't saying which! (See p. 350 for solutions.)

1. *Elderly steer* (6, 3, 3)
2. *Thin senile bore ran on* (6, 5, 8)
3. *A duller yes-man* (6, 1, 6)
4. *Carl Truhacker* (6, 1, 6)
5. *Christ, I'm a wonder!* (10, 5)
6. *Ax Heinlein's pa* (6, 7)
7. *Hid stomachs* (6, 5)
8. *Darin' man's porn* (6, 7)
9. *A shrill, neon LA* (6, 7)
10. *Nukes augur ill* (6, 1, 6)
11. *Shan't ham old jokes* (4, 6, 6)
12. *Now a saint* (3, 6) (alternatively: *I want a son!*)
13. *Feebler darts* (6, 6)
14. *The ostrich rippers* (11, 6)

(With thanks to Michael Coney, Colin Greenland and Pamela Sladek for certain of the above)

Twenty-two Double-Headed Pseudonyms

SF writers are pseudonym maniacs. There exists in fact a whole volume exclusively devoted to SF pseudonyms (and it is far from complete!). The following list points out where a pseudonym actually conceals two writers working in collaboration.

1. *Gordon Aghill* (Robert Silverberg and Randall Garrett)

2. *Eando Binder* (Earl Binder and Otto Binder)
3. *Alexander Blade* (Robert Silverberg and Randall Garrett) also a housename
4. *Thom Demijohn* (Thomas Disch and John Sladek)
5. *Howard Cory* (Jack Jardine and Julie Jardine)
6. *Norman Edwards* (Terry Carr and Ted White)
7. *Richard Greer* (Robert Silverberg and Randall Garrett)
8. *Charles Henneberg* (Charles Henneberg and Nathalie Henneberg)
9. *Kenneth Johns* (Kenneth Bulmer and John Newman)
10. *Cyril Judd* (C. M. Kornbluth and Judith Merril)
11. *Cassandra Knye* (Thomas Disch and John Sladek)
12. *Edson McCann* (Lester del Rey and Frederik Pohl)
13. *Clyde Mitchell* (Robert Silverberg and Randall Garrett)
14. *Jordan Park* (Frederik Pohl and C. M. Kornbluth)
15. *Mark Phillips* (Randall Garrett and Larry Harris)
16. *Robert Randall* (Robert Silverberg and Randall Garrett)
17. *Michael Barrington* (Michael Moorcock and Barrington J. Bayley)
18. *Alger Rome* (Algis Budrys and Jerome Bixby)
19. *Leonard G. Spencer* (Robert Silverberg and Randall Garrett)
20. *S. M. Tenneshaw* (Robert Silverberg and Robert Randall) also a housename
21. *Gerald Vance* (Robert Silverberg and Randall Garrett)
22. *John Jay Wells* (Marion Zimmer Bradley and Juanita Coulson)

Twenty-two SF Housenames

Housenames are the relic of the pulp age of 'factory writing' when a collective name was used for stories emerging from a variety of typewriters usually in some sort of house style. A surprising number of name writers have contributed to such pseudonymous prose, although exact attribution is sometimes difficult.

1. Victor Appleton (*Tom Swift* housename; used by Howard Garis and others)
2. William Arrow (used by Don Pfeil and William Rotsler)
3. Gabriel Barclay (used by Manly Wade Wellman and C. M. Kornbluth)
4. Alexander Blade (used by Robert Silverberg, Randall Garrett,

Howard Browne, Rog Phillips, Richard Shaver, Edmond Hamilton, William P. McGivern and many others)
5. Will Garth (used by Henry Kuttner, Edmond Hamilton, Eando Binder, Mort Weisinger, Manly Wade Wellman and others)
6. Maxwell Grant (*Spider* housename; used by Lester Dent and others)
7. S. D. Gottesman (used by C. M. Kornbluth, Frederik Pohl and Robert W. Lowndes)
8. Volsted Gridban (used by E. C. Tubb and John Russell Fearn)
9. Gill Hunt (used by E. C. Tubb, John Brunner and others)
10. E. K. Jarvis (used by Robert Silverberg, Paul Fairman, Harlan Ellison, Robert Moore Williams and possibly others)
11. Ivar Jorgenson/Jorgensen (used by Robert Silverberg, Paul Fairman, Harlan Ellison, Randall Garrett and others)
12. Paul Dennis Lavond (used by Frederik Pohl, C. M. Kornbluth, Robert Lowndes and Dirk Wylie)
13. Francis Lee (used by Howard Browne and others)
14. Jeffrey Lord (*Blade* housename; used by Roland Green, Ray Nelson and others)
15. Clyde Mitchell (used by Harlan Ellison, Robert Silverberg, Randall Garrett and others)
16. John E. Muller (Badger Books housename; used by R. L. Fanthorpe and others)
17. François Pagéry (used by Gérard Klein, Hervé Calixte and others)
18. Frank Patton (used by Ray Palmer, Richard Shaver and others)
19. Kenneth Robeson (*Doc Savage* housename; used by Lester Dent, Paul Ernst, Ron Goulart and others)
20. Brett Sterling (used by Ray Bradbury, Edmond Hamilton and others)
21. S. M. Tenneshaw (used by Robert Silverberg, Randall Garrett, Edmond Hamilton, Milton Lesser and others)
22. Ivar Towers (used by Richard Wilson, C. M. Kornbluth)

The Women In Disguise List

Contrary to a still popular belief, many women write science fiction and fantasy, among them major figures such as Ursula Le Guin,

Joanna Russ, Marion Zimmer Bradley, Pamela Sargent, André Norton, Kate Wilhelm, Josephine Saxton, Leigh Brackett, C. L. Moore, Octavia Butler, the list is endless. Many, however, have chosen, for reasons of their own, not to reveal their sex by using male pseudonyms or initials.

Paul Ash (Pauline Ashwell)
Philip Briggs (Phyllis Briggs)
Jayge Carr (Margery Krueger)
Jack Danvers (Camille Caseleyr)
C. J. Cherryh (Carolyn Janice Cherry)
Howard L. Cory (Julie Ann Jardine)
Adam Lukens (Diane Ditzer De Reyna)
Jorge De Reyna (Diane Ditzer De Reyna)
D. C. Fontana (Dorothy C. Fontana)
Simon Lang (Darlene Hartman)
Lee Hoffman (Shirley Lee Hoffman)
J. Hunter Holly (Joan Hunter Holly)
H. M. Hoover (forenames unknown but is a woman)
William Lamb (Margaret Jameson)
J. O. Jeppson (Janet Opal Jeppson)
A. Reynolds Long (Amelia Reynolds Long)
C. L. Moore (Catherine Lucille Moore)
March Cost (Margaret Morrison)
Cary Neeper (Carolyn Neeper)
Andrew North (Alice Mary Norton)
André Norton (Alice Mary Norton)
E. L. Arch (Rachel Payes)
Kit Reed (Lillian Craig Reed)
James Tiptree Jr (Alice Sheldon)
Francis Stevens (Gertrude Barrows Bennett)
S. J. Van Scyoc (Sydney Joyce Van Scyoc)
M. K. Wren (Martha Kay Renfroe)
John Jay Wells (Juanita Coulson and Marion Zimmer Bradley)
Jacob Transue (Joan Matheson)
A. M. Lightner (Alice Hopf)
G. MacDonald Wallis (Geraldine Wallis)

The Men In Disguise List

Alice Beecham (E. C. Tubb)
Joyce Churchill (M. John Harrison)
Leonie Hargrave (Thomas M. Disch)
Cassandra Knye (John Sladek on his own or with Thomas Disch)
Linda Lovecraft (Michel Parry)
Frances Lynch (D. G. Compton)

Eighteen Scottish SF or Fantasy Writers

1. Ruth M. Arthur
2. Chris Boyce
3. Robert Easson
4. Stuart Gordon (Richard Gordon)
5. Alasdair Gray
6. Nicholas Stuart Gray
7. Mollie Hunter
8. Duncan Lunan
9. J. T. McIntosh
10. Compton Mackenzie
11. Angus MacLeod
12. Sheila MacLeod
13. Paul MacTyre
14. Angus MacVicar
15. Donald Malcolm
16. David I. Masson
17. Naomi Mitchison
18. John Taine (Eric Temple Bell)

All the above hail from north of Hadrian's Wall, though both Easson and 'Taine' later became US citizens.

Sixteen Irish SF and Fantasy Authors

Certainly not to be confused with the more common English variety!

1. J. S. Andrews
2. Seamus Cullen
3. Lord Dunsany
4. Camilla Fegan
5. J. Sheridan Le Fanu
6. Steven E. Macdonald
7. Ch. R. Maturin
8. Brian Moore
9. Fitz James O'Brien
10. Flann O'Brien
11. Eimar O'Duffy
12. Bob Shaw
13. M. P. Shiel
14. Bram Stoker
15. James White
16. Leonard Wibberley

Twenty-two Canadian SF Writers

Because they write in English (or French), most Canadian SF authors are assumed by the general reader to be American (or French). This is often not so and Canada can boast an illustrious palette of national authors (as they do singers, viz. Neil Young and Joni Mitchell).

WRITING IN ENGLISH

1. John Aylesworth
2. Ben Barzman
3. Eleanor Cameron
4. Thomas B. Costain
5. Gordon R. Dickson
6. Wayland Drew
7. John Kenneth Galbraith
8. H. L. Gold
9. Phyllis Gottlieb
10. Alf Harris
11. Douglas Hill
12. Edna Mayne Hull
13. Ruth Nichols

14. Bruce Powe
15. A. E. Van Vogt

Although American by birth, Judith Merrill and Spider Robinson are resident in Canada, as are the British writers Michael Coney and Andrew Weiner

French Canadians

16. Jean-Pierre April
17. René Beaulieu
18. Michel Belil
19. Esther Rochon
20. Daniel Sernine
21. Jean-François Somcynski
22. Elisabeth Vonarburg

Eleven Ethnic Minorities SF Writers

Coloured Writers

1. Robert Lynn Asprin
2. Steven Barnes
3. Jesse Bone
4. Octavia Butler
5. Samuel R. Delany
6. Charles Saunders
7. Julian Jay Savarin

American Indian Writers

8. Russel Bates
9. Craig Strete

Asian Writers

10. Somtow Sucharitkul (who hails from Thailand although he writes in English)
11. Laurence Yep

Twenty-eight US Writers Born Overseas

1. Charles Angoff, Russia
2. Piers Anthony, England
3. Isaac Asimov, Russia
4. Jack Bertin, Italy
5. Reginald Bretnor, Russia
6. James Cook Brown, Philippines
7. Algis Budrys, East Prussia
8. Curtis Casewitt, Germany
9. Leslie Charteris, Malaysia
10. Arsen Darnay, Hungary
11. G. C. Edmondson, Mexico
12. Joseph Ferman, Lithuania
13. Charles Fontenay, Brazil
14. Hugo Gernsback, Luxembourg
15. John Hersey, China
16. Julie Jardine, Manchuria
17. Robert Magidoff, Russia
18. Ayn Rand, Russia
19. Marta Randall, Mexico
20. Robert Reginald, Japan
21. Hans Stefan Santesson, France
22. James H. Schmitz, Germany
23. Curt Siodmak, Germany
24. Idella Purnell Stone, Mexico
25. John Taine, Scotland
26. Manly Wade Wellman, Angola
27. Frederic Wertham, Germany
28. George Zebrowski, Austria

Seventeen British Writers Born Overseas

1. J. G. Ballard, China
2. John Bowen, India
3. Christine Brook-Rose, Switzerland
4. Alexander Cordell, Ceylon

5. Peter Dickinson, Zambia
6. Madelaine Duke, Switzerland
7. Lawrence Durrell, India
8. I. O. Evans, South Africa
9. Meir Gillon, Transylvania
10. Anna Kavan, France
11. Doris Lessing, Persia
12. Penelope Lively, Egypt
13. Michel Parry, Belgium
14. Mervyn Peake, China
15. Clifford C. Reed, South Africa
16. Andrew Stephenson, Venezuela
17. J. R. R. Tolkien, South Africa

SF Collaborators

SF writers meet each other more than most writers do – at conventions, workshops etc. – and collaborate apparently at the drop of a hat. A full list would run to many pages; what follows is confined to novels written by two people individually established as SF writers.

1. Poul Anderson and Gordon Eklund (*Inheritors of Earth*)
2. Poul Anderson and Gordon Dickson (*Earthman's Burden, Star Prince Charlie*)
3. Poul Anderson and Mildred Downey Broxon (*Demon of Scattery*)
4. Gregory Benford and Gordon Eklund (*Find the Changeling, If The Stars Are Gods*)
5. Gregory Benford and William Rotsler (*Shiva Descending*)
6. Michael Bishop and Ian Watson (*Under Heaven's Bridge* – one of the more unusual collaborations: one writer lives in the US, the other in the UK, and they have never met)
7. Ben Bova and Gordon Dickson (*Gremlins Go Home*)
8. Terry Carr and Ted White (*Invasion from 2500*, as 'Norman Edwards')
9. Avram Davidson and Ward Moore (*Joyleg*)
10. L. Sprague de Camp and Fletcher Pratt (*Incomplete Enchanter*, etc.)
11. L. Sprague de Camp and Lin Carter (various *Conan* novels)
12. L. Sprague de Camp and P. Schuyler Miller (*Genus Homo*)

13. Philip K. Dick and Ray Nelson (*The Ganymede Takeover*)
14. Philip K. Dick and Roger Zelazny (*Deus Irae*)
15. Gordon Dickson and Keith Laumer (*Planet Run*)
16. Thomas M. Disch and John Sladek (*Black Alice*)
17. Gardner Dozois and George Alec Effinger (*Nightmare Blue*)
18. David Gerrold and Larry Niven (*The Flying Sorcerers*)
19. Harry Harrison and Gordon Dickson (*Lifeship*)
20. Raymond F. Jones and Lester Del Rey (*Weeping May Tarry*)
21. C. M. Kornbluth and Judith Merril (*Gunner Cade* and others, as 'Cyril Judd')
22. Henry Kuttner and C. L. Moore (many novels)
23. Keith Laumer and Rosel George Brown (*Earthblood*)
24. Katherine McLean and Charles V. De Vet (*Second Game*)
25. George R. R. Martin and Lisa Tuttle (*Windhaven*)
26. Larry Niven and Jerry Pournelle (*The Mote in God's Eye*, etc.)
27. Frederik Pohl and C. M. Kornbluth (*The Space Merchants, Wolfbane*, etc.)
28. Frederik Pohl and Lester Del Rey (*Preferred Risk*, as 'Edson McCann')
29. Thomas Scortia and Frank Robinson (*The Glass Inferno*, etc.)
30. Robert Silverberg and Randall Garrett (*The Dawning Light*, as 'Robert Randall'
31. A. E. Van Vogt and E. M. Hull (*The Winged Man*, etc.)
32. Ted White and Dave Van Arnam (*Sideslip*)
33. Kate Wilhelm and Theodore L. Thomas (*The Clone, Year of the Cloud*)
34. Jack Williamson and Frederik Pohl (many novels)
35. Roger Zelazny and Fred Saberhagen (*Coils*)

The champion collaborator is Gordon Dickson, with four different partners – Poul Anderson, Ben Bova, Harry Harrison and Keith Laumer.

Eleven Brothers and Sisters

1. Gregory Benford and Jim Benford. Although both highly-regarded scientists, they have not written SF together. Gregory Benford has collaborated with Jim's wife, Hilary, on his novel *Timescape*

2. Earl Binder and Otto Binder are better known, collectively, as Eando Binder, although they have written separately
3. Igor Bogdanoff and Grichka Bogdanoff. These two French critics are identical twins and have always worked together
4. Marion Zimmer Bradley and Paul Zimmer. This rare brother and sister pair have collaborated on SF
5. Karel Capek and Joseph Capek. Although both are remembered for their solo efforts, these two brothers wrote *The Insect Play* and *Adam the Creator* together
6. John Dickson Carr and Robert S. Carr. They never wrote together
7. Howard Fast and Julius Fast. These brothers never collaborated; Julius principally worked as an anthologist
8. Joe Haldeman and Jack Haldeman. Although they usually write solo, they have collaborated on short stories and one novel
9. Alain Hilleret and André Hilleret. These two French brothers were known as 'Arcadius'
10. Arkady Strugatsky and Boris Strugatsky. The majority of their work is in collaboration; only a handful of short stories have appeared under a single name
11. John Coleman Burroughs and Hulbert Burroughs. Both sons of Edgar Rice Burroughs, they collaborated on several SF stories

The Joys of Married Life and the Typewriter

(c) Have collaborated on books or stories
(nc) Are not known to have collaborated on books or stories.
Where not indicated, both spouses are SF writers

Kingsley Amis-Elizabeth Jane Howard (KA has written SF and fantasy while EJH has written fantasy) (nc)
Poul Anderson-Karen Anderson (c)
Isaac Asimov-Janet O. Jeppson (c-on anthologies only)
James Blish-Virginia Kidd (c)
James Blish-Judith A. Lawrence (c)
Terry Carr-Carol Carr (c)
Claude F. Cheinisse-Christine Renard (c)
Avram Davidson-Grania Davis (nc)
L. Sprague de Camp-Catherine Crook de Camp (c)

Samuel R. Delany-Marilyn Hacker (c- on anthologies only)
Lester del Rey-Judy Lynn del Rey (née Benjamin) (nc-JLdR is
    editor)
Ted Dikty-Julian May (nc-TD is anthologist)
Charles Dye-Katherine McLean (nc)
Ed Emshwiller-Carol Emshwiller (nc-EH is illustrator/film maker)
R. Lionel Fanthorpe-Patricia Fanthorpe (c)
Herbert Franke-Charlotte Franke (nc)
James Frenkel-Joan D. Vinge (nc-JF is editor)
Stephen Goldin-Kathleen Sky (nc)
Joseph Green-Patricia Milton (c)
Edmond Hamilton-Leigh Brackett (c)
Charles Henneberg-Nathalie Henneberg (c)
Richard Hutton-Susan Allison (nc-RH is science writer, SA is
    editor)
Jack Jardine-Julie Jardine (c)
Stephen King-Tabitha King (nc)
Tappan King-Beth Meacham (c)
Damon Knight-Kate Wilhelm (nc)
Henry Kuttner-Catherine L. Moore (c)
David R. Mason-Katherine McLean (nc)
Michael Moorcock-Hilary Bailey (c)
Ward Moore-Raylin Moore (nc)
Claude Nunes-Rhoda Nunes (c)
Edgar Pangborn-Mary Pangborn (nc)
Alexei Panshin-Cory Panshin (née Seidman) (c)
Frederik Pohl-Judith Merrill (nc)
Frederik Pohl-Carol Pohl (c- anthologies only)
Chris Priest-Lisa Tuttle (nc)
Walt Richmond-Leigh Richmond (c)
Spider Robinson-Jeanne Robinson (c)
Hank Stine-Janrae Frank (nc)
Jeff Sutton-Jean Sutton (c)
Eric Van Lustbader-Victoria Schochet (nc-VS is editor)
A. E. Van Vogt-Edna Mayne Hull (c)
Vernor Vinge-Joan D. Vinge (nc)
Ian Watson-Judy Watson (c-although uncredited, JW co-wrote *The
    Woman Factory* in its first draft)
George Zebrowski-Pamela Sargent (c- not really married but live
    together)

A footnote to this list is that Harry Harrison married Evelyn Harrison who later married Lester del Rey, but she was not a writer.

Eighteen SF Parents and Children

(c) Have collaborated on books or stories
(nc) Are not known to have collaborated on books or stories

1. James Blish-Beth Blish (nc-Beth has published SF translations)
2. Edgar Rice Burroughs-John Coleman Burroughs (nc)
3. Edgar Rice Burroughs-Hulbert Burroughs (nc)
4. Howard Fast-Jonathan Fast (nc-Jonathan is married to well-known author Erica Jong)
5. William Murray Gradon-Murray Roberts (nc)
6. Frank Herbert-Brian Herbert (nc)
7. Fred Hoyle-Geoffrey Hoyle (c)
8. Fritz Leiber-Justin Leiber (nc)
9. Richard Matheson-Richard Christian Matheson (c)
10. John Middleton Murry-Richard Cowper (nc-JMM was a well-known literary critic and husband of Katherine Mansfield; RC is a pen-name for Colin Murry)
11. Rachel Cosgrove Payes-Robert Payes (nc)
12. Frederik Pohl-Frederik Pohl IV (c- on non-fiction)
13. Milton Rothman-Tony Rothman (nc)
14. Clifford D. Simak-Richard S. Simak (c)
15. Theodore Sturgeon-Robin Sturgeon (nc)
16. J. R. R. Tolkien-Christopher Tolkien (c- posthumously, when CT edited his father's notes and texts making up *The Silmarilion*)
17. Manly Wade Wellman-Wade Wellman (c)
18. Austin Tappan Wright-Tappan King (nc-Tappan King is in fact the grandson of the author of *Islandia*)

Twenty-six SF Writers Who Have Written Pornography

There is a strong dividing line between soft porn and hard-core pornography, often delineated by explicitness and language. Much of what was written before the 1967 US Supreme Court ruling abolishing most pornography laws is now considered rather mild and 'soft porn'. Many SF writers were active in this commercial field but few graduated to the harder stuff after 1967.

SOFT-CORE WRITERS

1. *Chester Anderson* wrote *The Pink Palace* on his own and *Faithful for Eight Hours* in collaboration with *Laurence Janifer* as Andrew Blake
2. *Marion Zimmer Bradley* was quite prolific in the soft-porn field (and romance and gothics) penning a variety of titles like *I Am a Lesbian, Spare Her Heaven, Knives of Desire, No Adam or Eve,* etc., under pen names Lee Chapman, Morgan Ives, John Dexter and Miriam Gardner
3. *Harlan Ellison* penned a short-story collection titled *Sex Gang* (1959) and used the pen-name Paul Merchant. A hard-core novel was announced by Essex House but never appeared
4. *David S. Garnett,* the young British writer is known to have contributed short stories to a variety of men's magazines
5. *Laurence Janifer* (see Chester Anderson – although is also likely to have penned various soft-porn novels under a pseudonym)
6. *David Mason,* the US sword and sorcery writer is also known to have worked pseudonymously in the field
7. *Mack Reynolds* is another SF writer active in the genre in the early 1960s, with at least a dozen novels, some as Maxine Reynolds and Todd Harding
8. *Robert Silverberg* wrote sex potboilers between 1959 and 1965, possibly sharing the Don Eliot pseudonym under which the following appeared: *Hot Rod Sinners, Sexteen, Sin for Solace, Wanton Web, Passion Thieves,* etc.
9. *George H. Smith* was active in almost every genre field and this one was no exception, both under his name and as Jan Hudson and Jerry Jason
10. *Bob Vardeman,* known to be Edward George (*Pleasure Planet*)
11. *Robert Anton Wilson* penned *The Sex Magicians*

Although not strictly pornography and not explicit enough to qualify as hard-core, novels by Brian Aldiss (*The Hand-Reared Boy* and sequels), Michael Moorcock (*The Brothel in Rosenstrasse*) and John Norman (the *Gor* series) are worth noting for their sexual content

1. *J. G. Ballard* The often controversial British writer is the author of *Crash*, a brutal and deliberately obsessive novel about sex fantasies centred on car crashes. A disquieting vision of the future in which sex and technology form a nightmare marriage, *Crash* was hailed by *New Scientist* as 'the first pornographic book dominated by 20th century technology'

2. *Raymond E. Banks* Highly active in the 1950s and 1960s as a reliable if unspectacular SF writer, Banks emerged with a torrid potboiler *The Moon Rapers* in 1979 for the notorious Hustler Paperbacks

3. *Samuel R. Delany* In 1973, US author Delany published *The Tides of Lust* (working title *Equinox*), a highly explicit if intensely symbolic novel with disturbing homosexual visions. When reprinted in England in 1980, the book was seized by the police. Another erotic novel *Hogg* written in 1973 remains unpublished

4. *Philip José Farmer* Already noted for his trail-blazing and taboo-breaking treatment of sex in SF (*The Lovers*, 'Mother', 'Riders of the Purple Wage'), Farmer abandoned all restrictions in the late 1960s and wrote a series of provocative sado-masochistic fantasies numbering *The Image of the Beast* and *Blown* featuring the sexual misadventures of a Los Angeles private eye facing a most disturbing, sexual invasion of the planet; *A Feast Unknown*, an adults-only updating of the Tarzan and Doc Savage personae. Another two novels continued in this vein of 'fleshing out' existing pulp characters, but were bowdlerized prior to publication. His unique pornographic novel outside SF is *Love Song*, a gothic, and torrid, romance of a man inveigled into an affair with a mother and daughter. *As You Desire* (1965, as William Norfolk) is soft-core

5. *Jane Gallion* The author of two pornographic novels for the famed Essex House imprint, Jane Gallion resurfaced on the SF scene with some 1980 *Galaxy* stories. Her *Biker* is an explicit tale of rape, domination and revenge in a post-nuclear context where Hell's Angels are on the rampage. She also wrote *Stoned*

6. *Richard E. Geis* The many times Hugo-winning fan publisher long made a living out of writing pornography. *Raw Meat, The Endless Orgy, The Sex Machine, Arena Women, Star Whores, The Corporation Strikes Back* are all bawdy, no holds-barred SF. Among

his many other pornographic novels: *Ravished, Male Mistress, Bedroom Backlist, Bongo Bum, In Bed We Lie, Eye at the Window, Girlsville, Sex Turned On*. He has also used the pen-name Peggy Swenson

7. *Langdon Jones* This young British writer revealed by stories in *New Worlds*, later collected in *The Eye of the Lens*, wrote a pornographic novel *Children of the Night* in the early 1970s under the name Michael Wesbury, which he has also used for short stories in men's magazines. This novel was sold to Essex House but never appeared

8. *Barry Malzberg* Prior to his iconoclastic career in SF, US writer Barry Malzberg was already a deft practitioner of erotica and pornography albeit in his own idiosyncratic way. His novels for Olympia are better-known: *Screen, In My Parents' Bedroom* and *Confessions of Westchester County*. He has however also written many other somewhat down-market novels of pornography, both under his name (*Oracle of the Thousand Hands, The Spread, Masochist*) and as Gerrold Watkins (*A Bed of Money, Giving it Away, A Satyr's Romance, Southern Comfort, The Art of the Fugue*). Although none of Malzberg's erotic output is SF, it is always challenging and unusual

9. *David Meltzer* The respected San Francisco poet published a few stories in SF magazines in the mid-1950s and became the foremost exponent of the highly-explicit Essex House line of novels, to which he contributed nine titles. Two series are SF: *The Agency*, which comprises *The Agency, The Agent* and *How Many Blocks in the Pile?* and the *Brain-Plant* quartet which included *Lovely, Healer, Out* and *Glue Factory*. *The Agency* trilogy unveils a vast underground network of sexual conspiracies ruling the world while the *Brain-Plant* series is a vision of a future city world gone mad. His other pornographic novels (non-SF) are *Orf* and *The Martyr*

10. *Andrew J. Offutt* The prolific ex-President of Science Fiction Writers of America is an old hand at the pornography game under his own name (*The Great 24 Hour Thing*) and a multitude of pseudonyms. John Cleve (*Barbarana, The Devoured, Fruit of the Loins, Jodinareh, The Juice of Love, Pleasure Us* – also known as *The Pleasure Principle* by Baxter Giles – *Manlib!, The Sexorcist* – a.k.a. *Unholy Revelry*, the Crusades retelling – *The Accursed Tower, The Passionate Princess* and sequels; as well as the recent sexy space-

opera series *Spaceways*. As Jeff Douglas: *The Balling Machine*. As
J. X. Williams: *Her*, *The Sex Pill*

11. *Charles Platt* Platt was another of the SF writers attracted by the
    innovations of the Essex House pornographic imprint in the late
    '60s. Most of his books in the field were written with Essex House
    in mind, but were finally published elsewhere, generally by
    Ophelia Press, a subsidiary of Olympia. His first three novels
    appeared under his own name: *The Gas*, where a secret nerve gas
    loosens all inhibitions and spreads through the English country-
    side, is the most traditionally SF one and was followed by *The
    Image Job* and *The Pleasure and the Pain*. He has also written a soft-
    core novel as Blakely St James, *A Song for Christina*

12. *Christopher Priest* Encouraged by Norman Spinrad, Priest was
    another British writer attracted by the Essex House formula. His
    novel was bought but never published due to the demise of the
    imprint

13. *Hank Stine* A one-time editor of *Galaxy*, Stine contributed two
    pornographic novels with SF themes to Essex House. They are
    Season of the Witch, highly praised by Harlan Ellison, where a
    criminal's brain is transferred into a woman's body and *Thrill
    City*, a novel of a future decadent America

14. *Theodore Sturgeon* The respected US author was commissioned
    to write a pornographic novel by Brian Kirby, the editor of the
    Essex House line. According to reliable sources close to Kirby,
    Sturgeon delivered the first draft of a book called *Godbody* late in
    1970. As Kirby was by then aware that his imprint was about to
    fold, he returned the manuscript to Sturgeon. The novel has
    never reappeared since and, according to Sturgeon, is still
    undergoing revisions. Should it ever appear it would be
    Sturgeon's first novel in almost twenty years, although there are
    doubts as to whether the pornographic elements will still be
    included. The resolution of Sturgeon's controversial short novel
    Some of your Blood is considered pornographic by some

15. *Ian Watson* British SF writer Ian Watson's first novel *The
    Woman Machine* (co-written with his wife Judy) depicts a future
    where women are exploited as sex objects and revolt. It has never
    seen the light of day in English due to its explicitness, but has
    appeared in France as *Orgasmachine* where it has gone into two
    editions. A revised version is expected from Berkley in 1983.

Thirty-two SF Writers Who Have Published Mystery Novels

1. Poul Anderson (*Murder Bound, Murder in Black Letter, Perish By The Sword*)
2. Isaac Asimov (*Murder at the ABA, A Whiff of Death*)
3. Robert Bloch (*Psycho*, and many others)
4. Anthony Boucher (*Rocket to the Morgue*, and many others)
5. Ben Bova (*The Multiple Man*)
6. Leigh Brackett (*An Eye For An Eye, No Good From A Corpse*)
7. Fredric Brown (*The Fabulous Clipjoint*, and many others)
8. John Brunner (*A Plague On Both Your Causes*, and others in *Max Curfew* series)
9. D. G. Compton (*And Murder Came Too*, and several others, as 'Guy Compton')
10. Thomas M. Disch (*Black Alice*, with John Sladek - published in the USA under the pseudonym 'Thom Demijohn')
11. Jack Finney (*5 Against The House*, and others)
12. Ron Goulart (*If Dying Was All, One Grave Too Many*, and others)
13. Harry Harrison (*Montezuma's Revenge, Queen Victoria's Revenge*)
14. Henry Kuttner (*The Brass Ring, The Day He Died*, and several others)
15. Keith Laumer (*Deadfall*)
16. Murray Leinster (*Murder in the Family, Murder Will Out*, and others under his real name, Will F. Jenkins)
17. Barry Malzberg (*The Running of Beasts*, with Bill Pronzini)
18. Richard Matheson (*Ride the Nightmare*)
19. Michael Moorcock (*Caribbean Crisis*, as 'Desmond Reid')
20. André Norton (*Murders For Sale*, as 'Allen Weston', in collaboration)
21. Edgar Pangborn (*A-100*, as 'Bruce Harrison')
22. H. Beam Piper (*Murder in the Gun Room*)
23. Mack Reynolds (*The Case of the Little Green Men*)
24. Robert Sheckley (*Calibre .50*, and several others)
25. John Sladek (*Black Aura, Invisible Green*)
26. Cordwainer Smith (*Atomsk*, as 'Carmichael Smith')
27. E. C. Tubb (*Assignment New York*, as 'Mike Langtry')
28. Wilson Tucker (*The Chinese Doll*, and many others)
29. Jack Vance (*The Man in the Cage* and several others, under his full name of John Holbrook Vance)

30. Manly Wade Wellman (*Find My Killer*, and others)
31. Kate Wilhelm (*City of Cain, More Bitter Than Death, The Nevermore Affair*)
32. John Wyndham (*Foul Play Suspected*, as 'John Beynon')

Seven Ellery Queen Novels Ghosted by SF Writers (and One Saint Novel)

It is not widely known that many of the novels published under the 'Ellery Queen' name are not the work of Frederick Dannay and Manfred Lee, whose pseudonym it originally was. At first it was thought that only some of the minor novels, published as paperback originals, were ghosted; more recently it has emerged that some of the more famous recent titles, featuring the detective Ellery Queen, were also by other hands. An uncertain number of Leslie Charteris's 'Saint' novels are also ghosted. The following are the work of well-known SF writers.

ELLERY QUEEN NOVELS:

1. *And On The Eighth Day* (by Avram Davidson – features Ellery Queen)
2. *Four Men Called John* (by Jack Vance)
3. *The Fourth Side of the Triangle* (by Avram Davidson – features Ellery Queen)
4. *The Madman Theory* (by Jack Vance)
5. *The Player on the Other Side* (by Theodore Sturgeon – features Ellery Queen)
6. *A Room to Die In* (by Jack Vance)
7. *A Study in Terror* (by Paul W. Fairman)

LESLIE CHARTERIS NOVEL:

Vendetta for the Saint (by Harry Harrison)

Nine SF Writers Who Have Also Published Westerns

It's often claimed that altogether too much SF consists of westerns in space, with blasters for six-guns. So it might be said that in publishing actual westerns these writers have simply come clean.

1. Leigh Brackett (*Rio Bravo*)
2. Lee Hoffman (*The Valdez Horses*, and many others)
3. Robert E. Howard (*A Gent From Bear Creek*)
4. Murray Leinster (*Cattle Rustlers* – and several more under his real name, 'Will F. Jenkins')
5. Noel Loomis (though he published a couple of SF novels, was best known as a western writer)
6. Chad Oliver (*The Wolf Is My Brother*)
7. Theodore Sturgeon (*The King and Four Queens, The Rare Breed, Sturgeon's West*)
8. E. C. Tubb (a great many under various pseudonyms)
9. Manly Wade Wellman (*Fort Sun Dance*, and many others)

Ten Writers of Humorous SF

1. Douglas Adams (*The Hitchhiker's Guide to the Galaxy* and sequels)
2. Fredric Brown (*What Mad Universe?* and many short stories)
3. Ron Goulart (innumerable novels)
4. Harry Harrison (*Bill, The Galactic Hero*, and *The Stainless Steel Rat* series, etc.)
5. R. A. Lafferty (*Space Chantey, The Reefs of Earth*, and many stories)
6. Eric Frank Russell (*Next of Kin, The Great Explosion* and many stories)
7. Robert Sheckley (*Dimension of Miracles, Mindswap* and most of his other work)
8. John Sladek (*The Reproductive System, The Muller-Fokker Effect, Roderick*)
9. William Tenn (the majority of his short stories)
10. Kurt Vonnegut (almost all his work)

Humour is very much an individual taste. All the above writers are notable for a significant number of humorous stories; others, such as Brian Aldiss, Piers Anthony, or Bob Shaw, may intersperse the occasional humorous piece with their more sober work. Some writers generally regarded as deeply serious – e.g. Ballard, Disch or Malzberg – are prized for their wit by some readers

Forty SF Writers Who Have Edited Fanzines

A great many writers started out as SF fans, and a healthy proportion of these went a step further and published their own amateur magazines, or fanzines. Most of these appeared in very small editions (often less than a hundred copies), and many are nowadays sought-after collectors' items. Here is a select list of writers and their fanzines:

1. Gregory Benford, *Void*
2. James Blish, *Tumbrils*
3. Ray Bradbury, *Futuria Fantasia*
4. Marion Zimmer Bradley, *Banneret*
5. John Brunner, *Noise Level*
6. Algis Budrys, *Slantasy*
7. Kenneth Bulmer, *Star Parade*
8. F. M. Busby, *Cry*
9. Linda Bushyager, *Granfalloon*
10. Terry Carr, *Fanac, Innuendo*
11. Jack Chalker, *Mirage*
12. John Christopher, *The Fantast*
13. Theodore Cogswell, *PITFCS*
14. Juanita Coulson, *Yandro*
15. Lester del Rey, *SF Forum*
16. Harlan Ellison, *Dimensions*
17. David Gerrold, *Otherworlds*
18. Jack C. Haldeman, *Tapeworm*
19. Lee Hoffman, *Quandry*
20. Robert Holdstock, *Macrocosm*
21. Damon Knight, *Snide*
22. Fritz Leiber, *New Purposes*
23. Richard Lupoff, *Xero*
24. Charles Eric Maine, *Gargoyle*
25. Michael Moorcock, *Burroughsania*
26. Charles Platt, *Garbistan*
27. Frederik Pohl, *Voice of the Gostak*
28. Christopher Priest, *Deadloss*
29. Tom Reamy, *Trumpet*
30. William Rotsler, *Tattooed Dragon*
31. Darrell Schweitzer, *Procrastination*

32. Robert Silverberg, *Spaceship*
33. Craig Strete, *Red Planet Earth*
34. E. C. Tubb, *Vector*
35. Wilson Tucker, *Le Zombie*
36. Lisa Tuttle, *Mathom*
37. Bob Vardeman, *Sandworm*
38. Ted White, *Pong*
39. Donald A. Wollheim, *The Phantagraph*
40. Chelsea Quinn Yarbro, *Dancing Gryphon*

Twenty Odd Books Out

Many SF authors have written outside the field. As the relevant list shows, many have also indulged in mysteries and thrillers. This is a list of some of the more unexpected titles to have been penned by writers better-known for their SF output.

1. Brian Aldiss, *Cities and Stones* (1966), a travel book on Yugoslavia
2. Poul Anderson, *Thermonuclear Warfare* (1963), just as it sounds
3. Alfred Bester, *The Life and Death of a Satellite* (1966), about the launch of an artificial satellite. Bester has also written a showbiz novel *Who He?/The Rat Race* (1953)
4. Marion Zimmer Bradley, *The Catch Trap* (1979), a massive novel about circus life. MZB has also written soft-porn, gothics and horror novels
5. L. Sprague de Camp, *Inventions and Their Management* (1937), and other books on inventions, weapons and patents, with A. K. Berle; de Camp has also written several popular archaeology books
6. Thomas M. Disch, *Clara Reeve* (1975, as Leonie Hargrave), a gothic pastiche
7. Joe Haldeman, *War Year* (1972) a partly autobiographical novel about Vietnam
8. Frank Herbert, *Without Me You're Nothing* (1981), with Max Bernard, a manual on home computers and their uses
9. Damon Knight, *Westerns of the 40s* (1977), an anthology of pulp western stories
10. Keith Laumer, *How to Design and Build Flying Models* (1960), a hobbyist's guide

11. Fritz Leiber, *Tarzan and the City of Gold* (1966), the only authorized Tarzan novel other than from E. R. Burroughs
12. Dan Morgan, *The Guitar* (1965), a popular instrument manual which is constantly reprinted
13. Frederik Pohl, *Edge of the City/A Man is Ten Feet Tall* (1957), the novelization of a Sidney Poitier movie. In collaboration with C. M. Kornbluth Pohl has also written some mainstream novels of social struggle (*A Town is Drowning*, *Presidential Year*, *Sorority House*)
14. Christopher Priest, *Your Book of Film-Making* (1974), a manual for children
15. Keith Roberts, *The Boat of Fate* (1971), an historical novel set in the death-throes of the Roman Empire
16. Robert Silverberg, *Ghosts Town of the American West* (1968). Like Asimov, Silverberg has written many books on many subjects in the soft sciences and historical field. This is one of the more unusual ones
17. John Sladek, *Judgement of Jupiter* (as Richard A. Tilms – 1980), a mock-serious scientific treatise blending astronomy, astrology, myth, political history, meteorology and blaming Jupiter for all earthly catastrophes. As James Vogh, Sladek has written other pseudo-science books, very much tongue-in-cheek (such as *Arachne Rising* in which a 13th sign of the zodiac is invented)
18. Cordwainer Smith, *The Political Doctrines of Sun-Yat-Sen* (1937, under his real name, Paul Linebarger), a book of political analysis
19. Theodore Sturgeon, *I, Libertine* (1956, as Frederick Ewing), a bawdy historical novel. Sturgeon has also written western novelizations and an Ellery Queen thriller
20. A. E. Van Vogt, *The Money Personality* (1972), how to become rich through developing your personality!

SF Writers For and Against the Vietnam War

In 1968 SF writers Judith Merril and Kate Wilhelm organized an advertisement signed by 82 writers stating, 'We oppose the participation of the United States in the war in Vietnam.' A counter-ad, signed by 72 writers, quickly appeared stating, 'We the undersigned believe the United States must remain in Vietnam to fulfill its responsibilities to the people in that country.' The two were published side by side in the June 1968 issue of *Galaxy Science Fiction*.

Among the writers who supported US involvement were:

Poul Anderson	R A Lafferty
Leigh Brackett	Larry Niven
Marion Zimmer Bradley	Jerry Pournelle
John W. Campbell	Fred Saberhagen
Hal Clement	Thomas Burnett Swann
L. Sprague de Camp	Jack Vance
Edmond Hamilton	Jack Williamson
Robert Heinlein	

Those who opposed the American presence included:

Isaac Asimov	Philip José Farmer
James Blish	Harry Harrison
Ray Bradbury	Damon Knight
Samuel R. Delany	Ursula Le Guin
Lester Del Rey	Fritz Leiber
Philip K. Dick	Robert Silverberg
Thomas M. Disch	Norman Spinrad
Harlan Ellison	Kate Wilhelm

Fifteen Nobel Prizewinners for Literature Who Have Written Science Fiction and Fantasy

1. Rudyard Kipling (Britain, 1907) Kipling was active in both science fiction and fantasy. His most famous SF stories are 'With the Night Mail' (1905) and its sequel 'As Easy as ABC' (1912), depicting a year 2,000 where flying has become so important that the whole world is ruled by the Aerial Board of Control (ABC). Fantasy and the supernatural are prominent in many of his short stories, most notable being 'The Phantom Rickshaw', 'The Strange Ride of Morrowbie Jukes' and 'The Lost Legion'
2. Selma Lagerlöf (Sweden, 1909) Although her novels *Herr Arne's Hoard* and *Thy Soul Shall Bear Witness* (1904 and 1912) are shot through by supernatural happenings, her contribution to SF lies in her children's book *The Wonderful Adventures of Nils* (1906) where the protagonist flies on gooseback, this long before the advent of aviation

3. Maurice Maeterlinck (Belgium, 1911) This Belgian poet's oeuvre was pervaded by fantasy, but his best remembered book is *The Blue Bird* (1908) an allegory often reminiscent of *Peter Pan*
4. Anatole France (France, 1921) in *Penguin Island* (1908), mankind's revolution comes in for a hefty dose of satire, while in *The Revolt of the Angels* (1914) the denizens of Paradise are driven to revolt
5. Wladislaw Reymont (Poland, 1924) Although generally known for his long sagas of peasant life in Poland, Reymont is also the author of *Bunt* (1914), a tale of animals' revolt against men, wherein they end up worshipping a gorilla, a precursor to Orwell's *Animal Farm*
6. George Bernard Shaw (Ireland, 1925) *Back to Methuselah* (1921) follows mankind's evolution from Genesis to the Far Future where humanity has become disembodied. *The Adventures of the Black Girl In Her Search for God* (1932) is fantasy, while many of the tales in *Buoyant Millions* (1950) are close to SF
7. Thomas Mann (Germany, 1929) *Doctor Faustus* is another variant on the classic fantasy theme of a pact with the devil
8. Sinclair Lewis (USA, 1930) His SF novel *It Can't Happen Here* (1935) predicts the rise of a fascist dictatorship in the USA of the near-future
9. Hermann Hesse (Germany, 1946) Although his present-day fame among younger generations is the result of other better-known books, his major utopian SF novel *The Glass Bead Game* (1943: also known as *Magister Ludi*) was the book which gained him his Nobel award. In a future land, a strange community resides whose entire role and purpose in life is dictated by a mysterious game
10. Bertrand Russell (Britain, 1950) The controversial philosopher's few incursions into fiction were pure SF: *Satan in the Suburbs* (1953), *Nightmares of Eminent Persons* (1954) and *Fact and Fiction* (1961) are all short story collections
11. Winston Churchill (Britain, 1953) *If Lincoln Had Not Lost at Gettysburg*, included in a 1931 anthology of alternate histories, is Churchill's contribution to SF. It is a sophisticated treatment, written as though by an inhabitant of a world where the South won the Civil War, speculating as to how things might have been if the North had won!
12. John Steinbeck (USA, 1962) *The Short Reign of Pippin IV* (1957)

is a fantasy satire where a descendant of Charlemagne is restored
to the throne of France

13. Jean-Paul Sartre (France, 1964)   The French philosopher's
marginal contribution to fantasy is his play *In Camera* (1945)
which takes place in hell

14. Harry Martinson (Sweden, 1974)   Perhaps the most advanced
example of SF from a Nobel prize-winner, albeit in the form of a
lengthy epic poem *Aniara* (1956) relating the tale of a generation
starship on an irreversible journey into the void

15. Isaac Bashevis Singer (USA, 1978)   The Yiddish writer now
resident in the United States has, through his treatment of traditional Jewish folklore, often treated the theme of the supernatural
in novels such as *Satan in Goray* (1934) and in innumerable short
stories, many of which have a contemporary setting

Keeping Up with the Brown(e)s

Alice Brown, author of *The Flying Teuton* (1918)

Charles Brockden Brown, America's first professional writer; created
fantasies and gothics amongst other genres

Charles N. Brown, editor and founder of *Locus*, the established
newspaper of the SF and fantasy field

Fredric Brown, a giant of both the SF and thriller fields. Best
remembered for his short short yarns and comic novels

George Sheldon Browne, British commercial writer of the 1950s

Harrison Brown, collaborator with Chloe Zerwick on *The Cassiopeia
Affair* (1967)

Howard Browne, famous editor and author of the *Tharn* prehistoric
series

Howard V. Brown, illustrator of the pulps

James Cook Brown, author of *The Troika Incident* (1970)

James Goldie Brown, New Zealand anthologist

Peter C. Brown, writer of *Smallcreep's Day* (1965)

Reginald Browne, author of the juvenile *School in Space* (1946)

Rosel George Brown, sadly-missed creator of the *Sybil Sue Blue*, planetary
policewoman series

Slater Brown, wrote the 1955 juvenile *Spaceward Bound*

Walter Browne, author of *2894 or the Fossil Man* (1894)

A Galaxy of Smiths

Clark Ashton Smith, a major contributor to the pulp magazines and creator of Zoothique, Hyperborea and other wondrous heroic fantasy lands

Cordelia Titcomb Smith, anthologist

Cordwainer Smith, Paul Linebarger's classic alter-ego who ushered a new baroque style and universe into modern SF

Dodie Smith, writer of juveniles and creator of *The 101 Dalmatians*

E. E. 'Doc' Smith, bestselling author of the *Grey Lensman* series

Lady Eleanor Furneaux Smith, fantasy writer, *Satan's Circus* (1932) and *Lovers' Meeting* (1940)

Ernest Bramah Smith, as Ernest Bramah, the creator of the Kai Lung series

Evelyn E. Smith, frequent US contributor to *Galaxy* and the author of several novels

Garret Smith, *Argosy* contributor and author of *Between Worlds* (1919) and *The Treasures of Tantalus* (1920)

George H. Smith, prolific US genre writer with a long list of novels

George O. Smith, *Astounding* contributor and creator of the classic *Venus Equilateral* series

Guy N. Smith, prolific British writer of horror novels

H. Allen Smith, author of *The Age of the Tail* (1955)

Keith Smith, Australian writer of *Ogf* (1965)

L. H. Smith, as Speedy Williams the author of *Journey Through Space* (1958)

L. Neil Smith, active Ballantine writer, *His Majesty's Bucketeers* (1981) and *The Probability Broach* (1980) are his better novels

Langdon Smith, poet of *Evolution* (1895)

Martin Cruz Smith, contemporary bestselling novelist of *Gorky Park*. He has written an SF alternate earth yarn *The Indians Won* (1970)

Ron Smith, Australian collaborator of John Baxter as Martin Loran

Surrey Smith, writer of *The Village That Wandered* (1960)

Thorne Smith, the classic light fantasy creator of the *Topper* books

Wayland Smith, author of *The Machine Stops* (1936)

W. J. Smith, writer of *The Grand Voyage* (1975)

Twelve SF Writers Who Are Also Illustrators, and Vice Versa

1. *Hannes Bok* One of the most popular SF illustrators of the 1940s and '50s, whose work is nowadays keenly collected, Bok also wrote three novels, and completed two left unfinished by A. Merritt

2. *John Coleman Burroughs* Son of ERB, he illustrated thirteen of his father's novels, drew a comic-strip version of 'John Carter of Mars' – and published an SF novel, *Treasure of the Black Falcon*

3. *James Cawthorn* Collaborator with Michael Moorcock (as 'Philip James') on *The Distant Suns*, Cawthorn has also been a magazine and book-jacket artist, and has illustrated comic-strip versions of Moorcock novels

4. *Hal Clement* A hobbyist painter, Clement has also had his work reproduced professionally – e.g. in *Space Art*, compiled by Ron Miller

5. *Elliott Dold* One of the most noted SF illustrators of the 1930s, Dold also published a story, 'The Bowl of Death', in the first issue of the rare *Miracle SF*

6. *Harry Harrison* Harrison was a professional comic-book illustrator before becoming a writer, and though he has largely abandoned illustration in recent years he did draw the covers for the British editions of two of his *Stainless Steel Rat* novels

7. *Damon Knight* Knight's first professional sale was a cartoon, and in the early 1940s he contributed a number of black-and-white illustrations to low-budget SF magazines

8. *Judith Ann Lawrence* Married to the late James Blish, Lawrence has published several SF stories and a *Star Trek* novel. A professional illustrator, she has executed a number of book jackets, including that of the British edition of Christopher Priest's *Fugue for a Darkening Island*

9. *Keith Roberts* Perhaps the most successful of these dual careerists, Roberts's simple, but stylish and distinctive illustrations were a feature of *New Worlds* and *Science Fantasy* in the 1960s

10. *Andrew Stephenson* Author of two novels and a number of stories, Stephenson has also contributed illustrations to *Galaxy* magazine, and to the US edition of Christopher Priest's *Inverted World*

11. *Joan Vinge* Although she has not published illustrations in books or magazines, Vinge has produced drawings to accompany her

stories, which have been sold in limited-edition portfolios
12. *Kurt Vonnegut* Perhaps Vonnegut's drawings would be more aptly characterized as 'doodles'; nonetheless, they are present in abundance in his novel *Breakfast of Champions*

The list might be extended in other ways. There are writers such as Thomas M. Disch, Fritz Leiber and Pamela Zoline who are also artists, though not SF artists. There are also two Hugo-winning fan artists – both cartoonists – who have published SF novels: Alexis Gilliland and William Rotsler

Twenty Leading British SF and Fantasy Artists

1. Jim Burns
2. Roger Dean
3. Les Edwards
4. Jim Fitzpatrick
5. Chris Foss
6. Brian Froud
7. Peter Goodfellow
8. David Hardy
9. Eddie Jones
10. Peter Jones
11. Josh Kirby
12. Alan Lee
13. Brian Lewis (1950s)
14. Ian Miller
15. Chris Moore
16. Bruce Pennington
17. Gerard Quinn (1950s)
18. Tony Roberts
19. Tim White
20. Patrick Woodroffe

Twenty Leading American SF and Fantasy Artists

1. George Barr
2. Earle Bergey (1940s)
3. Hannes Bok (1940s/'50s)
4. Howard Brown (1930s)
5. Vincent Di Fate
6. Leo and Diane Dillon
7. Ed Emshwiller (1950s/'60s)
8. Stephen Fabian
9. Virgil Finlay (1940s/'50s)
10. Frank Frazetta
11. Kelly Freas
12. Paul Lehr
13. Don Maitz
14. Frank R. Paul (1920s/'30s)
15. Richard Powers
16. John Schoenherr
17. Rick Sternbach
18. Boris Vallejo
19. 'Wesso' (H. Wessolowski) (1930s)
20. Michael Whelan

The dates indicate the period of major activity for artists no longer producing SF art

Ten Important British and American SF Comic-Strip Artists

1. Frank Bellamy (UK) – worked on both *Dan Dare* and *Garth*, among many others
2. Dick Calkins (US) – illustrated the original *Buck Rogers* comic strip
3. Howard Chaykin (US) – a highly regarded artist who has, among much else, illustrated comic-strip novels by Bester, Delany and Moorcock
4. Richard Corben (US) – his science-fantasy strips featuring the character Den have been highly popular, and were adapted for the movie *Heavy Metal*

5. Frank Hampson (UK) – the creator of Britain's best-loved strip, *Dan Dare*
6. Sydney Jordan (UK) – illustrated *Jeff Hawke*, probably the most sophisticated of all newspaper SF strips
7. Jack Kirby (US) – creator of *The Fantastic Four* and the major illustrator of the early Stan Lee Marvel Comics
8. Angus McKie (UK) – his strip, *So Beautiful and So Dangerous* was adapted to make another highlight of *Heavy Metal*
9. Alex Raymond (US) – hugely influential and much revered illustrator of *Flash Gordon*
10. James Steranko (US) – after Kirby the most highly regarded of Marvel Comics artists; also a noted historian of comics

Twenty Definitions of Science Fiction

Possibly because as a genre it has no bounds and is an open invitation for the imagination to run wild, science fiction has always proved very hard to define. The task of delineating what and what isn't SF has puzzled authors and critics for years already and all still have to agree on the ideal formula that could encompass the wide field of SF. Possibly, no one will ever agree and the mystery of what constitutes SF will remain whole and eternal.

1. *Brian Aldiss*: Science fiction is the search for a definition of man and his status in the universe which will stand in our advanced but confused state of knowledge (science), and is characteristically cast in the Gothic or post-Gothic mode
2. *Kingsley Amis*: Science fiction is that class of prose narrative treating of a situation that could not arise in the world we know, but which is hypothesized on the basis of some innovation in science or technology, or pseudo-science or pseudo-technology, whether human or extra-terrestrial in origin
3. *Isaac Asimov*: Science fiction is that branch of literature that deals with human responses to changes in the level of science and technology
4. *J. O. Bailey*: A piece of scientific fiction is a narrative of an imaginary invention or discovery in the natural sciences and consequent adventures and experience

5. *Reginald Bretnor:* [Fiction] in which the author shows awareness of the nature and importance of the human activity known as the scientific method, shows equal awareness of the great body of human knowledge already collected through that activity, and takes into account in his stories the effect and possible future effects on human beings of scientific methods and scientific fact

6. *John Clute and Peter Nicholls:* Science fiction is a label applied to a publishing category and its application is subject to the whims of editors and publishers

7. *L. Sprague de Camp:* Fiction based upon scientific or pseudo-scientific assumptions (space-travel, robots, telepathy, earthly immortality, and so forth) or laid in any patently unreal though non-supernatural setting (the future, or another world, and so forth)

8. *Hugo Gernsback:* Scientifiction [is] a charming romance intermingled with scientific fact and prophetic vision

9. *Robert A. Heinlein:* A handy short definition of almost all science fiction might read: realistic speculation about possible future events, based solidly on adequate knowledge of the real world, past and present, and on a thorough understanding of the scientific method. To make the definition cover all science fiction (instead of 'almost all') it is necessary only to strike out the word 'future'

10. *Barry N. Malzberg:* That branch of fiction that deals with the possible effects of an altered technology or social system on mankind in an imagined future, an altered present, or an alternative past

11. *Judith Merril:* Speculative fiction: stories whose objective is to explore, to discover, to *learn*, by means of projection, extrapolation, analogue, hypothesis-and-paper-experimentation, something about the nature of the universe, of man, of 'reality'

12. *Sam Moskowitz:* Science fiction is a branch of fantasy identifiable by the fact that it eases the 'willing suspension of disbelief' on the part of its readers by utilizing an atmosphere of scientific credibility for its imaginative speculations in physical science, space, time, social science, and philosophy

13. *Frederik Pohl:* It is that thing that people who understand science fiction point to, when they point to something and say "That's science fiction!'

14. *Fred Saberhagen:* A literary genre developed principally in the

20th Century, dealing with scientific discovery or development that, whether set in the future, in the fictitious present, or in the putative past, is superior to or simply other than that known to exist (*Encyclopedia Britannica*)

15. *Robert Scholes*: Fiction that offers us a world clearly and radically discontinuous from the one we know, yet returns to confront that known world in some cognitive way

16. *Tom Shippey*: Science fiction is hard to define because it is the literature of change and it changes while you are trying to define it

17. *Norman Spinrad*: There is only one definition of science fiction that seems to make pragmatic sense: 'Science fiction is anything published as science fiction'

18. *Theodore Sturgeon*: A science fiction story is a story built around human beings, with a human problem and a human solution, which would not have happened at all without its scientific content

19. *Darko Suvin*: A literary genre whose necessary and sufficient conditions are the presence and interaction of estrangement and cognition, and whose main formal device is an imaginative framework alternative to the author's empirical environment

20. *Donald A. Wollheim*: Science fiction is that branch of fantasy, which, while not true of present-day knowledge, is rendered plausible by the reader's recognition of the scientific possibilities of it being possible at some future date or at some uncertain period in the past

Lester Del Rey's Five Ages of Science Fiction

Lester Del Rey is an important figure in the SF field. His prestigious career as a writer began in 1938 and continues almost to this day; he has also been an influential, if conservative, critic, editor and historian of the genre. Although his last published novel dates back to 1971, he is still highly active in an important editorial position at Del Rey/Ballantine Books where he is responsible for the fantasy line and was the discoverer of Stephen Donaldson. His breakdown of the history of SF comes from his *The World of Science Fiction, 1926–1976*, a book-length study published in 1980

1. *The Age of Wonder* – 1926–37   Uncle Hugo and *Amazing* . . . *The Skylark of Space* . . . early fandom . . . spanning the galaxy at a half cent a word
2. *The Golden Age* – 1938–49   Campbell and *Astounding* . . . Heinlein, Asimov, and Sturgeon break new ground . . . atomic energy: fiction to fact . . . the first World SF Convention
3. *The Age of Acceptance* – 1950–61   The *Galaxy* years . . . the great magazine blight . . . the rise of the paperbacks
4. *The Age of Rebellion* – 1962–73   The New Wave, Harlan the Terrible and *Dangerous Visions* . . . the anthology explosion . . . SF in the schools . . . 2,000 plus at a World SF Convention
5. *The Fifth Age* – 1974–   'Sci-fi' hits the big time in books, films and TV . . . another boom in the making – and another burst? . . . a convention every week . . . *Star Wars* and after

Fifteen Pieces of SF Terminology

1. *Android*   A robot with humanoid appearance, or more commonly, an artificially created organic humanoid. Introduced in this modern usage by Jack Williamson in *The Cometeers* (1936)
2. *Ansible*   A communications device that transmits instantaneously by use of gravity waves; used by Ursula Le Guin in her Hainish stories
3. *BEM*   Bug-Eyed Monster: an abbreviation which has gone into widespread use
4. *Conapt* ('Condominium apartment')   An abbreviation used by Philip Dick in many of his novels
5. *Corpsicle*   A term coined by Frederik Pohl to describe bodies kept in cryonic suspension for future thawing and resuscitation
6. *Grok*   What people learn to do apropos of each other and the world in Robert Heinlein's *Stranger in a Strange Land*. It's a particularly deep and embracing understanding. You grok?
7. *Kipple*   'Kipple is useless objects, like junk mail or match folders after you use the last match or gum wrappers.' A form of detritus which breeds when nobody's looking. Your home can fill up with it in a matter of days. Introduced in Philip Dick's *Do Androids Dream of Electric Sheep?*

8. *Organlegger* Illegal supplier of human spare parts for transplant surgery. Used in several Larry Niven stories
9. *Robot* The Czech word meaning 'worker', given its SF meaning in Karel Capek's *RUR*
10. *Seetee* Contra-terrene (CT) matter: an alternative term to 'antimatter', introduced by Jack Williamson
11. *Spindizzies* Antigravity devices capable of moving whole cities in James Blish's *Cities in Flight* novels
12. *Tanj!* A Larry Niven coined acronym: There Ain't No Justice!
13. *Tanstaafl!* Acronym from the expression 'there ain't no such thing as a free lunch', which becomes a rallying cry in Robert Heinlein's *The Moon is a Harsh Mistress*
14. *Terraforming* Another Jack Williamson coinage, meaning to modify a planet to attain Earth-like conditions
15. *Waldo* A remote-control manipulator, introduced by Robert Heinlein in his short novel of the same title (1942); now in common use to describe such devices (which were developed subsequently)

Milestones in Bad Science Fiction

More than any other genre, SF has suffered a lot of bad writing. One could almost compile a whole volume of rather fun bad quotes from books and this list is anything but definitive. Most of the following choices were first published in *Vector*, the journal of the British Science Fiction Association where they appeared as amusing page-fillers. Our thanks to David Langford and all those who suffered to select them

The ships were so big, so vast, so fast. Faster than sounds. The noise reached you after the ship made it. That was why there was never any warning

And as the heads turned, Vawn began to giggle. For on top of each female head were the bonnets: and the bonnets resembled nothing so much as – what was the word – *brassières*, that was it, those things women wore in the twentieth century

'. . . Where do meteorites come from?' 'Space,' said Vawn, in a bored voice. 'Look, I'm hungry—' 'That's it! Space! So that tells you one important thing about meteorites!' said Ispex. 'What important thing? Is anyone else hungry?' Vawn said. But Tsu said, 'Go on!' 'It tells you,' said Ispex, impressively, 'that meteorites are spaceworthy!'

From *Starstormers* by Nicholas Fisk

'It's moving,' he said curtly. 'Heading for us. Just what we'd do if a strange spaceship appeared in our hunting grounds! . . . Thank God for the blasters!' 'Blasters, sir? What for?' The skipper grimaced at the empty visiplate. 'Because we don't know what they're like and can't take a chance!'

From 'First Contact' by Murray Leinster

He had to keep moving, it was like groping your way through a thick fog. The beams of your headlights throwing the fog back at you. It was like that, and yet it wasn't

If you could translate a problem into computer terms, then there was no problem you couldn't answer. It all depended on a man's ability to translate. To get the feel of a problem. To sense it. To view the whole cosmos as a huge mathematical equation. An enormous complex, and yet perfectly solvable, quadratic

He kept on feeding information and corrections. Looking at tapes and then re-feeding his answers. He worked in a series of concentric rectangles . . .

What the devil could it be? he asked himself over and over again. Only the length of the torch beam separated him from his objective now. He drew closer, and closer still. Then he recognized the peculiar gleaming object for what it was - a door handle!

From *The Asteroid Man* by R. L. Fanthorpe

Bruce the pilot acknowledged this with a bit of a grunt. 'Uh huh . . .' he managed to let out between his teeth

And now not a soul in the world would be any of the wiser as to what secret of the speechless minnows he held and had not divulged. And all because of the insalubriousness of a rock cavity

It was as if whatever device the object carried, induced in them a stupor of complete submission to another will more omnipotent than their own

Kurt Semen had been repeatedly jailed for disturbing the peace and inciting unnecessary pathos . . .

Many answers were tautologous as he and his colleagues had had to guess them

The echoing of the lesser explosions left the commando effete. The oubliette was surely nothing but a wreckage of worthless museum exhibits

Their rocket functions by means of a beam of photons projected fore and aft of the machine. The one serving to reduce pressure in an atmosphere from the nacelle of the craft, the latter to create a molecular pressure against elements in the tail of the craft by which method they were thrust forward much in the fashion of a jet

Man is an indefinable creature. The Ancient Greeks pondered over the amber glow that emanates from two materials in friction. Today we have the science of electronics

Was this a trap, the anticlimax, the bathos to it all. Final death?

It was to no avail. Rick was apparently dead. The fall was too great. Death had supined.

From *The Troglodytes* by Neal Rafcam

'I think you're cute too,' Zebbie answered, grabbed me by both shoulders, dragged me over the table, and kissed me hard. Our teeth grated and my nipples went *spung!*

'I'd be an idiot to risk competing with Deety's teats.'

My darling keeps her feelings out of her face, mostly, but those pretty pink spigots are barometers of her morale.

Her face remained calm but the light went out - and her nipples went down.

My nipples popped out; I grinned and stuck out my tongue at them. They stayed up; I was happy.

From *The Number of the Beast* by Robert Heinlein

'You may see the General now. Take the red carpet, please, and follow your shoes.'

'You will take the orange carpet to your left,' said a voice from his glass shoes.

'We landed on a sun,' he said slowly. 'A sun? . . . But why?' 'Probably for safety. What kind of being could come through this heat without a lot of preparation?' 'The dome must be a perfect insulator.' 'Either that, or they use the heat for refrigeration.'

'You make me ill!' Volmik said harshly and uttered the most insulting statement known to Alphirkians: 'You make my guts tired.'

From *The Man with Absolute Motion* by Silas Water

'Lothar! Ask him what the hell tigers are doing in an African jungle? Doesn't he know that tigers can only be found in Asia?' The tiger roared as Lothar spoke. 'What did he say?' 'He say: "You know it, and I know it - but do tigers know it?"'

'He says Tarzan hasn't bathed in 65 years - all jungle run in terror when Tarzan come - except bats, which have no olfactory nerves.'

From *Her* by J. X. Williams

Once it had landed the silence was gone - like an illusion that is destroyed when the curtains of a stage are pulled aside. The silence was broken by metallic noises. Harsh clanking, jarring, metallic noises. Things were stirring within the disc ship. Strange metallic things; things that were alien to the soft green grass of earth.

Terrifying things, steel things; metal things; things with cylindrical bodies and multitudinous jointed limbs. Things without flesh and blood. Things that were made of metal and plastic and transistors and valves and relays, and wires. Metal things. Metal things that could think. *Thinking metal things.* Terrifying in their strangeness, in their peculiar metal efficiency. Things the like of which had never been seen on earth before. Things that were sliding back panels . . . *Robots!* Robots were marching . . . Robots were marching; and were about to spread havoc and destruction across the earth, and as yet the sleeping earth knew nothing of their coming. As mysterious as anything in the great mysterious universe.

The robots in their disc ship had arrived . . . There were strange flickering lights all around the ship. Terrifying lights, weird lights, uncanny lights, awful lights, inhuman lights, alien lights, robot lights; and all around a great hemispherical glowing shield sprang up. A thing with pale greeny blue luminescence. An electronic thing, a mechanical thing. A thing that was part of the robot genius. A thing that was as strange as the ship and its occupants. A force field, a glowing greenish blue force field.

From *The Coming of the Robots* by Leo Brett

The foot remained where it was, drawn back lethal, loaded, deadly.

'The melbar instantaneous transmitter,' answered Knight, 'is not functioning. So we're like a blind man lost in a desert without a camel. . .'

'Don't threaten me with that thing,' said the dreadful bacteriologist, 'I can fire mine as quickly as you can fire that!'

Suddenly there was that strange feeling in the air. There was a weird sensation of *the presence of a presence*; they were no longer alone!

From *Micro Infinity* by John E. Muller

'I've said you're a chancroid, Hook, and a burst ulcer, and a candidate for advanced pustular syphiloderma, and I'll go on telling you you're a Pasturalla pestis . . .'

The Customs Man recovered his balance and, with the speed of a striking sex-crazed strooka, drew his weapon. The Tonota Eighty could vapourize a man's head at six hundred meters.

The two voices out there whispered fiercely as their owners squabbled. 'Oxymoron, Line! He's only an eczema-sniffing spirochaete sap! You should be able to rubberize him before your first tutorial!' 'It's all right for you, Taynor Sinker! You don't have the trouble I have with the rubberization process.'

Giffler melted.

His body deliquesced. It oozed. His head flowed and collapsed and sloughed. Still upright, he melted and shrank and collapsed, his body shimmered like a blood-drenched jelly. He shrank and oozed and formed a contracting pool of scum on the yard stones.

A robot vacuum cleaner and scrubber darted out on rubber wheels and began to suck and clean the spot where Giffler had died.

From the *Hook* series by Tully Zetford

The Launch Pad: A List of Authors' First SF/Fantasy Appearance in Print

Murray Leinster, *Oh, Aladdin!*, in *Argosy*, January 1919

John Taine, *The Purple Sapphire*, first book publication in 1924

Ralph Milne Farley, *The Radio Man*, in *Argosy*, June 1924

Edmond Hamilton, *The Monster-God of Mamurth*, in *Weird Tales*, August 1926

Donald Wandrei, *The Red Brain*, in *Weird Tales*, October 1927

Manly Wade Wellman, *Back to the Beast*, in *Weird Tales*, November 1927

David H. Keller, *The Revolt of the Pedestrians*, in *Amazing*, February 1928

Fletcher Pratt, *The Octopus Cycle*, in *Amazing*, May 1928

Stanton Coblentz, *The Sunken World*, in *Amazing Stories Quarterly*, Summer 1928

E. E. Smith, *The Skylark of Space*, in *Amazing*, August 1928

Jack Williamson, *The Metal Man* in *Amazing*, December 1928

Raymond Z. Gallun, *The Crystal Ray*, in *Air Wonder*, November 1929

John W. Campbell, *When the Atoms Failed*, in *Amazing*, January 1930

Laurence Manning, *City of the Living Dead*, in *Science Wonder*, May 1930

P. Schuyler Miller, *The Red Plague*, in *Wonder Stories*, July 1930

Nat Schachner, *The Tower of Evil*, in *Wonder Stories Quarterly*, Summer 1930

Philip Wylie, *Gladiator*, first book publication in 1930

Olaf Stapledon, *Last and First Men*, first book publication in 1930

John Beynon Harris (John Wyndham), *Worlds to Barter*, in *Wonder Stories*, May 1931

Clifford D. Simak, *The World of the Red Sun*, in *Wonder Stories*, December 1931

Donald Wandrei, *Raiders of the Universe*, in *Astounding*, September 1932

Eando Binder, *The First Martian*, in *Amazing*, October 1932

John Russell Fearn, *The Intelligence Gigantic*, in *Amazing*, June 1933

C. L. Moore, *Shambleau*, in *Weird Tales*, November 1933

Donald Wollheim, *The Man from Ariel*, in *Wonder Stories*, January 1934

Stanley G. Weinbaum, *A Martian Odyssey*, in *Wonder Stories*, July 1934

Robert Moore Williams (as Robert Moore), *Zero as a Limit* in *Astounding*, July 1934

H. L. Gold (as Clyde Crane Campbell), *Inflexure*, in *Astounding*, Octobr 1934

Robert Bloch, *Lilies*, in *Marvel Tales*, Winter 1934

William F. Temple, *The Kosso*, in *Thrills* (anthology), 1935

Forrest J. Ackerman, *Earth's Lucky Day*, in *Wonder*, March 1936

Henry Kuttner, *The Graveyard Rats*, in *Weird Tales*, March 1936

Eric Frank Russell, *The Saga of Pelican West*, in *Astounding*, February 1937

L. Sprague de Camp, *The Isolinguals*, in *Astounding*, September 1937

Frederik Pohl (as Elton V. Andrews), *Elegy to a Dead Satellite: Luna*, in *Amazing*, October 1937

Lester del Rey, *The Faithful*, in *Astounding*, April 1938

L. Ron Hubbard, *The Dangerous Dimension*, in *Astounding*, July 1938

Isaac Asimov, *Marooned off Vesta*, in *Amazing*, March 1939

Alfred Bester, *The Broken Axiom*, in *Thrilling Wonder*, April 1939

A. E. Van Vogt, *Black Destroyer*, in *Astounding*, July 1939

Robert A. Heinlein, *Life-Line*, in *Astounding*, August 1939

Fritz Leiber, *Two Sought Adventure*, in *Unknown*, August 1939

Theodore Sturgeon, *Ether Breather*, in *Astounding*, September 1939

Leigh Brackett, *Martian Quest*, in *Astounding*, February 1940

James Blish, *Emergency Refueling*, in *Super Science Stories*, March 1940

C. M. Kornbluth (with Richard Wilson as Ivar Towers), *Stepsons of Mars*, in *Astonishing*, April 1940

Fredric Brown, *Not Yet the End*, in *Captain Future*, January 1941

Damon Knight, *Resilience*, in *Stirring Science Stories*, February 1941

Wilson Tucker, *Interstellar Way-Station*, in *Super Science Stories*, May 1941

Ray Bradbury, *Pendulum*, in *Super Science Stories*, November 1941

Anthony Boucher, *Snulbug*, in *Unknown*, December 1941

Hal Clement, *Proof*, in *Astounding*, June 1942

George O. Smith, *QRM-Interplanetary*, in *Astounding*, October 1942

James H. Schmitz, *Greenface*, in *Unknown*, August 1943

A. Bertram Chandler, *This Means War*, in *Astounding*, May 1944
Jack Vance, *The World-Thinker*, in *Thrilling Wonder*, Summer 1945
Arthur C. Clarke, *Loophole*, in *Astounding*, April 1946
William Tenn, *Alexander the Bait*, in *Astounding*, May 1946
Margaret St Clair, *Rocket to Limbo*, in *Fantastic Adventures*, November 1946
Poul Anderson, *Tomorrow's Children*, in *Astounding*, March 1947
H. Beam Piper, *Time and Time Again*, in *Astounding*, April 1947
T. L. Sherred, *E for Effort*, in *Astounding*, May 1947
Ward Moore, *Greener Than You Think*, first book publication in 1947
Judith Merril, *That Only a Mother*, in *Astounding*, June 1948
Charles L. Harness, *Time Trap*, in *Astounding*, August 1948
John Christopher (as Christopher Youd), *Christmas Tree*, in *Astounding*, February 1949
Kris Neville, *The Hand from the Stars*, in *Super Science Stories*, July 1949
James Gunn (as Edwin James), *Communications*, in *Startling Stories*, September 1949
Katherine MacLean, *Defense Mechanism*, in *Astounding*, October 1949
Cordwainer Smith, *Scanners Live in Vain*, in *Fantasy Book*, January 1950
Gordon R. Dickson, *Trespass!* in *Fantastic Stories Quarterly*, March 1950
Mack Reynolds, *Isolationist*, in *Fantastic Adventures*, April 1950
Richard Matheson, *Born of Man and Woman*, in *F&SF*, Summer 1950
Chad Oliver, *The Land of Lost Content*, in *Super Science Fiction*, November 1950
J. T. McIntosh, *The Curfew Tolls*, in *Astounding*, December 1950
Kurt Vonnegut, *Report on the Barnhouse Effect*, in *Collier's*, 1950
Charles Beaumont, *The Devil, You Say?*, in *Amazing Stories*, January 1951
Walter M. Miller Jr, *The Secret of the Death Dome*, in *Amazing Stories*, January 1951
Harry Harrison, *Rock Diver*, in *World Beyond*, February 1951
Alan E. Nourse, *The High Threshold*, in *Astounding*, March 1951
Edgar Pangborn, *Angel's Egg*, in *Galaxy*, June 1951
E. C. Tubb, *No Short Cuts*, in *New Worlds*, June 1951
Zenna Henderson, *Come on, Wagon*, in *F&SF*, December 1951
Edmund Cooper, *The Unicorn*, in *Everybody's*, 1951
Stanislaw Lem, *The Astronauts*, first book publication in 1951
John Brunner (as Gill Hunt), *Galactic Storm*, first book publication in 1951
Daniel F. Galouye, *Rebirth*, in *Imagination*, March 1952

Ron Goulart, *Letters to the Editor*, in *F&SF*, April 1952
Frank Herbert, *Looking for Something*, in *Startling Stories*, April 1952
Mark Clifton, *What Have I Done?*, in *Astounding*, May 1952
Daniel Keyes, *Precedent*, in *Marvel SF*, May 1952
Robert Sheckley, *Final Examination*, in *Imagination*, May 1952
Theodore Cogswell, *The Spectre General*, in *Astounding*, June 1952
Philip K. Dick, *Beyond Lies the Wub*, in *Planet Stories*, July 1952
Philip José Farmer, *The Lovers*, in *Startling Stories*, August 1952
Algis Budrys, *Walk to the World*, in *Space SF*, November 1952
Christopher Anvil, *Cinderella Inc*, in *Imagination*, December 1952
Kenneth Bulmer (with A. V. Clarke), *Space Treason*, first book publicatiion in 1952
James White, *Assisted Passage*, in *New Worlds*, January 1953
Robert F. Young, *The Black Deep Thou Wingest*, in *Startling Stories*, June 1953
Marion Zimmer Bradley, *Keyhole* and *Women Only*, both in *Vortex*, October 1953
Anne McCaffrey, *Freedom of the Race*, in *SF Plus*, October 1953
Arthur Sellings, *The Haunting*, in *Authentic*, October 1953
Thomas N. Scortia, *The Prodigy*, in *SF Adventures*, February 1954
Robert Silverberg, *Gordon Planet*, in *Nebula*, February 1954
Barrington J. Bayley, *Combat's End*, in *Vargo Statten SF Magazine*, May 1954
Brian W. Aldiss, *Criminal Record*, in *Science Fantasy*, July 1954
Avram Davidson, *My Boy Friend's Name is Jello*, in *F&SF*, July 1954
William F. Nolan, *The Joy of Living*, in *If*, August 1954
Bob Shaw, *Aspect*, in *Nebula*, August 1954
Andrew J. Offutt, *And Gone Tomorrow*, in *If*, December 1954
G. C. Edmondson, *Blessed Are the Meek*, in *Astounding*, September 1955
Gérard Klein, *Une Place au Balcon*, in *Galaxie*, October 1955
Philippe Curval, *L'Oeuf d'Elduo*, in *Fiction*, December 1955
Harlan Ellison, *Glow-Worm*, in *Infinity*, February 1956
Lloyd Biggle Jr, *Gypped*, in *Galaxy*, July 1956
Kate Wilhelm, *The Pint-Sized Genie*, in *Fantastic*, October 1956
J. G. Ballard, *Prima Belladonna*, in *Science Fantasy*, December 1956
Stefan Wul, *Retour à O*, first book publication in 1956
Fred Hoyle, *The Black Cloud*, first book publication in 1957
Michael Moorcock, *Sojan the Swordsman*, in *Tarzan Adventures*, 1957
Thomas Burnett Swann, *Winged Victory*, in *Fantastic Universe*, July 1958
Richard McKenna, *Casey Agonistes*, in *F&SF*, September 1958

Keith Laumer, *Greylorn*, in *Amazing*, April 1959
Joanna Russ, *Nor Custom Stale*, in *F&SF*, September 1959
Ben Bova, *The Star Conquerors*, first book publication in 1959
Arkady and Boris Strugatsky, *The Country of the Purple Clouds*, first
   book publication in 1959
R. A. Lafferty, *Day of the Glacier*, in *Science Fiction*, January 1960
Michel Jeury (as Albert Higon) *Aux Etoiles du Destin*, first book publi-
   cation in 1960
Fred Saberhagen, *Volume Paa-Pyx*, in *Galaxy*, February 1961
Terry Carr, *Who Sups with the Devil?*, in *F&SF* May 1962
Roger Zelazny, *Passion Play*, in *Amazing*, August 1962
Ursula K. Le Guin, *April in Paris*, in *Fantastic*, September 1962
Thomas M. Disch, *The Double-Timer*, in *Fantastic*, October 1962
Samuel R. Delany, *The Jewels of Aptor*, first book publication in 1962
Piers Anthony, *Possible to Rue*, in *Fantastic*, April 1963
Norman Spinrad, *The Last of the Romany*, in *Analog*, May 1963
Alexei Panshin, *Down to the World of Men*, in *If*, July 1963
Langdon Jones, *Stormwater Tunnel*, in *New Worlds*, July 1964
Keith Roberts, *Escapism*, in *Science Fantasy*, September 1964
Larry Niven, *Coldest Place*, in *If*, December 1964
Charles Platt, *One of Those Days*, in *Science Fantasy*, December 1964
Gregory Benford, *Stand-In*, in *F&SF*, June 1965
Josephine Saxton, *The Wall*, in *Science Fantasy*, November 1965
Brian Stableford (as Brian Craig), in *Science Fantasy*, November 1965
Christopher Priest, *The Run*, in *Impulse*, May 1966
Gene Wolfe, *Mountains like Mice*, in *If*, May 1966
Gardner F. Dozois, *The Empty Man*, in *If*, September 1966
Doris Piserchia, *Rocket to Gehenna*, in *Amazing*, September 1966
John T. Sladek, *The Poets of Millgrove, Iowa*, in *New Worlds*,
   November 1966
Dean Koontz, *Soft Come the Dragons*, in *F&SF*, August 1967
Barry N. Malzberg (as K. M. O'Donnell), *We're Coming Through the
   Window*, in *Galaxy*, August 1967
Richard Cowper, *Breakthrough*, first book publication in 1967
Mark S. Geston, *Lord of the Starship*, first book publication in 1967
Richard A. Lupoff, *One Million Centuries*, first book publication in
   1967
James Tiptree Jr, *Birth of a Salesman*, in *Analog*, March 1968
M. John Harrison, *Baa Baa Blocksheep*, in *New Worlds*, November 1968
Robert P. Holdstock, *Pauper's Plot*, in *New Worlds*, November 1968

Joe Haldeman, *Out of Phase*, in *Galaxy*, September 1969
Ian Watson, *Roof Garden Under Saturn*, in *New Worlds*, November 1969
David Gerrold, *Oracle for a White Rabbit*, in *Galaxy*, December 1969
Michael Coney, *Symbiote*, in *New Writings in SF 15*, 1969
Edward Bryant, *Sending the Very Best*, in *New Worlds*, January 1970
Vonda N. McIntyre, *Breaking Point*, in *Venture*, February 1970
Jack Dann (with George Zebrowski), *Traps*, in *Worlds of If*, March 1970
Gordon Eklund, *Dear Aunt Annie*, in *Fantastic*, April 1970
Pamela Sargent, *Landed Minority*, in *F&SF*, September 1970
Michael Bishop, *Piñon Fall*, in *Galaxy*, October 1970
George Zebrowski, *The Water Sculptor*, in *Infinity One*, 1970
Tanith Lee, *The Dragon Hoard*, first book publication in 1971
George R. R. Martin, *The Hero*, in *Galaxy*, February 1971
George Alec Effinger, *The 8.30 to 9.00 Slot*, in *Amazing*, April 1971
Jerry Pournelle, *Peace with Honor*, in *Analog*, May 1971
Lisa Tuttle, *Stranger in the House*, in *Clarion 2*, 1972
Spider Robinson, *The Guy with Eyes*, in *Analog*, February 1973
John Varley, *Picnic on Nearside*, in *F&SF*, August 1974
Tom Reamy, *Twilla*, in *F&SF*, September 1974
Suzy McKee Charnas, *Walk to the End of the World*, first book publication in 1974
Joan D. Vinge, *Tin Soldier*, in *Orbit 14*, 1974
Cherry Wilder, *The Ark of James Carlyle*, in *New Writings in SF 24*, 1974
John Crowley, *The Deep*, first book publication in 1975
M. A. Foster, *The Warriors of Dawn*, first book publication in 1975
Jack Chalker, *A Jungle of Stars*, first book publication in 1976
C. J. Cherryh, *Gate of Ivrel*, first book publication in 1976
Carter Scholz, *The Eve of the Last Apollo*, in *Orbit 18*, 1976
Orson Scott Card, *Ender's Game*, in *Analog*, August 1977
Stephen Donaldson, *Lord Foul's Bane*, first book publication in 1977
Rudy Rucker, *Spacetime Donuts*, in *Unearth*, Summer 1978

Twenty Famous First Novels

Some authors arrive on the scene gradually; others announce themselves with a flourish. All the following first novels fall into the latter category, and in each case there are at least some critics who would claim that the first novel remains the author's best.

1. Brian Aldiss, *Non-Stop*
2. Piers Anthony, *Chthon*
3. Alfred Bester, *The Demolished Man*
4. Ray Bradbury, *Fahrenheit 451*
5. Arthur C. Clarke, *Against the Fall of Night (The City and the Stars)*
6. Daniel F. Galouye, *Dark Universe*
7. Joe Haldeman, *The Forever War*
8. Charles Harness, *The Paradox Men*
9. Harry Harrison, *Deathworld*
10. Frank Herbert, *The Dragon in the Sea (Under Pressure)*
11. Daniel Heyes, *Flowers for Algernon*
12. Fred Hoyle, *The Black Cloud*
13. David Lindsay, *A Voyage to Arcturus*
14. Walter Miller, *A Canticle for Leibowitz*
15. Alexei Panshin, *Rite of Passage*
16. Olaf Stapledon, *Last and First Men*
17. A. E. Van Vogt, *Slan*
18. Kurt Vonnegut, *Player Piano*
19. Ian Watson, *The Embedding*
20. H. G. Wells, *The Time Machine*

Twenty-two Famous Opening Lines

1. In the week before their departure to Arrakis, when all the final scurrying about had reached a nearly unbearable frenzy, an old crone came to visit the mother of the boy, Paul.

Dune, Frank Herbert

2. Once upon a time, there was a Martian named Valentine Michael Smith.

Stranger in a Strange Land, Robert Heinlein

3. Like a radar echo bounding from a distant object and returning to its source, the sound of Roy Complain's beating heart seemed to him to fill the clearing.

Non-Stop, Brian Aldiss

271

4. His name was Gaal Dornick and he was just a country boy who had never seen Trantor before.

Foundation, Isaac Asimov

5. Vaughan died yesterday in his last car-crash.

Crash, J. G. Ballard

6. He was one hundred and seventy days dying and not yet dead.

Tiger! Tiger! Alfred Bester

7. At three-thirty AM on the night of June 5, 1992, the top telepath in the Sol system fell off the map in the offices of Runciter Associates in New York City.

Ubik, Philip K. Dick

8. To wound the autumnal city.

Dhalgren, Samuel R. Delany

9. Even on the earth shadows are frequently good places to hide.

Needle, Hal Clement

10. His wife had held him in her arms as if she could keep death away from him.

To Your Scattered Bodies Go, Philip José Farmer

11. The volcano that had reared Taratua up from the Pacific depths had been sleeping now for half a million years.

Childhood's End, Arthur C. Clarke

12. With a gentle sigh the service tube dropped a message capsule into the receiving cup.

Deathworld, Harry Harrison

13. I loved the Captain in my own way, although I knew that he was insane, the poor bastard.

Beyond Apollo, Barry Malzberg

14. At 19.00 hours, ship's time, I made my way to the launching bay.

Solaris, Stanislaw Lem

15. I'll make my report as if I told a story, for I was taught as a child on my homeworld that Truth is a matter of the imagination.

The Left Hand of Darkness, Ursula K. Le Guin

16. In Cambodia, a country that lies between Vietnam and Thailand on the map, between n and zero on the time chart, is the

magic city of Angkor, where once the great Khmer race lived.

The Final Programme, Michael Moorcock

17. In the night-time heart of Beirut, in one of a row of general-address transfer booths, Louis Wu flicked into reality.

Ringworld, Larry Niven

18. To be honest, I haven't been able to remember clearly everything that happened to me before and during Trial, so where necessary I've filled in with possibilities - lies if you want.

Rite of Passage, Alexei Panshin

19. I had reached the age of six hundred and fifty miles.

Inverted World, Christopher Priest

20. They caught the kid doing something disgusting out under the bleachers at the high-school stadium and he was sent home from the grammar school across the street.

The Dreaming Jewels, Theodore Sturgeon

21. Two thousand million years or so ago two galaxies were colliding or, rather, were passing through each other.

Triplanetary, E. E. 'Doc Smith'

22. All this happened, more or less.

Slaughterhouse Five, Kurt Vonnegut

Famous First Issues

The first issue of a magazine may give a clear idea of the glories to come or it may bear no resemblance at all to what the magazine eventually evolves into. Here are the contents lists (stories only) of the first issues of a number of notable SF/fantasy magazines; judge for yourself which category they fall into.

Amazing Stories (USA. First issue April 1926)

Jules Verne - *Off on a Comet* (Part 1)
H. G. Wells - *The New Accelerator*
G. Peyton Wertenbaker - *The Man From the Atom*
George Allan England - *The Thing From - Outside*

Austin Hall - *The Man Who Saved The World*
Edgar Allan Poe - *The Facts in the Case of M. Valdemar*

Astounding Science Fiction (USA. First issue January 1930. Now **Analog**)

Victor Rousseau - *The Beetle Horde* (Part 1)
Captain S. P. Meek - *The Cave of Horror*
Ray Cummings - *Phantoms of Reality*
M. L. Staley - *The Stolen Mind*
C. V. Tench - *Compensation*
Murray Leinster - *Tanks*
Anthony Pelcher - *Invisible Death*

Fantastic (USA. First issue Summer 1952. Ceased publication 1980)

Walter M. Miller - *Six and Ten Are Johnny*
Sam Martinez - *For Heaven's Sake*
Paul W. Fairman - *'Someday They'll Give Us Guns'*
H. B. Hickey - *Full Circle*
Louise Lee Outlaw - *The Runaway*
Kris Neville - *The Opal Necklace*
Ray Bradbury - *The Smile*
H. L. Gold - *And Three To Get Ready*
Isaac Asimov - *What If*
Raymond Chandler - *Professor Bingo's Snuff*

Magazine of Fantasy and Science Fiction (USA. First issue Fall 1949)

Cleve Cartmill - *Bells on His Toes*
Perceval Landon - *Thurnley Abbey*
Philip MacDonald - *Private - Keep Out!*
Fitz-James O'Brien - *The Lost Room*
Theodore Sturgeon - *The Hurkle is a Happy Beast*
H. H. Holmes - *Review Copy*
Guy Endore - *Men of Iron*
Stuart Palmer - *A Bride for the Devil*
Oliver Onions - *Rooum*
Richard Sale - *Perseus Had a Helmet*
Winona McClintic - *In the Days of Our Fathers*

Galaxy (USA. First issue October 1950. Ceased publication 1980)

Clifford D. Simak - *Time Quarry* (Part 1)
Theodore Sturgeon - *The Stars Are the Styx*
Katherine MacLean - *Contagion*
Richard Matheson - *Third From the Sun*
Fritz Leiber - *Later Than You Think*
Fredric Brown - *The Last Martian*
Isaac Asimov - *Darwinian Pool Room*

If (USA. First issue March 1952. Ceased publication 1974)

Howard Browne - *Twelve Times Zero*
Ray Palmer - *The Hell Ship*
Walter M. Miller - *Bitter Victory*
Milton Lesser - *Black Eyes and the Daily Grind*
Richard Shaver - *Of Stegner's Folly*
Theodore Sturgeon - *Never Underestimate*
Rog Phillips - *The Old Martians*
Alvin Heiner - *The Stowaway*

Interzone (British. First issue Spring 1982)

M. John Harrison - *The New Rays*
Keith Roberts - *Kitemaster*
Angela Carter - *The Cabinet of Edgar Allan Poe*
John Sladek - *Guesting*
Michael Moorcock - *The Brothel in Rosenstrasse*

Isaac Asimov's Science Fiction Magazine (USA. First issue Spring 1977)

John Varley - *Good-bye, Robinson Crusoe*
Isaac Asimov - *Think!*
Arthur C. Clarke - *Quarantine*
Edward D. Hoch - *The Homesick Chicken*
Sally A. Sellers - *Perchance to Dream*
Herb Boehm (John Varley) - *Air Raid*
Fred Saberhagen - *Period of Totality*
Sherwood Springer - *The Scorch on Wetzel's Hill*
William Jon Watkins - *Coming of Age in Henson's Tube*
Gordon R. Dickson - *Time Storm*

New Worlds (British. First issue 1946. Ceased regular publication 1970)

Maurice G. Hugi - *The Mill of the Gods*
William F. Temple - *The Three Pylons*
Mark Denholm - *Solar Assignment*
K. Thomas - *Knowledge Without Learning*
John Russell Fearn - *Sweet Mystery of Life*
Thornton Ayre - *White Mouse*

Planet Stories (USA. First issue Winter 1939. Ceased publication 1955)

John Murray Reynolds - *The Golden Amazons of Venus*
Fletcher Pratt and Laurence Manning - *Expedition to Pluto*
Linton Davies - *Warlords of the Moon*
John Wiggin - *Cave-Dwellers of Saturn*

Science Wonder Stories (USA. First issue June 1929. Ceased publication - having become *Thrilling Wonder Stories*, 1955)

Irving Lester and Fletcher Pratt - *The Reign of the Ray* (Part I)
H. G. Wells - *The Diamond Maker*
James P. Marshall - *Warriors of Space*
Kennie McDowd - *The Marble Virgin*
David H. Keller - *The Threat of the Robot*
Stanton A. Coblentz - *The Making of Misty Isle*

Startling Stories (USA. First issue January 1939. Ceased publication 1955)

Stanley G. Weinbaum - *The Black Flame*
D. D. Sharp - *The Eternal Man*
Eando Binder - *Science Island*

Unknown (USA. First issue March 1939. Ceased publication 1943)

Eric Frank Russell - *Sinister Barrier*
Mona Farnsworth - *Who Wants Power?*
Frank Belknap Long - *Dark Vision*
H. L. Gold - *Trouble With Water*
Manly Wade Wellman - *Where Angels Fear*

A. B. L. Macfadyen Jr - *Closed Doors*
Robert Moore Williams - *Death Sentence*

Eleven Harlan Ellison Shock First Lines

Of all contemporary writers, Harlan Ellison is without the shadow of a doubt the most adept at grabbing your attention from the first line of a story onwards. He is the master of the hook and one could almost compile a whole anthology of his opening lines. These are some of our memorable favourites.

1. They flushed the niggers from underground bunkers, out near the perimeter, and Charlie Knox killed his because he thought the boogie was going for a gun ('Knox')

2. Because I had died of cancer of the lymph glands, I was the only one saved when the world disappeared ('Cold Friend')

3. He drank ice crystals laced with midnight and watched their world burn ('Kiss of Fire')

4. You'll pardon me but my name is Evsise and I'm standing here in the middle of the sand, talking to a butterfly, and if I sound like I'm talking to myself, again you'll pardon but what can I tell you? ('I'm Looking for Kadak')

5. In the third year of my death, I met Piretta ('The Time of the Eye')

6. It was half-past September when the red phone rang ('Santa Clause vs SPIDER')

7. I knew she was a virgin because she was able to ruffle the silken mane of my unicorn ('On the Downhill Side')

8. The King of Tibet was having himself a fat white woman ('At the Mouse Circus')

9. If God (or Whoever's in charge) had wanted Dr Netta Bernstein to continue living, He (or She) wouldn't have made it so easy for me to kill her ('Killing Bernstein')

10. When they unscrewed the time capsule, preparatory to helping temponaut Enoch Mirren to disembark, they found him doing a disgusting thing with a disgusting thing ('How's the Night Life on Cissalda?')

11. William Weisel pronounced his name why-*zell*, but many of the unfortunates for whom he had done remodeling and construction pronounced it *weasel* ('The Man Who Was Heavily into Revenge')

Editorial Boobs and Interference

Tales of editorial meddling abound in SF – particularly in the USA, where many editors emerged from the pulp magazines, in which the sign of a good editor was reckoned to be the amount of blue-pencilling he or she put on a typescript. These are a few varied examples of things going wrong.

1. Brian Aldiss's *Non-Stop* is an SF novel set in a mysterious environment which the characters explore. At the end the secret is revealed: they are aboard a giant starship. In order to enhance the mystery its American publisher retitled the novel *Starship*.

2. John Brunner's *The Productions of Time* was so badly mangled by its copy-editor when first published in the USA that the author felt obliged to issue a disclaimer, pointing to over fifty erroneous 'corrections' in the first chapter alone!

3. John Brunner's *The Shock-Wave Rider* had – in the manuscript – two characters who were brothers. Its American copy-editor, presumably deciding that the author had a bad memory, turned them into one

4. Stephen Donaldson's *The One Tree* reportedly got him into trouble with his American editor, Lester del Rey. Del Rey apparently objected to a sequence written in the first person by a woman character: fantasy readers, he maintained, would not stand for this! He seems to have got his way, for no such sequence appears in the published book

5. Edward Ferman and Barry Malzberg's *Final Stage* anthology received unauthorized attention from an overzealous copy-

editor, whose interference led to several authors, among them Harlan Ellison, disowning their stories as published in the original hardcover edition

6. H. L. Gold, influential editor of *Galaxy* magazine, is legendary for his inability to leave well alone. One of his regular contributors, Theodore Sturgeon, took to crossing through any phrase he (Sturgeon) was particularly pleased with, and then writing it in again over the top, so that there was no space left for Gold to make alterations

7. Damon Knight's story 'Eripmav' is a brief joke about a planet of vegetable creatures, whose punch line is that they kill their equivalent of vampires with a steak through the heart. It is reprinted in *One Hundred Great SF Short Short Stories*, edited by Isaac Asimov, Martin Greenberg and Joseph Olander, and for the British paperback edition some sharp-eyed proof-reader spotted his 'error', corrected 'steak' to 'stake', and thus made the entire thing completely meaningless

8. Michael Moorcock's *The Lives and Times of Jerry Cornelius* was so emasculated by its American paperback publisher that when they asked his approval of their wholesale changes he felt moved to write back suggesting that they make lots more

9. Robert Silverberg's *Dying Inside* is one novel out of several which have been bowdlerized for magazine serialization. Silverberg's novel suffers especially badly, and loses much of its impact. (Another sufferer was Robert Heinlein, who after 400 pages of *I Will Fear No Evil* steeled himself to write a four letter word only to have it changed to f—k by the magazine editor)

Six Novels Which Differ Substantially In Their British and American Editions

Minor differences between British and American editions of books are quite common; differing editorial requirements may make for differences of detail. In each of the following, however, the differences are quite considerable.

1. Piers Anthony, *Macroscope*   The British edition of this novel is substantially abridged

2. Arthur C. Clarke, *Imperial Earth* The British edition is substantially shorter than the American
3. Frederik Pohl, *Jem* The British edition has one lengthy chapter removed
4. Keith Roberts, *The Chalk Giants* The American edition was considerably cut and revised by its editor, to the point where the author disowned it
5. Keith Roberts, *Pavane* The American edition contains one long episode not incorporated in the earlier British edition
6. John Sladek, *Roderick* The American edition contains only the first two-thirds (approximately) of the British edition

The US edition of the present book also happens to contain a substantial number of additional lists! Buy both editions . . .

Four SF Books with Embarrassing Publishers' Errors

1. Ben Bova, *THX 1138* (Paperback Library, 1971) The first edition omitted the last three pages of typescript, making it end somewhat abruptly. Subsequent US editions correct the mistake, but the British edition (Granada, 1975) repeated it
2. Philip K. Dick, *The Penultimate Truth* (Jonathan Cape, 1967). The first British edition reproduces the blurb from the American paperback as the first page of the novel
3. Wilson Tucker, *The Time Masters* (SF Book Club, 1971). This edition omits the last page of typescript
4. Cherry Wilder, *The Luck of Brin's Five* (Pocket Books). The first paperback printing goes one up on any of the above and leaves out the entire final chapter

Sequels and Homages

Writers would not be human if, upon reading certain books by other authors, they feel they either would have loved to have written the book in question, written it differently or feel like writing a continuation of it. A few examples:

H. G. Wells' *The War of the Worlds* has been paraphrased by Christopher Priest with his *The Space Machine*

The late H. Beam Piper's *Fuzzy* novels have been continued by William Tuning and Ardath Mayhar

Jack Vance's *The Eyes of the Overworld* has a sequel by Michael Shea, titled *A Quest for Simbilis*

Chester Anderson's *The Butterfly Kid* has two sequels by two different friends of his: Michael Kurland's *The Unicorn Girl* and T. A. Waters' *The Probability Pad*

H. G. Wells' *The Time Machine* has seen a variety of sequels by other hands: Egon Friedell's *The Return of The Time Machine*, K. W. Jeter's *Morlock Night* and has been paraphrased (featuring Wells as a character) by Karl Alexander in *Time after Time* and Ion Hobana in 'A Kind of Space'

Brian Aldiss has offered two variations on books by other writers with *Frankenstein Unbound* inspired by Mary Shelley's *Frankenstein* and *Moreau's Other Island*, a modern adaptation of Wells' *The Island of Doctor Moreau*

Jules Verne's *20,000 Leagues Under the Sea* and Captain Nemo have inspired many other writers, including Thomas Monteleone's *The Secret Sea* and illustrator Jean-Claude Forest, creator of Barbarella, with his adult strip *Mystérieuse, Midi, Matin et Soir*

Many highly commercial characters or sagas have also been continued by other pens: Tarzan, Conan, the Cthulhu mythos, the *Lensman* series are prime examples. Philip José Farmer is a specialist of this with his *Hadon of Ancient Opar* imitations of Tarzan, his use of Jules Verne's Phileas Fogg and many other fictional characters created by other authors: Sherlock Holmes, Kilgore Trout, Doc Savage, etc . . .

While David Kyle has continued E. E. 'Doc' Smith's *Lensman* series, other notes by Smith have been expanded into series by Gordon Eklund and Stephen Goldin

Edgar Allen Poe's *Arthur Gordon Pym* was continued by no less than Jules Verne with *An Antarctic Mystery* and also directly inspired Lovecraft's *At The Mountains of Madness*

A further instalment of Jonathan Swift's *Gulliver's Travels* was produced by the Hungarian Frigyes Karinthy as *Voyage to Faremido and Capillaria*

Conan Authors

When Robert E. Howard, the creator of Conan, died by suicide in 1936, he left twenty-one adventures of the mighty-hewed barbarian warrior. Extensive notes and outlines were found in his belongings and with the approval of the estate, a whole Conan industry moved into gear, fleshing out the Howard ideas and excerpts and, later, even creating complete new books which owed nothing to Howard bar the use of Conan, the brutality and background. These are the writers who have worked in the Conan mines:

Robert E. Howard
L. Sprague de Camp
Bjorn Nyberg
Lin Carter
Karl Edward Wagner
Andrew J. Offutt
Poul Anderson
Robert Jordan

Other larger-than-life Howard characters have also been continued by other hands, principally Bran Mak Morn (by Karl Edward Wagner) and Cormac Mac Art (by Andrew J. Offutt)

The Jerry Cornelius Writers

Jerry Cornelius is an eponymous character created by Michael Moorcock who first introduced him in several short stories before making him the leading character in his novel *The Final Programme* which was followed by several others and story collections. As a particularly potent symbol of entropic decadence, Cornelius soon fascinated both readers and other writers close to Moorcock alike and, with Moorcock's approval, various writers used their personal vision of Jerry Cornelius in stories of their own. This in fact became the largest wholesale use of an imaginary character by a group of writers, excluding the pulp practitioners. The majority of the stories (and two comic strips) were collected by Moorcock and Langdon

Jones in *The Nature of the Catastrophe*. There have since been many more Cornelius stories from amateur writers.

Brian Aldiss, one short story
Michael Butterworth, short stories
Mal Dean, provided illustrations for many stories and drew part of the Jerry Cornelius comic strip
Jacques Guiod, French writer; one story in French edition of *Galaxy* as Jim Gwinn
M. John Harrison, three short stories and co-scripted the comic strip
Maxim Jakubowski, two stories, one published, the other announced in *New Worlds* and never published
R. Glyn Jones, illustrator and comic strip artist
Langdon Jones, a long Cornelius poem
Alex Krislov, one short story
Moebius, the well-known French artist featured Cornelius in his surrealist strip *Le Garage Hermétique de Jerry Cornelius*
Michael Moorcock, five novels, many short stories. JC also appears as an absent or secondary character in many of Moorcock's other titles. Co-scripted the comic strip
Charles Partington, one short story
James Sallis, one short story
Norman Spinrad, one short story

Ten Mark II Novels

For personal or commercial reasons, some writers have revised already-published novels, often quite substantially and published them under a new title.

1. Gregory Benford: *Deeper Than The Darkness* (1970) became *The Stars in Shroud* (1978)
2. Michael Bishop: *A Funeral for the Eyes of Fire* (1975) became *Eyes of Fire* (1980)
3. John Brunner: *The Hundredth Millennium* (1959) became *Catch a Falling Star* (1968)
4. John Brunner: *Echo in the Skull* (1959) became *Give Warning to the World* (1974)

5. John Brunner: *Secret Agent of Terra* (1962) became *The Avengers of Carrig* (1969)
6. John Brunner: *Castaway's World* (1963) became *Polymath* (1974) note: most of the books written by Brunner for Ace in the late 1950s-early 1960s were later expanded and revised and retitled. This is only a selection
7. Arthur C. Clarke: *Against the Fall of Night* (1953) became *The City and the Stars* (1956)
8. Philip José Farmer, in the guise of translating J. H. Rosny Ainé's *L'Etonnant Voyage de Hareton Ironcastle* (1922) in fact completely rewrote it as *Ironcastle* (1976)
9. Fritz Leiber: *You're All Alone* (1972) became *The Sinful Ones* (1980) (first appearance in a shorter magazine format as 'The Sinful Ones' in fact occurred as early as 1950)
10. Michael Moorcock: *Somewhere in the Night* (as by Bill Barclay, 1966) became *The Chinese Agent* (1970)

Twelve Remakes/Remodels

It has often been said by detractors of the genre that SF is no more than westerns in space; while this is often true of the worst kind of space operas, it is nonetheless a sweeping generalization. However, a fair number of SF books do consist of modernized versions of certain legends or prior books, whether in spirit or fact.

1. A. Bertram Chandler's series of novels featuring Commodore Grimes is inspired and closely modelled on C. S. Forester's character of Horatio Hornblower
2. Laurence Janifer's titles featuring amateur sleuth Gerald Knave are modelled on Leslie Charteris' The Saint
3. R. A. Lafferty's *Space Chantey* retells Homer's *Odyssey* in a crazy space setting
4. Michael Moorcock's *Ice Schooner* borrows its plot from Joseph Conrad's *Rescue*
5. Michael Moorcock's *The Final Programme* closely follows, for its first third, the plot of his own initial Elric novel *The Stealer of Souls*, substituting Jerry Cornelius and a modern setting for Elric and his barbarian environment

6. Alexei Panshin's three novels featuring Anthony Villiers are also modelled on the character of The Saint
7. Emil Petaja's *Saga of the Lost Earths* and its sequels is a space version of the Finnish Kalevala myths
8. Brian Stableford's *Dies Irae* trilogy carefully transposes on to a wider-than-life setting Homer's old stalwarts *The Odyssey* and *The Iliad*
9. Bruce Sterling's *Involution Ocean* borrows much of its plot from Melville's *Moby Dick*
10. W. J. Stuart novelized the script of the film of *Forbidden Planet*, which owed a lot to Shakespeare's *The Tempest*
11. Bob Swigart's *The Time Trip* is inspired by the *Epic of Gilgamesh*
12. Joan Vinge's award-winning *The Snow Queen* openly acknowledges its source, the Andersen fairy-tale

A List of Alternatives

Writers and, more often, publishers indulge in the very annoying spectator sport of modifying titles of their books at the drop of a hat; in some cases this is to advertise that a book has been revised or drastically rewritten (see list). However, in most instances, the text masquerading under title (b) is the same you have already read under title (a) and only the gaudy cover is different (and the price of the book, most likely!). An exhaustive list of examples of this dubious practice could go on for as long as this book. This is just a small selection of alternative titles, most centring on changes of title between US and British editions.

Brian W. Aldiss	*Non-Stop/Starship*
	Hothouse/The Long Afternoon of Earth
	Bow Down to Nul/The Interpreter
Poul Anderson	*War of the Wing-Men/The Man Who Counts*
	Star Ways/Peregrine
	Planet of No Return/Question and Answer
Isaac Asimov	*The 1,000 Year Plan /Foundation*
	The Rebellious Stars/The Stars Like Dust

J. G. Ballard	*The Burning World/The Drought*
	The Atrocity Exhibition/Love and Napalm: Export USA
Barrington J. Bayley	*Collision Course/Collision with Chronos*
Alfred Bester	*The Stars My Destination/Tiger! Tiger!*
	Extro/The Computer Connection/The Indian Giver
Michael Bishop	*And Strange at Ecbatan the Trees/Beneath the Shattered Moons*
James Blish	*The Triumph of Time/A Clash of Cymbals*
Leigh Brackett	*The Starmen/The Starmen of Llyrdis/The Galactic Breed*
Ray Bradbury	*The Silver Locusts/The Martian Chronicles*
	Dark Carnival/The Small Assassin
	A Medicine for Melancholy/The Day it Rained Forever
Fredric Brown	*Project Jupiter/The Lights in the Sky are Stars*
John Brunner	*The Whole Man/Telepathist*
Algis Budrys	*False Night/Some Will Not Die*
Mark Clifton and Frank Riley	*They'd Rather be Right/The Forever Machine*
D. G. Compton	*The Continuous Katherine Mortenhoe/The Unsleeping Eye*
	The Steel Crocodile/The Electric Crocodile
Michael Coney	*Hello Summer, Goodbye/Rax*
Edmund Cooper	*The Uncertain Midnight/Deadly Image*
L. Sprague de Camp	*A Planet Called Krishna/Cosmic Manhunt*
Philip K. Dick	*Solar Lottery/World of Chance*
Gordon R. Dickson	*Dorsai/The Genetic General*
Thomas M. Disch	*Mankind Under the Leash/The Puppies of Terra*
G. C. Edmondson	*Blue Face/Chapayeca*
Harlan Ellison	*Spider Kiss/Rockabilly*
Philip José Farmer	*A Woman A Day/Timestop/The Day of Timestop*
Jack Finney	*The Third Level/The Clock of Time*
Daniel Galouye	*Simulacron-3/Counterfeit World*
James Gunn	*The Dreamers/The Mindmaster*
Charles Harness	*Flight Into Yesterday/The Paradox Men*
Harry Harrison	*Tunnel Through the Deeps/A Transatlantic Tunnel, Hurrah!*
	The Daleth Effect/In Our Hands the Stars

Robert Heinlein	*The Day After Tomorrow/Sixth Column*
Frank Herbert	*The Dragon Under the Sea/Under Pressure/21st Century Sub*
Laurence Janifer	*You Sane Men/Bloodworld*
Raymond F. Jones	*Man of Two Worlds/Renaissance*
Damon Knight	*Hell's Pavement/Analogue Men*
	The People Maker/A for Anything
C. M. Kornbluth	*Not This August/Christmas Eve*
Henry Kuttner	*Fury/Destination Infinity*
C. S. Lewis	*Perelandra/Voyage to Venus*
J. T. McIntosh	*Born Leader/Worlds Apart*
Michael Moorcock	*The Sundered Worlds/The Blood Red Game*
	Elric of Melniboné/The Dreaming City
	The Fireclown/The Winds of Limbo
	The Wrecks of Time/The Rituals of Infinity
H. Beam Piper	*Lord Kalvan of Otherwhen/Gunpowder God*
Frederik Pohl and C. M. Kornbluth	*The Space Merchants/Gravy Planet*
Christopher Priest	*A Dream of Wessex/The Perfect Lover*
Eric Frank Russell	*The Space Willies/Next of Kin*
Arthur Sellings	*Telepath/The Silent Speakers*
Robert Sheckley	*Journey Beyond Tomorrow/The Journey of Joenes*
Robert Silverberg	*Hawksbill Station/The Anvil of Time*
	The Masks of Time/Vornan-19
Clifford D. Simak	*First He Died/Time and Again*
John T. Sladek	*Mechasm/The Reproductive System*
William Sloane	*The Edge of Running Water/The Unquiet Corpse*
George O. Smith	*The Fourth R/The Brain Machine*
Brian Stableford	*Optiman/War Games*
Theodore Sturgeon	*The Dreaming Jewels/The Synthetic Man*
Wilson Tucker	*Time Bomb/Tomorrow Plus X*
Jack Vance	*The Space Pirate/The Five Gold Bands*
A. E. Van Vogt	*The House That Stood Still/Aliens Among Us/The Mating Cry*
	One Against Eternity/The Weapon Makers
	200,000,000 AD/The Book of Ptath
	The Mixed Men/Mission to the Stars
Kurt Vonnegut	*Player Piano/Utopia 14*
Kate Wilhelm	*The Mile-Long Spaceship/Andover and the Android*

John Wyndham   *Out of the Deeps / The Kraken Wakes*
                 The Chrysalids / Re-Birth

A Long List of Long SF Story Titles

In the interests of art and otherwise, writers have often indulged in
the use of particularly long titles for their works, and SF practitioners
probably more than any other genre writers. Conversely there have
been a score of short titles with an assortment of one letter, digit or
'blob' choices, but any such list would prove rather restrictive so
we've made a particular effort to make this a long list of long titles.
We have not included fanzine appearances, only professional
publications.

1. On the Street of the Serpents or the Assassination of Chairman
   Mao as Effected by the Author in Seville, Spain in the Spring of
   1992 A Year of No Certain Historicity
   Michael Bishop (*31 words*)
2. Travels Into Several Remote Regions of the World by Lemuel
   Gulliver, First a Surgeon and Then a Captain of Several Ships
   (better known as Gulliver's Travels)
   Jonathan Swift (*21 words*)
3. A Fruteful and Pleasante Worke of the Beste State of a Publyque
   Weale, and of the New Yle Called Utopia (better known as
   Utopia)
   Thomas More (*20 words*)
4. Hot Wireless Sets, Aspirin Tablets, the Sandpiper Sides of Used
   Matchboxes, and Something That Might Have Been Castor Oil
   (sometimes known as Chronocules)
   D. G. Compton (*19 words*)
5. The Season the Lemmings Worshipped the Slime-God and Daisy
   Jack Found the Factory Had Swallowed His Quicksand People
   Harlan Ellison (*19 words*)
6. With Mingled Feelings of Anticipation and Apprehension The
   Emigrants Leave Their Native Earth for a Far-Off Destination
   Ward Moore (*18 words*)

The War List

A bellicose listing that spans many a frightening future and possibility . . .

The *War* of Two Worlds, Poul Anderson
War of the Wing Men, Poul Anderson
Cold Cash *War*, Robert Asprin
The *War* God Walks Again, F. Britten Austin
War With the Newts, Karel Capek
The *War* of Dreams, Angela Carter
The Ilearth *War*, Stephen R. Donaldson
The Riverworld *War*, Philip José Farmer
The Forever *War*, Joe Haldeman
War Games, Karl Hansen
War With the Robots, Harry Harrison
Cold *War* in a Country Garden, Lindsay Gutteridge
The Wonder *War*, Laurence Janifer
Space *War*, Neil R. Jones
The Overlords of *War*, Gérard Klein
Retief's *War*, Keith Laumer
War with the Gizmos, Murray Leinster
Star *Wars*, George Lucas (ghosted by Alan Dean Foster)
Space *War* Blues, Richard A. Lupoff
The Sex *War*, Sam Merwin
The Grail *War*, Richard Monaco
City *Wars*, Dennis Palumbo
The Cool *War*, Frederik Pohl
The Earth *War*, Mack Reynolds
The *War* Book, James Sallis (ed)
War Games, Brian Stableford
War Against the Rull, A. E. Van Vogt
The Texas-Israeli *War*: 1999, Howard Waldrop and Jake Saunders
The *War* in the Air, H. G. Wells
War in Heaven, Charles Williams

The Dark List

One of the main criticisms of modern science fiction is that it has too much of a tendency to gloom and doom. An analysis of book titles apparently bears this out with the words 'dark' or 'darkness' occurring surprisingly often among the clusters of 'worlds', 'time', 'eternity', 'infinity' and other old reliables. This is just a selection.

We Are for the *Dark*, Robert Aickman
The *Dark* Light Years, Brian W. Aldiss
Queen of Air and *Darkness*, Poul Anderson
Deeper Than the *Darkness*, Gregory Benford and Gordon Eklund
The *Dark* Side of Earth, Alfred Bester
Watchers of the *Dark*, Lloyd Biggle Jr
All the Colours of *Darkness*, Lloyd Biggle Jr
This *Darkening* Universe, Lloyd Biggle Jr
City of *Darkness*, Ben Bova
Dragons of *Darkness*, Orson Scott Card (ed)
The Man in the *Dark* Suit, Dennis Caro
The *Dark* Dimension, A. Bertram Chandler
All *Darkness* Met, Glen Cook
Dark December, Alfred Coppel
Lest *Darkness* Fall, L. Sprague de Camp
A Handful of *Darkness*, Philip K. Dick
A Scanner *Darkly*, Philip K. Dick
Dark Dominion, David Duncan
The *Dark* Design, Philip José Farmer
Dark is the Sun, Philip José Farmer
The *Dark* World, Henry Kuttner
The Left Hand of *Darkness*, Ursula K. Le Guin
Gather *Darkness*, Fritz Leiber
Our Lady of *Darkness*, Fritz Leiber
Journey Into *Darkness*, Frank Belknap Long
The *Darkest* of Nights, Charles Eric Maine
Shot in the *Dark*, Judith Merril (ed)
Fugue for a *Darkening* Island, Christopher Priest
Dark Tides, Eric Frank Russell
Haven of *Darkness*, E. C. Tubb

Demon of the *Dark* Ones, Bob Vardeman and Victor Milan
Darkness Weaves, Karl Edward Wagner
Dark Inferno, James White
Darker Than You Think, Jack Williamson
The *Dark* Bright Water, Patricia Wrightson
Fall Into *Darkness*, Nicholas Yermakov
Creatures of Light and *Darkness*, Roger Zelazny
The *Dark* Tower, C. S. Lewis
Dark Universe, Daniel F. Galouye
Darkness and Dawn, George Allan England
Dark Atlantis, David Craigie
The *Dark* Beasts, Frank Belknap Long
The *Dark* Brotherhood, H. P. Lovecraft
Dark Carnival, Ray Bradbury
The *Dark* Chateau, Clark Ashton Smith
The *Dark* Destroyers, Manly Wade Wellman
Dark Enchantment, Dorothy Macardle
Dark Encounters, William Croft Dickinson
The *Dark* Enemy, Joan Hunter Holly
The *Dark* Entries, Robert Aickman
The *Dark*-Eyed Lady, A. E. Coppard
Dark Fantastic, Margaret Echard
The *Dark* Fantastic, Whit Masterton
The *Dark* Fire, Elinor Mordaunt
Dark Gateway, John Burke
The *Dark* Intruder, Marion Zimmer Bradley
The *Dark* Man, Robert E. Howard
The *Dark* Menace, Charles Birkin
The *Dark* Millennium, A. J. Merak
The *Dark* Mind, Colin Kapp
Dark Mind, *Dark* Heart, August Derleth (ed)
Dark Music, Jack Snow
Dark Nights, Thomas Burke
Dark Odyssey, Donald Wandrei
Dark of the Moon, August Derleth (ed)
The *Dark* Other, Stanley G. Weinbaum
The *Dark* Page, Neil Bell
Dark Piper, André Norton
The *Dark* Planet, Joan Hunter Holly

The *Dark* Returners, Joseph Payne Brennan
The *Dark* Side, Damon Knight (ed)
The *Darkest* Night, Peter Saxon
Darkness and Light, Olaf Stapledon
The *Darkness* Before Tomorrow, Robert Moore Williams
After *Dark*, Wilkie Collins
Beyond the Curtain of *Dark*, Peter Haining (ed)
In A Glass *Darkly*, J. Sheridan le Fanu
Candles in the *Dark*, Dorothy Black
Beware After *Dark*, T. Everett Harre (ed)
In *Dark* Places, John Russell
Powers of *Darkness*, Robert Aickman

The Light List

To counterpoint the dark list, here is a similar one to show that there is after all still some ground for optimism in SF and fantasy!

The Dark *Light* Years, Brian Aldiss
Star *Light*, Star Bright, Alfred Bester
The *Light* That Never Was, Lloyd Biggle Jr
Dragons of *Light*, Orson Scott Card (ed)
The *Light* at the End of the Universe, Terry Carr
Seed of *Light*, Philip José Farmer
Light a Last Candle, Vincent King
Seek*light*, K. W. Jeter
A Different *Light*, Elizabeth Lynn
The Dying of the *Light*, George R. R. Martin
The *Light* Bearer, Sam Nicholson
Creatures of *Light* and Darkness, Roger Zelazny
Lord of *Light*, Roger Zelazny
The *Light* Fantastic, Harry Harrison (ed)
The *Light* Fantastic, Alfred Bester
The *Lights* in the Skies are Stars, Fredric Brown
The *Light* Invisible, R. H. Benson
The *Light* of Lilith, G. McDonald Wallis

The Dawning *Light*, Robert Randall
Keep On the *Light*, Christine Campbell Thomson (ed)
The Children of *Light*, Henry Lionel Lawrence

The Cosmic Season List

For a genre that is supposed to be imaginative, SF has somewhat
fallen down on the task when it comes to inventing new seasons.
Planetary building and ecology devising are one thing, but new,
original seasons are in short supply. This is a list of books using
existing seasons as part of their titles.

SPRING

Helliconia Spring, Brian W. Aldiss (further seasons are to follow . . .)
I Love Galesburg in the Springtime, Jack Finney

SUMMER (by all accounts, SF writers' favourite season!)

Midsummer Tempest, Poul Anderson
Hello Summer, Goodbye, Michael Coney
Engine Summer, John Crowley
The Last Rose of Summer, Steve Gallagher
The Door Into Summer, Robert A. Heinlein
The End of Summer, Barry N. Malzberg and Bill Pronzini (eds)
Blind Summer, Tom Reamy
Eve of Midsummer, Jack Shackleford
Summer Rising, Sheila Sullivan
Summer in 3,000, Peter Martin

AUTUMN (seemingly out-of-fashion these days . . .)

Autumn Angels, Arthur Byron Cover
The Autumn People, Ray Bradbury

WINTER

The World in Winter, John Christopher
The Sound of Winter, Arthur Byron Cover
The Garden of Winter, Gordon Eklund
Winter Among the Ice, Jules Verne
The Winter People, Gilbert Phelps
Winter's Children, Michael Coney

A Calendar for the Future

Or novels and stories featuring a year to come in their title.

'1937, A.D.!', John Sladek
'A 1950 Marriage', David H. Keller
'The Revolution of 1960', Stanley G. Weinbaum and Ralph Milne
   Farley
'Wednesday, November 15, 1967', George Alec Effinger
'The Man Who Collected the 1st September, 1973', Tor Age
   Bringsvaerd
'January 1975', Barry N. Malzberg
1984, George Orwell
1985, Anthony Burgess
Pioneer 1990, Vargo Statten
Crisis! – 1992, Benson Herbert
The Texas-Israeli War, 1999, Howard Waldrop and Jake Saunders
'Crisis, 1999', Fredric Brown
The City 2000 AD, Clem, Greenberg and Olander (eds)
'Agoraphobia, AD 2000', Ian Watson
'The Year 2000', Robert Abernathy
The Year 2000, Harry Harrison (ed)
'Crimes of the Year 2,000', Ray Cummings
Crisis 2000, Charles Eric Maine
Looking Backwards from the Year 2000, Mack Reynolds
AD 2000, Alvarado M. Fuller
2001: A Space Odyssey, Arthur C. Clarke

2010: Odyssey Two, Arthur C. Clarke
Year 2018!, James Blish
2018 AD or the King Kong Blues, Sam J. Lundwall
2020 Vision, Jerry Pournelle (ed)
Ultimatum in 2050 AD, Jack Sharkey
'2066, Election Day', Michael Shaara
Norman Conquest 2066, J. T. McIntosh
2076: The American Tricentennial, Edward Bryant (ed)
War in 2080, David Langford
Revolt in 2100, Robert A. Heinlein
Enterprise 2115, Charles Grey
Crisis in 2140, H. Beam Piper and John J. McGuire
Daybreak 2250 AD, André Norton
A Saga of 2270 AD, Volsted Gridban
'A Happy Day in 2381', Robert Silverberg
Armageddon 2419 AD, Philip Nowlan
'2430 AD', Isaac Asimov
The Year 2440, Louis-Sebastien Mercier
Invasion from 2500, Norman Edwards
'New York: AD 2660', Hugo Gernsback
'The Great Catastrophe of 2947', Woods Peters
Summer in 3000, Peter Martin
Year 3097, R. D. Miller
Fugitives from Year 4000, Jacques Spitz
Lords of 9016, John Russell Fearn
'20,000 AD', Nathan Schachner and Arthur Leo Zagat
'5,000,000 AD', Miriam Allen deFord
200,000,000 AD, A. E. Van Vogt

Spider Robinson's All-Time-Favourite Larry Niven Titles

Science Fiction Story: 'Neutron Star'
Fantasy Story: 'Not Long Before the End'
Science Fact Essay: 'Theory and Practice of Time Travel'
Science Fiction Essay: 'Man of Steel – Woman of Kleenex'
Non-Science Fiction Story: 'The Deadlier Weapon'

Bar Story: 'The Fourth Profession'
Disaster Novel: *Lucifer's Hammer* (with Jerry Pournelle)
Disaster Short Story: 'Inconstant Moon'
Humorous SF Novel: *The Flying Sorcerer* (with David Gerrold)
Humorous SF Short Story: 'Flight of the Horse'
SF Detective Story: 'The Organleggers'

Source: Introduction to 'Inconstant Moon' in the Spider Robinson
The Best Of All Possible Worlds anthology (1980)

Favourite Pulp Titles

They don't title them like this anymore!

Ghouls of the Green Death (Wyatt Blassingame, 1934)
Death Calls from the Madhouse (Hugh B. Cave, 1935)
The House of Doomed Brides (Ray Cummings, 1935)
The Chair Where Terror Sat (Arthur J. Burks, 1936)
Moaning on the Styx (Arthur J. Burks, 1938)
Dance of the Blood Drinkers (J. O. Quinliven, 1938)
Black Pool for Hell Maidens (Hal K. Wells, 1938)
Coming of the Faceless Killers (Francis James, 1938)
Slave of the Swamp Satan (Dale Clark, 1938)
Nameless Brides of Forbidden City (Frederick C. Davis, 1939)
Pawn of Hideous Desire (Ray Cummings, 1939)
When the Death-Bat Flies, (Norvell W. Page, 1937)
Mistress of the Murder Madmen (Vernon James, 1939)
Death's Lips are Hot (Nathan Schachner, 1938)
The Goddess of Crawling Horrors (Wyatt Blassingame, 1937)
Food for the Fungus Lady (Ralston Fields, 1939)
The Wind Monster Wants Me (Gabriel Wilson, 1938)

The Lost Novels of Kilgore Trout

The importance of the SF works of Kilgore Trout (1907-81) has been disputed by many reputable critics, including Kurt Vonnegut and Philip José Farmer. Unfortunately, with the exception of *Venus on the Half-Shell* which appeared in *The Magazine of Fantasy and Science Fiction* and later in paperback format, his works remain unknown through virtue of having mainly been published by pornographic imprints with utterly misleading covers and are eagerly sought after by collectors of both the erotic and the SF genre as a result. The following list of Trout's known titles was compiled by Philip José Farmer, from primary research by Vonnegut principally published in *God Bless You, Mr Rosewater* and *Breakfast of Champions*. A question mark surrounds the actual length of Trout's *The Baring-gaffner of Bagnialto or This Year's Masterpiece*, which Farmer lists as a short story but Vonnegut describes as a novel in *B of C*.

NOVELS

The Gutless Wonder (1932)
2BRO2B
Venus on the Half-Shell
Oh Say Can You Smell?
The First District Court of Thankyou
Pan-Galactic Three-Day Pass
Maniacs in the Fourth Dimension (1948)
The Gospel From Outer Space
The Big Board
Pan Galactic Straw-Boss (Mouth Crazy)
Plague on Wheels
Now It Can Be Told
The Son of Jimmy Valentine
How You Doin'?
The Smart Bunny
The Pan-Galactic Memory Bank
The Baring-gaffner of Bagnialto or This Year's Masterpiece

SHORT STORIES

The Dancing Fool (in April 1962 issue of *Black Garterbelt,* a magazine published by World Classics Library)
This Means You
Gilgongo!
Hail to the Chief

The Unpublished Novels of R. A. Lafferty

That most original of SF writers, Raphael Aloysius Lafferty, only came to writing at the mature age of forty-six, and his first novel *Past Master* appeared in 1968 when he was already fifty-four. As Sandra Miesel puts it in her essay on Lafferty in *Twentieth Century Science Fiction Writers* '. . . (he) is science fiction's most prodigious teller of tall tales'. His iconoclastic qualities also make him supremely uncommercial for the mainstream of publishing and many of his novels remain unpublished. Here, to whet the appetite of Lafferty fans, are their titles.

More Than Melchisedech (third part of *The Devil Is Dead* trilogy, which
    also includes *Archipelago*)
Esteban
Half A Sky
Mantis
Iron Tongue of Midnight
When All The World Was Young
To Aurelia With Horns
The Elliptical Grave
Dark Shine
Dotty
In A Green Tree – a tetralogy comprising:
    My Heart Leaps Up
    Grasshoppers and Wild Honey
    Deep Scars of the Thunder
    Incidents of Travel in Flatland

The Unpublished Novels of Philip K. Dick

The untimely death on 2 March 1982 of Philip K. Dick robbed science fiction and modern literature of one of its most precious and enquiring talents. In 1972, Dick donated many of his manuscripts and papers to the Special Collections Library, California State University, Fullerton. These include many unpublished books, not always SF, and it is to be hoped some enterprising publishers may over the years come to bring these novels into print.

The Man Whose Teeth Were All Exactly Alike (358 page manuscript)
Mary and the Giant (315 pages)
Gather Yourselves Together (481 pages)
Puttering about in a Small Land (416 pages)
In Milton Lumky Territory (293 pages)
The Broken Bubble of Thisbe Holt (350 pages)
Voices from the Street (652 pages)

Sixteen Eagerly Awaited Harlan Ellison Books

1. *The Crackpots* (listed in *Ellison Wonderland*, 1962)
2. *Don't Speak of Rope* – collaboration with Avram Davidson (listed in *Ellison Wonderland*)
3. *Demon With a Glass Hand* (listed in *I Have No Mouth and I Must Scream*, 1967, and others)
4. *Dial 9 to Get Out* (listed in *I Have No Mouth and I Must Scream*, and others)
5. *The Harlan Ellison Hornbook* (listed in *Over the Edge*, 1970, and others)
6. *The Prince of Sleep* (listed in *Over the Edge*, 1970; *Locus* 195, Oct 1976, reports the book sold to Dell for $20,000)
7. *The Wars of Love* – essays on the battle of the sexes (listed in *Over the Edge*)
8. *The Sound of a Scythe* (listed in *Over the Edge*, and others)
9. *The Last Dangerous Visions* (listed in *Over the Edge*, and frequently since)

10. *The Unknown Book of Harlan Ellison* (listed in *Approaching Oblivion*, 1974)
11. *The Dark Forces 1: The Salamander Enchantment* (listed in *Approaching Oblivion*, and others)
12. *Rif* (listed in *Approaching Oblivion*, and others)
13. *Impossible Dreams* – a textbook of imaginative literature, edited with Arnold R. Kunert (listed in *Approaching Oblivion*, and others)
14. *Brain Movies* (*Locus* 185, Feb 1976 reports that this book, a collection of scripts, was sold to Pyramid Books)
15. *A Boy and His Dog* (listed in *No Doors, No Windows* (1976: the book *Blood's A Rover*, to which this may refer, was announced for 1979 publication but later cancelled)
16. *Medea: Harlan's World* (anthology sold to Bantam for $20,000, reported *Locus* in 1977)

(The unique and controversial Ellison has a tendency to start publicizing his books long before they are actually written. Sometimes they duly appear. Sometimes not.)

The Hundred Top Grossing SF, Fantasy and Horror Films
(in US $ – as of end of December 1981 – Source: *Variety*)

1.	*Star Wars*, George Lucas, 1977	185,138,000
2.	*The Empire Strikes Back*, Irvin Kershner, 1980	135,209,000
3.	*Raiders of the Lost Ark*, Steven Spielberg, 1981	90,434,000
4.	*The Exorcist*, William Friedkin, 1978	88,500,000
5.	*Superman 1*, Richard Donner, 1978	82,500,000
6.	*Close Encounters Of The Third Kind*, Steven Spielberg	77,000,000
7.	*Superman 2*, Richard Lester, 1981	64,000,000
8.	*Star Trek – The Movie*, Robert Wise, 1979	56,000,000
9.	*Heaven Can Wait*, Warren Beatty/Buck Henry, 1978	49,000,000
10.	*Alien*, Ridley Scott, 1979	39,800,000
11.	*Young Frankenstein*, Mel Brooks, 1975	38,800,000
12.	*King Kong*, John Guillermin, 1976	36,900,000
13.	*The Amityville Horror*, Stuart Rosenberg, 1979	35m
14.	*Moonraker*, Lewis Gilbert, 1979	33.9m
15.	*The Shining*, Stanley Kubrick, 1980	30.8m

16. *The Omen*, Richard Donner, 1976   28.54m
17. *The Black Hole*, Gary Nelson, 1979   25.48m
18. *2001: A Space Odyssey*, Stanley Kubrick, 1968   24.1m
19. *Love at First Bite*, Stan Dragoti, 1979   20.6m
20. *Halloween*, John Carpenter, 1978   18.5m
21. *Herbie Rides Again*, Robert Stevenson, 1974   17.5m
22. *Friday the 13th*, Sean Cunningham, 1980   17.1m
23. *Excalibur*, John Boorman, 1981   17m
24. *Flash Gordon*, Mike Hodges, 1980   16.1m
25.= *A Clockwork Orange*, Stanley Kubrick, 1971   16m
25.= *Time Bandits*, Terry Gilliam, 1981   16m
27. *Clash of the Titans*, Desmond Davis, 1981   15.6m
28.= *Planet Of The Apes*, Franklin Schaffner, 1968   15m
28.= *Carrie*, Brian De Palma, 1976   15m
28.= *Rosemary's Baby*, Roman Polanski, 1960   15m
31. *Herbie Goes to Monte Carlo*, Vincent McEveety, 1977   14m
32. *Exorcist 2: The Heretic*, John Boorman, 1977   13.9m
33. *Lord of the Rings*, Ralph Bakshi, 1978   13.7m
34. *Omen 2: Damien*, Don Taylor, 1978   13.6m
35.= *Dracula*, John Badham, 1979   12.4m
35.= *Altered States*, Ken Russell, 1980   12.4m
37. *The Rocky Horror Picture Show*, Jim Sharman, 1975   12.21m
38. *The Fury*, Brian De Palma, 1978   12.1m
39. *Buck Rogers in the 25th Century*, Daniel Haller, 1979   12.01m
40. *Capricorn One*, Peter Hyams, 1978   12m
41. *An American Werewolf in London*, John Landis, 1981   11.6m
42. *Invasion Of The Body Snatchers*, Philip Kaufman, 1978   11.13m
43. *The Absent-Minded Professor*, Robert Stevenson, 1961   11.1m
44.= *20,000 Leagues Under the Sea*, Richard Fleischer, 1954   11m
44.= *The Fog*, John Carpenter, 1980   11m
46. *Mysterious Monsters*, R. Guenette, 1975   10.9m
47.= *Escape From New York*, John Carpenter, 1981   10.5m
47.= *The Shaggy DA*, Robert Stevenson, 1976   10.5m

47.= *Halloween 2*, Rick Rosenthal, 1981 10.5m
50. *The Prophecy*, John Frankenheimer, 1979 10.49m
51. *Son of Flubber*, Robert Stevenson, 1963 10.45m
52. *Island At The Top Of The World*, Robert Stevenson, 1974 10.2m
53. *Friday the 13th Part 2*, Steve Miner, 1981 10.1m
54. *Battle Beyond the Stars*, Jimmy Murakami, 1980 10m
55.= *Escape to Witch Mountain*, John Hough, 1975 9.5m
55.= *Logan's Run* Michael Anderson, 1976 9.5m
55.= *The Incredible Shrinking Woman*, Joel Schumacher, 1981 9.5m
55.= *Outland*, Peter Hyams, 1981 9.5m
59.= *Heavy Metal*, Gerald Potterton, 1981 9.3m
59.= *Willard*, Delbert Mann, 1971 9.3m
61. *The Final Conflict*, Graham Baker, 1981 9.1m
62. *Rollerball*, Norman Jewison, 1975 9.05m
63. *The Late, Great Planet Earth*, Robert Amram, 1977 8.8m
64. *Beneath The Planet Of The Apes*, Ted Post, 1970 8.6m
65. *The Cat From Outer Space*, Norman Tokar, 1978 8.4m
66. *The Andromeda Strain*, Robert Wise, 1971 8.34m
67. *Darby O'Gill And The Little People*, Robert Stevenson, 1969 8.3m
68. *The Howling*, Joe Dante, 1981 8.2m
69. *Sleeper*, Woody Allen, 1973 8m
70. *Silent Scream*, Denny Harris, 1979 7.9m
71.= *Sinbad And The Eye Of The Tiger*, Sam Wanamaker, 1977 7.7m
71.= *The Swarm*, Irwin Allen, 1978 7.7m
73. *Herbie Goes Bananas*, Vincent McEveety, 1980 7.5m
74. *Return From Witch Mountain*, John Hough, 1978 7.3m
75.= *It's Alive*, Larry Cohen, 1977 7.1m
75.= *Battlestar Galactica*, Richard Colla, 1979 7.1m
77. *Westworld*, Michael Crichton, 1973 7m
78. *The Final Countdown*, Don Taylor, 1980 6.6m
79. *The Sword In The Stone*, Wolfgang Reitherman, 1963 6.5m
80. *Time After Time*, Nicholas Meyer, 1979 6.3m
81.= *Dragonslayer*, Matthew Robins, 1981 6m
81.= *Phantasm*, Don Coscarelli, 1979 6m

81.= *Meteor*, Ronald Neame, 1979 — 6m
81.= *Prom Night*, Paul Lynch, 1980 — 6m
81.= *Scanners*, David Cronenberg, 1981 — 5.8m
86. *Race With The Devil*, Jack Starrett, 1975 — 5.75m
87. *Hangar 18*, James L. Conway, 1980 — 5.708m
88. *Close Encounters: The Special Edition*, Steven Spielberg, 1980 — 5.56m
89. *Escape From The Planet Of The Apes*, Don Taylor, 1971 — 5.5m
90.= *Barbarella*, Roger Vadim, 1968 — 5.5m
90.= *Fantastic Voyage*, Richard Fleischer, 1966 — 5.5m
92.= *Flesh Gordon*, Howard Ziehm, 1974 — 5.3m
92.= *The Changeling*, Peter Medak, 1980 — 5.3m
94. *Death Race 2000*, Paul Bartel, 1970 — 5.25m
95. *Damnation Alley*, Jack Smight, 1977 — 5.031m
96.= *The Birds*, Alfred Hitchcock, 1963 — 5m
96.- *Dr Strangelove*, Stanley Kubrick, 1964 — 5m
96.= *King Kong*, Meriam C. Cooper, 1933 — 5m
96.= *The Golden Voyage of Sinbad*, Gordon Hessler, 1974 — 5m
96.= *The Reincarnation of Peter Proud*, J. Lee Thompson, 1975 — 5m

Note: Since this list was compiled Steven Spielberg's latest two movies *ET* and *Poltergeist* have made him the world's number one box-office movie maker and *ET* is set to become the biggest grossing movie in history

Six SF and Fantasy Film Flops

1. *Meteor* (1979) lost $15.8 million
2. *The Island* (1980) lost $12.4 million
3. *The Wiz* (1978) lost $10.4 million
4. *Lost Horizon* (1973) lost $8.2 million
5. *Dracula* (1979) lost $4.5 million
6. *Xanadu* (1980) lost $2.3 million

Loss figures have been reached by deducting available rental revenue in USA and Canada from the films' negative cost

Source: *Anatomy of the Movies*, 1981

The Dramatic Presentation Hugos

1958
The Incredible Shrinking Man (Movie) Jack Arnold

1959
No Award

1960
The Twilight Zone (TV Series)

1961
The Twilight Zone (TV Series)

1962
The Twilight Zone (TV Series)

1963
No Award

1964
No Award

1965
Dr Strangelove (Movie) Stanley Kubrick

1966
No Award

1967
The Menagerie (*Star Trek* TV Episode)

1968
City On The Edge of Forever (*Star Trek* TV Episode)

1969
2001: A Space Odyssey (Movie) Stanley Kubrick

1970
TV Coverage of Apollo XI

1971
No Award

1972
A Clockwork Orange (Movie) Stanley Kubrick

1973
Slaughterhouse Five (Movie) George Roy Hill

1974
Sleeper (Movie) Woody Allen

1975
Young Frankenstein (Movie) Mel Brooks

1976
A Boy and his Dog (Movie) L. Q. Jones

1977
No Award

1978
Star Wars (Movie) George Lucas

1979
Superman (Movie) Richard Donner

1980
Alien (Movie) Ridley Scott

1981
The Empire Strikes Back (Movie) Irvin Kershner

Stephen King's Favourite Horror and Fantasy Films

Alien (Ridley Scott, 1979)
Black Sunday (Mario Bava, 1961)
The Brood (David Cronenberg, 1979)
Lady in a Cage (Walter Graumann, 1961)
Carrie (Brian De Palma, 1976)
Creature from the Black Lagoon (Jack Arnold, 1954)
The Creeping Unknown (Val Guest, 1955)
Curse of the Demon (Jacques Tourneur, 1957)
Dawn of the Dead (George A. Romero, 1979)
Deliverance (John Boorman, 1972)
Dementia-13 (Francis Ford Coppola, 1963)
Duel (Steven Spielberg, 1971)
Enemy From Space (Val Guest, 1957)

The Exorcist (William Friedkin, 1973)
Frenzy (Alfred Hitchcock, 1972)
Halloween (John Carpenter, 1978)
The Haunting (Robert Wise, 1963)
I Bury the Living (Albert Band, 1958)
Invasion of the Body Snatchers (Don Siegel, 1956)
It Came From Outer Space (Jack Arnold, 1953)
Jaws (Steven Spielberg, 1975)
Let's Scare Jessica to Death (John Hancock, 1971)
Martin (George A. Romero, 1977)
The Night of the Hunter (Charles Laughton, 1955)
Night of the Living Dead (George A. Romero, 1968)
Picnic at Hanging Rock (Peter Wein, 1978)
Psycho (Alfred Hitchcock, 1960)
Rabid (David Cronenberg, 1976)
Repulsion (Roman Polanski, 1965)
Rosemary's Baby (Roman Polanski, 1968)
The Seventh Seal (Ingmar Bergman, 1956)
The Shining (Stanley Kubrick, 1980)
Sisters (Brian De Palma, 1973)
Suspiria, (Dario Argento, 1977)
The Texas Chainsaw Massacre (Tobe Hooper, 1974)
Them! (Gordon Douglas, 1954)
The Thing (Christian Nyby, 1951)
Wait Until Dark (Terence Young, 1967)
Whatever Happened to Baby Jane? (Robert Aldrich, 1961)
The Man with X-ray Eyes (Roger Corman, 1963)

(From *Danse Macabre*, 1981)

The Best Frankenstein Monsters of the Screen

Charles Ogle   Contrary to popular belief, Boris Karloff was not the
first cinematic incarnation of Mary Shelley's pitiful but powerful
monster. Charles Ogle interpreted him in an early, Edison Company-
produced version directed by J. Searle Dawley in 1910

Boris Karloff   William Henry Pratt, an amiable British actor working
in Hollywood, made Frankenstein's monster his very own in 1931,
thanks to the imaginative make-up of Jack Pierce. He was to play the

Baron's doomed creation in three movies: *Frankenstein* (1931), *The Bride of Frankenstein* (1935), both directed by James Whale and *Son of Frankenstein* (1939) directed by Rowland V. Lee. A final, apocryphal appearance as the Monster occurred in a *Route 66* television episode in 1962, where he played himself playing the Monster. Curiously enough, Karloff also played Dr Neumann, creator of the monster in *House of Frankenstein* (1944) and Baron Frankenstein himself in *Frankenstein 1970* (1957)

Lon Chaney Jr Better known for his other horror and fantasy roles, Lon Chaney Jr was Karloff's successor in *The Ghost of Frankenstein*, directed by Erle Kenton in 1942

Bela Lugosi Usually remembered for his seminal incarnation as Dracula, Lugosi had already starred in the previous two Frankenstein movies as sidekick Igor. However, in *Frankenstein Meets the Wolf Man*, directed by Roy Neill in 1943, he played the perennial Monster against Lon Chaney Jr in a change of casting as the Wolf Man

Glenn Strange With Karloff, Glenn Strange was the longest serving Monster, appearing in three successive films: *House of Frankenstein* (1944), *House of Dracula* (1945) and *Abbott and Costello Meet Frankenstein* (1948)

Christopher Lee Lee was the first choice for the Monster when British producers Hammer Films resurrected the Frankenstein mythos in 1957 with Terence Fisher's *The Curse of Frankenstein*. Christopher Lee's greater claim to fame was, of course, in the Hammer productions of Dracula films

Kiwi Kingston An erstwhile wrestler, Kingston played the Monster in *The Evil of Frankenstein* (1964) facing Peter Cushing as one of the more perennial and suave Barons

Michael Sarrazin A youthful-looking Hollywood leading-man of the 1970s, Michael Sarrazin was the surprising, but effective choice for the Monster, in the 1973 made-for-TV film *Frankenstein: The True Story*, directed by Jack Smight and co-scripted by Christopher Isherwood

Peter Boyle The talented character actor Peter Boyle was the Monster in Mel Brooks' affectionate parody *Young Frankenstein* (1974)

Joe Dallesandro More accustomed to contemporary cinéma-vérité movies, Joe Dallesandro was the strikingly effete Monster of the Andy Warhol-produced, Paul Morrissey-directed 1975 *Flesh for Frankenstein*

Thirteen Generations of Dracula

Or the successive actors to have played the role of the sinister Transylvanian Count of Darkness:

1. *Max Schreck*, not strictly Dracula but his archetypal predecessor Count Orlok, otherwise known as *Nosferatu* (Friedrich Murnau, 1922)
2. *Bela Lugosi*, in *Dracula* (Todd Browning, 1931)
3. *Lon Chaney Jr*, as Count Alucard aka you-know-who in *Son of Drucula* (Robert Siodmak, 1943)
4. *John Carradine*, in *House of Dracula* (Erle C. Kenton, 1945) and *Billy The Kid versus Dracula* (William Beaudine, 1966)
5. *Francis Lederer*, in *The Return of Dracula* (Paul Landers, 1958)
6. *Christopher Lee*, the modern incarnation of the vampire par excellence; in *The Horror of Dracula* (Terence Fisher, 1958) and countless sequels
7. *William Marshall*, as a black Dracula, in *Blacula* (William Crain, 1973)
8. *Udo Kier*, in the Warhol production of *Dracula* (Paul Morrissey, 1974)
9. *Jack Palance*, in the TV movie *Dracula* (Dan Curtis, 1974)
10. *Louis Jourdan*, in the BBC TV adaptation (Gerald Savory, 1976)
11. *George Hamilton*, in the spoof *Love at First Bite* (Stan Dragoti, 1979)
12. *Klaus Kinski*, in the remake of *Nosferatu* (Werner Herzog, 1979)
13. *Frank Langella*, in *Dracula* (1979)

Eleven Jekyll-to-Hyde Transformations

Like the eternal theme of Dorian Gray whose mirror image retains the scars and infamies of time and debauchery, Robert Louis Stevenson's tale of Dr Jekyll and his savage alter ego strikes a responsive chord and reveals the dark side to man's character. It has long fascinated movie-makers (and special-effects-cum-trick-photography buffs). Indeed, it is, with Victor Hugo's *Les Misérables*, the most adapted novel in film history. Before this list even begins, there are records of at least six versions of the story, with now forgotten actors (James Cruze, King Baggott, Alwin Neuss).

1. *Conrad Veidt* in *Der Januskopf*, 1920
2. *John Barrymore*, in 1920, directed by John S. Robertson
3. *Fredric March*, in 1932, directed by Rouben Mamoulian
4. *Spencer Tracy*, in 1941, directed by Victor Fleming
5. *Sylvester the Cat*, in a cartoon version titled *Dr Jekyll's Hyde*, probably late 1940s
6. *Boris Karloff*, in *Abbott and Costello meet Dr Jekyll and Mr Hyde*, 1953
7. *Paul Massie*, in *The Two Faces of Dr Jekyll* (Terence Fisher, 1960)
8. *Jerry Lewis*, in the comic spoof *The Nutty Professor* (Jerry Lewis, 1963)
9. *Christopher Lee*, in *I, Monster*, 1970
10. *Ralph Bates* and *Martine Beswick*, in an unorthodox but effective version as *Dr Jekyll and Sister Hyde*, 1971
11. *David Hemmings*, in the 1980 BBC TV production

Generations of Kong: A List of Giant Ape Movies

Whether or not man is descended from the ape, film-makers have certainly taken the simian species to their hearts and featured apes to their heart's delight on the screen. Excluding the relatively-normal-sized denizens of *The Planet of the Apes* and its sequels, we have deliberately restricted the following list to giant apes, more often than not on some form of joyful rampage to pass the (boring) time of day.

The Lost World (Harry Hoyt, 1925)
The Unholy Three (Tod Browning, 1925)
Stark Mad (Lloyd Bacon, 1929)
The Unholy Three (Jack Conway, 1930)
King Kong (Merian Copper and Ernest Schoedsack, 1933)
Song of Kong (Ernest Schoedsack, 1933)
White Pongo (Sam Newfield, 1945)
Unknown Island (Jack Bernhard, 1948)
Mighty Joe Young (Ernest Schoedsack, 1949)

Konga (John Lemont, 1961)
Tor, King of Beasts (Don Glut, 1962)
King Kong versus Godzilla (Inoshiro Honda and Thomas Montgomery, 1962)
Mad Monster Party (Saul Bass, 1967)
King Kong Escapes (Inoshiro Honda, 1967)
The Mighty Gorga (D. Hewitt, 1970)
Schlock (John Landis, 1972)
Ape (Paul Leder, 1976)
King Kong (John Guillermin, 1976)
Queen Kong (Frank Agrama, 1977)
Baby Kong (Mario Bava, 1977)
Bye Bye Monkey! (Marco Ferreri, 1977)

Forrest J. Ackerman's Ten Favourite Scientifilms

1. *Metropolis* – A thing of beauty is a joy forever. The city! the laboratory! the robotrix! the genius of Fritz Lang!
2. *Things To Come* – A vision of futurity once seen never forgotten. (Still, I've seen it probably fifty times. Ditto *Metropolis*)
3. *War of the Worlds* – Wells once more. George Pal's enthralling realization of a masterpiece of scientifiction
4. *The Invisible Man* – And again, Wells. Claude Rains' voice alone would have made it a favourite of a blind man
5. *Close Encounters of the Third Kind* – Don't believe in Flying Saucers and am a confirmed atheist but the climax filled me with exultation of a 'spiritual' nature
6. *The Empire Strikes Back* – Derived more excitement from it than even its mind-boggling predecessor, *Star Wars*
7. *Alien* – It's 'alienity' made my hair stand on end more than once
8. *King Kong* –More than a movie, an experience to re-experience again and again
9. *High Treason* – The one film on the list probably virtually no one reading this list ever saw. A pacifistic vision in 1929 of the world on the verge of war in 1940; Britain's second talking feature
10. *Fantastic Voyage* – A trip into the 'interior' that fascinated me with its special effects

Forrest J. Ackerman's Hate List (Sans Parole)

1. *2001: A Space Odyssey*
2. *Zardoz*
3. *The Illustrated Man*
4. *The Incredible Shrinking Woman*
5. *The Four-Sided Triangle*
6. *Village of the Giants*
7. *King Kong* (remake)
8. *Conquest of Space*
9. *Time Bandits*
10. *Silent Running*

Chickens in Space

Cluck! The True Story of Chickens in the Cinema is possibly the most unusual book devoted to the art of the cinema. Conceived by the young American writer Jon-Stephen Fink and published in England in 1981, it analyses crucial chicken scenes in famous (and more obscure) movies and also lists an impressive array of films featuring chicken scenes, grading them by order of significance.

° Elementary Incident
°° Useful Insight
°°° Notable Significance
°°°° Awesome Consequence

Our list selects all films with a science fiction or fantasy element thus assessed!

Alien	°°°°
All That Jazz	°°
The Bride of Frankenstein	°°°
Close Encounters of the Third Kind	°°°
Dark Star	°°°°
Doctor Dolittle	°°°
Eraserhead	°°°
The Exterminating Angel	°°°
Food of the Gods	°°°°

313

The Ghost of Mr Chicken	oooo
Jason and the Argonauts	o
King Kong	ooo
Let's Scare Jessica to Death	oo
Love at First Bite	ooo
The Mysterious Island	ooo
Nosferatu	ooo
The Prophecy	ooo
Rosemary's Baby	oo
Sleeper	oo
The Texas Chainsaw Massacre	ooo
2001: A Space Odyssey	oooo
Village of the Giants	ooo
The Wizard of Oz	oooo

The SF and Fantasy Golden Turkeys

Harry and Michael Medved's *The Golden Turkey Awards* (1980) reminds us, tongue well in cheek, of the worst achievements in Hollywood history. Some of the amusing categories chosen are relevant to Fantasy and Science Fiction and they are listed hereunder. The real fun, however, is the Medveds' hilarious text recalling the untold masochistic pleasures many of these movies are fully responsible for. So, if the idea appeals to you, we can only recommend your obtaining the book by hook or by crook.

THE MOST EMBARRASSING MONSTER IN SCREEN HISTORY

Robot Monster (1953) *Winner*
The Alligator People (1959)
Attack of the Fifty-Foot Woman (1958)
The Creeping Terror (1964)
From Hell It Came (1959)
Gamera, The Invincible (1962)
Teenagers from Outer Space (1959)

THE MOST BRAINLESS BRAIN MOVIE OF ALL TIME

They Saved Hitler's Brain (1964) *Winner*

314

The Brain Eaters (1958)
The Brain from Planet Arous (1957)
The Brain That Wouldn't Die (1963)

THE MOST BADLY BUMBLED BEE MOVIE OF ALL TIME

The Swarm (1978) *Winner*
The Bees (1978)
The Deadly Bees (1962)
The Invasion of the Bee Girls (1963)

THE WORST TWO-HEADED TRANSPLANT MOVIE EVER MADE

The Thing with Two Heads (1972) *Winner*
The Incredible Two-Headed Transplant (1971)
The Manster: Half Man and Half Monster

THE WORST RODENT MOVIE OF ALL TIME

The Food of the Gods (1976) *Winner*
The Killer Shrews (1959)
The Mole People (1956)
The Nasty Rabbit (1965)
Night of the Lepus (1972)

THE WORST VEGETABLE MOVIE OF ALL TIME

Attack of the Mushroom People (1963) *Winner*
Attack of the Killer Tomatoes (1978)
Invasion of the Star Creatures (1965)
Please Don't Eat My Mother (1973)

The SF Movies of Méliès

George Lucas, Steven Spielberg, Stanley Kubrick and Ridley Scott are the names on everyone's lips when it comes to SF movies today. But the man who made it all possible was Georges Méliès (1861–1938). In a whirlwind career which ended as early as 1913, he produced over 800 films, some of them just clips, and was the first magician of fantasy and special effects. Unfortunately, very few of his films have survived. This is a list of his major science fiction ones:

315

The Laboratory of Mephistopheles (1897) in which Méliès himself
played the madcap inventor in a laboratory full of wonderful
tricks

The Clown and the Automaton (1897) the first appearance of a robot on
the silver screen

A Novice at X-Rays (1898) where a skeleton separates itself from its
body with dire effects

The Astronomer's Dream (1898) in which the Moon comes down to
Earth

Cleopatra (1899) in a sequence inspired by *She*, the heroine changes
from beauty to hag while passing through a magical flame

Coppelia (1900) in this version of the ballet, the mechanical dancer is
a miniature

A Trip to the Moon (1902) a naïve but exhilarating voyage to our
satellite by an unlikely bunch of explorers

An Impossible Voyage (1904) the exploration of the solar system

The Tunnel Under the Channel (1907) an early attempt at joining
France and England

20,000 Leagues Under the Sea (1907) an adaptation of the Jules Verne
classic

The Conquest of the Pole (1912) another Jules Verne screen version

Twelve Early Movies about the Destruction of the World

1. *Seven Days to Noon* (Roy Boulting, 1950) Distraught scientist
   tries to destroy London with an atom bomb
2. *Five* (Arch Oboler, 1951) Five survivors of radiation attack
   squabble among themselves; only two make it
3. *When Worlds Collide* (Rudolph Mate, 1951) Planetoid
   approaches and hits our planet. Survivors escape by rocketship to
   the unknown
4. *The War of the Worlds* (Byron Haskin, 1953) The Martian
   invades as per H. G. Wells' famous novel
5. *Invaders from Mars* (William Cameron Menzies, 1954) Flying
   saucer invasion attempt with assorted mayhem and havoc
6. *The Invasion of the Body Snatchers* (Don Siegel, 1956) Pods borne
   by space spores take over humanity by counterfeiting people's
   appearance

7. *The 27th Day* (William Asher, 1957)   Five earthmen are given lethal capsules capable of destroying the world. Track them down or else is the hero's task
8. *The World, the Flesh and the Devil* (Ranald McDougall, 1959)   A trio survive a nuclear holocaust. One is black
9. *On the Beach* (Stanley Kramer, 1959)   The slow, but inexorable approach of nuclear armageddon
10. *The Day the Earth Caught Fire* (Val Guest, 1962)   Atomic experiments push the world out of orbit and nearer to the sun
11. *Dr Strangelove* (Stanley Kubrick, 1963)   Madcap black comedy about the sad inevitability of nuclear destruction through the follies of politicians and military personnel
12. *The Omega Man* (Boris Sagal, 1971)   Germ warfare transforms the majority of humanity into vampires. Charlton Heston is the lone 'normal' being who fights on but eventually succumbs

A List of Invisible Films

The theme of H. G. Wells' *The Invisible Man* has always held much attraction for film-makers with its potential for sleight of hand and trickery. James Whale, who directed the original *Frankenstein* movie, was the first director to tackle the subject, featuring Claude Rains in the title role, although for obvious reasons he only appears briefly (and dead) at the end of the film. This was soon followed by many other visible personages.

The Invisible Man (1933)
The Invisible Man Returns (1940)
The Invisible Ghost (1941)
The Invisible Woman (1941)
The Invisible Agent (1942)
The Invisible Man's Revenge (1944)
Slaves of the Invisible Monster (1950)
Abbott and Costello Meet the Invisible Man (1951)
The Invisible Boy (1957)
The Invisible Creature (1959)
The Invisible Terror (1963)
The Invisible Man (1975) TV movie, pilot for the subsequent series

317

Twenty Famous Robots of Filmland

C3 PO and *R2 D2* in *Star Wars*, 1977 and *The Empire Strikes Back*, 1980
Maria in *Metropolis*, 1972
Robby in *Forbidden Planet*, 1956 and *The Invisible Boy*, 1957
Gort in *The Day the Earth Stood Still*, 1951
Huey, Dewie and Louie in *Silent Running*, 1972
The Cyclons in *Battlestar Galactica*, 1978
The Ice Robot in *Logan's Run*, 1976
Gunslinger (Yul Brynner), in *Westworld*, 1973
The Wives in *The Stepford Wives*, 1975
Woody Allen as *Miles Monroe* impersonating a robot servant in *Sleeper*, 1973
Twiki and *Dr Theopolis* in *Buck Rogers in the 25th Century*, 1979
Marvin the Paranoid Android in the television version of *The Hitchhiker's Guide to the Galaxy*, 1980
Tobor the Great in an unidentified movie
Bubbo, in *Clash of the Titans*, 1981
Vincent in *The Black Hole*, 1979

Thirteen Famous Female Monsters of the Screen

1. Acquanetta as *The Ape Woman*
2. Mari Blanchard in the title role of *The She Devil* (Kurt Neumann, 1957)
3. Susan Cabot in *The Wasp Woman*
4. Yvonne de Carlo as the sinister Lily in *The Munsters* TV series, also in the feature length *Munster Go Home* (Earl Bellamy, 1966)
5. Gloria Holden as *Dracula's Daughter* (Lambert Hillyer, 1936)
6. Elsa Lanchester as the electric *Bride of Frankenstein* (James Whale, 1935)
7. Jacqueline Pearce as the Cobra Girl in *The Reptile* (John Gilling, 1966). She also portrays the treacherous but classy Servalan in *Blake's 7*
8. Ingrid Pitt became a Hammer film female monster fixture with

vampire roles in *The Vampire Lovers* (1971), *The House that Dripped Blood* (1971) and *Countess Dracula* (1970)

9. Simone Simon was the mysterious Irena Dubrovna in Val Lewton's *The Cat People* (1942) and *The Curse of the Cat People* (1944)

10. Coleen Gray played the eminently forgettable *Leech Woman* (Edward Dehn, 1960)

11. The nubile Natasha Kinski is the most modern avatar of screen lady-monsters in her feline incarnation in Paul Schrader's *Cat People* (1982)

12. Gale Sondergaard as *The Spider Woman Strikes Back*, also *Sherlock Holmes and the Spider Woman* (1946 and 1944 (Roy Neill and Arthur Lubin))

13. Barbara Steele as the sulphurous witch who returns to haunt innocents after a painful death in Mario Bava's classic *Black Sunday* (1960)

Forrest J. Ackerman's Ten Favourite Filmonsters

1. *Erik, the Phantom of the Opera*, as portrayed by Lon Chaney Sr. The ultimate *human* incarnation of horror

2. *Kong*, King of the animated prehistoriccreatures surviving from the Dawn of Time, birthed by his 'god' fathers Delgado and O'Brien

3. *Frankenstein*, the Karloffian 'body that never lived, taken from the graves, the gallows' and indelibly etched in my memory

4. *Dracula*, the cold Transylvanian count, undead 500 years and nightly replenishing his corpse with warm blood, as personified by Bela Lugosi

5. *The Mummy*, Im-ho-tep, risen from the sands of ancient Egypt after 3,700 years, incarnated by Boris Karloff

6. *The Id*, the electrifying force-field monster of Altair-4, created by the artful animators of Disney Studios for *The Forbidden Planet*

7. *The Metaluna Mutant*, the macrocephalonic monster of *This Island Earth*

8. *The Chestburster*, Roger Dicken's revolting 'thing from inner space' in *Alien*

9. *The Alien*, H. R. Giger's unforgettable monstrosity in the film of the same name
10. *The Face Behind the Mask*, Lionel Atwill, so scarily scarred in *The Mystery of the Wax Museum*

My Favourite Nude SF Scenes

A male chauvinist list here, I fear. I cannot remember which French critic or film director (either Truffaut or Godard) who said, a long time ago, that the ultimate in film-making was to reveal the bodies of beautiful women. As a keen fan of both the movies and beautiful women, I have taken unashamed pleasure in watching certain actresses disrobe or show just a square inch of tantalizing flesh in many a film. Such moments are all too rare in SF movies and so here is my list. I have deliberately excluded fantasy and horror films, where the amount of flesh on view is certainly much more generous and liberal but which, for me, lack the concentrated intensity of nudity in a SF context

1. Jenny Agutter, in loose, revealing, almost transparent and then wet gowns, in *Logan's Run*, an otherwise rotten film
2. Julie Christie, one of my major feminine obsessions (ah! *Don't Look Now*, *Dr Zhivago*, *Darling*, ah again!) is spied on by the sinister computer in *Demon Seed* as she takes a shower
3. Jessica Lange in the clutches of *King Kong*, in the de Laurentis version. Not strictly nude, although I gather from reports on the shooting of the movie that her top kept slipping off under the pressure of the mechanical hand of the giant ape. I leave my imagination to do the rest and conjure up a delightful breast and nipple. Also a nice wet scene
4. Brooke Adams in Kaufman's version of *The Invasion of the Body Snatchers*, walking in a naked daze among the shelves and shelves of pods
5. Sigourney Weaver's stripping down to her underwear under the watchful eye of the monster in *Alien*. Again, not strictly a nude scene, but full of potent eroticism
6. Sara Kestelman in *Zardoz*, freckles and all

7. The running girl in the fantasy sequence of *A Clockwork Orange*. The slow motion, her anonymity and the full frontal effect all combine to make this another strong scene

8. Valerie Perrine on Trafalmadore in *Slaughterhouse-Five*. Playing Billy Pilgrim's dream-girl Montana Wildhack, Valerie Perrine showed much more in the *Playboy* pictorial of the shooting and almost everywhere elsewhere since, but there's a delightful hint of puppy fat and such a mischievous twinkle in her eye!

9. Judi Bowker, almost virginal in the horrendous *Clash of the Titans* but offers us a brief back view of her compact body before indulging bra-less in the spray, which, although not on a par with Jacqueline Bisset's famous wet tee-shirt scene in *The Deep*, nevertheless provides some guilty pleasure . . .

Maxim Jakubowski alone - Malcolm Edwards had nothing to do with this one . . .

Twenty-four SF Novels that became Twenty-four SF Movies

Science fiction fans often complain of the lack of quality of SF on the silver screen and all too often moan that film-makers should adapt well-known books rather than trusting Hollywood hacks generally ignorant of the genre it rules. What is not often realized, however, is how many SF novels have in fact already been adapted for the screen (as well as many short stories):

1. Balmer and Wylie's *When Worlds Collide* was filmed by Rudolph Mate

2. Pierre Boulle's *Planet of the Apes* was filmed by Franklin Schaffner

3. Ray Bradbury's *Fahrenheit 451* was filmed by François Truffaut

4. Ray Bradbury's *The Illustrated Man* was filmed by Jack Smight

5. Anthony Burgess' *A Clockwork Orange* was filmed by Stanley Kubrick

6. John W. Campbell Jr's *The Thing* was filmed by John Carpenter

7. D. G. Compton's *The Unsleeping Eye/The Continuous Katherine Mortenhoe* was filmed as *Deathwatch* by Bertrand Tavernier

8. Michael Crichton's *The Andromeda Strain* was filmed by Robert Wise

9. Philip K. Dick's *Do Androids Dream of Electric Sheep?* was filmed as *Blade Runner* by Ridley Scott
10. Harlan Ellison's *A Boy and His Dog* was filmed by L. Q. Jones
11. Harry Harrison's *Make Room, Make Room* was filmed as *Soylent Green* by Richard Fleischer
12. Daniel Keyes' *Flowers for Algernon* was filmed as *Charly* by Ralph Nelson
13. Stanislaw Lem's *Solaris* was filmed by Andrei Tarkovsky
14. Ira Levin's *The Stepford Wives* was filmed by Bryan Forbes
15. Richard Matheson's *Bid Time Return* was filmed as *Somewhere in Time* by Jeannot Szwarc
16. Richard Matheson's *I, Legend* was filmed as *The Omega Man* by Boris Sagal
17. Richard Matheson's *The Incredible Shrinking Man* was filmed by Jack Arnold
18. Michael Moorcock's *The Final Programme* was filmed by Robert Fuest
19. William Nolan and George Clayton Johnson's *Logan's Run* was filmed by Michael Anderson
20. Walter Tevis' *The Man Who Fell to Earth* was filmed by Nicolas Roeg
21. Kurt Vonnegut's *Slaughterhouse-Five* was filmed by George Roy Hill
22. John Wyndham's *Revolt of the Triffids* was filmed by Steve Sekely
23. John Wyndham's *The Midwich Cuckoos* was filmed as *The Village of the Damned* by Wolf Rilla
24. Roger Zelazny's *Damnation Alley* was filmed by Jack Smight

This list is far from restrictive, but doesn't cover Jules Verne, H. G. Wells (see separate lists), TV productions and many foreign language films

The Ray Harryhausen Special Effects List

Ray Harryhausen is the acknowledged master of stop-motion animation in the cinema of the fantastic. He has peopled many films with a varied assortment of monsters, animals and magic tricks and his art spans many years. This is a list of his special effects in science fiction and fantasy movies:

The Beast from 20,000 Fathoms (Eugene Lourie, 1953)
It Came From Beneath the Sea (Robert Gordon, 1955)
The Animal World (Irwin Allen, 1956)
Earth versus the Flying Saucers (Fred F. Sears, 1956)
Twenty Million Miles to Earth (Nathan Juran, 1957)
The Seventh Voyage of Sinbad (Nathan Juran, 1958)
The Three Worlds of Gulliver (Jack Sher, 1960)
Mysterious Island (Cy Endfield, 1961)
Jason and the Argonauts (Don Chaffey, 1963)
First Men in the Moon (Nathan Juran, 1964)
One Million Years BC (Don Chaffey, 1966)
The Valley of Gwangi (James O'Conolly, 1969)
The Golden Voyage of Sinbad (Gordon Hessler, 1973)
Sinbad and the Eye of the Tiger (Sam Wanamaker, 1977)
Clash of the Titans (Desmond Davis, 1981)

As can be seen, the director of the film is seldom remembered whereas Harryhausen (often also acting as associate or co-producer) and his effects are still fond memories

A List of Gimmicks

As if the thrills and spills that SF and horror movies can offer were not enough, the film industry has indulged in 'technical advances' to enrich movies in many a way. These have ranged from the sublime to the ridiculous but apart from format improvements such as Cinemascope, Vistavision or the short-lived Cinerama, most of these innovations barely lived a season or two and are now relegated to dusty celluloid dungeons, although the occasional would-be mogul resurfaces every few years or so with another gimmick to tickle our jaded senses:

1. *3-D*, introduced in the early '50s with forgettable movies like *Bwana Devil* (1952) and *House of Wax* (1953). Hitchcock's *Dial M*

323

for Murder (1954) was filmed as a 3-D movie but released with a normal print due to the tepid public reaction to the process which has been resuscitated a few times since – but never for very long

2. *Emergo* emerged from the fertile brain of master showman William Castle who had already inaugurated the idea of insuring spectators against the incidence of heart attacks at his horror movies. During the showing of his *House on Haunted Hill* (1958), an illuminated plastic skeleton slid over the audience's heads

3. *Percepto* consisted of low-voltage electric shocks applied to seats in the audience during a crucial part of *The Tingler* (1959)

4. *The Fright Break*, yet another Castle concoction devised for *Homicidal* (1961) consisted of a row of seats fitted with seat belts hopefully to prevent spectators from going on the rampage out of sheer fear!

5. *Illusion-O* was a Castle variation on 3-D where special glasses were provided to enable the spectator to see or not to see the ghosts of *13 Ghosts* (1960) according to their courage

6. *Smell-O-Vision* was developed by Mike Todd Jr to enhance *The Scent of Mystery* (1960) by piping specific smells into the auditorium. Early attempts in US cinemas were a mess, with the varying perfumes mixing badly or erupting at the wrong plot moment. This has been modernized with *Odorama*, a palette of smells encapsulated on a card on the scratch and sniff principle (*Polyester*, 1981)

7. *Psychorama* flashed subliminal information on the screen which only the subconscious could read in *My World Dies Screaming* (1958)

8. *Hallucinogenic Hypnovision* despite its fantabulous name merely consisted of a member of the cinema staff running screaming up and down the aisles in a phosphorescent mask pretending to be a madman who had escaped from the reels of *The Maniacs are Loose* (1971)!

9. *Sensurround* was developed by Universal-MCA for *Earthquake* (1974). To make you feel as if you were at the very epicentre of the quake, the film's soundtrack had low-frequency electronic impulses simulating strong vibrations. Comments on the process have been mixed, but the gimmick was used again (albeit with less relevant subjects) on *Midway* (1976) and *Rollercoaster* (1977)

Alakazam the Great (Taiji Yabushita and Osamu Tezuka, 1961)
Eegah! (Nicholas Meeriwether, 1962)
Godzilla versus the Smog Monster (Yoshimitu Banno, 1972)
The Horror of Party Beach (Del Tenney, 1964)
Last Year at Marienbad (Alain Resnais, 1962)
Lost Horizon (Charles Jarrott, 1973)
The Omen (Richard Donner, 1976)
Robot Monster (Phil Tucker, 1953)
Santa Claus Conquers the Martians (Nicholas Webster, 1964)
The Story of Mankind (Irwin Allen, 1957)

In 1978, Californian film-buff Harry Medved published *The Fifty Worst Movies of All Time* (and how they got that way), an awesome collection of articles on awful movies. Ten out of the fifty movies honoured thus fall into the SF and Fantasy category. They are listed above.

Readers were invited to submit their own 'worst' choices and the results were published in Harry and Michael Medved's *The Golden Turkey Awards* (1980). The following SF and Fantasy movies came high in the list:

Plan Nine from Outer Space (Edward Wood Jr, 1959) *Poll Winner*
Exorcist II: The Heretic (John Boorman, 1977) *Runner-Up*
King Kong (John Guillermin, 1976)
The Swarm (Irwin Allen, 1978)
Orca (Michael Anderson, 1977)
Damien: Omen II (Don Taylor, 1978)
Godzilla's Revenge (1969)

The Star Wars Saga

At the time of writing, George Lucas's massive 9-part *Star Wars* cinematic saga hadn't even reached its first third, with *Star Wars* and

The Empire Strikes Back released and *The Return of The Jedi* still in the process of being filmed. In the world of books, however, the saga is much more advanced, even if not all the stories are to be part of the filmed series.

Star Wars, George Lucas (in fact written by Alan Dean Foster)
Splinter of the Mind's Eye, Alan Dean Foster
Han Solo at Star's End, Brian Daley
Han Solo's Revenge, Brian Daley
Han Solo and the Lost Legacy, Brian Daley
The Empire Strikes Back, Donald F. Glut
Return of the Jedi, James Kahn

And, no doubt, many more to come . . .

Ten SF Writers Who Have Appeared in Movies

1. *Forrest J. Ackerman*   Has made a number of cameo appearances, most recently in *The Howling* (where he is the customer in the occult bookshop). In John Landis's *Schlock* he is the popcorn-eating character next to the apeman in the movie theatre
2. *Martin Amis*   Son of Kingsley Amis and author of the SF novel *Dead Babies*, Martin Amis was also a child actor, appearing in the movie *A High Wind in Jamaica*
3. *Charles Beaumont*   Makes an appearance in the movie *The Intruder*
4. *Arthur C. Clarke*   Clarke achieves belated movie fame for his part as Leonard Woolf (husband of Virginia) in the movie *Village in the Jungle*
5. *Harlan Ellison*   'Harlan Ellison has a bit part in an orgy scene in Bill Rotsler's movie *The Godson* . . . The scene was filmed in Harlan's house.' Report in *Locus* 99
6. *Stephen King*   King has a bit part in buddy George Romero's *Knightriders*, and also appears in *Creepshow*, scripted by King and directed by Romero
7. *Fritz Leiber*   A professional actor, Leiber has made small appearances in films, most notably the Greta Garbo *Camille*
8. *Richard Matheson*   Makes a brief appearance in *Somewhere in Time*, a movie based on one of his novels

9. *William F. Nolan* Like Beaumont, appears in *The Intruder*
10. *Tom Reamy* Has a small part in *The Goddaughter*, another Bill Rotsler movie (see Ellison, above); may also appear in *Flesh Gordon*, a movie on which he worked

Stephen King's Guilty Pleasures

The American movie magazine *Film Comment* runs an irregular column of 'Guilty Pleasures' by guest film critics, writers and film-makers. This allows the writer to select and comment on a list of bad films he has liked. Stephen King's selection appeared in the May/June 1981 issue.

Bring Me the Head of Alfredo Garcia (Sam Peckinpah)
Bloody Mamma (Jonathan Demme)
Killers Three (AIP production featuring Dick Clark)
Sorcerer (William Friedkin)
The Horror of Party Beach (low-budget horror movie)
The Amityville Horror (Stuart Rosenberg)
The Wild Angels (Roger Corman)
Suspiria (Dario Argento)
Night of the Juggler (features James Brolin)

Danny Peary's Cult Movies

Cult movies are those that elicit passion in moviegoers, regardless of their intrinsic artistic worth. Danny Peary, a leading US film writer brought a hundred such films together in 1981 in his book *Cult Movies*, subtitled *The Classics, the Sleepers, the Weird and the Wonderful*. The movies he selected represented a highly idiosyncratic choice of films from the silent era to the present that fans see again and again. This list details the SF and fantasy choices:

Beauty and the Beast (Jean Cocteau, 1946)
Black Sunday (Mario Bava, 1960)
The Brood (David Cronenberg, 1979)

El Topo (Alexandro Jodorowsky, 1971)
Eraserhead (David Lynch, 1978)
Fantasia (Walt Disney, 1940)
Forbidden Planet (Fred McLeod Wilcox, 1956)
Freaks (Tod Browning, 1932)
Halloween (John Carpenter, 1978)
House of Wax (André de Toth, 1953)
I Married a Monster from Outer Space (Gene Fowler Jr, 1958)
I Walked with a Zombie (Jacques Tourneur, 1943)
Invasion of the Body Snatchers (Don Siegel, 1956)
Jason and the Argonauts (Don Chaffey, 1963)
King Kong (Merian Cooper and Ernest Schoedsack, 1933)
Kiss Me, Deadly (Robert Aldrich, 1955)
The Little Shop of Horrors (Roger Corman, 1960)
Mad Max (George Miller, 1979)
Night of the Living Dead (George Romero, 1968)
The Nutty Professor (Jerry Lewis, 1963)
Peeping Tom (Michael Powell, 1960)
Plan 9 from Outer Space (Edward D. Wood Jr, 1956)
The Red Shoes (Michael Powell and Emeric Pressburger, 1948)
The Rocky Horror Picture Show (Jim Sharman, 1975)
Tarzan and his Mate (Cedric Gibbons, 1934)
The Texas Chainsaw Massacre (Tobe Hooper, 1974)
The Wizard of Oz (Victor Fleming, 1939)
2001: A Space Odyssey (Stanley Kubrick, 1968)
Witchfinder General (Michael Reeves, 1968)

A List of Hammer Movies

Although Hammer Films' reputation is upheld these days by their vampire and horror movies of the 1960s and '70s, the film company was begun in 1947 and was for a long time a major force in movie-making in England. This is a list of our favourite Hammer movies, some of which deserve rehabilitating.

1. *The Mystery of the Mary Celeste*, a spooky thriller filmed in 1935 by Will Hammer for his then company Hammer Production which

was later to become Hammer Films proper. This featured Hollywood's Count Dracula, Bela Lugosi

2. *Stolen Face*, an early Terence Fisher effort, 1952, with the eponymous mad scientist at work and play

3. *Four-Sided Triangle*, an adaptation of the William F. Temple story by house director Terence Fisher, 1953

4. *Spaceways*, a forgotten Hammer realistic film based on a Charles Eric Maine radio-play (later novelized) about a murder on a space launch establishment, 1953 (Terence Fisher)

5. *The Quatermass Experiment*, the first film adaptation of the Nigel Kneale television serial, 1955 (Val Guest). Was followed by two other Quatermass movies in 1957 and 1967

6. *The Curse of Frankenstein*, Terence Fisher's 1957 first incursion into the horror genre which was soon to become a Hammer trade mark. Peter Cushing was the Baron and Christopher Lee the monster

7. *Dracula*, with Lee as the sinister bloodthirsty Count and Cushing as his urbane opponent; Terence Fisher again in 1958. The success of this movie set Hammer on a steadfast path of horror and it was succeeded by *The Mummy* (1959), *The Curse of the Werewolf* (1960), *The Phantom of the Opera* (1962) and a whole battery of further Dracula and Frankenstein movies

8. *The Damned*, Joseph Losey's bleak classic allegory on nuclear power, 1962

9. *One Million Years BC*, Raquel Welch's classic fur bikini movie, 1966

10. *To the Devil a Daughter*, a 1976 late return to form by Fisher, this time finding inspiration in Dennis Wheatley's satanic opus

The Roger Corman/Edgar Allan Poe List

At one time an incredibly prolific film director, Roger Corman has for many years now restricted his activities to producing and film distribution. A master of the low-budget movie who worked with equal ease in all genres: SF, war, fantasy, motorcycle movies, psychedelia, horror, thrillers, westerns, etc. He excelled in the elegiac but sinister mood of his films adapted or inspired by Edgar Allan Poe.

1. *Fall of the House of Usher*, 1960, w. Vincent Price
2. *The Pit and the Pendulum*, 1961, w. Vincent Price, Barbara Steele, John Kerr, Luana Anders
3. *The Premature Burial*, 1962, w. Ray Milland, Hazel Court
4. *Tales of Terror*, 1962, w. Vincent Price, Basil Rathbone, Debra Paget
5. *The Raven*, 1963, w. Vincent Price, Boris Karloff, Peter Lorre, Jack Nicholson, Hazel Court
6. *The Haunted Palace*, 1963, w. Vincent Price, Debra Paget, Lon Chaney Jr
7. *The Masque of the Red Death*, 1964, w. Vincent Price, Hazel Court, Jane Asher
8. *The Tomb of Ligeia*, 1964, w. Vincent Price, Elizabeth Shepherd

Many of the above films were scripted by Richard Matheson, Charles Beaumont and Robert Towne (who much later wrote *Chinatown* for Polanski). The scripts are far from faithful to Poe but remain always innovative. *The Pit and the Pendulum* also includes episodes from Poe's *Fall of the House of Usher* poem as well as the story in question. *Tales of Terror* incorporated adaptations of *Morella, The Strange Case of Mr Valdemar* and *The Black Cat/A Cask of Amontillado. The Raven* had in fact little to do with Poe's poem, and *The Haunted Palace* while acknowledging the Poe poem as its title was in fact heavily derived from H. P. Lovecraft's *The Case of Charles Dexter Ward.*

Jules Verne at the Movies

A Trip to the Moon (Méliès, 1902)
The Conquest of the Pole (Méliès, 1907)
20,000 Leagues Under the Sea (Stuart Paton, 1916)
Mysterious Island (Lucien Hubbard, 1928)
Michel Strogoff (w. Curt Jurgens, early 1950s)
20,000 Leagues Under the Sea (Richard Fleischer, 1954)
Around the World in 80 Days (Mike Todd, 1956)
From the Earth to the Moon (Byron Haskin, 1958)
The Deadly Invention (Karel Zeman, 1958)
Journey to the Center of the Earth (Henry Levin, 1959)

330

Master of the World (William Witney, 1961)
Mysterious Island (Cy Endfield, 1961)
Five Weeks in a Balloon (1962)
Captain Nemo's Underwater City (James Hill, 1969)
In Search of the Castaways (Walt Disney prod w. Maurice Chevalier
and Hayley Mills, late 1960s)

H. G. Wells at the Movies

A Trip to the Moon (Méliès, 1902)
First Men in the Moon (J. V. Leigh, 1919)
The Man Who Could Work Miracles (Lothar Mendes, ?)
The Invisible Man (James Whale, 1931)
Island of Lost Souls (Erle Kenton, 1932)
Things to Come (William Cameron Menzies, 1936)
'Golfing' in The Dead of Night (Charles Crichton, 1945)
The War of the Worlds (Byron Haskin, 1953)
The Time Machine (George Pal, 1960)
First Men in the Moon (Nathan Juran, 1964)
Food of the Gods (Bert Gordon, 1976)
The Island of Doctor Moreau (Don Taylor, 1977)
Time After Time (Nicholas Meyer, 1979)

The Great SF Serials

A touch of nostalgia here! When rip-roaring adventure yarns could
be seen over weeks and weeks with cliff-hangers galore and thrills by
the dozen. So you thought Star Wars and its saga was all-original?

The Airmail Mystery, 1932, where the Black Hawk's plane is sent into
mission at the end of an Aerial Catapult
Whispering Shadows, 1933, whose villain transmits his voice and
sinister silhouette
The Vanishing Shadow, 1934, where the hero controls invisibility
The Miracle Rider, 1935, sees Tom Mix handle a death-ray

331

The Phantom Empire, 1935, has Gene Autry seeking lost civilizations underneath the earth

Undersea Kingdom, 1935, Crash Corrigan conquers Atlantis

Flash Gordon, 1936, the first, the one, the only Flash against nasty old Ming

Flash Gordon's Trip to Mars, 1938, all on board to fight Ming and his Nitron Ray

Buck Rogers, 1939, thwarts the evil schemes of Killer Kane

Flash Gordon Conquers the Universe, 1940, versus the Purple Death

The Adventures of Captain Marvel, 1941, see the hero fly!

Batman, 1943, see the hero win!

Captain America, 1944, see the hero triumph!

The Phantom of the Air, 1944, defies gravity with his fabulous Contragrav

The Purple Monster Strikes, 1945, beware the invaders from Mars

Brick Bradford, 1947, see the hero cross the Crystal Door and save the world, the universe and everything!

Superman, 1948, fights the Spider Lady and her Reducer Ray

Batman and Robin, 1949, see the heroes win!

King of the Rocket Men, 1949, attired in his jet-suit to oppose Vulcan and his Decimator

The Invisible Monster, 1950, see the hero become invisible!

Captain Video, 1951, with colour for the space sequences

Flying Disc from Mars, 1951, the saucers are coming

Radar Men from the Moon, 1952, Commando Cody, Sky Marshal of the Universe, flies in his jet-suit and disposes of Retik the Ruler

Zombies of the Stratosphere, 1952, Larry Martin of the Interplanetary Patrol flies in his rocket suit and disposes of Marez and Nareb

The Lost Planet, 1953, Columbia's last serial

Commando Cody, 1953, returns for Republic's last serial

These we have loved!

The SF and Fantasy Telemovie List

Films made specially for television are too often overlooked by most film specialists. They are often shown unheralded (despite respectable star line-ups and seasoned directors at the helm) and their repeat schedule is most haphazard. The major source of information for telemovies is *Movies Made For Television* by Alvin H. Marill (Arlington House, 1980). Because of the high costs of special effects and sets, there have not been many telemovies in the SF and fantasy field, but those that have been made and shown are certainly worth knowing about, in the hope of that elusive repeat.

Shadow On the Land (Richard C. Sarafian, 1968)   America under the grip of a totalitarian government. A secret underground force battles an iron-fisted dictator (w. Jackie Cooper, Gene Cooper, Carol Lynley, John Forsythe, Janice Rule)

Fear No Evil (Paul Wendkos, 1969)   From a Guy Endore story, a supernatural thriller where a man is possessed by an antique mirror (w. Louis Jourdan, Carroll O'Connor, Bradford Dillman, Wilfrid Hyde-White)

The Immortal (Joseph Sargent, 1969)   From *The Immortals* by James Gunn. A test driver possesses a rare blood type that makes him immortal. But many seek his gift, through transfusion, for dubious motives. A short-lived series followed in 1970–71 (w. Christopher George, Barry Sullivan, Ralph Bellamy, Carol Lynley)

Night Gallery (Boris Sagal, Steven Spielberg and Barry Shear, 1969)   A three part fantasy anthology, which was to spawn a popular series (1971–3) (w. Joan Crawford, Ossie Davis, Roddy McDowell)

Daughter Of The Mind (Walter Grauman, 1969)   Based on *The Hand of Mary Constable* by Paul Gallico. A cybernetics professor believes his dead daughter is trying to reach him from beyond the grave (w. Gene Tierney, Don Murray, Ray Milland, Edward Asner)

Sole Survivor (Paul Stanley, 1970)   The ghosts of a bomber crew haunt the survivor (w. William Shatner, Vince Edwards, Richard Basehart)

The Challenge (Allen Smithee, 1970)   A lone representative each for the USA and an Asian country fight out a war on a deserted island; shades of Fredric Brown's *Arena*! (w. Darren McGavin, Broderick Crawford, James Whitmore)

Ritual of Evil (Robert Day, 1970)   A sequel to *Fear No Evil*. Further excursions into black magic (w. Louis Jourdan, Anne Baxter, Diana Hyland, Wilfred Hyde-White)

The Love War (George McCowan, 1970)   Aliens from two warring planets take on human form and battle it out in a small Californian town (w. Lloyd Bridges, Angie Dickinson)

How Awful About Allan (Curtis Harrington, 1970)   Strange voices from the dead haunt the hero (w. Anthony Perkins, Julie Harris, Joan Hackett)

Night Slaves (Ted Post, 1970)   Based on a Jerry Sohl novel. Zombies populate a small western town and a mysterious woman holds the key to the mystery (w. James Franciscus, Lee Grant, Tisha Sterling, Leslie Nielsen)

The Aquarians (Don McDougall, 1970)   Underwater adventures with mad nerve-gas-controlling scientist (w. Ricardo Montalban, José Ferrer, Leslie Nielsen)

The House That Would Not Die (John Llewellyn Moxey, 1970)   Witchcraft, black magic and ghosts in a derelict house (w. Barbara Stanwyck, Richard Egan)

Hauser's Memory (Boris Sagal, 1970)   From the Curt Siodmak novel; Cold War thriller with brain transplant and Nazis (w. David McCallum, Susan Strasberg, Lilli Palmer, Leslie Nielsen)

Crowhaven Farm (Walter Grauman, 1970)   Supernatural goings-on on a farm (w. Hope Lange, John Carradine)

City Beneath the Sea (Irwin Allen, 1971)   The underwater twenty-first-century city of Pacifica combats aliens (w. Stuart Whitman, Robert Wagner, Joseph Cotten, Rosemary Forsyth, Richard Basehart)

The Deadly Dream (Alf Kjellin, 1971)   A scientist sees his dreams taking shape (w. Lloyd Bridges, Janet Leigh)

The Last Child (John Llewellyn Moxey, 1971)   A couple defy the government's strict population control laws (w. Van Heflin, Harry Guardino, Janet Margolin, Edward Asner, Michael Cole)

Death Takes a Holiday (Robert Butler, 1971)   Death takes a human form and comes to Earth and falls in love with a beautiful woman (w. Yvette Mimieux, Monte Markham, Myrna Loy, Melvyn Douglas, Kerwin Matthews)

Black Noon (Bernard Kowalski, 1971)   An occult western (w. Roy Thinnes, Yvette Mimieux, Gloria Grahame, Ray Milland, Henry Silva)

Duel (Steven Spielberg, 1971)   Adapted from the Richard Matheson short story, this telemovie has since attained classic status and been given theatrical release. The relentless pursuit of an innocent driver in his car by a leviathan of a lorry (w. Dennis Weaver)

Earth II (Tom Gries, 1971)   Soap opera antics on a space station of the future (w. Gary Lockwood, Anthony Franciosa, Lew Ayres, Mariette Hartley, Gary Merrill)

The Devil and Miss Sarah (Michael Caffey, 1971)   A western outlaw with satanic powers possesses a woman's soul (w. Gene Barry, Slim Pickens, Janice Rule)

The Astronaut (Robert Michael Lewis, 1972)   A space exploration cover-up conspiracy movie (w. Jackie Cooper, Monte Markham, Susan Clark)

The Night Stalker (John Llewellyn Moxey, 1972)   Modern-day vampire terrorizes Las Vegas. Script by Richard Matheson. A brief series followed in 1974–5. (w. Darren McGavin, Carol Lynley, Ralph Meeker, Claude Atkins, Simon Oakland)

Something Evil (Steven Spielberg, 1972)   Haunted farmhouse yarn; early Spielberg TV effort (w. Sandy Dennis, Jeff Corey, Darren McGavin)

The People (John Korty, 1972)   Based on the Zenna Henderson stories collected in *Pilgrimage*. Backwoods folk have mysterious powers (w. William Shatner, Kim Darby, Diane Varsi)

She Waits (Delbert Mann, 1972)   A murdered woman possesses her husband's new bride (w. David McCallum, Patty Duke, Lew Ayres, Dorothy McGuire)

The Screaming Woman (Jack Smight, 1972)   Based on a Ray Bradbury story about a woman being buried alive and spooking a whole family (w. Olivia de Havilland, Joseph Cotten, Walter Pidgeon, Alexandra Hay, Ed Nelson, Laraine Stephens)

Probe (Russ Mayberry, 1972)   Space-age detective Marlowe-like capers. Pilot for the *Search* series (1972–3) (w. Hugh O'Brian, Elke Sommer, John Gielgud, Burgess Meredith)

The Eyes of Charles Sand (Reza Badiyi, 1972)   Occult murder investigation where the hero sees visions from beyond the grave (w. Peter Haskell, Joan Bennett, Bradford Dillman, Adam West)

Moon of the Wolf (Daniel Petrie, 1972)   Werewolf lurks in a Louisiana bayou (w. David Janssen, Barbara Rush, Bradford Dillman)

Visions of Death (Lee H. Katzin, 1972)   A clairvoyant academic foresees his own death (w. Telly Savalas, Monte Markham, Barbara Anderson)

Sandcastles (Ted Post, 1972)   A lonely young girl has a romance with a dead man (w. Bonnie Bedelia, Herschel Bernardi, Jan-Michael Vincent, Mariette Hartley)

Gargoyles (B. W. L. Norton, 1972)   Anthropological demonic yarn (w. Cornel Wilde, Jennifer Salt, Scott Glenn)

The Devil's Daughter (Jeannot Szwarc, 1973)   Devil-worshipping hi-jinxes (w. Shelley Winters, Joseph Cotten, Belinda Montgomery, Robert Foxworth)

Frankenstein (Glenn Jordan, 1973)   Another adaptation of the classic horror yarn (w. Robert Foxworth, Susan Strasberg, Bo Svenson)

The Night Strangler (Dan Curtis, 1973)   Richard Matheson teleplay for this sequel to *The Night Stalker* originated the *Kolchak* series (1974–5). Monster-chasing reporter battles with terror and his colleagues' incredulity (w. Darren McGavin, Jo Ann Pflug, Simon Oakland, John Carradine, Scott Brady)

A Cold Night's Death (Jerrold Freedman, 1973)   Snowbound Arctic scientists stalked by unknown force (w. Robert Culp, Eli Wallach)

Baffled! (Philip Leacock, 1973)   Another clairvoyant protagonist

336

thriller (w. Leonard Nimoy, Susan Hampshire, Rachel Roberts, Vera Miles)

The Horror at 37,000 Feet (David Lowell Rich, 1973)   Ghosts haunt a plane's hold (w. Chuck Connors, Buddy Ebsen, William Shatner, Roy Thinnes, Tammy Grimes)

Poor Devil (Robert Scheerer, 1973)   An apprentice demon bungles all his attempts at snaring a soul (w. Sammy Davis Jr, Christopher Lee, Jack Klugman, Adam West)

The Norliss Tapes (Dan Curtis, 1973)   William F. Nolan script of reporter discovering the walking dead and peril (w. Roy Thinnes, Angie Dickinson, Claude Akins, Michele Carey)

The Stranger (Lee H. Katzin, 1973)   An astronaut crash lands on a replica of Earth planet (w. Glen Corbett, Sharon Acker, Lew Ayres, Dean Jagger, Cameron Mitchell)

The Six-Million Dollar Man (Richard Irving, 1973)   Based on Martin Caidin's *Cyborg*, the feature-length pilot for the now-famous series (1973-8) (w. Lee Majors, Martin Balsam, Barbara Anderson, Darren McGavin, Dorothy Green)

Genesis II (John Llewellyn Moxey, 1973)   Sleeper wakes up in future society film from *Star Trek* producer Gene Roddenberry (w. Alex Cord, Mariette Hartley)

The Picture of Dorian Gray (Glenn Jordan, 1973)   Eighth film version of the Oscar Wilde story (w. Shane Briant, Nigel Davenport)

Satan's School for Girls (David Lowell Rich, 1973)   The title gives the whole plot away! (w. Pamela Franklin, Roy Thinnes, Kate Jackson, Lloyd Bochner, Cheryl Ladd)

Don't Be Afraid of the Dark (John Newland, 1973)   Another haunted house yawn (w. Kim Darby, Jim Hutton, Barbara Anderson)

Scream, Pretty Peggy (Gordon Hessler, 1973)   Horror tale by Amicus-expatriate (w. Bette Davis, Allan Arbus)

Catholics (Jack Gold, 1973)   From the Brian Moore novel, religious drama set in the future (w. Trevor Howard, Martin Sheen, Raf Vallone, Cyril Cusack, Andrew Keir)

Frankenstein: The True Story (Jack Smight, 1973) Four-hour painstaking version of the classic tale. Superb production values and Christopher Isherwood teleplay (w. James Mason, Leonard Whiting, David McCallum, Jane Seymour, Nicola Paget, Michael Sarrazin, John Gielgud, Ralph Richardson, Agnes Moorhead, Tom Baker, Margaret Leighton). Later cut down to two hours for US theatrical release

The Cat Creature (Curtis Harrington, 1973) Robert Bloch story inspired this tale of mummy theft and Oriental baddies (w. Meredith Baxter, Stuart Whitman, John Carradine, Gale Sondergaard)

The Borrowers (Walter C. Miller, 1973) Based on the Mary Norton novel, a tale of little people who live between the floorboards of a Victorian mansion (w. Eddie Albert, Tammy Grimes)

Scream of the Wolf (Dan Curtis, 1974) Another Richard Matheson–Dan Curtis collaboration for this modernized werewolf tale (w. Peter Graves, Clint Walker, Jo Ann Pflug)

The Questor Tapes (Richard A. Colla, 1974) Gene Roddenberry pilot which never turned into a series although a novelization by Dorothy (DC) Fontana did ensue. An android seeks his identity and creator (w. Robert Foxworth, John Vernon, Lew Ayres)

Killdozer (Jerry London, 1974) The Ted Sturgeon tale of man vs alien-controlled machine (w. Clint Walker, Neville Brand)

Dracula (Dan Curtis, 1974) Richard Matheson teleplay of the Bram Stoker perennial tale of terror (w. Jack Palance, Simon Ward, Nigel Davenport, Fiona Lewis)

Killer Bees (Curtis Harrington, 1974) Yet another title-reveals-all telemovie (w. Gloria Swanson, Kate Jackson, Eddie Albert)

Wonder Woman (Vincent McEveety, 1974) This feature has in fact no connection with the TV series of some years later featuring Lynda Carter as the pneumatic heroine (w. Cathie Lee Crosby, Ricardo Montalban, Kaz Garas)

Turn of the Screw (Dan Curtis, 1974) This time around, William F. Nolan adapts a classic tale for Dan Curtis, the haunting Henry James horror story filmed in 1961 as *The Innocents* (w. Lynn

Redgrave, Jasper Jacob, Eva Griffith)

Planet Earth (Marc Daniels, 1974) Rodenberry remakes his own *Genesis II* of the previous year. Sleeper awakes to confront future society (w. John Saxon, Janet Margolin, Diana Muldaur, Ted Cessidy)

The Strange and Deadly Occurrence (John Llewellyn Moxey, 1974) Haunted home strikes the boob tube, again (w. Robert Stack, Vera Miles, L. Q. Jones, Herb Edelman)

The Stranger Within (Lee Phillips, 1974) Richard Matheson adapts his own short story about a baby still inside the womb, controlling his mother's actions to strange effect (w. Barbara Eden, David Doyle, Nehemiah Persoff)

The Disappearance of Flight 412 (Jud Taylor, 1974) UFO vs uncomprehending airforce yarn (w. Glenn Ford, Bradford Dillman, David Soul)

Where Have All The People Gone? (John Llewellyn Moxey, 1974) Survival after the nuclear holocaust for an American family (w. Peter Graves, Verna Bloom, Kathleen Quinlan)

Stowaway To The Moon (Andrew V. McLaglen, 1975) Juvenile astronaut story (w. Lloyd Bridges, John Carradine)

The Dead Don't Die (Curtis Harrington, 1975) Robert Bloch teleplay of 1930s sailor drawn to the netherworld (w. George Hamilton, Ray Milland, Ralph Meeker, Joan Blondell)

Satan's Triangle (Sutton Roley, 1975) Bermuda triangle under another name (w. Doug McClure, Kim Novak, Jim Davis, Alejandro Rey)

Trilogy of Terror (Dan Curtis, 1975) Three vehicles for Karen Black in this anthology of Matheson stories; two adapted by William Nolan and one by Matheson himself. Only one is specifically fantasy (w. Karen Black, Robert Burton, John Karlen)

Search for the Gods (Jud Taylor, 1975) Ancient astronaut theories investigated by a trio of students (w. Kurt Russell, Ralph Bellamy, Stephen McHattie)

The Invisible Man (Robert Michael Lewis, 1975) Pilot for the 1973 series, with little left of the H. G. Wells original story (w. David McCallum, Jackie Cooper, Melinda Fee)

Strange New World (Robert Butler, 1975)   Three astronauts return, after a bout of suspended animation, to a planet now in the far future. Pilot for a series which never emerged (w. John Saxon, Martine Beswick, James Olson, Kathleen Miller)

The UFO Incident (Richard A. Colla, 1975)   UFO-kidnapping supposedly based on fact (w. James Earl Jones, Estelle Parsons)

Beyond the Bermuda Triangle (William A. Graham, 1975)   Retired businessman probes Triangle disappearances (w. Fred McMurray, Sam Groom, Donna Mills, Suzanne Reed)

The New, Original Wonder Woman (Leonard J. Horn, 1975)   Return of the comic-strip heroine in pilot for the later series (1975-8) (w. Lynda Carter, Lyle Waggoner, Stella Stevens, Cloris Leachman)

Time Travelers (Alex Singer, 1976)   An Irwin Allen production sees a time traveller returning to the great Chicago fire (w. Sam Groom, Tom Halick, Richard Basehart)

Future Cop (Jud Taylor, 1976)   Cop with android partner thriller comedy; more were to follow (w. Ernest Borgnine, Michael Shannon)

Gemini Man (Alan Levi, 1976)   US secret agent with powers of invisibility strikes again; a short-lived series followed in 1976-7 (w. Ben Murphy, Katherine Crawford)

Look What's Happened to Rosemary's Baby (Sam O'Steen, 1976)   The growth to adulthood of the famous demonic spawn (w. Stephen McHattie, Patty Duke, Broderick Crawford, Ruth Gordon, Ray Milland, George Maharis)

Beauty and the Beast (Fielder Cook, 1976)   New adaptation of the classic children's fairy-tale (w. George Scott, Trish Van Devere, Virginia McKenna, Bernard Lee)

The Last Dinosaur (Alex Grasshoff and Tom Kotani, 1977) Rich hunter is given the opportunity to travel back in time, albeit without weapons, to meet a dinosaur and a marauding pre-historic tribe (w. Richard Boone)

The Spell (Lee Philips, 1977) Overweight teenager turns the tables on her tormentors thanks to her supernatural psychic powers (w. Lee Grant, James Olson, Lelia Goldoni, Susan Myers)

The Strange Possession of Mrs Oliver (Gordon Hessler, 1977) Richard Matheson scripts another possession yarn (w. Karen Black, George Hamilton, Robert F. Lyons)

Man From Atlantis (Lee H. Katzin, 1977) Pilot for brief series of last survivor of the underwater mythical kingdom (w. Patrick Duffy, Victor Buono, Belinda Montgomery)

The Possessed (Jerry Thorpe, 1977) Good versus Evil tale in a girls' school (w. James Farentino, Joan Hackett, P. J. Soles, Harrison Ford, Ann Dusenberry)

Red Alert (William Hale, 1977) Accident in a nuclear power plant (w. William Devane, Adrienne Barbeau, Michael Brandon, Ralph Waite)

Spectre (Clive Donner, 1977) London-based tale of demonology (w. Robert Culp, Gig Young, John Hurt, Gordon Jackson, Jenny Runacre)

Good Against Evil (Paul Wendkos, 1977) Another exorcism movie (w. Dack Rambo, Elyssa Davalos, Dan O'Herlihy)

The Man With The Power (Nicholas Sgarro, 1977) Bodyguard inherits hidden powers from faraway planet (w. Bob Neill, Tim O'Connor, Vic Morrow, Persis Khambatta)

Exo-Man (Richard Irving, 1977) Paralysed academic creates special suit which provides him with super-human powers. Never made it into a series (w. David Ackroyd, José Ferrer, Kevin McCarthy)

The Magnificent Magnet of Santa Mesa (Hy Averback, 1977) Naïve young boffin invents energy-saving device (w. Michael Burns)

Spider-Man (E. W. Swackhamer, 1977) Pilot feature-length for series (w. Nicholas Hammond, David White)

Curse of the Black Widow (Dan Curtis, 1977) Mysterious killer leaves victim in stranger spider-like web (w. Tony Franciosa, Donna Mills, Patty Duke, June Allyson, Jeff Corey)

The Incredible Hulk (Kenneth Johnson, 1977)   Pilot for popular series; how the Hulk became the Hulk (w. Bill Bixby, Lou Ferrigno, Susan Sullivan, Jack Colvin)

It Happened at Lake Wood Manor (Robert Scherer, 1977)   Ants attack holiday mansion (w. Suzanne Somers, Robert Foxworth, Myrna Loy, Lynda Day George)

Tarantulas: The Deadly Cargo (Stuart Hagmann, 1978)   Tarantulas attack town (w. Claude Akins, Pat Hingle, Charles Frank)

The Dark Secret of Harvest Home (Leo Penn, 1978)   Five-hour version of the Thomas Tryon novel *Harvest Home* of strange doings in the genteel countryside (w. Bette Davis, David Ackroyd, René Auberjonois, Rosanna Arquette)

The Bermuda Depths (Tom Kotani, 1978)   Back to the Triangle! (w. Burl Ives, Leigh McCloskey)

Night Cries (Richard Lang, 1978)   A dead baby haunts its mother (w. Susan St James, Michael Parks)

Cruise Into Terror (Bruce Kessler, 1978)   Spirit from an old sarcophagus terrorizes cruise ship (w. Christopher George, Lynda Day George, Ray Milland, Stella Stevens, Hugh O'Brian)

The Ghost of Flight 401 (Stephen Hilliard Stern, 1978)   Supernatural occurrences involving an actual plane crash, adapted from the John G. Fuller book (w. Ernest Borgnine, Gary Lockwood)

Dr Scorpion (Richard Lang, 1978)   Mad scientist rises and strikes again! (w. Nick Mancuso, Christine Lahti, Roscoe Lee Brown)

Cops and Robin (Allen Reisner, 1978)   Cop and android sidekick on the beat again (w. Ernest Borgnine, Michael Shannon, Carol Lynley, John Amos, Natasha Ryan)

Death Moon (Bruce Kessler, 1978)   Supernatural goings-on in Hawaii (w. Robert Foxworth, Frances Nuyen)

Dr Strange (Philip DeGuere, 1978)   The *Marvel* comics character makes it to the screen (w. Peter Hooten)

The Clone Master (Don Medford, 1978)   Scientist makes duplicates of himself to fight for the good ole USA (w. Art Hindle, Robyn Douglass, Ralph Bellamy)

Human Feelings (Ernest Pintoff, 1978) God as a woman, angels, whimsy. Morality tale gone wrong (w. Nancy Walker, Pamela Sue Martin, Armand Assante, Billy Crystal)

Kiss Meets The Phantom Of The Park (Gordon Hessler, 1978) Rock group versus mad scientist and his replica robots (w. Kiss, Anthony Zerbe, Carmine Caridi)

Devil Dog: The House of Hell (Curtis Harrington, 1978) The devil inhabits a dog and leashes out (w. Richard Crenna, Yvette Mimieux, Martine Beswick, Kim Richards)

Stranger in our House (Wes Craven, 1978) Telemovie by splatter film specialist. Witchcraft in the countryside (w. Linda Blair, Lee Purcell, Jeremy Slate)

The Time Machine (Henning Schellerup, 1978) An adaptation of the H. G. Wells classic (w. John Beck, Priscilla Barnes)

The Thief of Baghdad (Clive Donner, 1978) Star-studded remake of the Korda classic Arabian fantasy (w. Roddy McDowall, Kabir Bedi, Frank Finlay, Marina Vlady, Peter Ustinov, Terence Stamp, Ian Holm, Pavla Ustinov, Daniel Emilfork)

A Fire In The Sky (Jerry Jameson, 1978) Three-hour SF disaster as comet falls on Phoenix, Arizona, based on a Paul Gallico story (w. Richard Crenna, Elizabeth Ashley, Lloyd Bochner)

The Terror Out of the Sky (Lee H. Katzin, 1978) Sequel to *The Savage Bees*, wherein 'they' return (w. Efrem Zimbalist Jr, Dan Hagerty, Tovah Feldshuh)

Captain America (Ron Holcomb, 1979) Another comic-strip super-hero comes to life screen-wise (w. Reb Brown, Len Birman, Heather Menzies, Steve Forrest)

Salvage (Lee Philips, 1979) Junk merchant builds rocket to journey to the Moon to retrieve valuable wrecks. Gave birth to series *Salvage 1* (w. Andy Griffith, Joel Higgins, Trish Stewart, Richard Jaeckel)

Mandrake (Harry Falk, 1979) Comic-strip hero versus the obligatory villains and mad scientist (w. Anthony Herrera, Simone Griffith, Gretchen Corbett)

Gold of the Amazon Women (Mel Damski, 1979)   Legendary tribe of women warriors is found in South American deepest jungle (w. Bo Svenson, Anita Ekberg, Donald Pleasence)

The Darker Side of Terror (Gus Trikonis, 1979)   Scientist clones himself but experiment goes wrong when his replica goes nasty (w. Robert Forster, Adrienne Barbeau, Ray Milland)

The Billion Dollar Threat (Barry Shear, 1979)   Super secret agent meets ultra-mad scientist and saves world again (w. Dale Robinette, Ralph Bellamy, Keenan Wynn, Patrick McNee)

The Ultimate Imposter (Paul Stanley, 1979)   Secret agent is linked to computer and faces Russian foes (w. Joseph Hacker, Keith Andes, Erin Gray)

Tise Vahimagi's Villains from TV's Past

Dr Who
The Daleks
Cybermen
The Master

The Avengers
The Cybernauts

The Bionic Woman
The Fembots

Batman
Joker
Catwoman
Penguin
Riddler
King Tut
Shame
Louie
Mr Freeze
Mad Hatter
Marsha
Egghead

Star Trek
Klingons
Romulans
Harry Mudd

The Man From Atlantis
Mr Schubert

The Man from UNCLE
Thrush
Gervaise Ravel

Land of the Giants
Inspector Kobick

Voyage to the Bottom of the Sea
Mr Pem

Lost in Space
Franum B.
Athena

A columnist with *Starburst* and the author of several books on television Tise Vahimagi is a foremost specialist of TV series and history

---

Seven Actors Who Have Played Doctor Who

1. William Hartnell   was the first Doctor Who in the television series, appearing in the initial four-part programme *An Unearthly Child* broadcast on 23 November 1963. His final appearance was in Part 4 of *The Tenth Planet*, 29 October 1966. Worn out by the strain of a battle with the Cybermen, he suddenly grows older when returning to the Tardis and begins to change . . .
2. Peter Cushing   played the Doctor in two motion pictures, *Doctor Who and the Daleks* (1965) and *The Daleks: Invasion Earth 2150 AD* (1966)
3. Patrick Troughton   was the second television Doctor, replacing William Hartnell. His first appearance was in *The Power of the Daleks*, 5 November 1966 and his final one in the tenth part of

The War Games shown on 21 June 1969. The Doctor, a renegade Time Lord, has had to summon the assistance of his peers in battle; after the inevitable outcome, he is tried and exiled to Earth after having his appearance changed

4. Jon Pertwee   succeeded Patrick Troughton. He was first seen in *Spearhead from Space*, 3 January 1970 and left the scene in *Planet of the Spiders*, 8 June 1974. Following a confrontation with a giant mutated spider, the Doctor's body suffers irreparable damage. A Tibetan monk accelerates his regeneration and he changes appearance again

5. Trevor Martin   played the Doctor in the theatre on the occasion of the only stage production of a Doctor Who story, *Doctor Who and the Daleks* in *Seven Keys to Doomsday*, which ran at the Adelphi Theatre, London, between 16 December 1974 and 12 January 1975

6. Tom Baker   was the fourth television incarnation of the Doctor and the actor to hold the role longest. His first appearance was in *Robot*, 28 December 1974 and his final bow occurred in *Logopolis*, 21 March 1981, where he fell to his death after a fight with the Master and his body began regenerating

7. Peter Davison   is the present Doctor Who. Although a glimpse of him was caught in Tom Baker's last foray in *Logopolis*, his initial appearance on British television screens in his own right was on 4 January 1981 in the first episode of *Castrovalva*

Sixteen Recognized SF Writers Who Have Authored Star Trek Scripts

Created by Gene Roddenberry (who himself penned eleven scripts), *Star Trek* remains, despite its many shortcomings, the major TV SF series and its legion of fans still keep the flame well alive. A number of established US authors wrote for the series and/or its animated offshoot. We detail their contributions:

1. *Russell Bates* One script (in coll with David Wise): 'How Sharper than a Serpent's Tooth' (animated)

2. *Jerome Bixby* Four scripts: 'Mirror, Mirror', 'By Any Other Name' (with D. C. Fontana), 'Day of the Dove' and 'Requiem for Methuselah'
3. *Robert Bloch* Three scripts: 'Wolf in the Fold', 'What are Little Girls Made Of?' and 'Catspaw'
4. *Fredric Brown* His classic story 'Arena' was adapted into a *Star Trek* episode of the same name by Gene Coon
5. *Mike Dolinsky* (writing as Meyer Dolinsky) One script: 'Plato's Stepchildren'
6. *Max Ehrlich* One script: 'The Apple' (with Gene Coon)
7. *Harlan Ellison* One script: 'The City on the Edge of Forever'
8. *Dorothy C. Fontana* Nine scripts: 'Tomorrow is Yesterday', 'Charlie X', 'This Side of Paradise' (w Nathan Butler), 'Journey to Babel', 'Friday's Child', 'By Any Other Name' (w Jerome Bixby), 'The Ultimate Computer' (w Lawrence N. Wolfe), 'The Enterprise Incident', and 'Yesteryear' (animated)
9. *David Gerrold* Five scripts: 'The Trouble with Tribbles', 'More Tribbles, More Troubles' (animated), 'Bem' (animated), 'I Mudd' (w Stephen Kandel), 'The Cloud-Minders' (co-wrote story w Oliver Crawford, but *not* script)
10. *George Clayton Johnson* One script: 'The Man Trap' (first-ever episode)
11. *Richard Matheson* One script: 'The Enemy Within'
12. *Larry Niven* One script: 'Slaver Weapon' (animated)
13. *Jerry Sohl* Two scripts: 'The Corbomite Manoeuver' and 'Whom Gods Destroy' (w Lee Erwin – story only)
14. *Norman Spinrad* One script: 'The Doomsday Machine'
15. *Theodore Sturgeon* Two scripts: 'Shore Leave' and 'Amok Time'
16. *Howard Weinstein* One script: 'The Pirates of Orion' (animated)

Six SF Writers Who Have Recorded Rock Music

1. *Robert Calvert* Lyricist for rock group Hawkwind and its later offshoot the Hawklords, Robert Calvert also occasionally performed on stage with them (as did Moorcock; see below). After leaving the group he recorded two solo albums *Captain Lockheed and the Star-Fighters* and *Lucky Lief and the Longships*. He has

published SF short stories and texts in underground magazines and *New Worlds*. His recent rock novel *Hype* was accompanied by an album of music and he has a SF novel due for publication in the UK

2. *Mick Farren* A music journalist and author of six SF novels (*The Feelies, The Texts of Festival, The Quest of the DNA Cowboys, Synaptic Manhunt, The Neural Atrocity* and *The Song of Phaid the Gambler*), Farren was first active between 1967 and 1970 in British underground rock band The Deviants, for whom he sang and wrote lyrics. An album *The Deviants* was released in 1969, including songs such as 'Death of a Dream Machine', 'Junior Narco Rangers', 'Metamorphosis Exploration' and 'Billy the Monster'. A solo album 'Vampires Stole My Lunch Money' appeared in 1978

3. *David Meltzer* Better known as a poet, Meltzer has authored several SF novels with strong erotic connotations: *The Agency* (1968), *The Agent* (1968) and *How Many Blocks in the Pile* (1968) forming the 'Agency' trilogy; the 'Brain-Plant' series features *Lovely, Healer, Out* and *Glue Factory* (all 1969). He has recorded two albums of self-penned material (with his wife Tina): *Serpent Power* (1968) and *Poet Song* (1969), both released on the then prestigious folk label Vanguard

4. *Michael Moorcock* Having performed in clubs as a blues singer in his youth, Moorcock intermittently appeared on stage with rock group Hawkwind in the early 1970s. He has written lyrics for the following Hawkwind songs: 'The Wizard Blew His Horn', 'Standing at the Edge' and 'Warriors' on the *Warrior at the Edge of Time* album, 1975. He also performs on the record. He plays banjo on Robert Calvert's album *Lucky Lief and the Long Ships*, 1975. Other songs for Hawkwind include 'The Black Corridor' and 'Sonic Attack' on the *Space Ritual* album, 1973

In 1975, Moorcock put together the Deep Fix group, comprising Steve Gilmore, erstwhile SF writer Graham Charnock and himself. This line-up recorded an album *The New World's Fair* released on United Artists in 1975. On this record, Moorcock plays guitar, mandolin and banjo and sings the following self-penned tracks: 'Candy Floss Cowboy', 'Fair Dealer', '16-year Old Doom', 'Last Merry-Go-Round' and 'Dude's Dream (Rolling in the Ruins)'. Two other songs were recorded, 'Star Cruiser' and 'Dodgem Dude' for a single not released at the time, but since out on Independent label Flick Knife in 1981. This same small label issued a compilation album in 1982 under the title *Hawkwind – Friends and Relations*, featuring Moorcock on 'Good Girl, Bad Girl' and 'Time Centre'. A limited edition single of 'The Brothel in Rosenstrasse' was also issued in 1982.

Moorcock has also penned lyrics for US heavy metal outfit Blue Oyster Cult. 'The Great Sun Jester' on *Mirrors* (1979); 'Black Blade' on *Cultosaurus Erectus* (1980) and 'Veteran of the Psychic Wars' on *Fire of Unknown Origin* (1981)

5. *John Shirley* Young New York author John Shirley plays the NY professional club scene with his band Obsession. He has recorded songs for the independent label Dorian

6. *Norman Spinrad* Spinrad has written words for the musical piece 'Houston 69 – The Crash Landing' by French electronic synthesizer player Richard Pinhas and performs through a vocoder on the track, which is included on Pinhas' album *East-West* (1980)

Many other writers of SF are adept musicians and have played on a professional or semi-professional basis, although there are no recorded instances of their work (except for a cassette of the Sucharitkul piece with Malzberg on violin),

Jean-Pierre Andrevon, the French author is also known as a folk singer

Lloyd Biggle Jr, is a respected musicologist and has taught at US universities

Jerome Bixby has been known to compose classical music

Marc Bourgeois, another French writer, has played with the groups Gong and Green

John F. Burke, an old-established British hack is an accomplished player of various instruments

Graham Charnock, well-known as author, fan and bookshop manager, was a member of Moorcock's Deep Fix and plays semi-professionally at weekends and conventions with his group

Los Gonococcos is a ribald, impromptu group of French fans and critics who play conventions and other events

Laurence Janifer is another writer who has performed in a dance band

Langdon Jones was, before the *New Worlds* days, a professional
   musician and played in an army band
James Kahn has played as singer-songwriter with local folk-rock group
   Silver City
John Kippax used to play the saxophone in a dance band
Sam Lundwall had his own pop/folk group and recorded in Sweden.
   Some of his compositions have been sung by Abba
Barry Malzberg has played violin with a symphonic orchestra on the
   occasion of a Sucharitkul composition performance, *Starscapes*
Janet E. Morris plays bass in her husband's rock band
Josephine Saxton plays bongos with local Coventry bands
Somtow Sucharitkul has established a healthy reputation as a composer
   of classical and modern music and many of his pieces have had
   public performances
Elisabeth Vonarburg, the Canadian novelist and critic, has performed
   as a folk-singer

Anagram Solutions

Lester del Rey
Robert Anson Heinlein
Samuel R. Delany
Arthur C. Clarke
Cordwainer Smith
Alexei Panshin
Thomas Disch
Norman Spinrad
Harlan Ellison
Ursula K. Le Guin
John Thomas Sladek
Ian Watson
Alfred Bester
Christopher Priest

Nine Asian Invasions

1. Robert Heinlein, *Sixth Column*
2. Philip K. Dick, *The Man in the High Castle*
3. M.J. Engh, *Arslan*
4. C.M. Kornbluth, *Not This August*
5. R. MacKay, *The Yellow Wave*
6. J.H. Palmer, *The Invasion of New York*
7. M.P. Shiel, *The Yellow Peril*
8. M.P. Shiel, *The Yellow Danger*
9. M.P. Shiel, *The Dragon*

Eight Russian Invasions

1. Kingsley Amis, *Russian Hide and Seek*
2-4. Clive Egleton, *A Piece of Resistance*
    Last Post for a Partisan
    The Judas Mandate
5. John Gardner, *Golgotha*
6. Oliver Lange, *Vandenberg*
7. C.M. Kornbluth, *Not This August*
8. Allyn Thompson, *The Azriel Uprising*

Rudy Rucker's Ten Mathematics Favourites

1. *Archytas's Duplication of the Cube* The Greeks were interested in how one might go about constructing a line segment of length equal to the cube root of two. This is impossible with ruler and compass alone, but Archytas found a way of doing it by looking at the common intersection of a cone, cylinder and torus.
2. *Hinton's Tessaract* Charles H. Hinton coined the word "tessaract," for a four-dimensional hypercube. By playing with a set of 81 small coloured cubes he learned how to visualize it. He also invented a gun for shooting baseballs.

3. *The Klein Bottle*   This was the idea of Felix Klein, a 19th-century German mathematician. Many people have heard of it, but few really understand it. In a nutshell, the Klein bottle is to four-dimensional space as the Mobius strip is to three-dimensional space.

4. *Poincaré's Model of the Hyperbolic Plane*   In order to prove the consistency of non-Euclidean geometry, Poincaré constructed this mathematical model. Here we have an infinite space squeezed inside the bounds of a circle. Someone who starts out from the center of the circle shrinks in such a way that he can never reach the circumference.

5. *The Grandi Series*   This is the infinite series $1 - 1 + 1 - 1 + \ldots$ Viewed in one way, the Grandi series adds up to zero (you start with nothing and then subtract one for every one you add in). Viewed another way, it adds up to one (you start with one and then add on another one for every one you take away). Grandi claimed that God had used this series to create the Universe out of nothingness.

6. *Cantor's Theorem*   In 1874 Georg Cantor proved a startling fact: there are different levels of infinity. In particular, there are more points in continuous space than there are integers. This theorem leads to a very interesting problem, the Continuum Problem: exactly which level of infinity best characterises continuous space?

7. *Hilbert Space*   This is an infinite dimensional space used in quantum mechanics. There is reason to believe that the mind is best represented as a pattern in Hilbert space.

8. *Minkowski Spacetime*   Hermann Minkowski introduced the idea of four-dimensional spacetime in order to simply explain Einstein's Special Theory of Relativity. Thinking in terms of spacetime is a good way to lessen one's fear of death. Minkowski, not that it matters, died of drowning.

9. *Gödel's Incompleteness Theorem*   In 1930 Kurt Gödel proved a remarkable thing: mathematics is open-ended. There can never be a final, best theory of mathematics (or of anything else important, for that matter). Truth is undefinable and infinitely elusive.

10. *Conway's Number Line*   John Horton Conway recently discovered what is, in a sense, the largest possible number system, called *No*. *No* has infinitely big numbers marching all the way out to the Absolute, and seething little infinitesimals everywhere you look.

Michael Moorcock's Nine Favourite Characters

By and large, it's the villains I remember best!

1. *Steerpike*—in Mervyn Peake's *Ghormenghast Trilogy*
2. *Jim*—in Joseph Conrad's *Lord Jim*
3. *Axel Heyst*—in Joseph Conrad's *Victory*
4. *Nostromo*—in Joseph Conrad's *Nostromo*
5. *Strangman*—in J.G. Ballard's *The Drowned World*

But then there are also strong ones I remember well, like

6. *Cheri*—in Colette's *Cheri*
7. *Mrs. Dalloway*—in Virginia Woolf's *Mrs. Dalloway*

The characters in D.H. Lawrence also come over strongly, but are all very much the same Lawrentian characters!
And then there's

8. *Pip*—in Charles Dickens' *Great Expectations*
9. *Gully Foyle*—in Alfred Bester's *The Stars My Destination.*

Nine Futuristic Arts

1. *Cloud-sculpture*—in J.G. Ballard's "The Cloud Sculptors of Coral D"
2. *Computer assisted comic art*—in Harry Harrison's *Portrait of the Artist*
3. *Dream construction*—in Isaac Asimov's *Dreaming is a Private Thing*
4. *Free-fall dancing*—in Spider and Jeanne Robinson's *Stardance*
5. *Holographic sculpture*—in William Rotsler's *Patron of the Arts*
6. *Mask making*—in Jack Vance's *The Moon Moth*
7. *Novel-writing by machine*—in Fritz Leiber's *The Silver Eggheads*
8. *Psycho-sculpture*—in Robert Silverberg's *The Second Trip*
9. *Sonic sculpture*—in J.G. Ballard's *The Singing Statues*

Ten Novels and Stories Featuring SF Writers and SF Fandom

1. Robert Bloch, "A Way of Life"—in which the only artifacts surviving from our civilisation are SF fanzines, which are viewed with awe by a future civilisation.
2. Ben Bova, *The Starcrossed*—a *roman à clef* based on Bova's experiences working on the illfated TV series *The Starlost,* conceived by Harlan Ellison.
3. Robert Coulson and Gene De Weese, *Now You See It/Him/Them*
4. Robert Coulson and Gene De Weese, *Charles Fort Never Mentioned Wombats*—two humourous collaborative novels set in the SF fan world.
5. Harlan Ellison, "All The Lies That Are My Life"—a fictionalisation of certain aspects of Ellison's career, and his friendship with Robert Silverberg, partly set at a world SF convention.
6. L. Ron Hubbard, *Typewriter in the Sky*—in which a pulp writer finds himself trapped in the world of his creation.
7. Barry Malzberg, *Herovit's World*—a novel about a hack SF writer and his descent into insanity, with funny and devastating *roman à clef* elements.
8. Larry Niven and Jerry Pournelle, *Inferno*—in which an SF writer is catapulted from a convention into hell, in a humourous reworking of Dante.
9. K.M. O'Donnell, *Dwellers of the Deep*
10. K.M. O'Donnell, *Gather in the Hall of the Planets*—Barry Malzberg, writing under a pseudonym, published these two novels of aliens at SF conventions before he had ever visited one.

1950

Best Short Stories of the Year

The Santa Claus Planet	Frank Morton Robinson
The Gnurrs Come from the Voodvork Out	Reginald Bretnor
The Mindworm	C.M. Kornbluth
The Star Ducks	Bill Brown
Not to be Opened	Roger F. Young

Process	A.E. Van Vogt
Forget-Me-Not	William F. Temple
Contagion	Katherine MacLean
Trespass	Poul Anderson & Gordon Dickson
Oddy and Id	Alfred Bester
To Serve Man	Damon Knight
Summer Wear	L. Sprague de Camp
Born of Man and Woman	Richard Matheson
Fox in the Forest	Ray Bradbury
The Last Martian	Fredric Brown
The New Reality	Charles L. Harness
Two Face	Frank Belknap Long
Coming Attraction	Fritz Leiber

(E.F. Bleiler and T.E. Dikty's *The Best Science Fiction Stories 1951*)

The Best Novels of Robert A. Heinlein

In 1976, Maxim Jakubowski polled a group of writers and critics on the best novels of Robert A. Heinlein for the short-lived *SF Digest* magazine. The following rated the novels (and collections): Brian Aldiss, John Clute, the late Andy Ellsmore, M. John Harrison, Jakubowski, Peter Nicholls, Christopher Priest, Tom Shippey, Ian Watson and Peter Weston. After computing the ratings, the following order of preference emerged:

1. *The Door Into Summer*
2. *The Puppet Masters*
3. *Citizen of the Galaxy*
4. *Double Star*
5. *The Green Hills of Earth*
6. *The Man Who Sold the Moon*
7. *The Star Beast*
8. *Have Space Suit, Will Travel*
9. *Starship Troopers*
10. *The Moon Is a Harsh Mistress*
11. *Revolt in 2100*

12. *Methuselah's Children*
13. *Rocket Ship Galileo*
14. *Stranger in a Strange Land*
15. *Glory Road*
16. *Podkayne of Mars*
17. *Farnham's Freehold*
18. *Time Enough for Love*
19. *I Will Fear No Evil*

(Note: *The Number of the Beast* and *Friday* were not published at the time of this poll)

Isaac Asimov's Best SF Books

The following order of importance arose from the same *SF Digest* poll of British authors and critics of 1976 (see *The Best Novels of Robert A. Heinlein* list)

1. *Foundation*
2. *I, Robot*
3. *Caves of Steel*
4. *Foundation and Empire*
5. *The End of Eternity*
6. *The Naked Sun*
7. *Earth Is Room Enough*
8. *Second Foundation*
9. *The Martian Way*
10. *Pebble in the Sky*
11. *Nightfall*
12. *The Stars Like Dust*
13. *The Rest of the Robots*
14. *Asimov's Mysteries*
15. *The Currents of Space*
16. *The Gods Themselves*
17. *The Early Asimov*
18. *Fantastic Voyage*

A List of A. E. Van Vogt's Best Science Fiction

1. *Slan*
2. *Destination: Universe*
3. *Voyage of the Space Beagle*
4. *The Weapon Shops of Isher*
5. *The World of Null-A*
6. *The Weapon Makers*
7. *Players of Null-A*
8. *The Mind Cage*
9. *War Against the Rull*
10. *The Wizard of Linn*
11. *The House That Stood Still*
12. *The Universe Maker*
13. *Empire of the Atom*
14. *The Silkie*
15. *The Book of Ptath*
16. *Future Glitter*
17. *Siege of the Unseen*
18. *The Darkness on Diamondia*

Thirty Very Expensive SF and Fantasy First Editions

Before you book a world cruise on the strength of having copies of any of the books listed below, be warned that these prices are what a top bookseller might hope to get for copies in fine condition, and that identifying true first editions is sometimes a very tricky job. For instance, several later reprints of Frank Herbert's *Dune* have the words "first edition" on the copyright page, but are only of ordinary secondhand book value. Country of origin of the relevant edition is given in brackets.

1. Richard Adams, *Watership Down* (UK), $750
2. Ray Bradbury, *Fahrenheit 451*, limited asbestos-bound edition (US), $1250
3. Edgar Rice Burroughs, *Tarzan of the Apes* (US), $7500
4. Philip José Farmer, *The Green Odyssey* (US), $750
5. Robert Heinlein, *Stranger in a Strange Land* (US), $400

6. Frank Herbert, *Dune* (US), *$500*
7. William Hope Hodgson, *The House on the Borderland* (UK), *$350*
8. William Hope Hodgson, *The Night Land* (UK), *$350*
9. Robert E. Howard, *A Gent From Bear Creek* (UK), *$3000*
10. Ursula Le Guin, *A Wizard of Earthsea* (US), *$350*
11. David Lindsay, *A Voyage to Arcturus* (UK), *$350*
12. H.P. Lovecraft, *The Outsider* (US), *$900*
13. H.P. Lovecraft, *The Shadow Over Innsmouth* (US), *$1500*
14. H.P. Lovecraft, *The Shunned House* (US), *$2000*
15. Walter M. Miller, *A Canticle for Leibowitz* (US), *$400*
16. George Orwell, *Animal Farm* (UK), *$850*
17. George Orwell, *Nineteen Eighty-Four* (UK), *$900*
18. Edgar Allan Poe, *Narrative of Arthur Gordon Pym* (US), *$2000*
19. Edgar Allan Poe, *Tales of the Grotesque and Arabesque* (US), *$3500*
20. Mary Shelley, *Frankenstein* (UK), *$13,000*
21. E. E. Smith, *The History of Civilization* (special limited edition of the "Lensman" series) (US), *$2000*
22. William Timlin, *The Ship That Sailed to Mars* (UK), *$1500*
23. J.R.R. Tolkien, *The Hobbit* (UK), *$3000*
24. J.R.R. Tolkien, *Lord of the Rings* (3 vols) (UK), *$3500*
25. Jack Vance, *To Live Forever* (US), *$350*
26. Stanley Weinbaum, *Dawn of Flame* (US), *$750*
27. H.G. Wells, *The Invisible Man* (UK), *$500*
28. H.G. Wells, *The Island of Dr. Moreau* (UK), *$500*
29. H.G. Wells, *The Time Machine* (UK), *$750*
30. H.G. Wells, *War of the Worlds* (UK), $500

(Note: These prices were arrived at in consultation with various specialist booksellers. As some of the books—e.g., the Robert E. Howard—have never been offered for sale, prices are inevitably speculative. On the other hand, the top price—for *Frankenstein*—was actually attained at auction early in 1982.)

Sought-After SF Paperbacks

Reliant as it is on the paperback format, it's no surprise that science fiction in paperback is already becoming a collector's medium. Values at the top end do not approach those of rare hardcovers but are nevertheless increasing fast. The following list was compiled by using prices quoted in Kevin Hancer's *The Paperback Price Guide* (Overstreet, 1980), and pertain to books in mint condition. Many titles missing from this list could well reach a higher value in specialised auctions; these would include many titles written by SF writers outside the field, often under pen-names: the rare first edition of Larry Niven's *Ringworld* (Ballantine) in which the world turns in the wrong direction, many of the pornographic Essex House titles, particularly those by Philip José Farmer, etc . . .

$80.00—*Topper* by Thorne Smith (Pocket Books 4, 1939)
$75.00—*Rocket to the Morgue* by H. H. Holmes (Anthony Boucher) (Phantom Mystery, 1942)
$60.00—*The Judas Goat* by Leslie Edgley & *Cry Plague!* by Theodore S. Drachman (Ace Double D13, 1953)
$60.00—*An Earthman on Mars* by Ralph Milne Farley (Avon 285, 1950)
$60.00—*Tarzan in the Forbidden City* by Edgar Rice Burroughs (Bantam 23, 1939)
$60.00—*The Dunwich Horror* by H.P. Lovecraft (Bart House 12, 1945)
$60.00—*The Dying Earth* by Jack Vance (Hillman 41, 1950)
$55.00—*The Weird Shadow Over Innsmouth* by H. P. Lovecraft (Bart House 4, 1944)
$50.00—*The Conquest of the Amazon* by John Russell Fearn (Harlequin 218, 1952)
$45.00—*The Ship of Ishtar* by Abraham Merritt (Avon 324, 1951)

This list is far from restrictive, a book's worth being what an avid collector is willing to go up to . . . so start checking those trunks in cellars and attics!

The Ten Most Expensive Comics in the World

Title	1981 value (in US $)
1. *Marvel Comics* No. 1 (1939) First appearance of the Sub-Mariner.	14,000
2. *Action Comics* No. 1 (1938) First appearance of Superman.	11,500
3. *Motion Picture Funnies Weekly* No. 1 (1939) Given out free in cinemas. There are only allegedly 7 copies extant.	7,500
4. *Superman* No. 1 (1939) Reprint with six new pages of *Action Comics* No. 1.	7,000

5. *Whiz Comics* No. 1 (1940)   6,500
   First appearance of Captain Marvel. An issue No. 0 with
   only 10 copies printed is alleged to have been published,
   but this has never been corroborated.
6. *Detective Comics* No. 27 (1939)   6,000
7. *Double Action Comics* No. 1 (1940)   4,500
   Only 5 copies in existence.
8. *Captain America* No. 1 (1941)   3,600
   First appearance of the eponymous character.
9. *Captain Marvel Adventures* No. 1 (1941)   3,600
   Captain Marvel by Jack Kirby.
10. *Wow Comics* No. 1 (1941)   3,500
    This comic's cover having been printed on very poor
    quality paper, there are very few now to be found in good
    condition.

Twenty-six Clarion Alumni

The Clarion writers workshop created by Damon Knight and Kate Wilhelm,
and continued by Robin Scott Wilson and many other SF academics and
writers, has proved a great way of nurturing new talent. Four anthologies
featuring work by young authors originating at the workshop have so far
appeared, but a great many of these writers have since broken into print
elsewhere—some of them to already high acclaim. No doubt more will
emerge in the fullness of time to make this list incomplete.

1. Russell Bates
2. C. Davis Belcher
3. Alan Brennert
4. Mildred Downey Broxon
5. Edward Bryant
6. F.M. Busby
7. Octavia Butler
8. Dennis Caro
9. Gerald F. Conway
10. Glen Cook
11. George Alec Effinger

12. Mel Gilden
13. Steve Herbst
14. P.C. Hodgell
15. Evelyn Lief
16. Vonda N. McIntyre
17. J. Michael Reaves
18. Kim Stanley Robinson
19. Carter Scholz
20. John Shirley
21. Kathleen M. Sidney
22. Dave Skal
23. James Sutherland
24. Robert Thurston
25. Lisa Tuttle
26. Robert Wissner

Kings of the Ace Doubles

In many minds, the Ace Double series remains the epitome of pulp science fiction with their gaudy back-to-back covers and most evocative titles. Although many a respectable title was also published as part of an Ace Double, it is the more forgettable wham-bam-thank-you-ma'am space operas which made the imprint so memorable. Many writers were heavy contributors to the series, under their own names as well as under pen-names. (Titles published on their own by Ace have not been included.)

John Brunner, 24 titles (3 as Keith Woodcott)
Andre Norton, 17 titles (3 as Andrew North)
Louis Trimble, 13 titles (only one SF + 1 western + 11 thrillers)
Robert Silverberg, 13 titles (9 as RS, 3 as Calvin Knox, 1 as Ivar
     Jorgenson)
Kenneth Bulmer, 13 titles
A. Bertram Chandler, 12 titles
Poul Anderson, 12 titles
Jack Vance, 11 titles
Robert Moore Williams, 11 titles
Donald A. Wollheim, 10 titles (5 as DAW, 5 as David Grinnell)

SF Recipes

In 1973, Anne McCaffrey canvassed other writers of SF and fantasy for their favourite cooking recipes, preferably of a creative and extraterrestrial nature. The results were published in what Ballantine Books termed a "very original" volume entitled *Cooking Out of this World*. Many authors revealed highly conservative tastes (Moorcock's traditional Xmas pudding, or Frank Herbert's Sukiyaki and other Japanese dishes), but the majority did exhibit a salutary—if stomach-curdling—imagination in the culinary domain. Here are some of the more outlandish choices.

Brian Aldiss, Serbian Fishermen's Soup
Alfred Bester, Baked Striped Bass Caponata
Marion Zimmer Bradley, Breakfast Cookies
John Brunner, Squid with Pine Nuts
Edward Bryant, Granola Nisbet
Avram Davidson, Peasant Pottage
Gordon Dickson, Emergency Paté
Thomas Disch, Shaker Spinach
George Alec Effinger, Ginger Peachy Soup
Harlan Ellison, Café Ellison Diabolique
Ursula K. Le Guin, Crab Nebula
Fritz Leiber, Fish Stew in its infinite varieties
Anne McCaffrey, Irish Clear Lamb Stew
Walter M. Miller, Jr., Gopher Stew
Larry Niven, Busted Kneecap
Joanna Russ, Hamburger and Stewed Tomatoes
Josephine Saxton, Fiddly Prawns and Mussels
Bob Shaw, Deadline Stew
Robert Silverberg, Beefsteak Tartare
John Sladek, Caligula Salad with Muttered Dressing
E. C. Tubb, Orange Wine
Kate Wilhelm, The World's Biggest Crab Cake
Chelsea Quinn Yarbro, Chicken in Port Wine Sauce

Seriously, though, many of the recipes sound delicious, and we can only direct you to Anne's anthology (?) for further information and how-to.

Fifteen SF Writers Who Are Also Important Editors

1. Anthony Boucher (edited the magazine *F & SF* for ten years)
2. Ben Bova (editor of *Analog*, and subsequently *Omni*)
3. John W. Campbell (editor of *Astounding/Analog* for over 30 years)
4. Terry Carr (editor at Ace Books, and of the *Universe* series)
5. Lester Del Rey (editor of several 1950s magazines, and now fantasy editor of Del Rey Books)
6. Samuel Delany (editor of the *Quark* series of anthologies)
7. Harry Harrison (editor of various magazines in the 1950s and 60s)
8. Damon Knight (editor of the magazine *Worlds Beyond* and the *Orbit* series)
9. Michael Moorcock (editor of *New Worlds*)
10. Frederik Pohl (editor of *Galaxy*, *If* and various other magazines)
11. Keith Roberts (editor of *Impulse*)
12. Robert Sheckley (fiction editor of *Omni*)
13. Robert Silverberg (editor of the *New Dimensions* series)
14. E. C. Tubb (editor of *Authentic SF* in the 1950s)
15. Ted White (editor of *Amazing* and *Fantastic* 1969-78)

The First Twenty Ace SF Titles

Ace Books, despite many changes in ownership and a distinguished roll call of SF editors (Donald Wollheim, Terry Carr, James Baen, Susan Allison, etc.), has always been a paperback imprint with a particular devotion to science fiction. Although best remembered for their now highly-collectible Ace Doubles, which presented for the price of a single book two titles back to back, Ace also published many titles in their early days in a "solo" format, as this list shows.

D13. Theodore S. Drachman, *Cry Plague!*
      (Leslie Edgley, *The Judas Goat*) mystery title, 1953
D31. A. E. Van Vogt, *The Universe Maker*
      A. E. Van Vogt, *The World of Null-A*, 1953
D36. Robert E. Howard, *Conan the Conqueror*
      Leigh Brackett, *The Sword of Rhiannon*, 1953
D43. Paul Eldridge & George Sylvester Viereck, *Salome, My First 2,000 Years of Love*, 1954

D44. Eric Frank Russell, *Sentinels of Space*
Donald A. Wollheim (ed.), *The Ultimate Invader*, 1954
D53. Murray Leinster, *Gateway to Elsewhere*
A. E. Van Vogt, *The Weapon Shops of Isher*, 1954
D61. L. Sprague de Camp, *Cosmic Manhunt*
Clifford D. Simak, *Ring Around the Sun*, 1954
D66. L. Ron Hubbard, *Return to Tomorrow*, 1954
D69. C. L. Moore & Lewis Padgett, *Beyond Earth's Gates*
Andre Norton, *Daybreak 2250 A.D.*, 1954
D73. Donald A. Wollheim (ed.), *Adventures in the Far Future*
Donald A. Wollheim (ed.), *Tales of Outer Space*, 1954
D79. Francis R. Bellamy, *Atta*
Murray Leinster, *The Brain Stealers*, 1954
D84. Isaac Asimov, *The Rebellious Stars (The Stars Like Dust)*
Roger Dee, *An Earth Gone Mad*, 1954
D90. Robert Moore Williams, *The Chaos Fighters*, 1955
D94. Murray Leinster, *The Other Side of Here*
A. E. Van Vogt, *One Against Eternity (The Weapon Makers)*, 1955
D96. Andre Norton, *The Last Planet*
Alan E. Nourse, *A Man Obsessed*, 1955
D96. Andre Norton, *The Last Planet* (also published as a single book)
D99. Leigh Brackett, *The Galactic Breed (The Starmen)*
Robert Moore Williams, *Conquest of the Space Sea*, 1955
D103. Philip K. Dick, *Solar Lottery*
Leigh Brackett, *The Big Jump*, 1955
D110. Poul Anderson, *No World of their Own*
Isaac Asimov, *The 1,000 Year Plan (Foundation)*, 1955
D110. Isaac Asimov, *The 1,000 Year Plan* (also published as a single book)

The First Ten SF and Fantasy Titles from Avon Books

Although one of the earliest houses on the American paperback scene, Avon has never had a consistent SF policy, and this already reflected in the above list representing their first eight years, with a strong emphasis on fantasy.

Avon 6. *The Haunted Hotel & 25 Other Ghost Stories* by Wilkie Collins (edited by Bob Holland), 1941

Avon 26. *Seven Footprints to Satan* by Abraham Merritt, 1942
Avon 43. *Burn Witch Burn* by Abraham Merritt, 1944
Avon 69. *The Stray Lamb* by Thorne Smith, 1945
Avon 90. *The Avon Ghost Reader* edited by Herbert Williams, 1946
Avon 110. *Terror at Night* (anthology), 1947
Avon 117. *Creep Shadow Creep* by Abraham Merritt, 1947
Avon 136. *The Lurking Fear* by H. P. Lovecraft, 1948
Avon 184. *The Girl with the Hungry Eyes* edited by Donald Wollheim, 1949
Avon 195. *Out of the Silent Planet* by C. S. Lewis, 1949

The First Sixteen SF Titles from Ballantine Books

From the outset, Ballantine Books has been most strongly identified with science fiction, due to the obvious appreciation of the genre by its founders, Ian and Betty Ballantine. The imprint is now owned by Random House, and the SF and fantasy lines go under the name of Del Rey Books, in recognition of the strong contribution of SF Editor Judy-Lynn Del Rey (whose husband, writer Lester Del Rey, edits the fantasy line).

16. *Star Science Fiction Stories* edited by Frederik Pohl, 1953
21. *The Space Merchants* by Frederik Pohl & C. M. Kornbluth, 1953
25. *The Undying Fire* by Fletcher Pratt, 1953
28. *The Secret Masters* by Gerald Kersh, 1953
30. *Ahead of Time* by Henry Kuttner, 1953
33. *Childhood's End* by Arthur C. Clarke, 1953
36. *Earthly Creatures* edited by Charles Jackson, 1953
38. *Bring the Jubilee* by Ward Moore, 1953
41. *Fahrenheit 451* by Ray Bradbury, 1953
46. *More Than Human* by Theodore Sturgeon, 1953
50. *Out of the Deeps* by John Wyndham, 1953
52. *Expedition to Earth* by Arthur C. Clarke, 1953
55. *Star Science Fiction Stories 2* edited by Frederik Pohl, 1954
56. *Dark Dominion* by David Duncan, 1954
58. *Riders to the Stars* by Curt Siodmak, 1954
61. *Search the Sky* by Frederik Pohl & C.M. Kornbluth, 1954

The First Ten SF and Fantasy Titles from Bantam Books

Launched in 1945, Bantam Books today is one of the largest US paperback houses with a worthy SF program. In its early days, however, its interest in the genre was somewhat patchy, with the exception of Ray Bradbury and Fredric Brown's (whose mystery titles Bantam also published) presence.

Bantam 143.	*The She-Wolf, a Saki Sampler* by Saki, 1948
Bantam 502.	*The Unexpected* edited by Bennett Cerf, 1948
Bantam 751.	*Shot in the Dark* edited by Judith Merril, 1950
Bantam 819.	*Donovan's Brain* by Curt Siodmak, 1950
Bantam 835.	*What Mad Universe* by Fredric Brown, 1950
Bantam 886.	*The Martian Chronicles* by Ray Bradbury, 1951
Bantam A944.	*Timeless Stories for Today and Tomorrow* edited by Ray Bradbury, 1951
Bantam 991.	*The Illustrated Man* by Ray Bradbury, 1952
Bantam A1071.	*Brave New World* by Aldous Huxley, 1953
Bantam 1077.	*Space On My Hands* by Fredric Brown, 1953

The First Fifteen SF Titles from Berkley Books

Although a relative latecomer to the ranks of the major US paperback houses, Berkley's interest in SF was strong from the outset and has remained so to this day.

344.	*Mission to the Stars* by A. E. Van Vogt, 1955
G3.	*Possible Worlds of Science Fiction* edited by Groff Conklin, 1955
G31.	*Science Fiction Omnibus* edited by Groff Conklin, 1956
G41.	*The Astounding SF Anthology* edited by John W. Campbell Jr., 1956
G47.	*Astounding Tales of Space and Time* edited by John W. Campbell Jr., 1956
G53.	*The Big Book of Science Fiction* edited by Groff Conklin, 1956
G63.	*A Treasury of Science Fiction* edited by Groff Conklin, 1956
380.	*The Time Machine* by H. G. Wells, 1957
G71.	*Strangers in the Universe* by Clifford D. Simak, 1957
G77.	*Beachheads in Space* edited by August Derleth, 1957
G104.	*Beyond Time and Space* edited by August Derleth, 1958

G116. *The Outer Reaches* edited by August Derleth, 1958
G131. *Strange Ports of Call* edited by August Derleth, 1958
G148. *Men, Martians and Machines* by Eric Frank Russell, 1958
G103. *Worlds of Tomorrow* edited by August Derleth, 1958

The First Twenty Daw Titles

Daw Books was founded in 1971 by Donald A. Wollheim after a sterling career editing the Ace SF line. It was, and still is, the only major paperback imprint exclusively devoted to science fiction (the only exceptions to this rule have been two John Norman, author of the Gor books, titles *Ghost Dance* and *Imaginative Sex*). Although often decried by critics, the Daw line has always been characterized by sound commercial acumen in assessing public taste; furthermore, Don Wollheim has been instrumental in discovering a great many writers such as Tanith Lee, C. J. Cherryh, and Jo Clayton, as well as publishing many distinguished writers such as Moorcock, Jack Vance, Barrington J. Bayley, and Marion Zimmer Bradley.

1. *Spell of the Witch World*, Andre Norton
2. *The Mind Behind the Eye*, Joseph Green
3. *The Probability Man*, Brian N. Ball
4. *The Book of Van Vogt*, A. E. Van Vogt
5. *The 1972 Annual World's Best SF*, edited by Donald A. Wollheim
6. *The Day Star*, Mark Geston
7. *To Challenge Chaos*, Brian M. Stableford
8. *The Mindblocked Man*, Jeff Sutton
9. *Tactics of Mistake*, Gordon R. Dickson
10. *At the Seventh Level*, Suzette Haden Elgin
11. *The Day Before Tomorrow*, Gérard Klein
12. *A Darkness in my Soul*, Dean R. Koontz
13. *The Year's Best Horror Stories: 1*, edited by Richard Davis
14. *We Can Build You*, Philip K. Dick
15. *The World Menders*, Lloyd Biggle, Jr.
16. *Genius Unlimited*, John T. Phillifent
17. *Blue Face*, G. C. Edmondson
18. *Century of the Manikin*, E. C. Tubb
19. *The Regiments of Night*, Brian N. Ball
20. *Ole Doc Methuselah*, L. Ron Hubbard

The First Eight SF and Fantasy Titles from Pocket Books

The first purely paperback format US imprint remained uninterested in SF for a very long time. Despite the ground-breaking Wollheim anthology listed, very few titles were published by Pocket in its first ten years. Now owned by Simon & Schuster, and presented as Timescape Books, headed by David G. Hartwell, it is one of the SF market leaders.

4. *Topper* by Thorne Smith, 1938
123. *Dr. Jekyll and Mr. Hyde* by Robert Louis Stevenson, 1941
214. *The Pocket Book of Science Fiction*, edited by Donald Wollheim, 1943
384. *The Pocket Book of Short Stories*, edited by Philip Van Doren Stern, 1947
428. *The Night Life of the Gods* by Thorne Smith, 1947
447. *Turnabout* by Thorne Smith, 1947
452. *Dracula* by Bram Stoker, 1947
498. *Mr. Adam* by Pat Frank, 1948

Colours Out of Space

Black
The Black Cloud, Fred Hoyle
The Black Flame, Stanley G. Weibaum
Rhapsody in Black, Brian Stableford
The Black Flame, Lynn Abbey
Black Hearts in Battersea, Joan Aiken
Black Easter, James Blish
The Black Ferris, Ray Bradbury
The Black Hole, Alan Dean Foster
Black August, Dennis Wheatley
The Black Cauldron, Lloyd Alexander
The Black Galaxy, Murray Leinster
Black Heart and White Heart, H. Rider Haggard
The Black Doctor, A. Conan Doyle
The Black Star Passes, John W. Campbell, Jr.
The Novel of the Black Sea, Arthur Machen
Secret of the Black Planet, Milton Lesser
Treasure of the Black Falcon, John Coleman Burroughs
The Black Death, Cravens & Marr

Black in Time, John Jakes
The Black Wheel, Abraham Merritt
Red Moon and Black Mountain, Joy Chant
The Black Lion, Patricia & Lionel Fanthorpe

Blonde
The Blonde Goddess, R.P.J. Richards
My Blonde Princess of Space, John N. Will

Blue
Adventure in the Blue Room, S. Fowler Wright
The Blue Atom, Robert Moore Williams
The Blue Barbarians, Stanton Coblentz
Blue Juggernaut, Bron Fane
Nightmare Blue, George Alec Effinger & Gardner Dozois
Blue Face, G.C. Edmondson
Beyond the Blue Event Horizon, Frederik Pohl
Blue Moon, Douglas Lindsay, ed.
The Blue World, Jack Vance
Blue Adept, Piers Anthony
Sybil Sue Blue, Rosel George Brown

Crimson
The Crimson Capsule, Stanton Coblentz
The Crimson Planet, John E. Muller

Gold
The Golden Amazon (and various sequels), John Russell Fearn
The Golden Apples of the Sun, Ray Bradbury
The Golden People, Fred Saberhagen
Beyond the Golden Stair, Hannes Bok
The Golden Sword, Janet E. Morris
The Golden Apple, Robert Shea & Robert Anton Wilson
The Golden Space, Pamela Sargent
The Golden Torc, Julian May
The Golden Man, Philip K. Dick
Capella's Golden Eyes, Chris Evans
The Golden Shadow, Leon Garfield
Gold the Man, Joseph Green
Rule Golden, Damon Knight
The Golden Apple, David Lindsay

The Golden Barge, Michael Moorcock
Golden Vanity, Rachel Pollack
The Golden Slave, Poul Anderson
The Golden Horn, Poul Anderson
The Golden Helix, Theodore Sturgeon
The Golden Naginata, Jessica Amanda Salmonson
Five Gold Bands, Jack Vance
Golden Blood, Jack Williamson

Green
The Case of the Little Green Men, Mack Reynolds
The Coming of the Green, Leonard Wibberley
Lord of the Green Planet, Emil Petaja
The Green Child, Herbert Read
The Green Drift, John Lymington
The Green Fire, John Taine
The Green Man of Kilsona, Festus Pragnell
The Green Hills of Earth, Robert A. Heinlein
The Green Planet, Joan Hunter Holly
The Green Ray, Jules Verne
Green Phoenix, Thomas Burnett Swann
The Green Brain, Frank Herbert
The Green Millennium, Fritz Leiber
The Green Queen, Margaret St. Clair
Greener Than You Think, Ward Moore
The Green Gods, Nathalie-Charles Henneberg
The Green Man, Kingsley Amis
The Green Odyssey, Philip José Farmer
In Memory Still Green, Isaac Asimov
Green Destiny, Kenneth Bulmer
The Green Gene, Peter Dickinson
Greencomber, Peter Tate
The Green Suns, Henry Ward
The Green Rain, Paul Tabori

Grey
The Grey Mahatma, Talbot Mundy
The Grey Ones, Sax Rohmer
Greylorn, Keith Laumer
The Grey King, Susan Cooper

Grey Lensman, E. E. "Doc" Smith
The Grey Prince, Jack Vance
The Grey Mane of Morning, Joy Chant
The Grey Aliens, Joan Hunter Holly
Greybeard, Brian W. Aldiss
Grey Matters, William Hjortsberg

Orange
A Clockwork Orange, Anthony Burgess

Pink
Lucy in her Pink Packet, A.E. Coppard

Purple
The Purple Pirate, Talbot Mundy
The Purple Pterodactyls, L. Sprague de Camp
The Purple Armchair, Olga Hesky

Red
The Masque of the Red Death, Edgar Allen Poe
The Moon is Red, Sax Rohmer
Operation Red Carpet, John Boland
Red Alert, Peter George
The Red One, Jack London
The Red Planet, Russ Winterbotham
The Red Peri, Stanley G. Weinbaum
Red Planet, Robert A. Heinlein
The Red Planet, Charles Chilton
Hunters of the Red Moon, Marion Zimmer Bradley
Red Tide, Chapman & Tarzan
The Red Napoleon, Floyd Gibbons
Red Shift, Alan Garner
Red Moon and Black Mountain, Joy Chant

Sable
The Sable Moon, Nancy Springer

Scarlet
Doctors Wear Scarlet, Simon Raven

Silver
Beyond the Silver Sky, Kenneth Bulmer
Silverlock, Roy Myers
Silver on the Tree, Susan Cooper
The Silver Eggheads, Fritz Leiber
Cloud on Silver, John Christopher
The Silver Stallion, James Cabell
The Silver Metal Lover, Tanith Lee
The Silver Chair, C.S. Lewis
The Silver Sun, Nancy Springer

Vermilion
Vermilion Sands, J.G. Ballard

Violet
The Violet Apple, David Lindsay

White
The Lair of the White Worm, Bram Stoker
The Novel of the White Powder, Arthur Machen
White August, John Boland
White Lily, John Taine
The White Mountains, John Christopher
The White Dragon, Anne McCaffrey
White Light, Rudy Rucker
The Great White Space, Basil Copper
Quest of the White Witch, Tanith Lee
The Weird of the White Wolf, Bram Stoker
Snow White and the Giants, J. T. McIntosh
The Snow White Soliloquies, Sheila McLeod
The White Hart, Nancy Springer
Tales from the White Hart, Arthur C. Clarke

Yellow
The King in Yellow, Robert Chambers
Yellow Claw, Sax Rohmer
The Yellow God, H. Rider Haggard
The Yellow Fraction, Rex Gordon
The Yellow Peril, Richard Jaccoma
The Yellow Danger, M. P. Shiel

This list is dedicated to John D. McDonald.

Seventeen Faces of Boris Karloff

Although made immortal by his various portrayals of the pitiful but dangerous monster created by Baron Frankenstein, Boris Karloff also played a wide variety of sinister characters, villains or victims in his long film career.

1. Frankenstein's monster, in *Frankenstein* (1931), *The Bride of Frankenstein* (1935) and *Son of Frankenstein* (1939)
2. The Mesmerist, in *The Bells* (1926)
3. Im-Ho-Tep, in *The Mummy* (1932)
4. Fu Manchu, in *The Mask of Fu-Manchu*
5. The Ghoul, in *The Ghoul* (1933)
6. Dr. Scarabus, in *The Raven* (1963)
7. Mother Muffin, in *The Girl from U.N.C.L.E.* (TV—1967)
8. Mord the Axe-Man, in *Tower of London* (1939)
9. The Devil Worshipper, in *The Black Cat* (1933)
10. Count Gregor, in *The Black Room* (1935)
11. Bateman, in *The Raven* (1935)
12. Dr. Jekyll, in *Abbott & Costello Meet Dr. Jekyll & Mr. Hyde* (1953)
13. Gruesome, in *Dick Tracy Meets Gruesome* (1947)
14. Master Simms, in *Bedlam* (1946)
15. Mad Scientist, in *The Invisible Ray*
16. Deaf Mute Servant, in *The Old Dark House* (1932)
17. Mad Scientist, in *The Devil Commands* (1941)

Lugosi Times Eight

Despite Christopher Lee and many more modern rivals, Bela Lugosi remains *the* Dracula, a potent archetype of the horror movies. Though his portrayal of the sinister vampire Count is a cornerstone of his fame, Lugosi also interpreted various other roles in the horror and fantasy field.

1. *Dracula,* in *Dracula* (Todd Browning, 1931)—Lugosi had previously played the role on stage in New York in 1927. He interpreted the vampire part again in *Mask of the Vampire,* also by Todd Browning, 1935.
2. *Legendre, the Master of the Zombies,* in *White Zombie* (Victor Halperin, 1932)

3. *The Ape Man,* in *Island of Lost Souls* (Erle C. Kenton, 1932)
4. *Dr. Mirakle,* in *Murders in the Rue Morgue* (Robert Florey, 1932)
5. *Dr. Vitus Verdegast,* in *The Black Cat* (Edgar Ulmer, 1934)
6. *Dr. Vollin, the Mad Surgeon,* in *The Raven* (Lew Landers, 1935)
7. *Ygor,* in *Son of Frankenstein* (Rowland V. Lee, 1939)
8. *Frankenstein's monster,* in *Frankenstein Meets the Wolf-Man* (Roy William Neill, 1943)

The Many Faces of Lon Chaney

Lon Chaney (1886-1930) was often called the Man of the Thousand Faces. A classic character actor, he lent his often grotesquely disguised features to a variety of roles, many in the fantasy and horror film field. These are some of his most memorable incarnations.

1. *Frog,* a bogus cripple who plans to exploit a blind faith-healer, in *The Miracle Man* (1919)
2. *Blizzard,* the legless ruler of San Francisco's underworld, in *The Penalty* (1920)
3. *Dr. Lamb,* a mad scientist whose alter-ego is an ape-like hunchback, in *Blind Bargain* (1922)
4. *Quasimodo,* the tortured and pathetic anti-hero of *The Hunchback of Notre Dame* (1923)
5. *The Phantom of the Opera,* the disfigured wretch on a mad quest for vengeance (1925)
6. *Mrs. O'Grady,* a crooked ventriloquist masquerading as a seller of parrots, in *The Unholy Three* (1925; talkie remake in 1930)
7. *Alonzo,* the armless knife-throwing circus star, in *The Unknown* (1927)
8. *The Vampire,* stalking the night alleys of Whitechapel, in *London After Midnight* (1927)

Seven Faces of Lon Chaney, Jr.

As time sadly passes and the memory of both fades, many people now assume wrongly that there was only one Lon Chaney and that all the famous roles of villains and monsters concealed the same person. Lon Chaney, Jr.

(1906-1973) succeeded his father and carved a healthy niche in the annals of the movies with as wide a variety of roles as this list shows. Ironically, Lon Chaney, Jr. finally died of the same illness as his father—cancer of the throat.

1. *The Wolf-Man* in *The Wolf-Man* (1941—George Waggner) and sequels *(Frankenstein Meets the Wolf-Man*, 1943; *House of Dracula*, 1945; *House of Frankenstein*, 1945)
2. *A Caveman* in *One Million B.C.* (1940—D.W. Griffith & Hal Roach— not to be confused with Raquel Welch's immortal fur-bikini version)
3. *Frankenstein's Monster* in *The Ghost of Frankenstein* (Erle Kenton, 1942)
4. *Kharis the Mummy* in *The Mummy's Tomb* (Harold Young, 1942) and sequels *(The Mummy's Ghost*, 1944; *The Mummy's Curse*, 1945)
5. *Dracula,* in *Son of Dracula* (Robert Siodmak, 1943)
6. *Quasimodo,* in the *Route 66* TV series episode *Lizard's Leg and Owlet's Wing,* (1962)
7. *The Phantom of the Opera* in *The Black Castle* (Nathan Juran, 1952)

Barbara Steele: Ten Facets of Beauty and Horror

Fantasy and horror movies have had many would-be kings: Karloff, Lugosi, the two Lon Chaneys, Veidt, Christopher Lee, but no actress has ever dominated the field like Barbara Steele, an American actress who principally worked in Italy and captured the heart and soul of European (and later American) filmgoers with her wide-eyed, erotic portrayals of witches and aristocratic beauties. She is still sadly underrated today, even despite appearances in more serious movies like Fellini's *8½,* Demme's *Caged Heat* or Louis Malle's *Pretty Baby.* Until the arrival on the scene of arch-screamer Jamie Lee Curtis, Barbara Steele reigned supreme (and still does in many hearts). This is a selection of her more remarkable films; even when they were truly awful, they were worth seeing for the look in Barbara's eyes.

1. *Black Sunday* (Mario Bava, 1961)
2. *The Pit and the Pendulum* (Roger Corman, 1961)
3. *The Horrible Secret of Dr. Hitchcock* (Ricardo Freda, 1962)
4. *Danse Macabre* (aka *Castle of Blood*) (Antonio Marghereti, 1963)

5. *The Spectre* (Ricardo Freda, 1964)
6. *The Long Hair of Death* (Antonio Marghereti, 1964)
7. *Revenge of the Blood Beast* (Michael Reeves, 1965)
8. *The Crimson Cult* (Vernon Sewell, 1968)
9. *They Came From Within* (David Cronenberg, 1976)
10. *Piranha* (Joe Dante, 1978)

The Expressionist Faces of Conrad Veidt

A tremendously effective actor, Conrad Veidt is very much a forgotten man today, unlike his peers Karloff, Chaney or Lugosi. His acting style was deeply rooted in the traditions of German Expressionism, and he has contributed much to fantasy and horror roles.

1. *Cesare,* the hypnotized, murderous somnambulist, in *The Cabinet of Dr. Caligari* (1919)
2. *Ivan the Terrible,* a depraved waxwork figure of the infamous czar, in *Waxworks* (1924)
3. *Orlac,* the pianist who believes a murderer's hands have been grafted on to him after an accident, in *The Hands of Orlac* (1925)
4. *The Student,* he makes a pact with the devil and his mirror image begins to take on a life of its own, in *The Student of Prague* (1926)
5. *Gwynplaine,* the mutilated and deformed actor with a huge, distorted grin, in *The Man Who Laughs* (1928)
6. *The Sheik,* a villainous Arabian potentate, in *Bella Donna* (1934)
7. *The Stranger,* a saintly figure of unknown origin whose presence changes people's lives, in *The Passing of the Third Floor Back* (1935)
8. *The Grand Vizier,* the dazzling master of cunning and nastiness, in the first (and still by far the best) version of *The Thief of Baghdad* (1940)

SF and Fantasy Rock on Film

Rock films are slowly coming into their own as a new cinematic genre. This is a list of rock movies with SF or fantasy plotlines or elements.

Americathon (Neil Israel, 1979)
1998. The USA is bankrupt and the President organises a telethon spectacular to save the economy (with Elvis Costello, Eddie Money, Meatloaf, Harvey Korman, John Ritter).

Brewster McCloud (Robert Altman, 1970)
Altman's magical modern fable of a kid who wishes to fly, his alien godmother and killer birds featured a soundtrack by the legendary John Phillips and songs by Merry Clayton (with Bud Cort, Shelley Duvall, Sally Kellerman, Stacy Keach).

The Committee (Peter Sykes, 1968)
Short and bleak view of a mysterious and totalitarian future. Music by The Crazy World of Arthur Brown (with Paul Jones, Tom Kempinski).

Gas! Or It Became Necessary to Destroy the World in Order to Save It (Roger Corman, 1970)
Corman's last known directorial job. An apocalyptic comedy where a mysterious gas kills all adults. Songs by Country Joe and the Fish (with Cindy Williams, Talia Shire, Ben Vereen, Bud Cort).

The Ghost in the Invisible Bikini (Don Weis, 1966)
Beach party movie where a ghoul's house is taken over by a group of teenagers. Soundtrack by the Bobby Fuller Four (with Boris Karloff, Nancy Sinatra, Francis X. Bushman).

Gonks Go Beat (Robert Hartford-Davis, 1965)
Alien visitor reconciles warring parties on earth through the virtues of love and pop music. Wide cast of early British popsters including Lulu, the late Graham Bond, and the Nashville Teens (with Kenneth Connor, Frank Thornton).

Heavy Metal (Gerald Potterton, 1981)
Adult animated feature inspired by the comic strips of French magazine *Métal Hurlant*, but all material is American. Various SF and fantasy stories are connected by a thematic link. Soundtrack features Devo, Grand Funk Railroad, Blue Oyster Cult, Black Sabbath, and Trust.

The Horror of Party Beach (Del Tenney, 1964)
Monsters from the radioactive deep invade teenager-infested beach. Guess who wins? Music by the Del-Aires. Who? (With John Scott, Alice Lyon.)

How to Stuff a Wild Bikini (William Asher, 1965)
Witchcraft, telekinesis and telepathy in this beach movie. Music by the Kingsmen (with Buster Keaton. Annette Funicello, Frankie Avalon).

Jubilee (Derek Jarman, 1978)
Punk showcase where Elizabeth I is transported by time travel to a London of riots and civil anarchy (with Jenny Runacre, Toyah, Adam Ant, Little Nell, Lindsay Kemp, Wayne County, Ian Charleson, Jordan).

The Man Who Fell to Earth (Nicolas Roeg, 1976)
Not quite a rock movie, but we like it. David Bowie as alien who seeks salvation on our planet. From the Walter Tevis novel. Music by John Phillips and Stomu Yamashta (with David Bowie, Candy Clark, Rip Torn, Buck Henry).

The Phantom of the Paradise (Brian De Palma, 1974)
Splendid rock remake of the classic film (and Leroux book) with a scintillating soundtrack (and performance) by Paul Williams (with William Finley, Jessica Harper, Gerrit Graham).

Privilege (David Watkins, 1967)
In a future, fascist England, a rock singer's image is exploited to keep youth under control. Mike Leander score (with Paul Jones, Jean Shrimpton).

The Rocky Horror Picture Show (Jim Sharman, 1975)
Cult film version of a musical spoof of the old Hammer movies (with Tim Curry, Susan Sarandon, Little Nell, Richard O'Brien, Charles Gray).

Son of Dracula (Freddie Francis, 1974)
Little-seen pastiche of the classic vampire movie (with Harry Nilsson, Ringo Starr).

Tomorrow (Val Guest, 1970)
Pop group is kidnapped by UFO schlock (with Olivia Newton-John).

Village of the Giants (Bert I. Gordon, 1965)
"Teenagers zoom to supersize and terrorise a town!" says the poster of this youth exploitation remake of Wells' *Food of the Gods*. Score by Jack Nitzsche; music and appearance by The Beau Brummels, Freddie Cannon and Mike Clifford (with Ron Howard, Beau Bridges, Tommy Kirk).

Wild in the Streets (Barry Shear, 1968)
Pop singer battles for the Presidency on an exterminate over-30s campaign.
Songs by Barry Mann and Cynthia Weill (with Christopher Jones, Shelley
Winters, Diane Varsi, Hal Holbrook, Richard Pryor).

The Wiz (Sidney Lumet, 1978)
Black remake of the classic children's tale, a showcase for Diana Ross (with
Diana Ross, Richard Pryor, Michael Jackson, Lena Horne).

Wonderwall (Joe Massot, 1968)
Splendid George Harrison instrumental soundtrack for this fantasy of things
beyond a wall (with Jack MacGowran, Jane Birkin, Irene Handl).

Xanadu (Robert Greenwald, 1980)
Angel comes down to Earth to promote love and disco-mania. Mucho pop
hits on soundtrack and appearance by The Tubes (with Olivia Newton-
John, Michael Beck, Gene Kelly).

Yellow Submarine (George Dunning, 1968)
Enchanted Beatles animated feature taking our heroes into other lands of
wonder, music, and fantasy. Superlative soundtrack (of course . . .).

A Small Selection of SF Song Titles

Apeman	The Kinks
Atlantis	The Shadows
Atlantis	Donovan
Breakfast on Pluto	Don Partridge
Calling Occupants of Interplanetary Craft	The Carpenters
Diamond Dogs	David Bowie
Doomsday	Evelyn Thomas
End of the World	Skeeter Davis
Everybody's Gone to the Moon	Jonathan King
Fireball XL5	Don Spencer
Frankenstein	Edgar Winter Group
I'm the Urban Spaceman	Bonzo Dog Doo Dah Band
Night of the Vampire	The Moontrekkers

Venus and Mars	Paul McCartney & Wings
Robot	The Tornados
Robot Man	Connie Francis
Rocket Man	The Spotnicks
Rocket Man	Elton John
Silver Machine	Hawkwind
Soul Dracula	Hot Blood
Supersonic Rocket Ship	The Kinks
Telstar	The Tornados
Across the Universe	The Beatles
Astro Man	Jimi Hendrix
Up From the Skies	Jimi Hendrix
Transmaniacon	Blue Oyster Cult
Yellow Submarine	The Beatles
The Beatle Flying Saucer	Ed Solomon
Frankenstein Meets the Beatles	Jeckyll and Hyde
Martian Hop	The Ran-Dells
Flying Saucer Rock and Roll	Billy Lee Riley
Skylab	The Ventures
Riders in the Sky	The Ramrods
Mr. Spaceman	The Byrds
CTA 102	The Byrds
5D	The Byrds
In the Year 2525	Zager and Evans
Starsailor	Tim Buckley
Longer Boats	Cat Stevens
Wooden Ships	Crosby, Stills and Nash
Rocket Man	Pearls Before Swine
Stardancer	Pearls Before Swine
For the Dead in Space	Pearls Before Swine
Crown of Creation	Jefferson Airplane
Have You Seen the Stars Tonight?	Jefferson Starship
Dark Star	Grateful Dead
Star's End	David Bedford
Children of the Future	Steve Miller
Space Oddity	David Bowie
Lemmings	Van Der Graaf Generator
After the Flood	Van Der Graaf Generator
Dark Side of the Moon	Pink Floyd
Set the Controls for the Heart of the Sun	Pink Floyd

380

The Cygnet Committee	David Bowie
Bionic Man	The Fabulous Poodles
The Eggplant That Ate Chicago	Dr. West's Medicine Show
Here Come the Martians	Jonathan Richman
It Came Out of the Sky	Creedence Clearwater Revival
King Kong	Frank Zappa
Looking Out My Back Door	Creedence Clearwater Revival
Pure and Easy	The Who
The Purple People Eater	Sheb Wooley & Jackie Dennis
This Time Tomorrow	The Kinks
2,000 Light Years from Home	The Rolling Stones
In Another Land	The Rolling Stones
2000 Man	The Rolling Stones
The Moon is a Harsh Mistress	Jimmy Webb
Chronolyse	Richard Pinhas
Cosmic Slop	Funkadelic
Beam Me Up Scotty	Fingerprintz
Mothership Connection	Parliament
The Atrocity Exhibition	Joy Division
Another Green World	Eno
The Attack of the Giant Ants	Blondie
Stairway to the Stars	Blue Oyster Cult
Workshop of the Telescopes	Blue Oyster Cult
Flaming Telepaths	Blue Oyster Cult
Extra Terrestrial Intelligence	Blue Oyster Cult
Godzilla	Blue Oyster Cult
The Man Who Sold the World	David Bowie
Life on Mars	David Bowie
Superman	David Bowie
Starman	David Bowie
1984	David Bowie
Vermilion Sands	The Buggles
Robot	Hawkwind
Space Age Love Song	A Flock of Seagulls

and more . . . and more . . . and more . . .

Readers are invited to investigate their record sleeves and complete this list at their leisure.

Six SF Writers Who Have Recorded Rock Music

1. Robert Calvert

Lyricist for rock group Hawkwind and its later offshoot the Hawklords, Robert Calvert also occasionally performed on stage with them (as did Moorcock; see further on). After leaving the group he recorded two solo albums, *Captain Lockheed and the Star-Fighters* and *Lucky Lief and the Longships*. He has published SF short stories and texts in underground magazines and *New Worlds*. His recent rock novel *Hype* was accompanied by an album of music, and he has a SF novel due for publication in the UK.

2. Mick Farren

A music journalist and author of six SF novels (*The Feelies, The Texts of Festival, The Quest of the DNA Cowboys, Synaptic Manhunt, The Neural Atrocity* and *The Song of Phaid the Gambler*), Farren was first active between 1967 and 1970 in the British underground rock band The Deviants, for whom he sang and wrote lyrics. An album, *The Deviants* was released in 1969, including songs such as 'Death of a Dream Machine,' 'Junior Narco Rangers,' 'Metamorphosis Exploration' and 'Billy the Monster.' A solo album, *Vampires Stole My Lunch Money*, appeared in 1978.

3. David Meltzer

Better known as a poet, Meltzer has authored several SF novels with strong erotic connotations: *The Agency*, 1968, *The Agent*, 1968, and *How Many Blocks in the Pile?*, 1968, forming the 'Agency' trilogy. The 'Brain-Plant' series features *Lovely, Healer, Out* and *Glue Factory*, all 1969. He has recorded two albums of self-penned material (with his wife Tina): *Serpent Power*, 1968, and *Poet Song*, 1969, both released on the then prestigious Vanguard label.

4. Michael Moorcock

Having performed in clubs as a blues singer in his youth, Moorcock intermittently appeared on stage with rock group Hawkwind in the early 1970s. He has written lyrics for the following Hawkwind songs: 'The Wizard Blew His Horn,' 'Standing at the Edge' and 'Warriors' on the *Warrior at the Edge of Time* album, 1975. He also performs on the record. He plays banjo on Robert Calvert's album *Lucky Lief and the Longships* (1975). Other songs for Hawkwind include 'The Black Corridor' and 'Sonic Attack' on the *Space Ritual* album, 1973.

In 1975, Moorcock put together the Deep Fix group, comprising Steve

Gilmore, erstwhile SF writer Graham Charnock and himself. This line-up recorded an album *The New World's Fair* released on United Artists in 1975. On this record, Moorcock plays guitar, mandolin and banjo, and sings the following self-penned tracks: 'Candy Floss Cowboy,' 'Fair Dealer,' '16-year-old Doom,' 'Last Merry-Go-Round' and 'Dude's Dream (Rolling in the Ruins).' Two other songs–'Star Cruiser' and 'Dodgem Dude'–were recorded for a single not released at the time, but since out on independent label Flick Knife in 1981. This same small label issued a compilation album in 1982 under the title *Hawkwind–Friends and Relations* featuring Moorcock on 'Good Girl, Bad Girl' and 'Time Centre.' A limited edition single of 'The Brothel in Rosenstrasse' was also issued in 1982.

Moorcock has also penned lyrics for the US heavy metal outfit Blue Oyster Cult. 'The Great Sun Jester' on 'Mirrors,' 1979; 'Black Blade' on 'Cultosaurus Erectus,' 1980 and 'Veteran of the Psychic Wars' on 'Fire of Unknown Origin,' 1981.

5. John Shirley

Young New York author John Shirley plays the NY professional club scene with his band Obsession. He has recorded songs for the independent label Dorian.

6. Norman Spinrad

Spinrad has written words for the musical piece *Houston 69—The Crash Landing* by French electronic synthesizer player Richard Pinhas and performs through a vocoder on the track, which is included on Pinhas' album *East-West*, 1980.

Many other writers of SF are adept musicians and have played on a professional or semi-professional basis, although there are no recorded instances of their work (except for a cassette of the Sucharitkul piece with Malzberg on violin).

Jean-Pierre Andrevon, the French author is also known as a folk singer.
Lloyd Biggle, Jr. is a respected musicologist and has taught at US universities.
Jerome Bixby has been known to compose classical music.
Marc Bourgeois, another French writer, has played with the groups Gong and Green.
John F. Burke, an old established British hack, is an accomplished player of various instruments.

Graham Charnock, well-known as author, fan and bookshop manager, was a member of Moorcock's Deep Fix and plays semi-professionally at weekends and conventions with his group.

Los Gonococcos is a ribald, impromptu group of French fans and critics who play conventions and other events.

Langdon Jones was, before the *New Worlds* days, a professional musician, and played in a regimental band.

James Kahn has played as singer-songwriter with local folk-rock group Silver City.

John Kippax used to play the saxophone in a dance band.

Barry Malzberg has played violin with a symphonic orchestra on the occasion of a Sucharitkul composition performance, *Starscapes.*

Laurence Janifer is another writer who has performed in a dance band.

Sam Lundwall had his own pop/folk group and recorded in Sweden. Some of his compositions have been sung by Abba.

Janet E. Morris plays bass in her husband's rock band.

Josephine Saxton plays bongos with local Coventry bands.

Somtow Sucharitkul has established a healthy reputation as a composer of classical and modern music and many of his pieces have had public performances.

Elisabeth Vonarburg, the Canadian novelist and critic, has performed as a folk-singer.

About the Authors

Maxim Jakubowski is a well-known editor and critic who occasionally writes SF and fantasy. A London-based publisher, he has edited a dozen anthologies and written several humour titles and books on rock and roll music. He has also contributed to major SF magazines and reference books.

Malcolm Edwards studied anthropology at Cambridge. He is a publisher's editor, was Administrator of the Science Fiction Foundation, and was a contributing editor to *The Encyclopedia of Science Fiction* (also available from Granada Paperbacks).